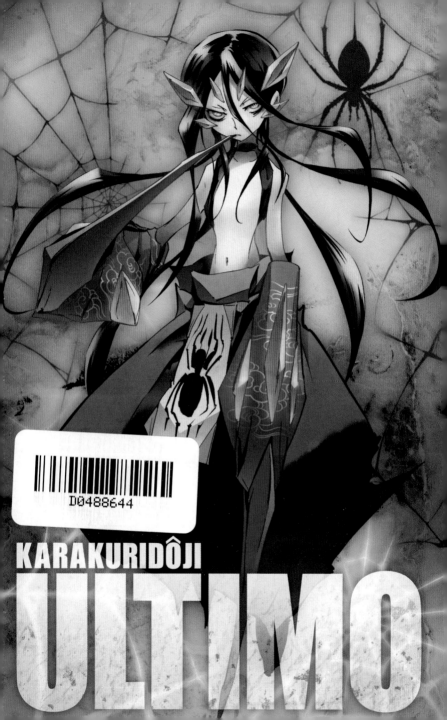

KARAKURIDÔJI
ULTIMO

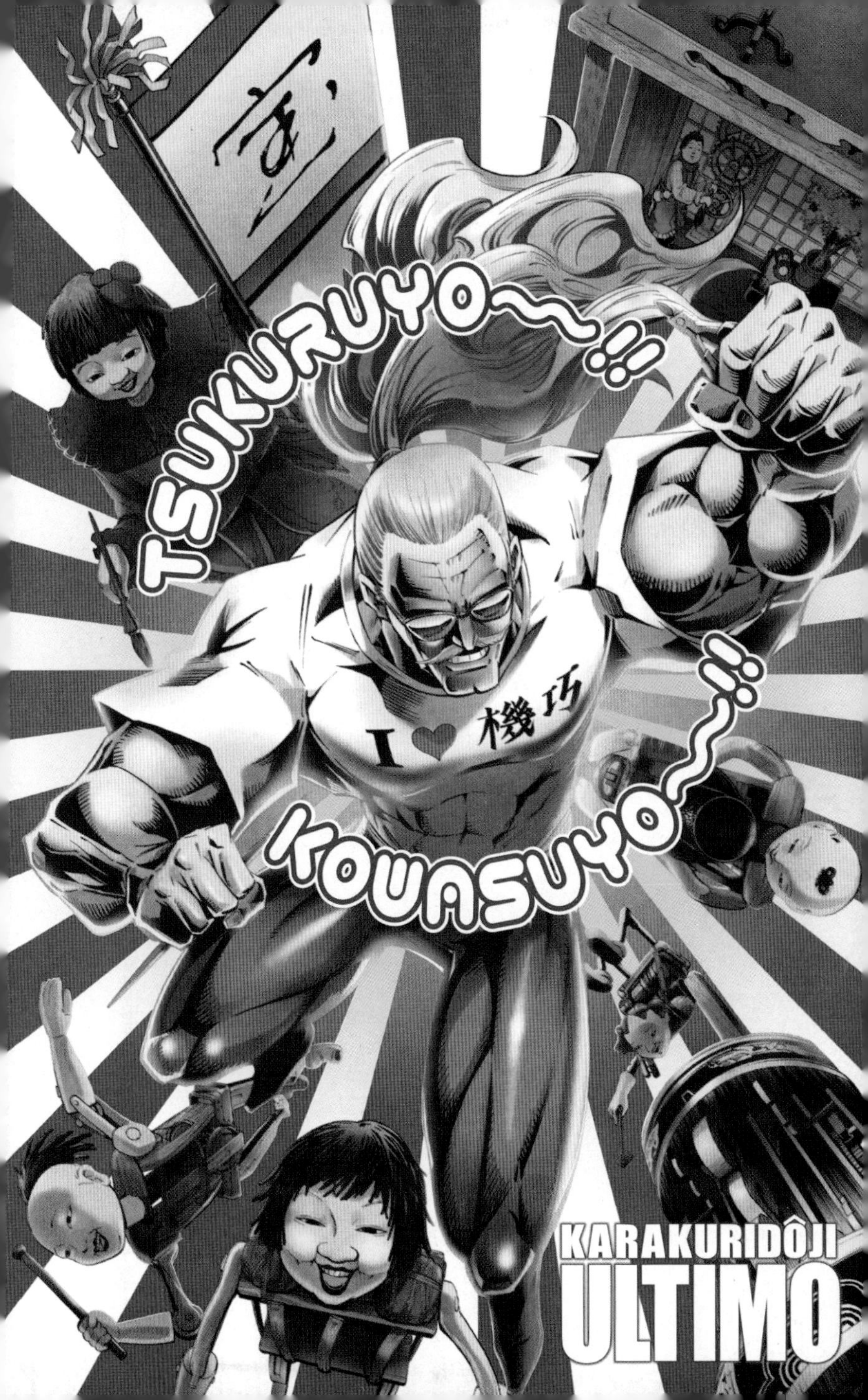
TSUKURUYO~~!!
KOWASUYO~~!!
I ♥ 機巧
KARAKURIDÔJI
ULTIMO

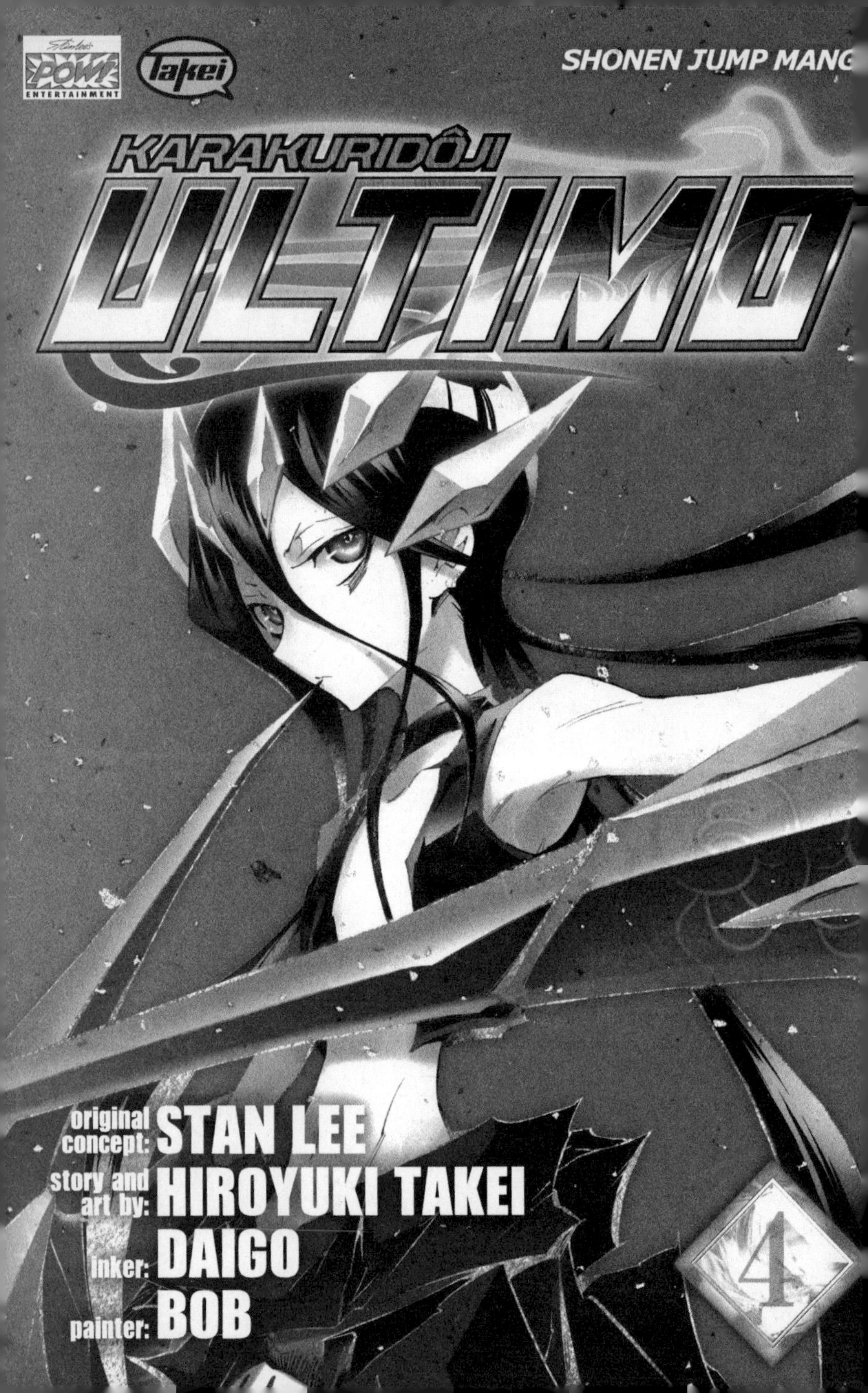
Stan Lee's POW! ENTERTAINMENT
Takei
SHONEN JUMP MANG
KARAKURIDÔJI
ULTIMO
original concept: STAN LEE
story and art by: HIROYUKI TAKEI
inker: DAIGO
painter: BOB
4

Karakuri Dôji Ultimo

Characters

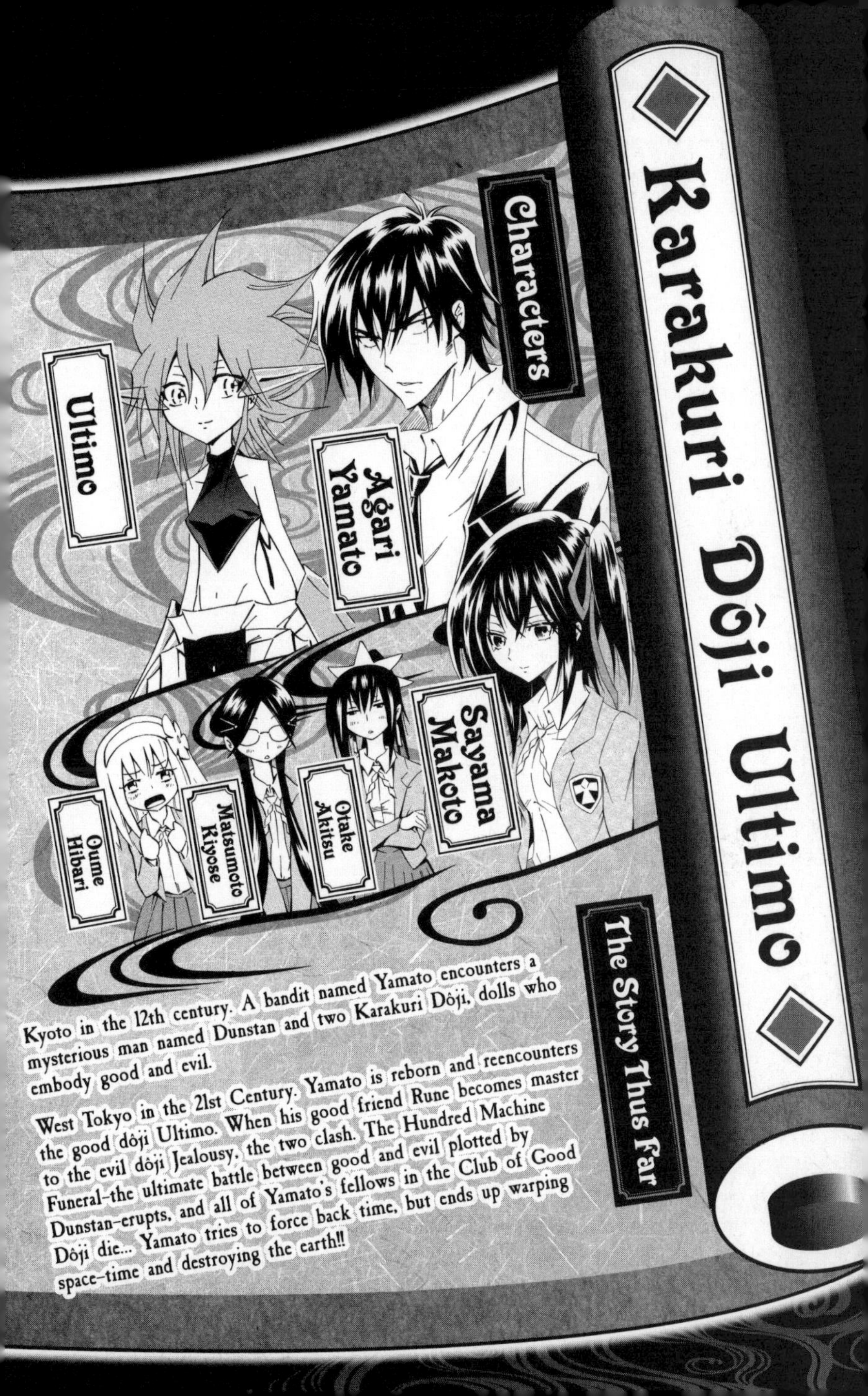
Agari Yamato
Ultimo
Sayama Makoto
Otake Akitsu
Matsumoto Kiyose
Oume Hibari

The Story Thus Far

Kyoto in the 12th century. A bandit named Yamato encounters a mysterious man named Dunstan and two Karakuri Dôji, dolls who embody good and evil.

West Tokyo in the 21st Century. Yamato is reborn and reencounters the good dôji Ultimo. When his good friend Rune becomes master to the evil dôji Jealousy, the two clash. The Hundred Machine Funeral–the ultimate battle between good and evil plotted by Dunstan–erupts, and all of Yamato's fellows in the Club of Good Dôji die... Yamato tries to force back time, but ends up warping space-time and destroying the earth!!

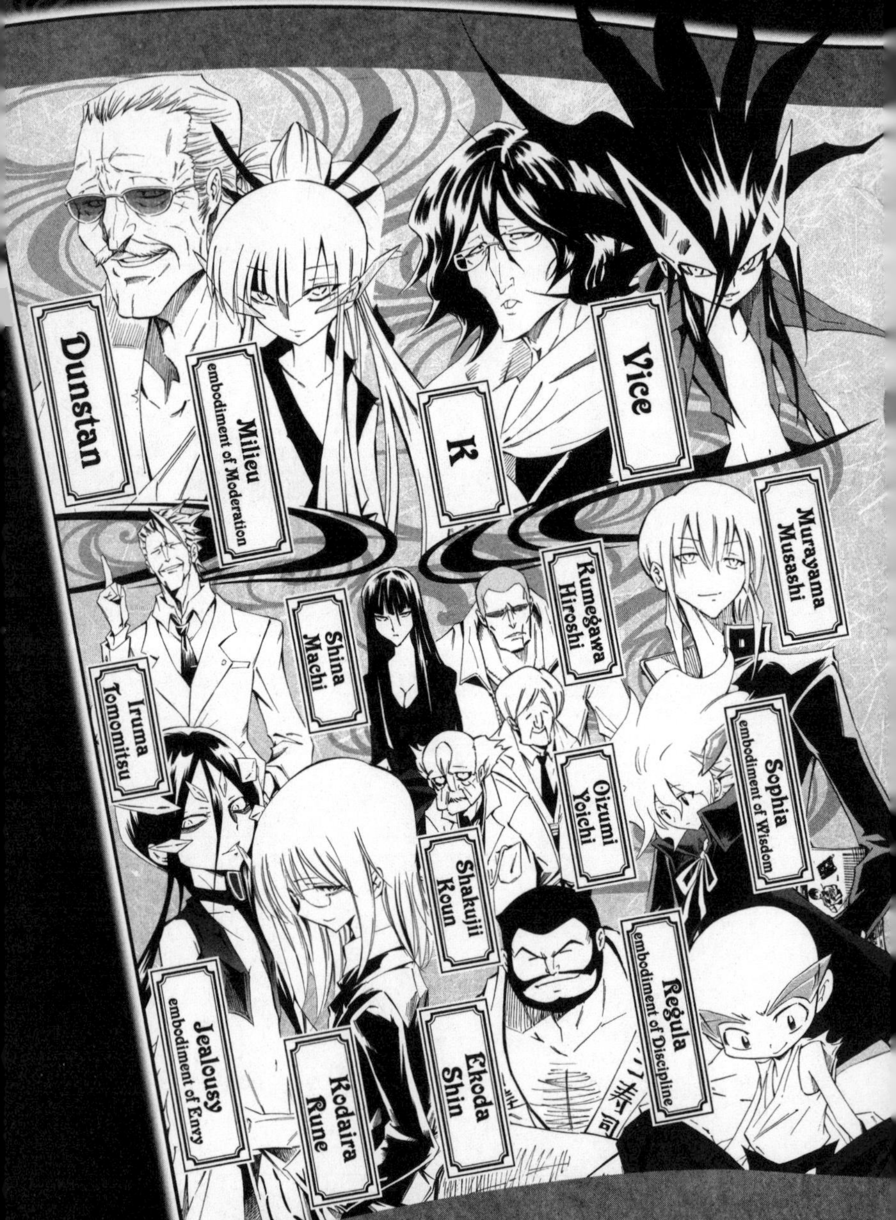
Vice
K
Milieu
embodiment of Moderation
Dunstan
Murayama
Musashi
Kumegawa
Hiroshi
Shina
Machi
Iruma
Tomomitsu
Sophia
embodiment of Wisdom
Oizumi
Yoichi
Shakujii
Koun
Regula
embodiment of Discipline
Ekoda
Shin
Kodaira
Rune
Jealousy
embodiment of Envy

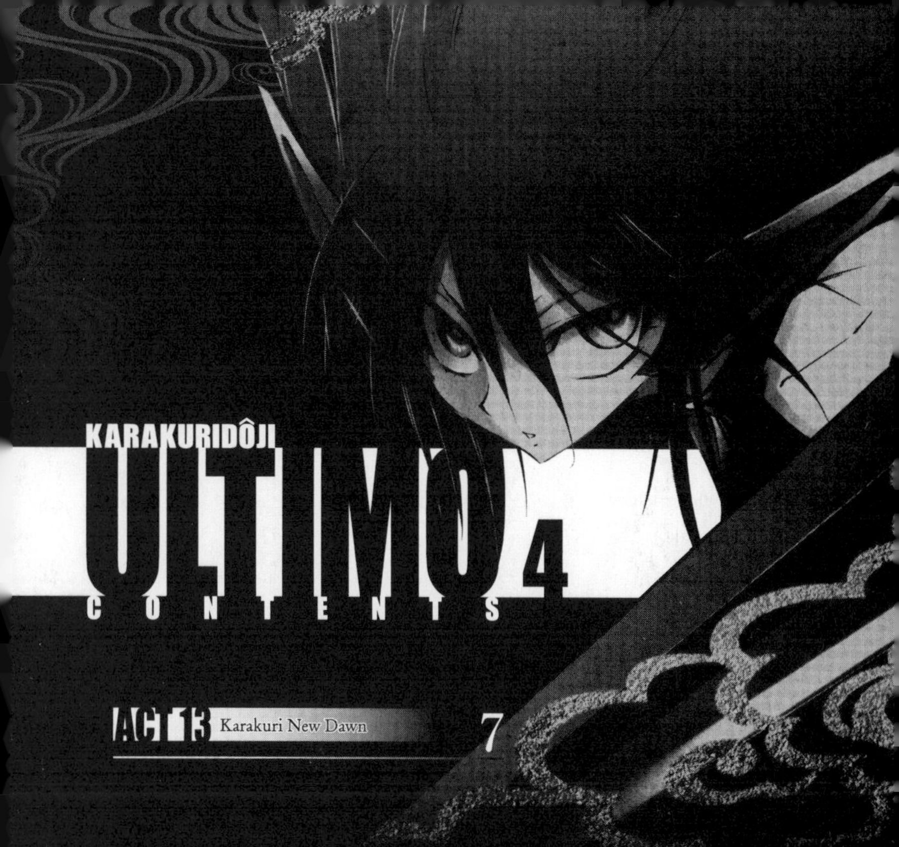

KARAKURIDÔJI

ULTIMO 4

CONTENTS

ACT 13 Karakuri New Dawn   7

ACT 14 Love Wasabi   53

ACT 15 Battle at the Antique Shop   99

ACT 16 Time Traveler Yamato   145

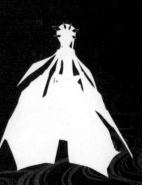

ACT 13
KARAKURI NEW DAWN

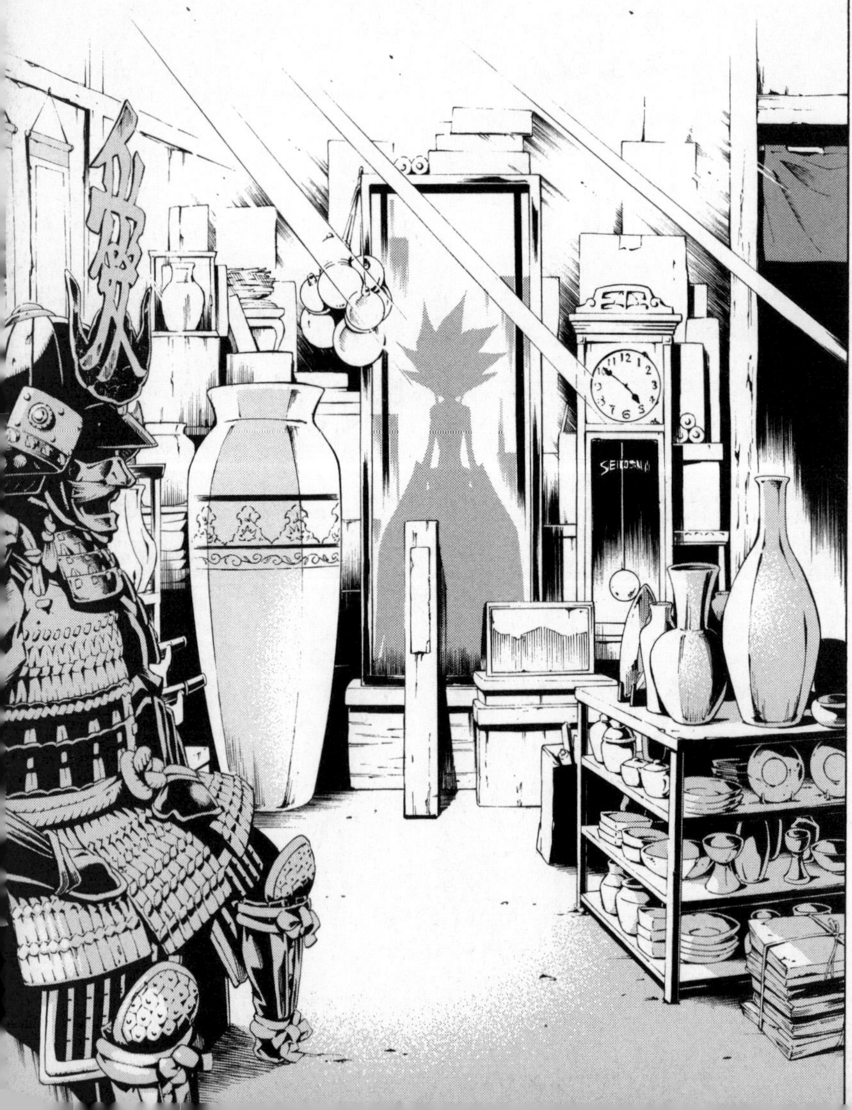

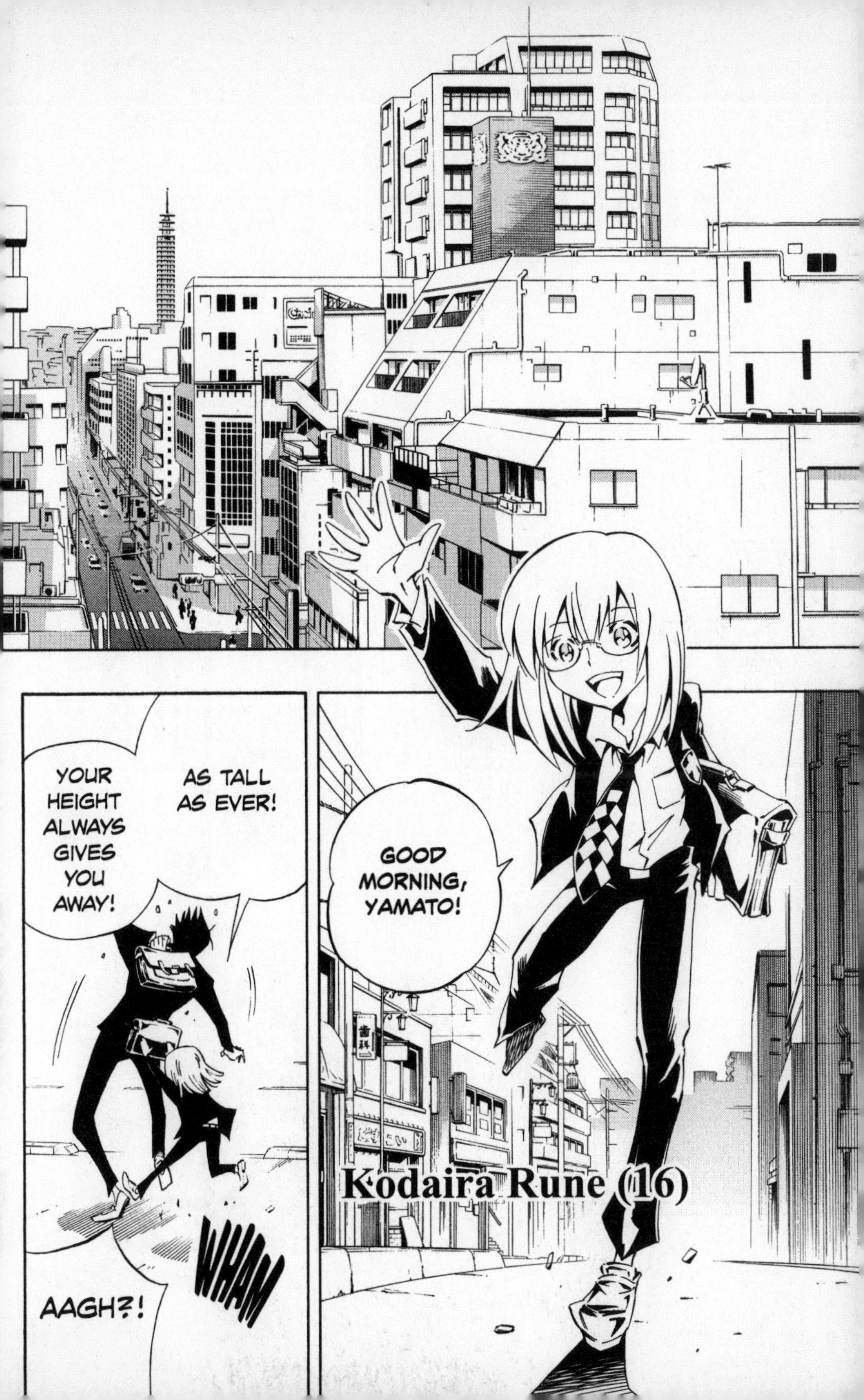
GOOD MORNING, YAMATO!
Kodaira Rune (16)
AS TALL AS EVER!
YOUR HEIGHT ALWAYS GIVES YOU AWAY!
WHAM
AAGH?!

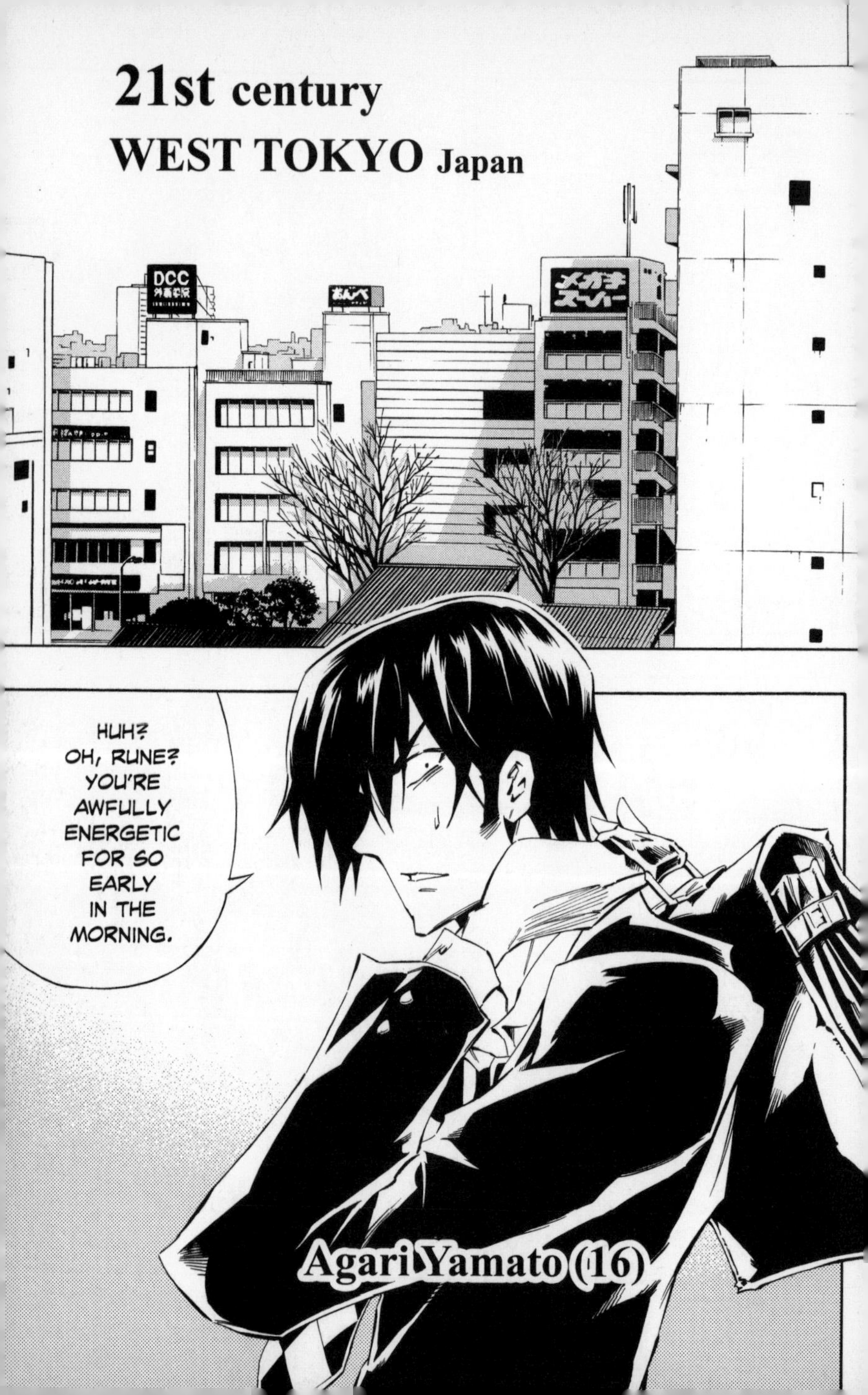
21st century
WEST TOKYO Japan
HUH? OH, RUNE? YOU'RE AWFULLY ENERGETIC FOR SO EARLY IN THE MORNING.
Agari Yamato (16)

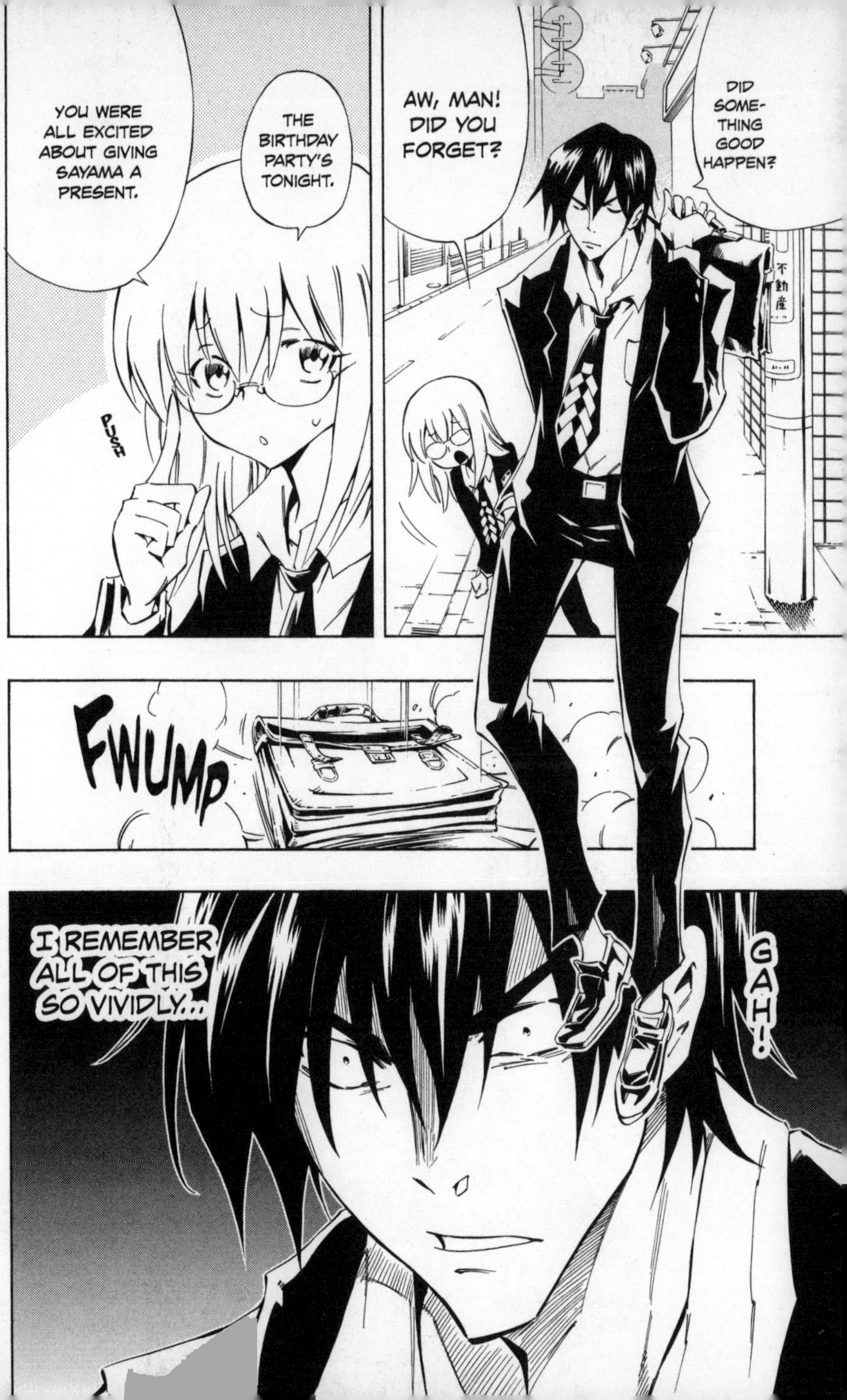
DID SOMETHING GOOD HAPPEN?
AW, MAN! DID YOU FORGET?
不動産
THE BIRTHDAY PARTY'S TONIGHT.
YOU WERE ALL EXCITED ABOUT GIVING SAYAMA A PRESENT.
PUSH
FWUMP
GAH!
I REMEMBER ALL OF THIS SO VIVIDLY...

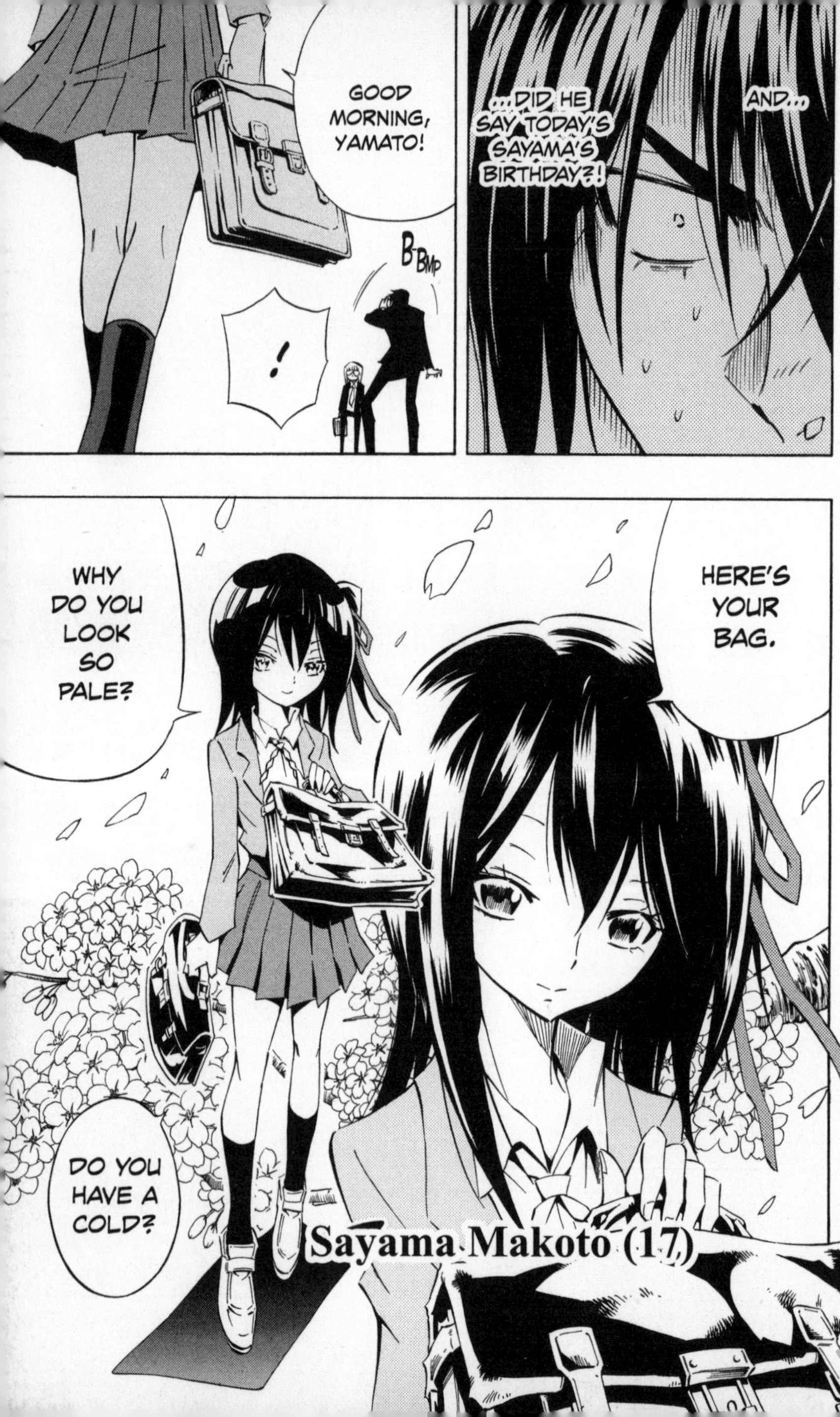
AND...
...DID HE SAY TODAY'S SAYAMA'S BIRTHDAY?!
GOOD MORNING, YAMATO!
B-BMP
!
HERE'S YOUR BAG.
WHY DO YOU LOOK SO PALE?
DO YOU HAVE A COLD?
Sayama Makoto (17)

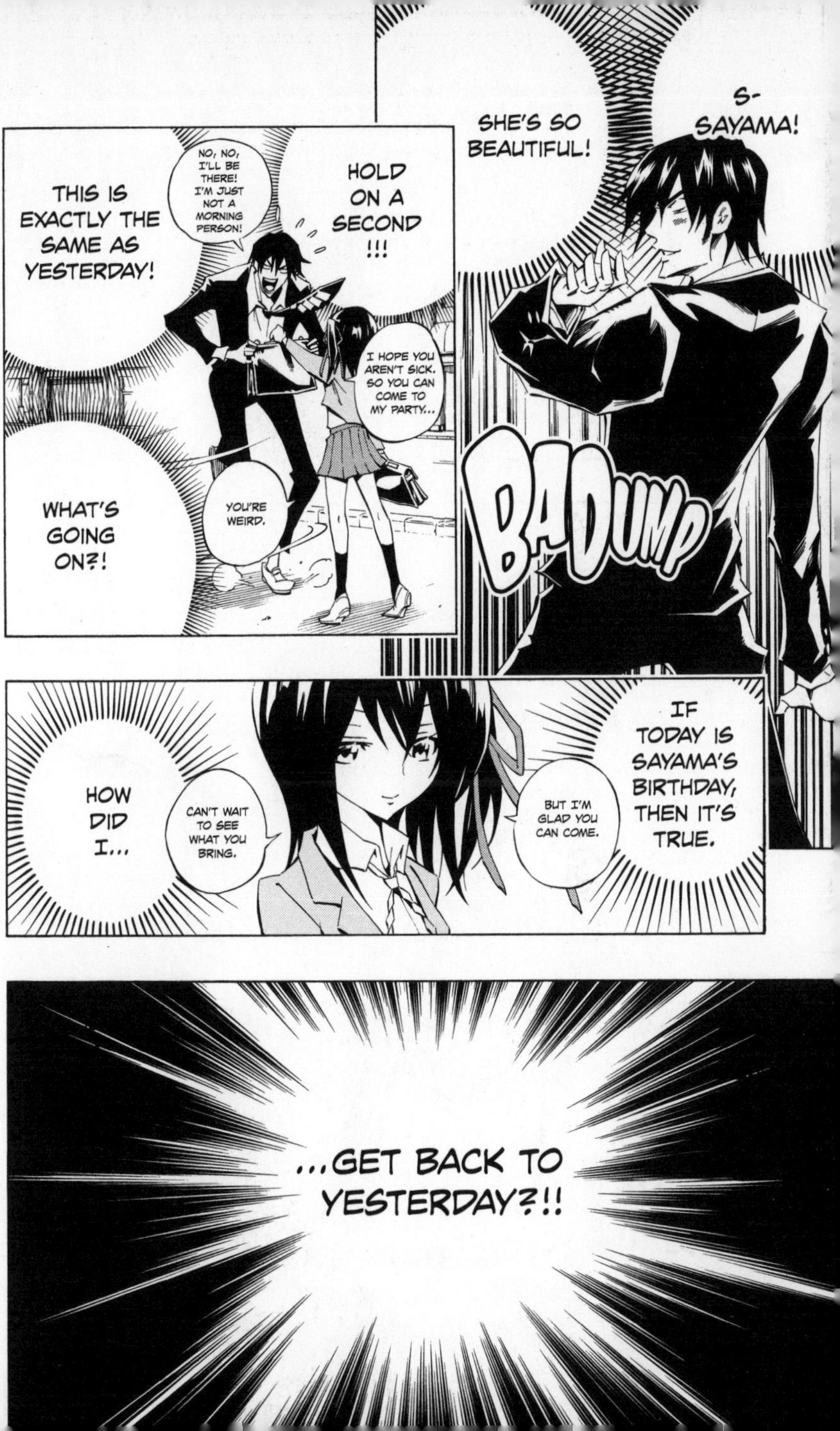
S-SAYAMA!
SHE'S SO BEAUTIFUL!
BADUMP
HOLD ON A SECOND!!!
NO, NO, I'LL BE THERE! I'M JUST NOT A MORNING PERSON!
THIS IS EXACTLY THE SAME AS YESTERDAY!
I HOPE YOU AREN'T SICK. SO YOU CAN COME TO MY PARTY...
YOU'RE WEIRD.
WHAT'S GOING ON?!
IF TODAY IS SAYAMA'S BIRTHDAY, THEN IT'S TRUE.
BUT I'M GLAD YOU CAN COME.
CAN'T WAIT TO SEE WHAT YOU BRING.
HOW DID I...
...GET BACK TO YESTERDAY?!!

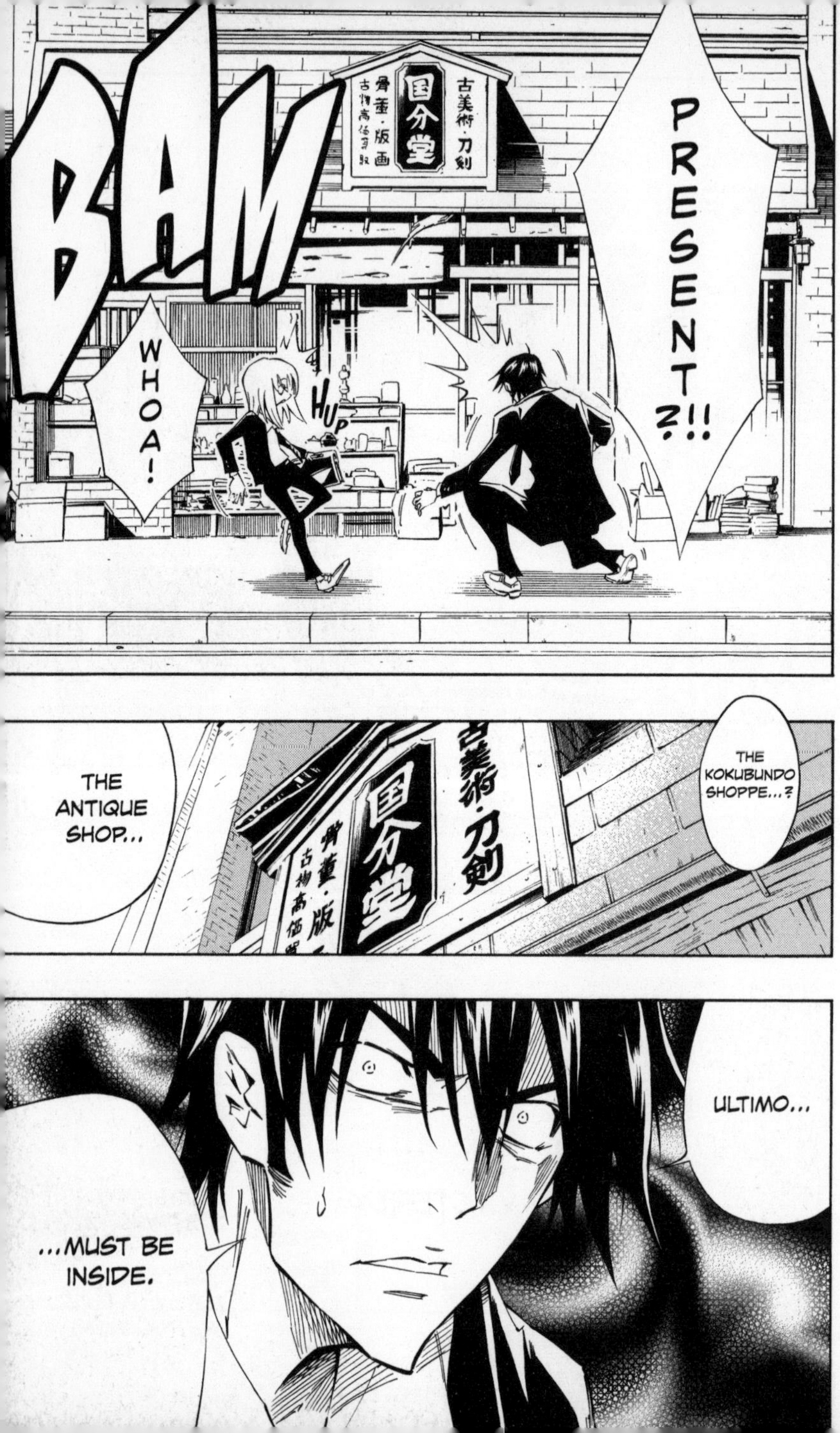
PRESENT?!!
古美術・刀剣
国分堂
骨董・版画
古物高価買取
BAM
HUP
WHOA!
THE KOKUBUNDO SHOPPE...?
THE ANTIQUE SHOP...
ULTIMO...
...MUST BE INSIDE.

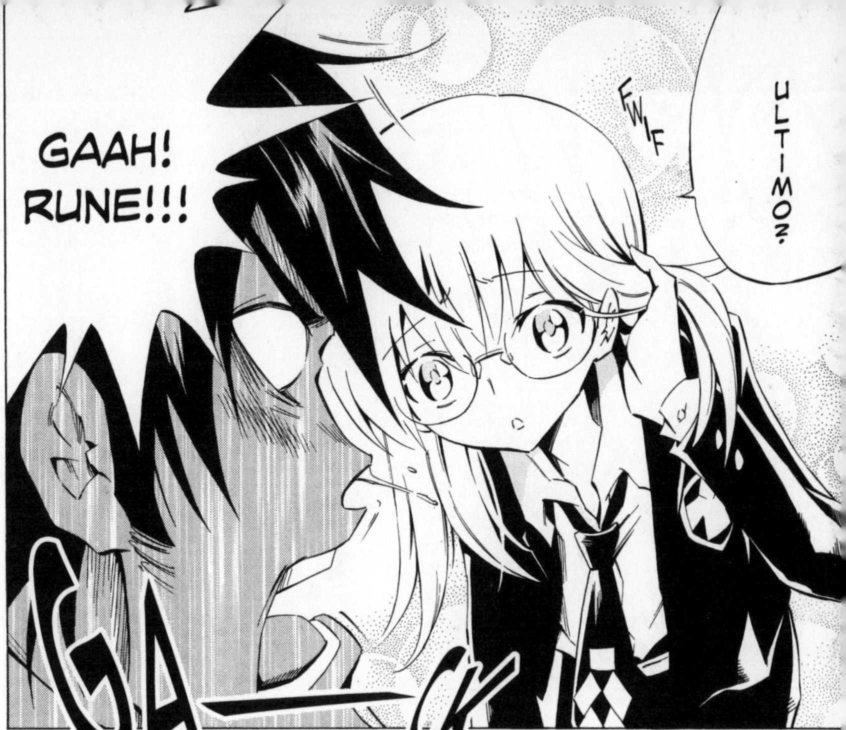
ULTIMO?
FWIF
GAAH! RUNE!!!
GA—CK

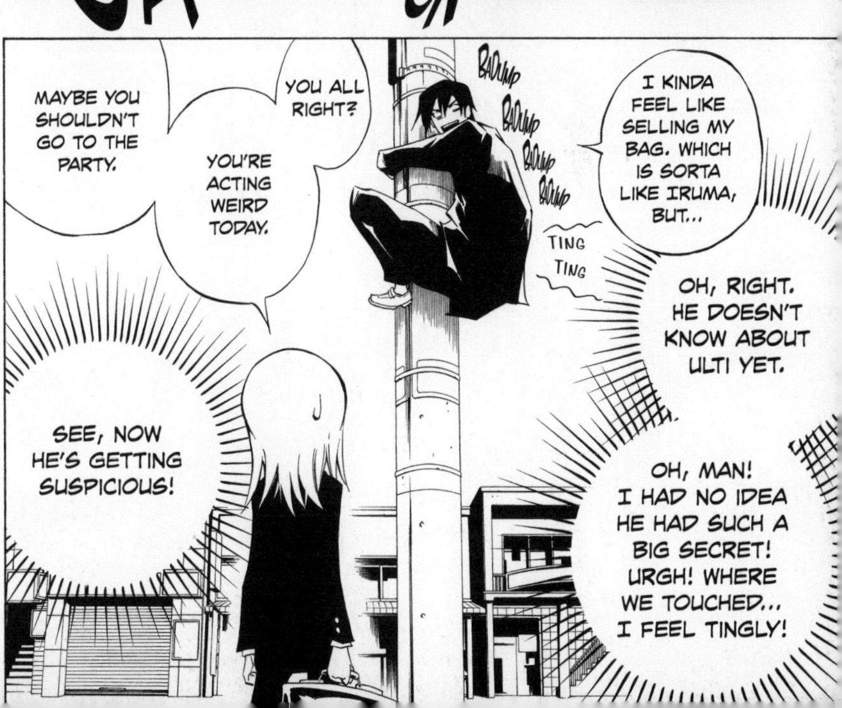
I KINDA FEEL LIKE SELLING MY BAG. WHICH IS SORTA LIKE IRUMA, BUT...
BADUMP BADUMP BADUMP BADUMP
YOU ALL RIGHT?
YOU'RE ACTING WEIRD TODAY.
MAYBE YOU SHOULDN'T GO TO THE PARTY.
TING TING
OH, RIGHT. HE DOESN'T KNOW ABOUT ULTI YET.
OH, MAN! I HAD NO IDEA HE HAD SUCH A BIG SECRET! URGH! WHERE WE TOUCHED... I FEEL TINGLY!
SEE, NOW HE'S GETTING SUSPICIOUS!

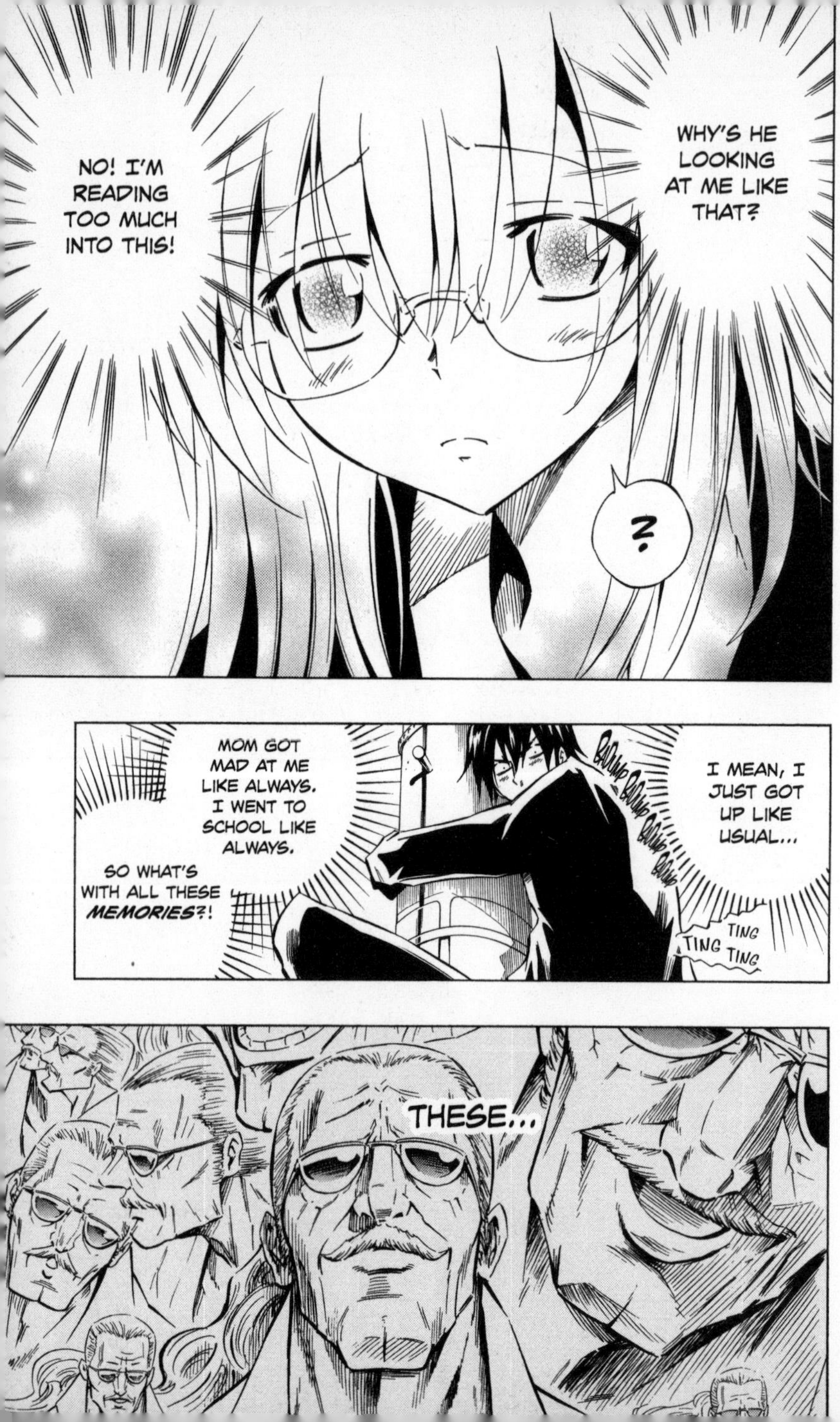
WHY'S HE LOOKING AT ME LIKE THAT?
NO! I'M READING TOO MUCH INTO THIS!
?
I MEAN, I JUST GOT UP LIKE USUAL...
BADUMP BADUMP BADUMP BADUMP BADUMP
TING TING TING TING
MOM GOT MAD AT ME LIKE ALWAYS. I WENT TO SCHOOL LIKE ALWAYS.
SO WHAT'S WITH ALL THESE *MEMORIES*?!
THESE...

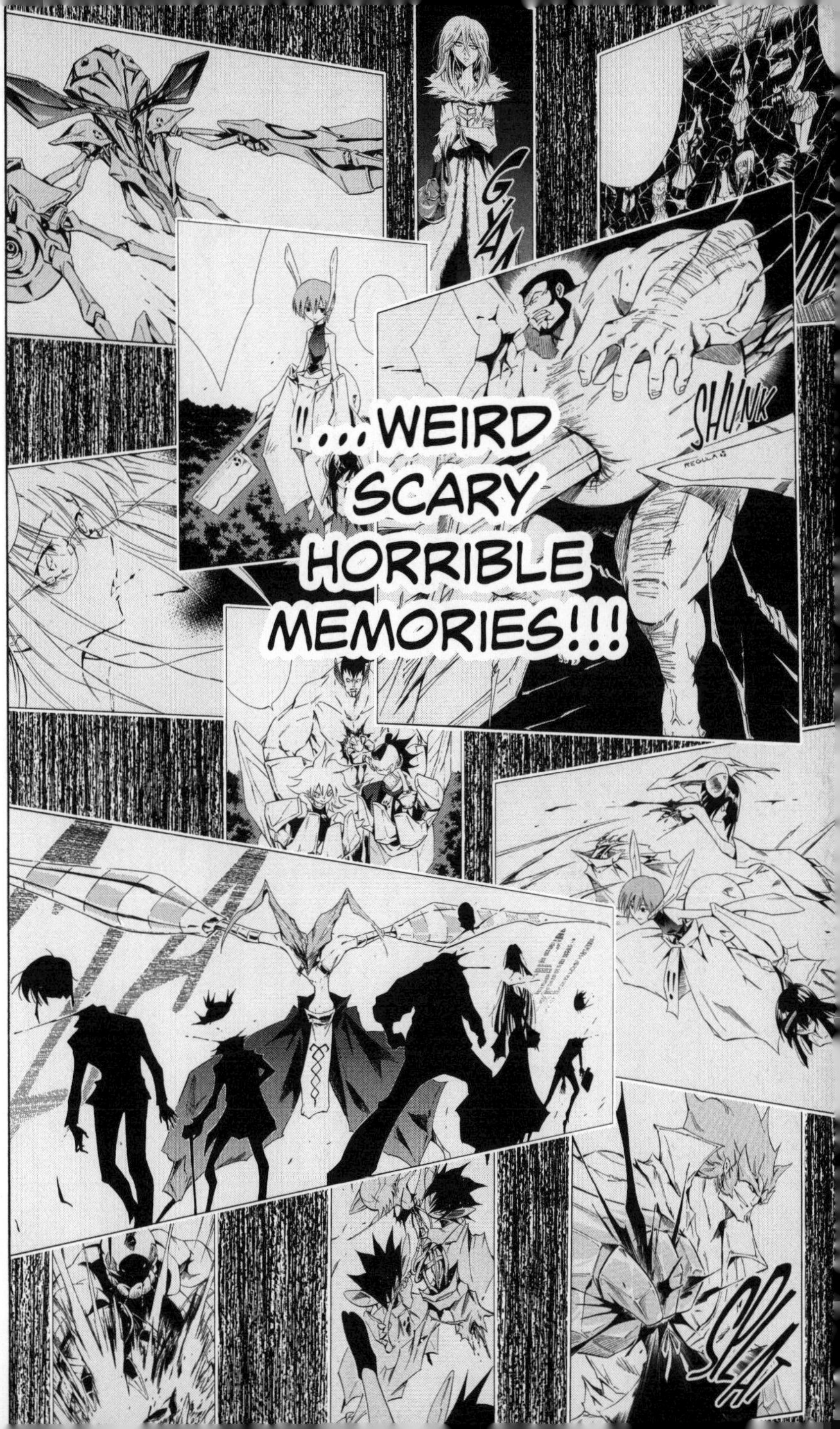
GYAA
SHUNK
!!
...WEIRD SCARY HORRIBLE MEMORIES!!!

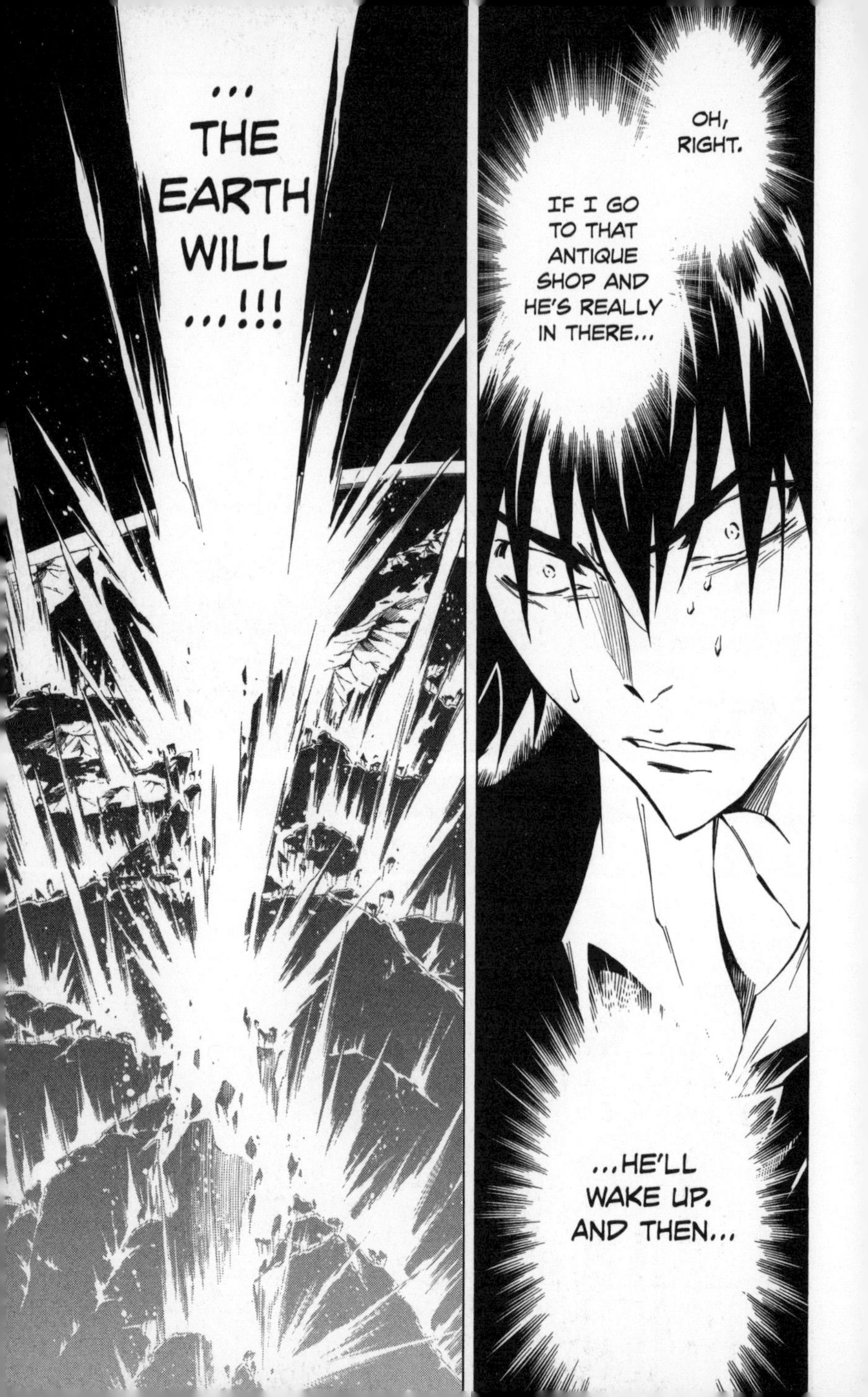
OH, RIGHT.
IF I GO TO THAT ANTIQUE SHOP AND HE'S REALLY IN THERE...
...HE'LL WAKE UP. AND THEN...
... THE EARTH WILL ...!!!

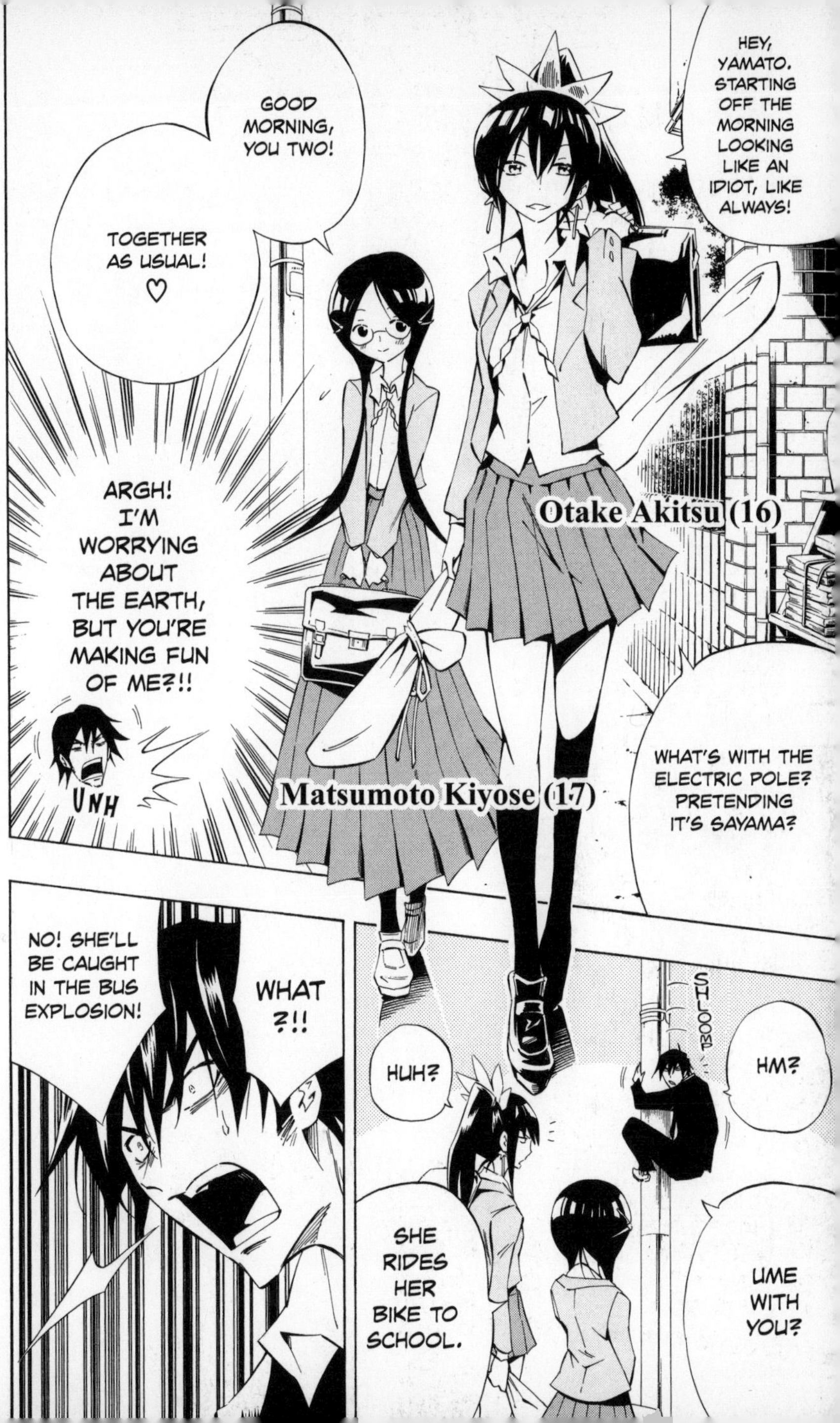
HEY, YAMATO. STARTING OFF THE MORNING LOOKING LIKE AN IDIOT, LIKE ALWAYS!
GOOD MORNING, YOU TWO!
TOGETHER AS USUAL! ♡
Otake Akitsu (16)
WHAT'S WITH THE ELECTRIC POLE? PRETENDING IT'S SAYAMA?
ARGH! I'M WORRYING ABOUT THE EARTH, BUT YOU'RE MAKING FUN OF ME?!!
UNH
Matsumoto Kiyose (17)
SHLOOMP
HM?
HUH?
UME WITH YOU?
SHE RIDES HER BIKE TO SCHOOL.
WHAT ?!!
NO! SHE'LL BE CAUGHT IN THE BUS EXPLOSION!

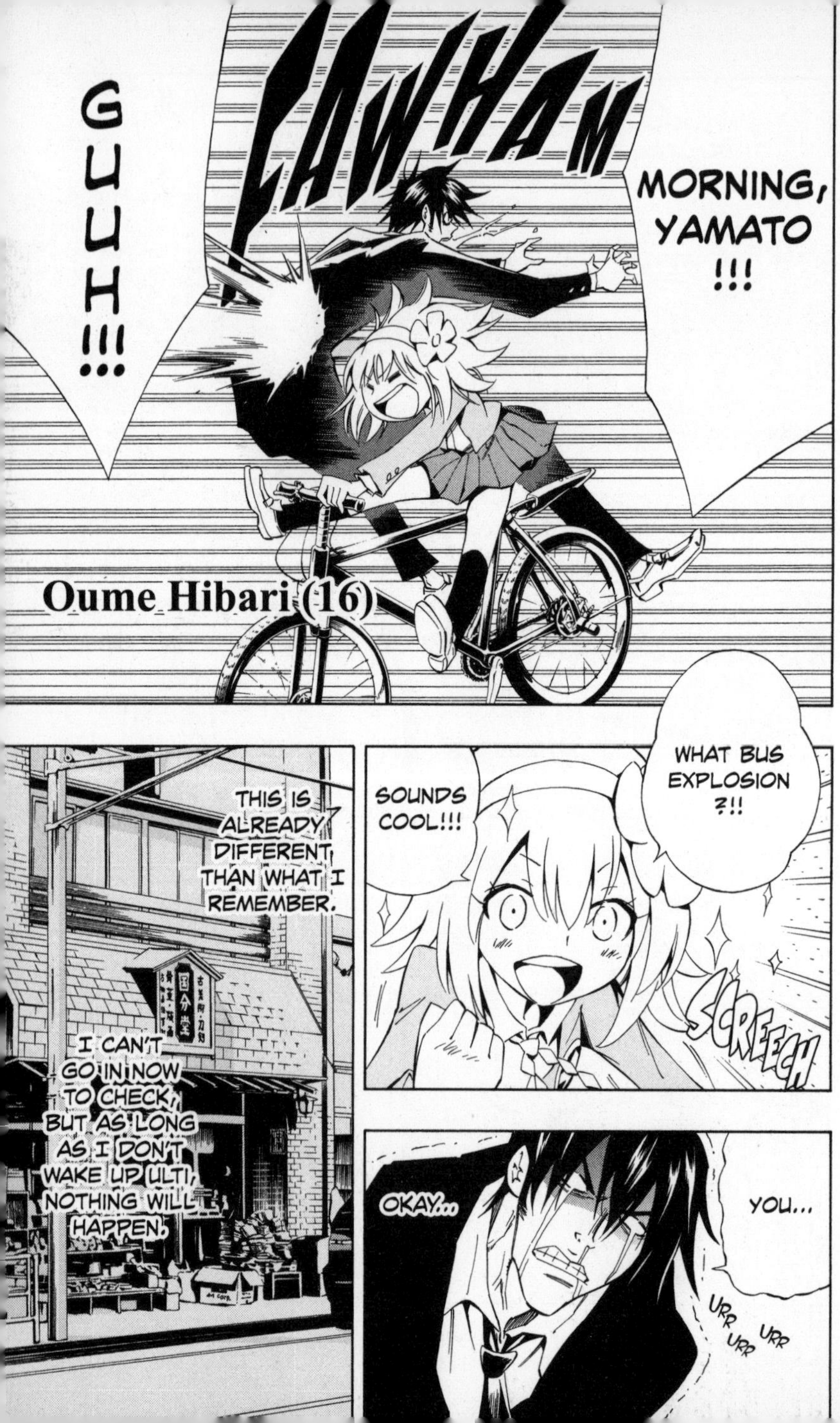
MORNING, YAMATO !!!
GUUH!!!
Oume Hibari (16)
WHAT BUS EXPLOSION ?!!
SOUNDS COOL!!!
SCREECH
YOU...
OKAY...
URR URR URR
THIS IS ALREADY DIFFERENT THAN WHAT I REMEMBER.
I CAN'T GO IN NOW TO CHECK, BUT AS LONG AS I DON'T WAKE UP ULTI, NOTHING WILL HAPPEN.

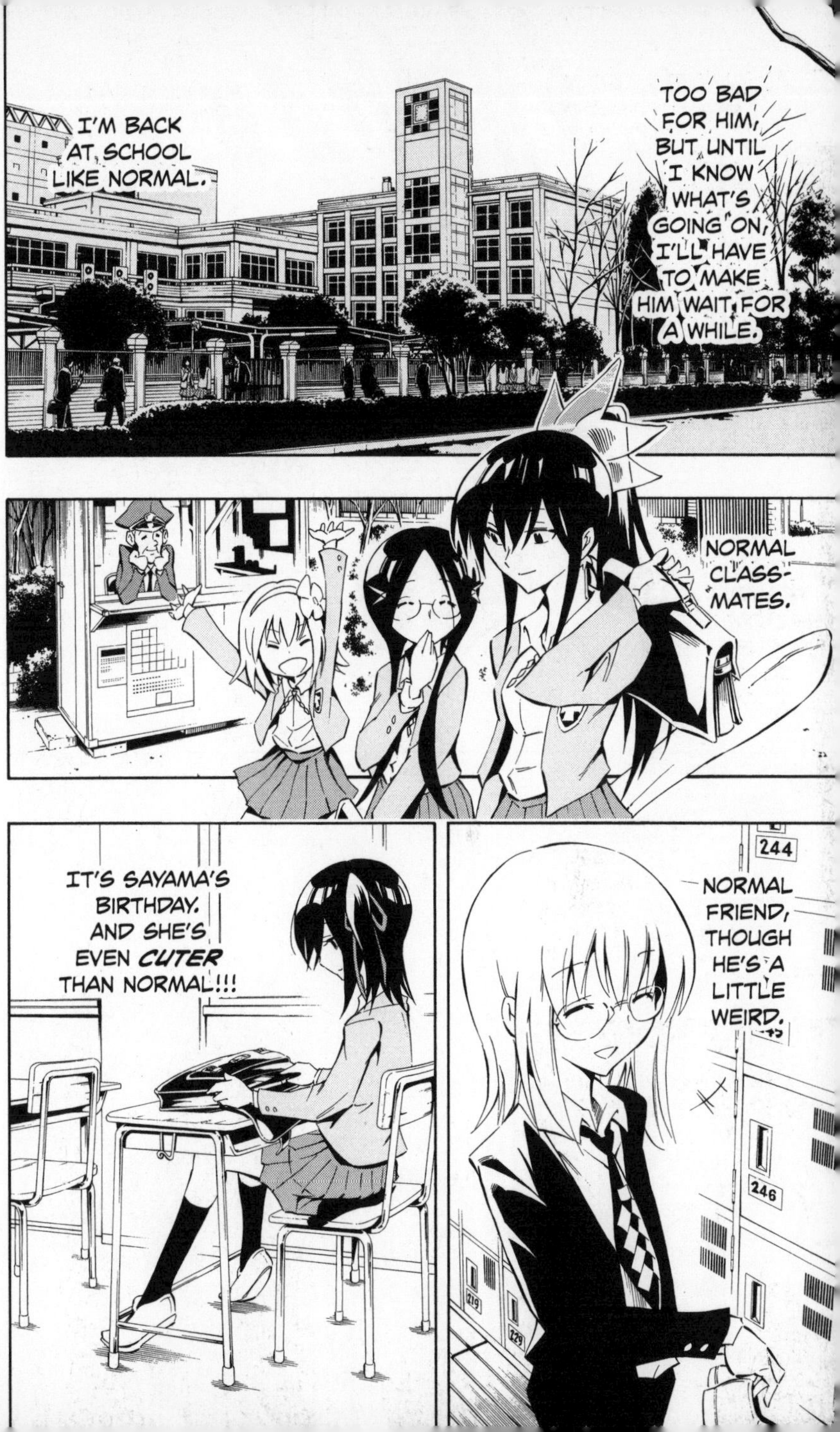
TOO BAD FOR HIM, BUT UNTIL I KNOW WHAT'S GOING ON, I'LL HAVE TO MAKE HIM WAIT FOR A WHILE.
I'M BACK AT SCHOOL LIKE NORMAL.
NORMAL CLASSMATES.
NORMAL FRIEND, THOUGH HE'S A LITTLE WEIRD.
IT'S SAYAMA'S BIRTHDAY. AND SHE'S EVEN *CUTER* THAN NORMAL!!!

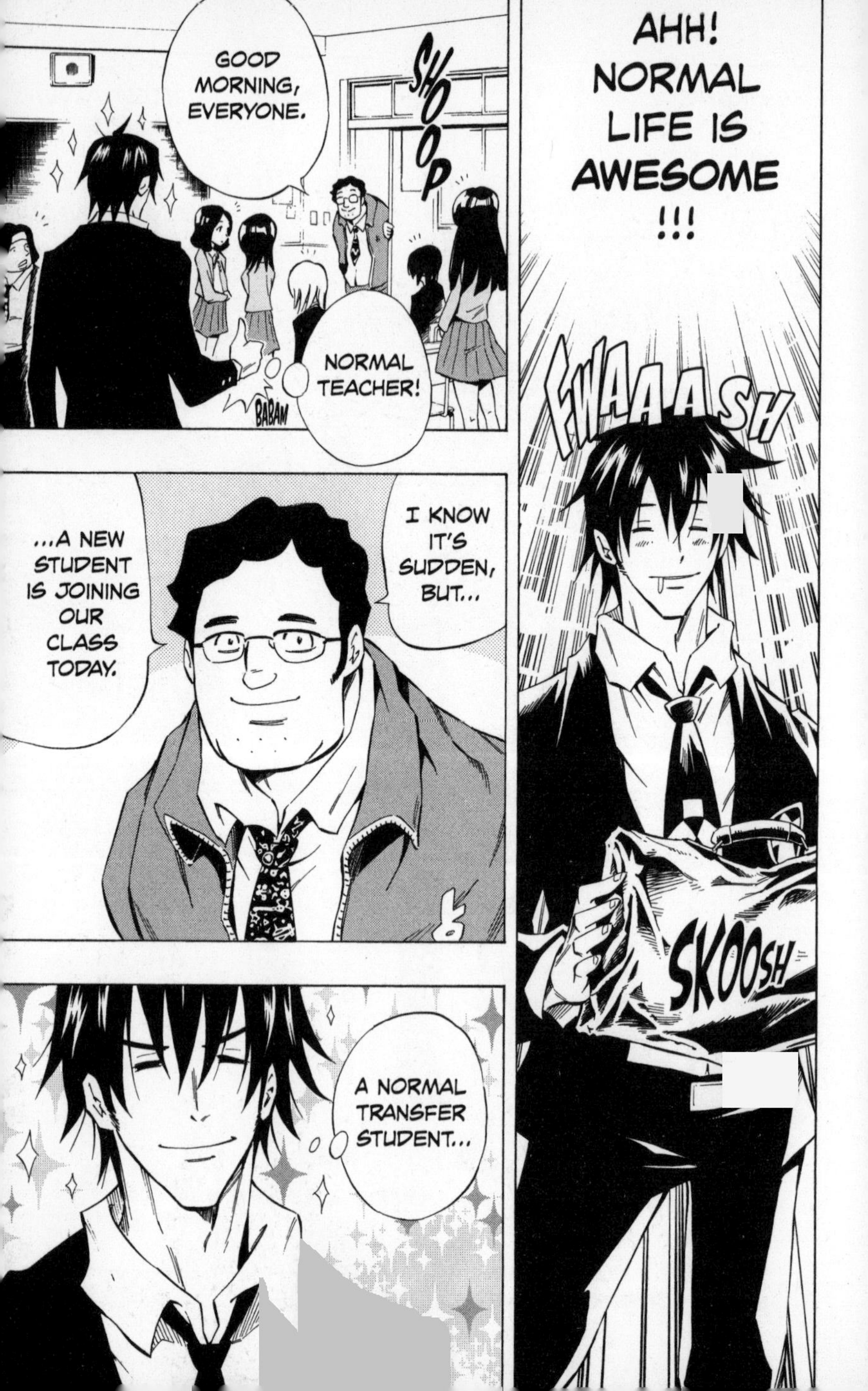
AHH! NORMAL LIFE IS AWESOME !!!
FWAAASH
SKOOSH
SHOOP
GOOD MORNING, EVERYONE.
NORMAL TEACHER!
BABAM
I KNOW IT'S SUDDEN, BUT...
...A NEW STUDENT IS JOINING OUR CLASS TODAY.
A NORMAL TRANSFER STUDENT...

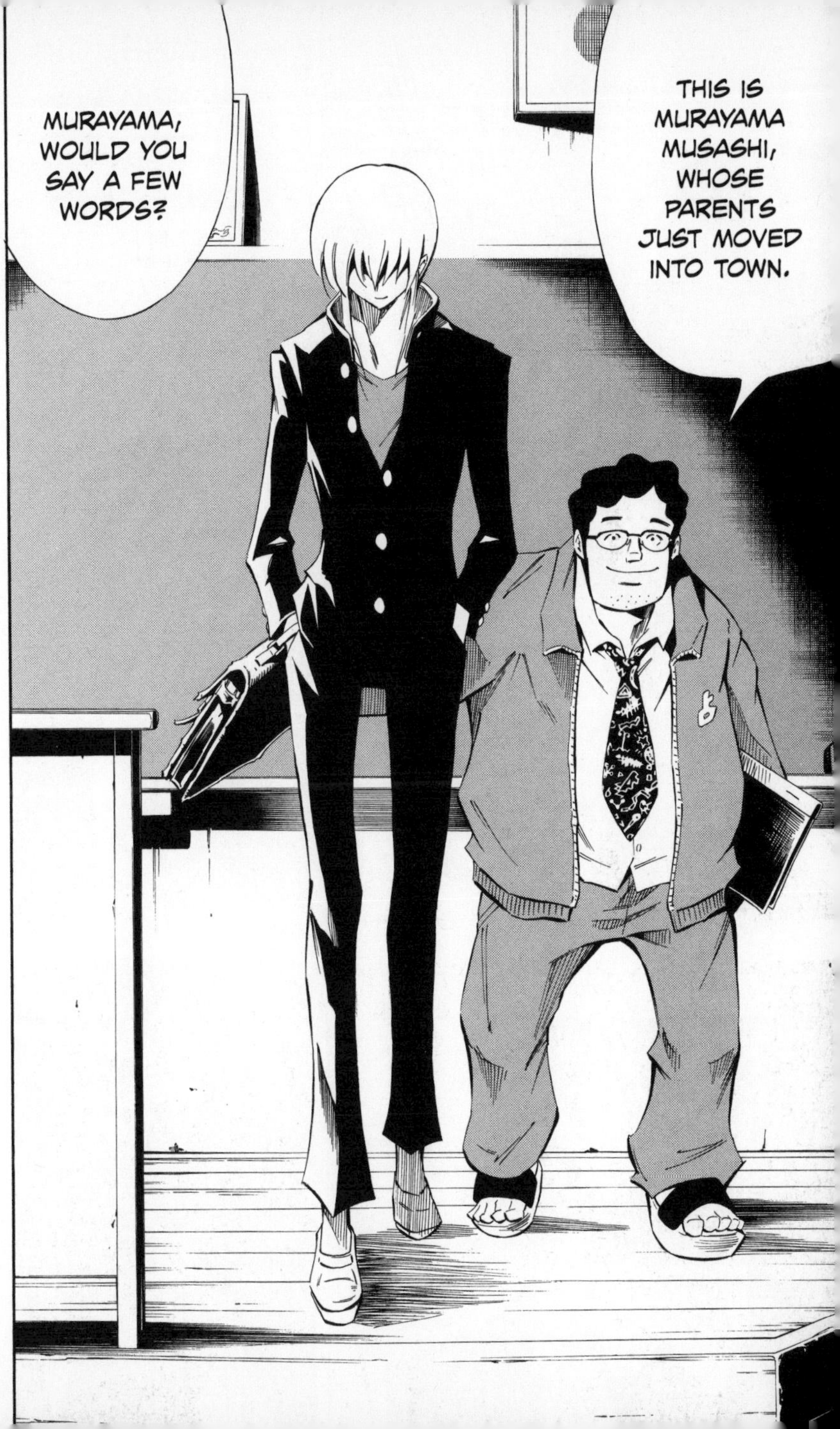
THIS IS MURAYAMA MUSASHI, WHOSE PARENTS JUST MOVED INTO TOWN.
MURAYAMA, WOULD YOU SAY A FEW WORDS?

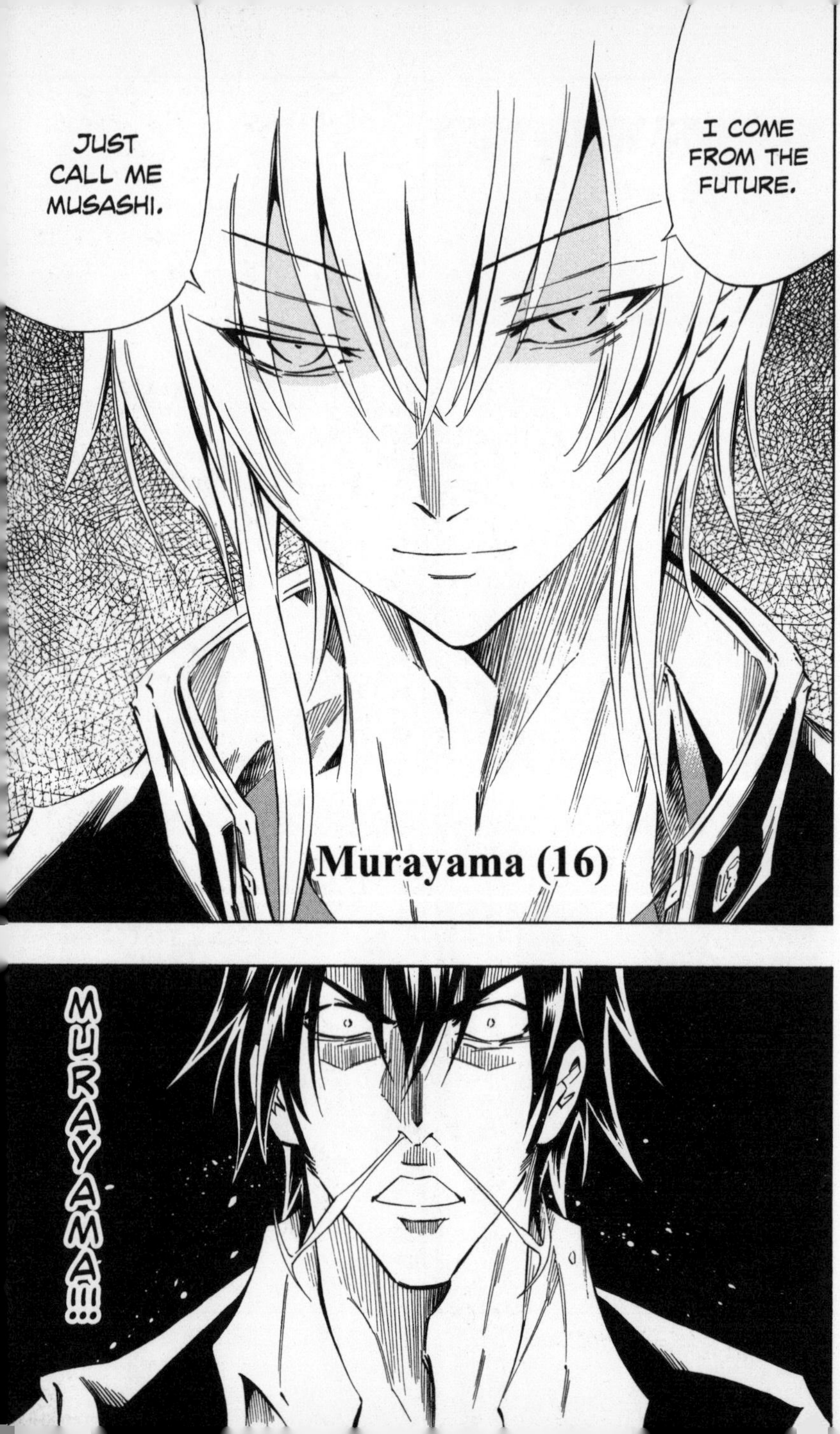
I COME FROM THE FUTURE.
JUST CALL ME MUSASHI.
Murayama (16)
MURAYAMA!!!

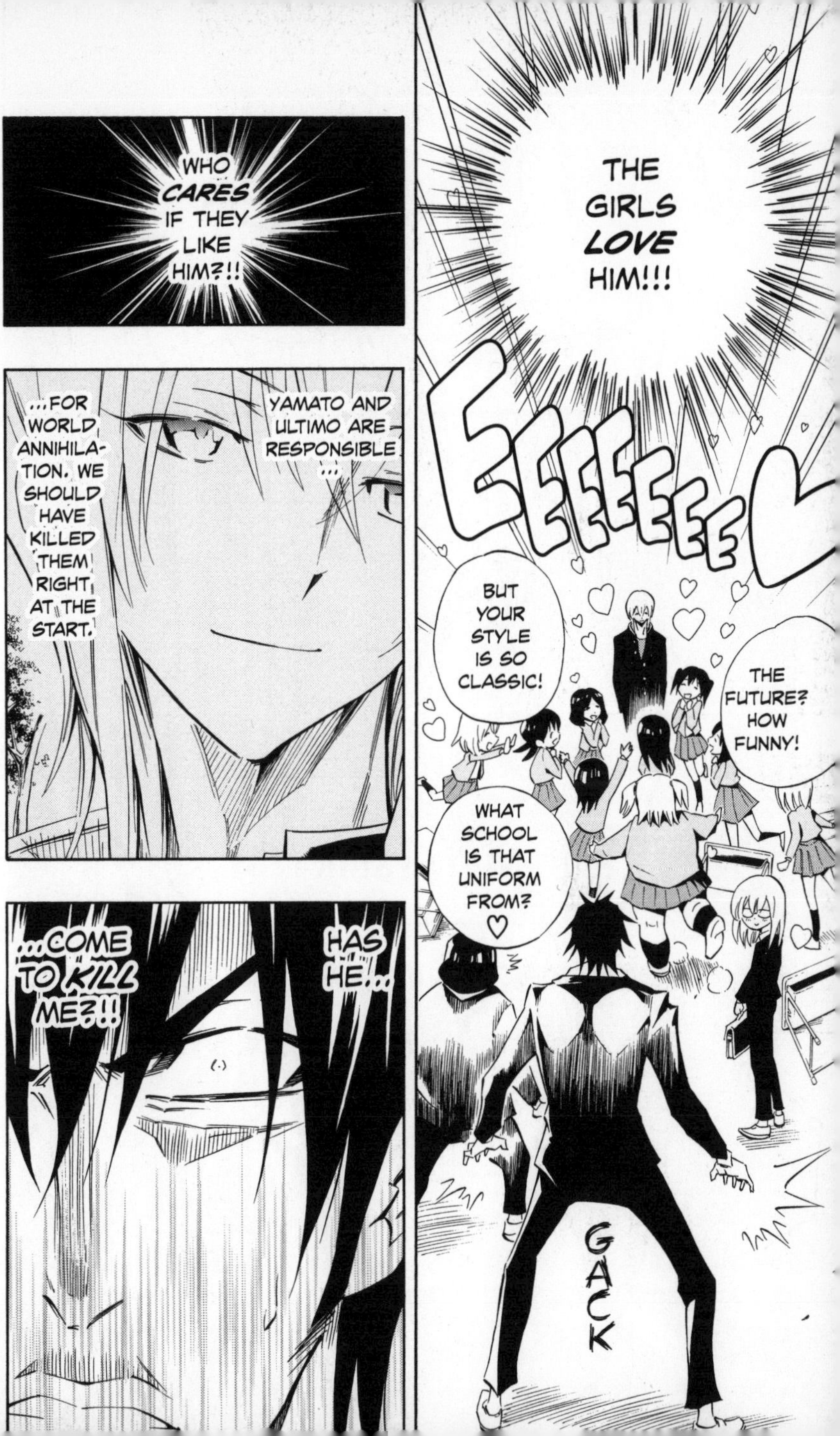
THE GIRLS LOVE HIM!!!
EEEEEEE♡
THE FUTURE? HOW FUNNY!
BUT YOUR STYLE IS SO CLASSIC!
WHAT SCHOOL IS THAT UNIFORM FROM? ♡
GACK
WHO CARES IF THEY LIKE HIM?!!
YAMATO AND ULTIMO ARE RESPONSIBLE...
...FOR WORLD ANNIHILATION. WE SHOULD HAVE KILLED THEM RIGHT AT THE START.
HAS HE...
...COME TO KILL ME?!!

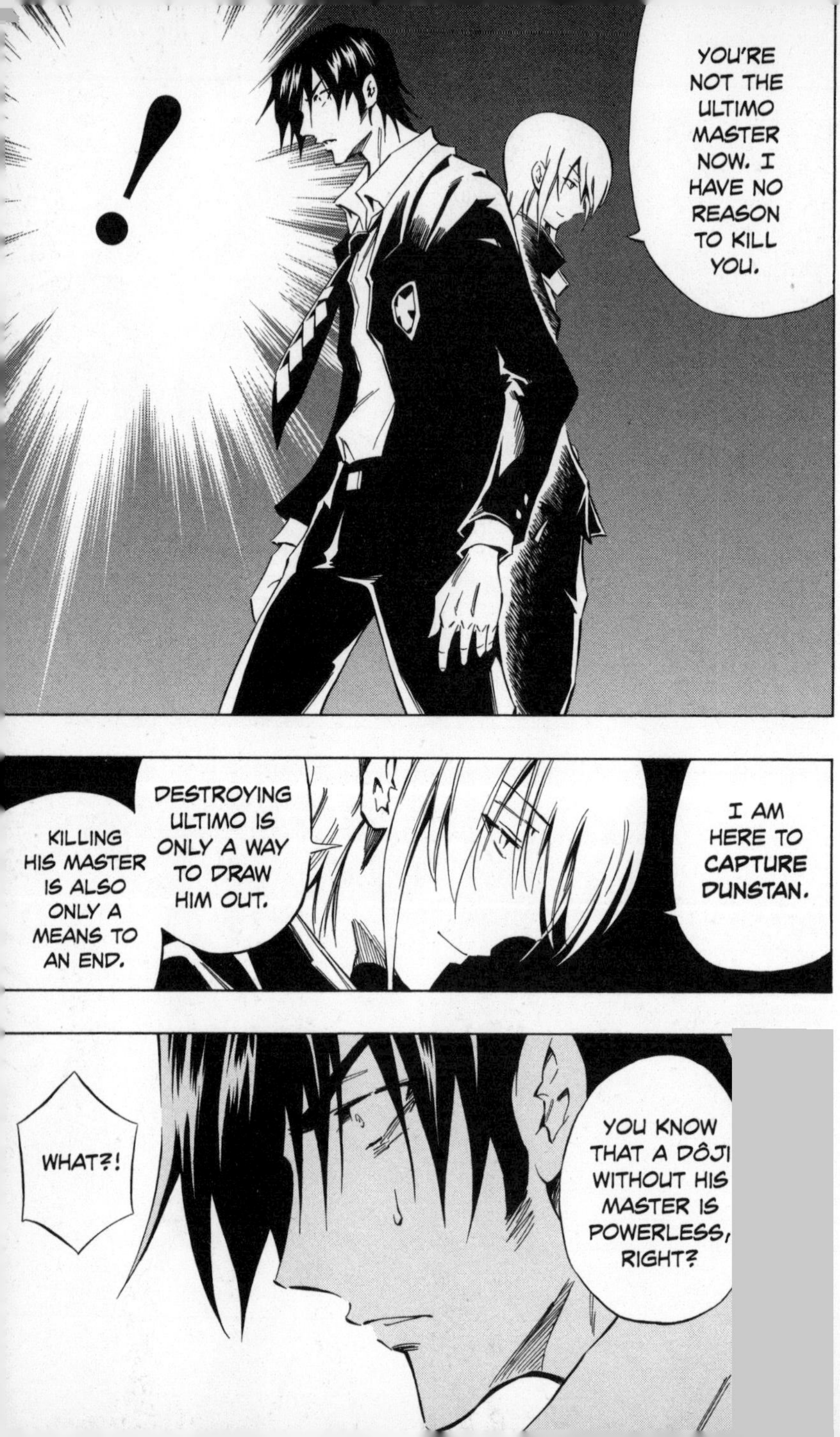
YOU'RE NOT THE ULTIMO MASTER NOW. I HAVE NO REASON TO KILL YOU.
!
I AM HERE TO CAPTURE DUNSTAN.
DESTROYING ULTIMO IS ONLY A WAY TO DRAW HIM OUT.
KILLING HIS MASTER IS ALSO ONLY A MEANS TO AN END.
YOU KNOW THAT A DÔJI WITHOUT HIS MASTER IS POWERLESS, RIGHT?
WHAT?!

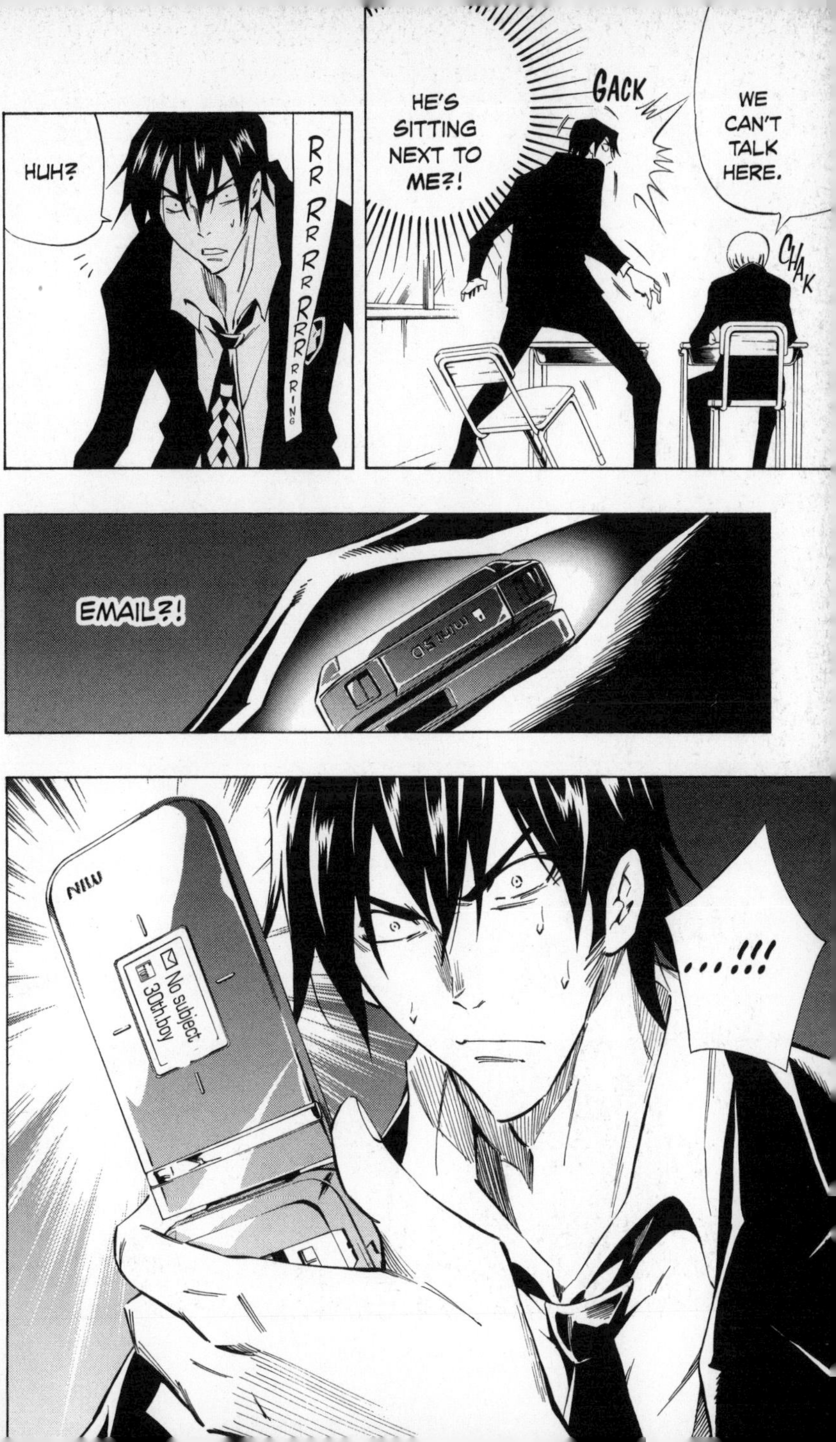
WE CAN'T TALK HERE.
CHAK
GACK
HE'S SITTING NEXT TO ME?!
RRRRRRRRRRRRRRRING
HUH?
EMAIL?!
miniSD
NIW
No subject
30th.boy
...!!!

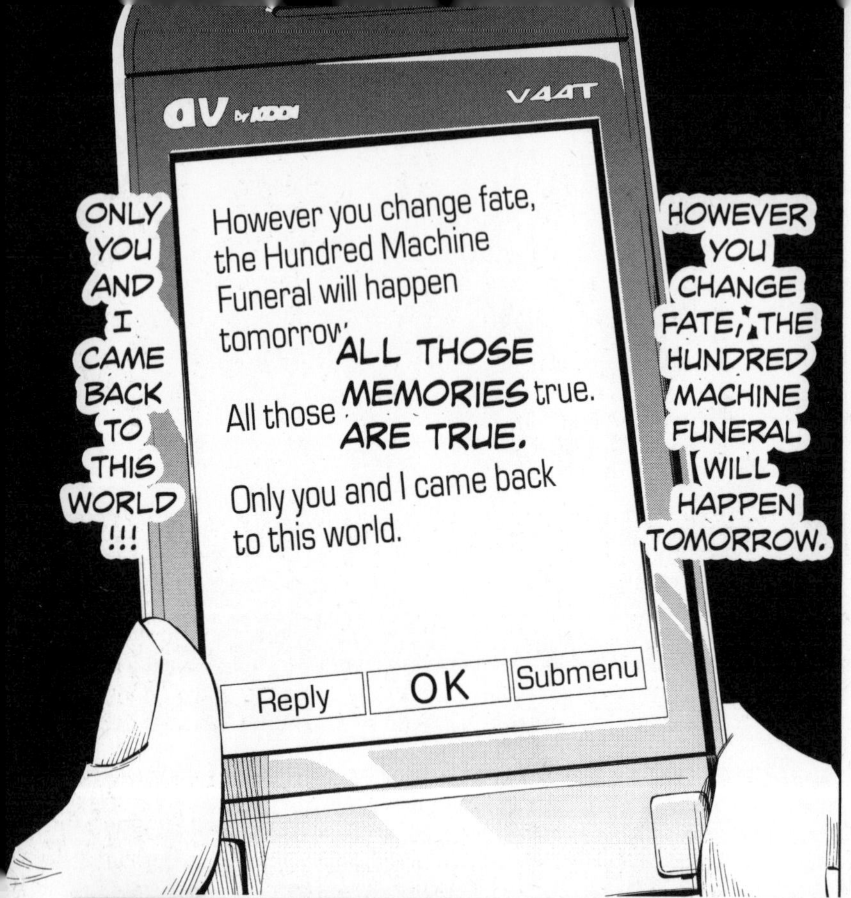
HOWEVER YOU CHANGE FATE, THE HUNDRED MACHINE FUNERAL WILL HAPPEN TOMORROW.
However you change fate, the Hundred Machine Funeral will happen tomorrov
ALL THOSE MEMORIES ARE TRUE.
All those
true.
Only you and I came back to this world.
Reply
OK
Submenu
ONLY YOU AND I CAME BACK TO THIS WORLD!!!

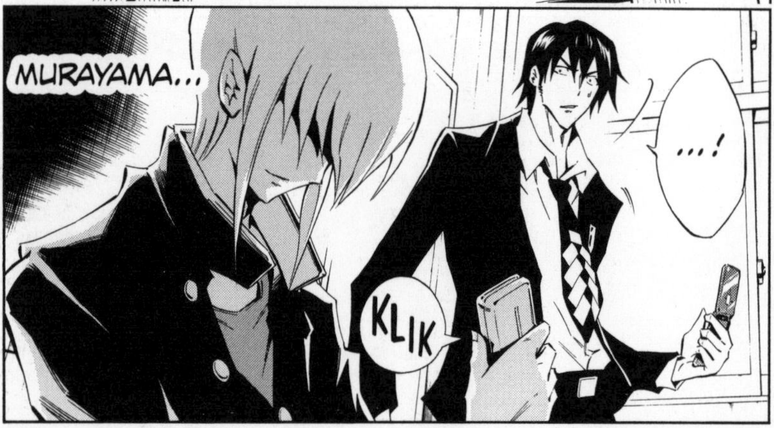
...!
MURAYAMA...
KLIK

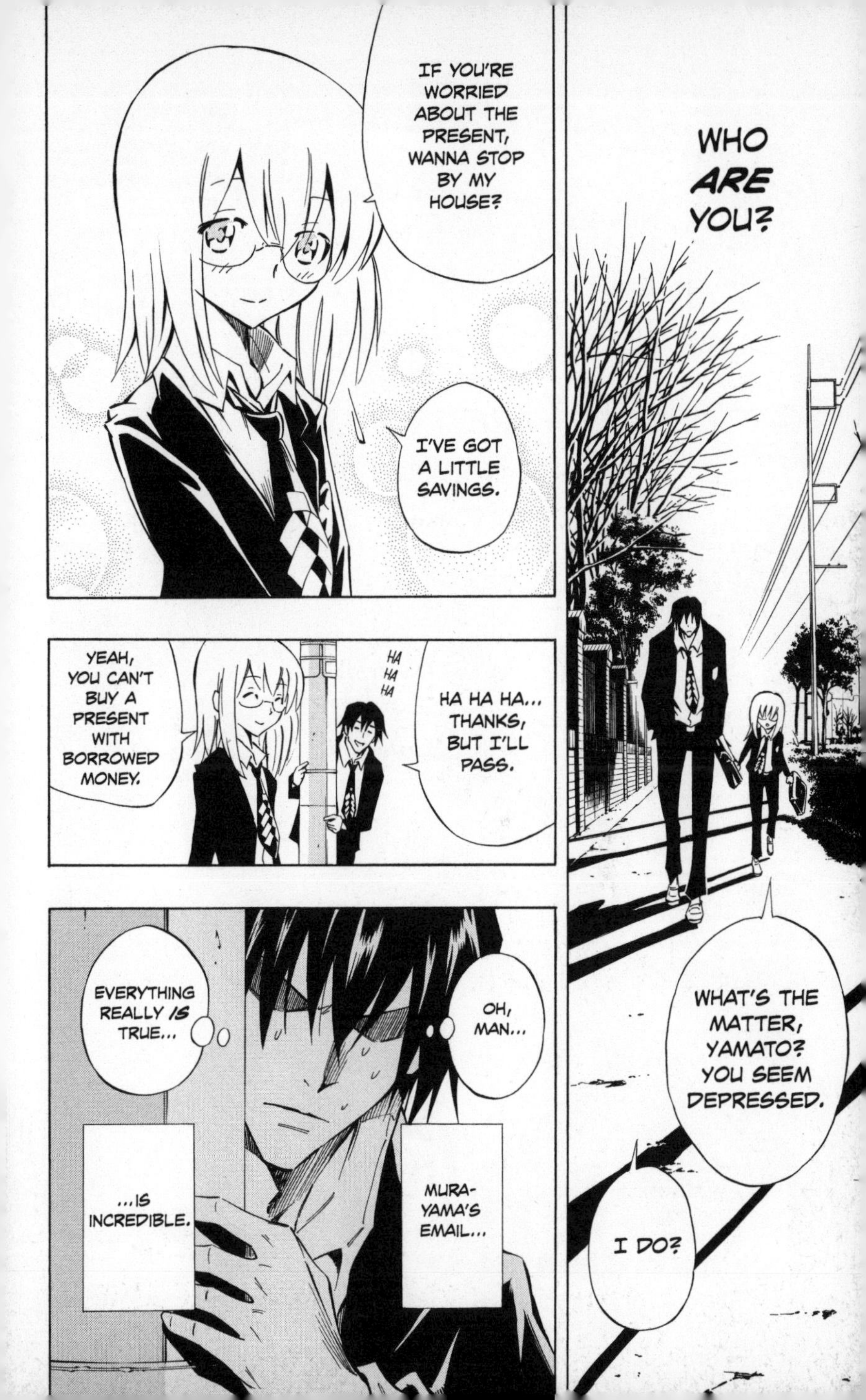
WHO *ARE* YOU?
WHAT'S THE MATTER, YAMATO? YOU SEEM DEPRESSED.
I DO?
IF YOU'RE WORRIED ABOUT THE PRESENT, WANNA STOP BY MY HOUSE?
I'VE GOT A LITTLE SAVINGS.
HA HA HA
HA HA HA... THANKS, BUT I'LL PASS.
YEAH, YOU CAN'T BUY A PRESENT WITH BORROWED MONEY.
OH, MAN...
EVERYTHING REALLY *IS* TRUE...
MURA-YAMA'S EMAIL...
...IS INCREDIBLE.

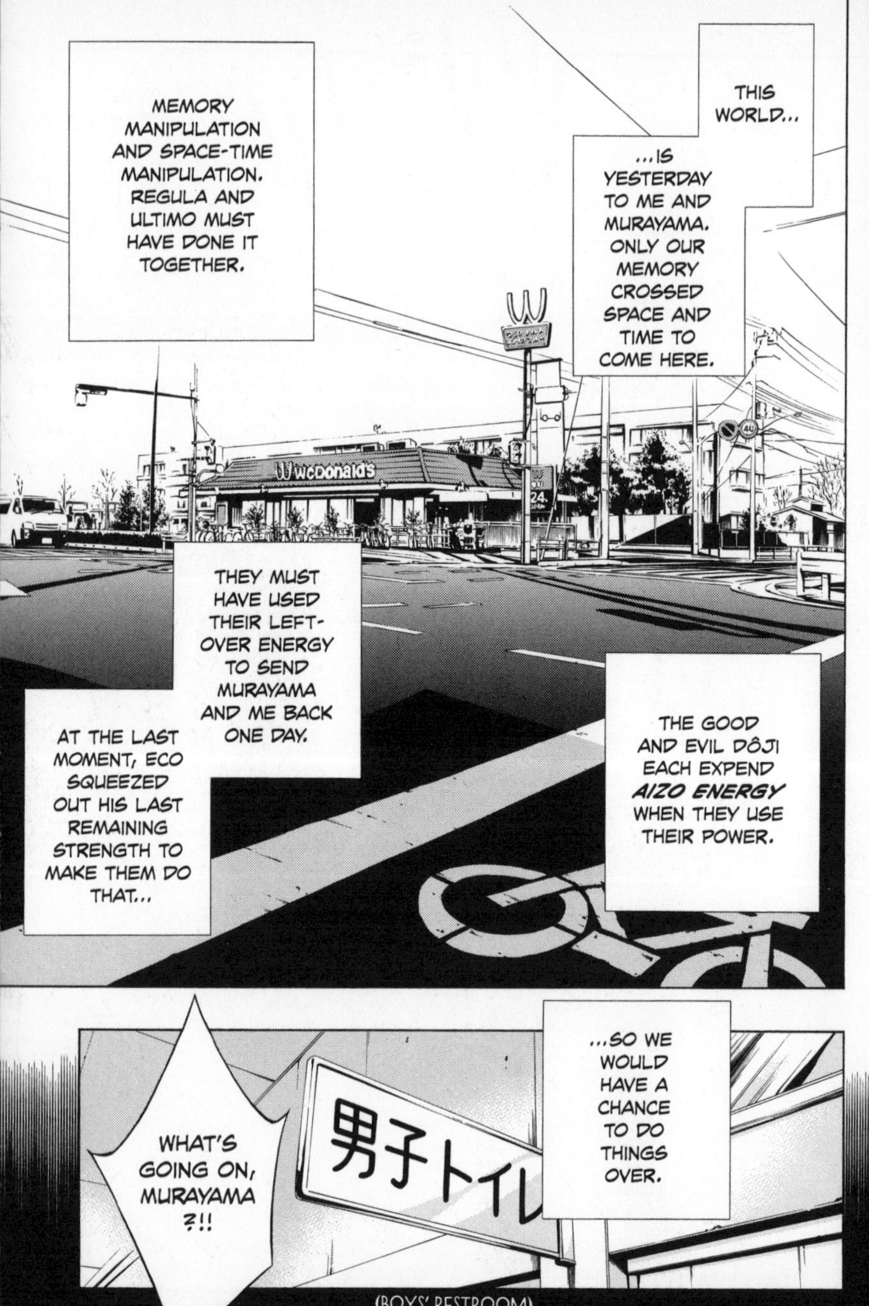
THIS WORLD...
...IS YESTERDAY TO ME AND MURAYAMA. ONLY OUR MEMORY CROSSED SPACE AND TIME TO COME HERE.
MEMORY MANIPULATION AND SPACE-TIME MANIPULATION. REGULA AND ULTIMO MUST HAVE DONE IT TOGETHER.
THE GOOD AND EVIL DÔJI EACH EXPEND *AIZO ENERGY* WHEN THEY USE THEIR POWER.
THEY MUST HAVE USED THEIR LEFT-OVER ENERGY TO SEND MURAYAMA AND ME BACK ONE DAY.
AT THE LAST MOMENT, ECO SQUEEZED OUT HIS LAST REMAINING STRENGTH TO MAKE THEM DO THAT...
...SO WE WOULD HAVE A CHANCE TO DO THINGS OVER.
男子トイレ
WHAT'S GOING ON, MURAYAMA?!!

(BOYS' RESTROOM)

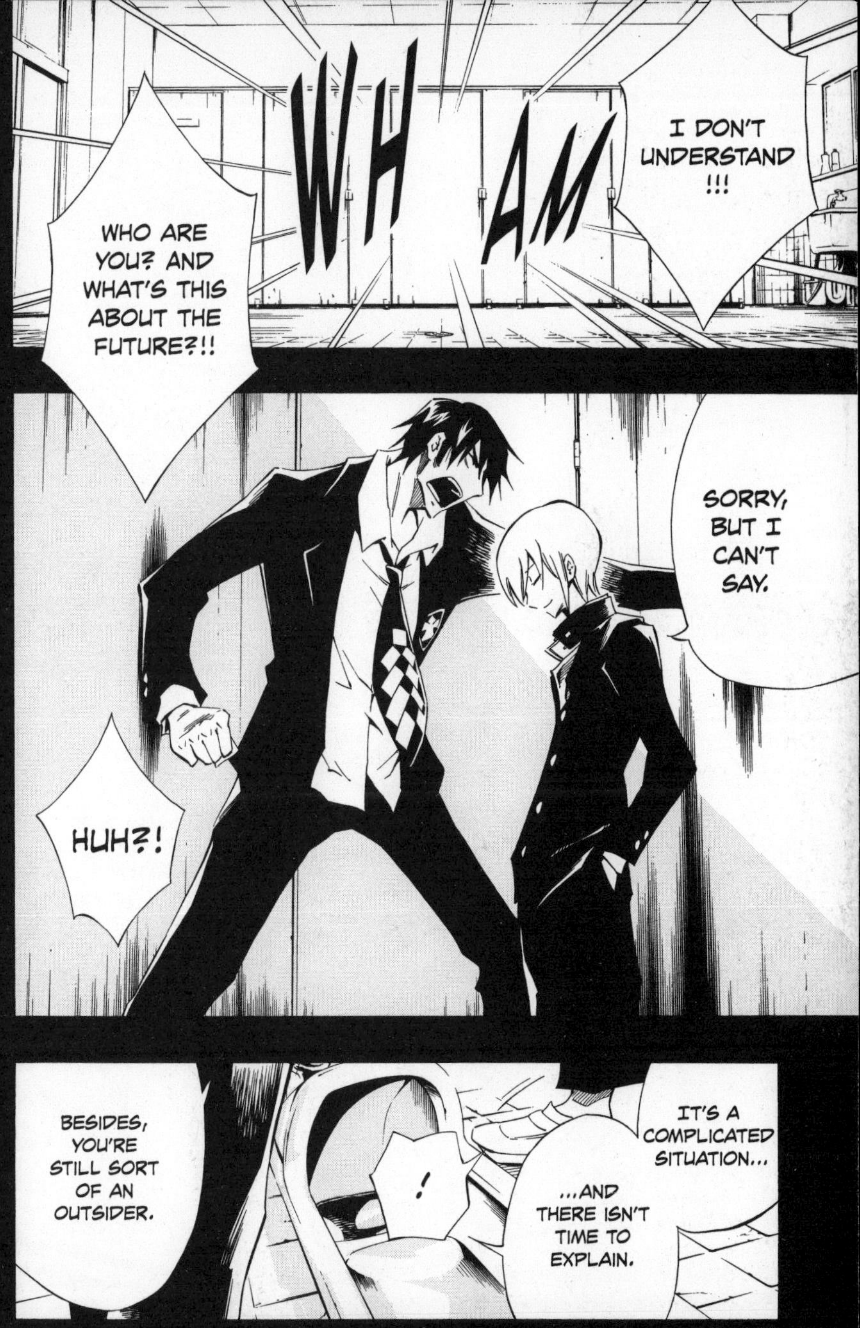
I DON'T UNDERSTAND!!!
WHAM
WHO ARE YOU? AND WHAT'S THIS ABOUT THE FUTURE?!!
SORRY, BUT I CAN'T SAY.
HUH?!
IT'S A COMPLICATED SITUATION...
...AND THERE ISN'T TIME TO EXPLAIN.
!
BESIDES, YOU'RE STILL SORT OF AN OUTSIDER.

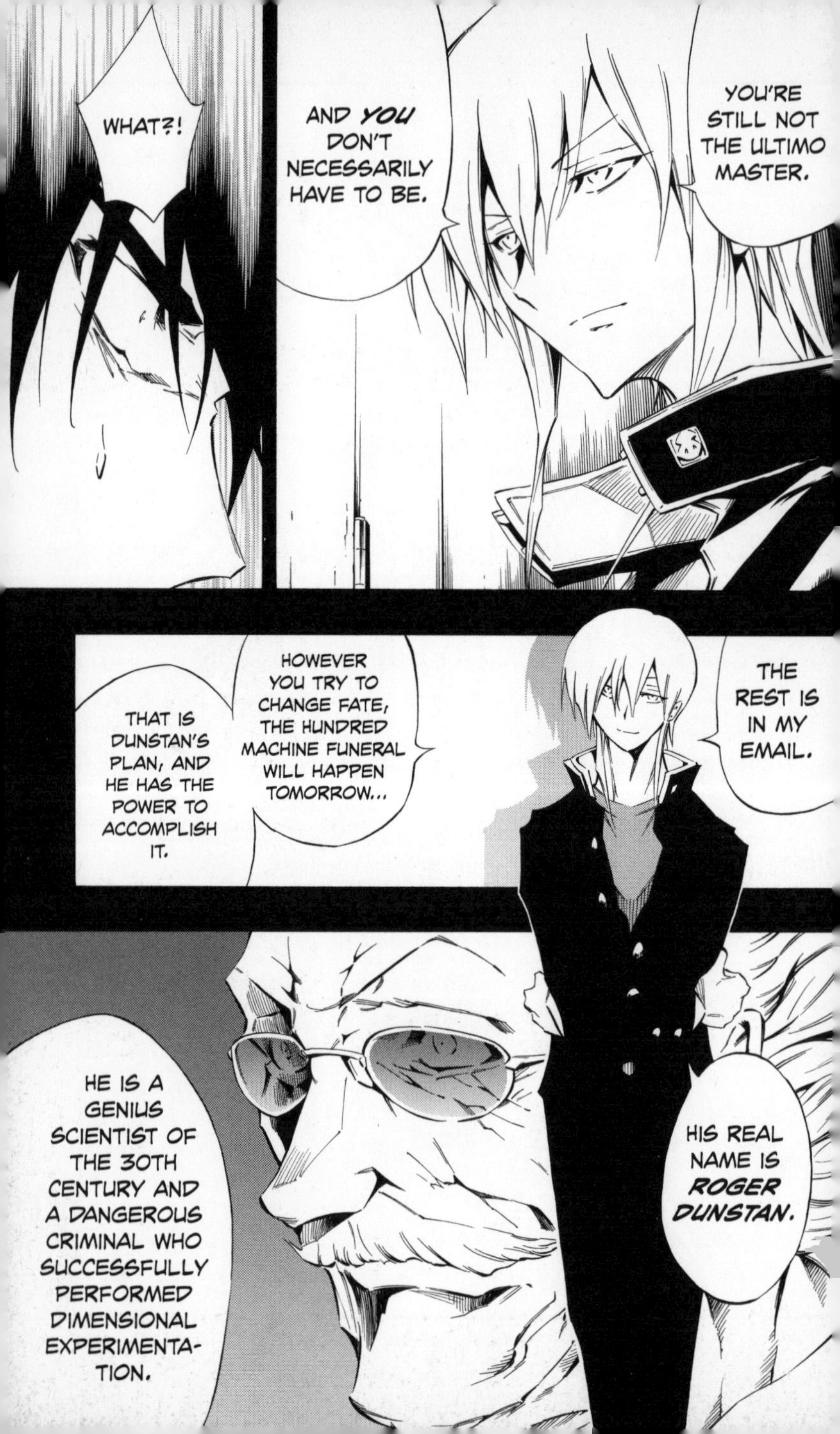
YOU'RE STILL NOT THE ULTIMO MASTER.
AND *YOU* DON'T NECESSARILY HAVE TO BE.
WHAT?!
THE REST IS IN MY EMAIL.
HOWEVER YOU TRY TO CHANGE FATE, THE HUNDRED MACHINE FUNERAL WILL HAPPEN TOMORROW...
THAT IS DUNSTAN'S PLAN, AND HE HAS THE POWER TO ACCOMPLISH IT.
HIS REAL NAME IS *ROGER DUNSTAN.*
HE IS A GENIUS SCIENTIST OF THE 30TH CENTURY AND A DANGEROUS CRIMINAL WHO SUCCESSFULLY PERFORMED DIMENSIONAL EXPERIMENTA-TION.

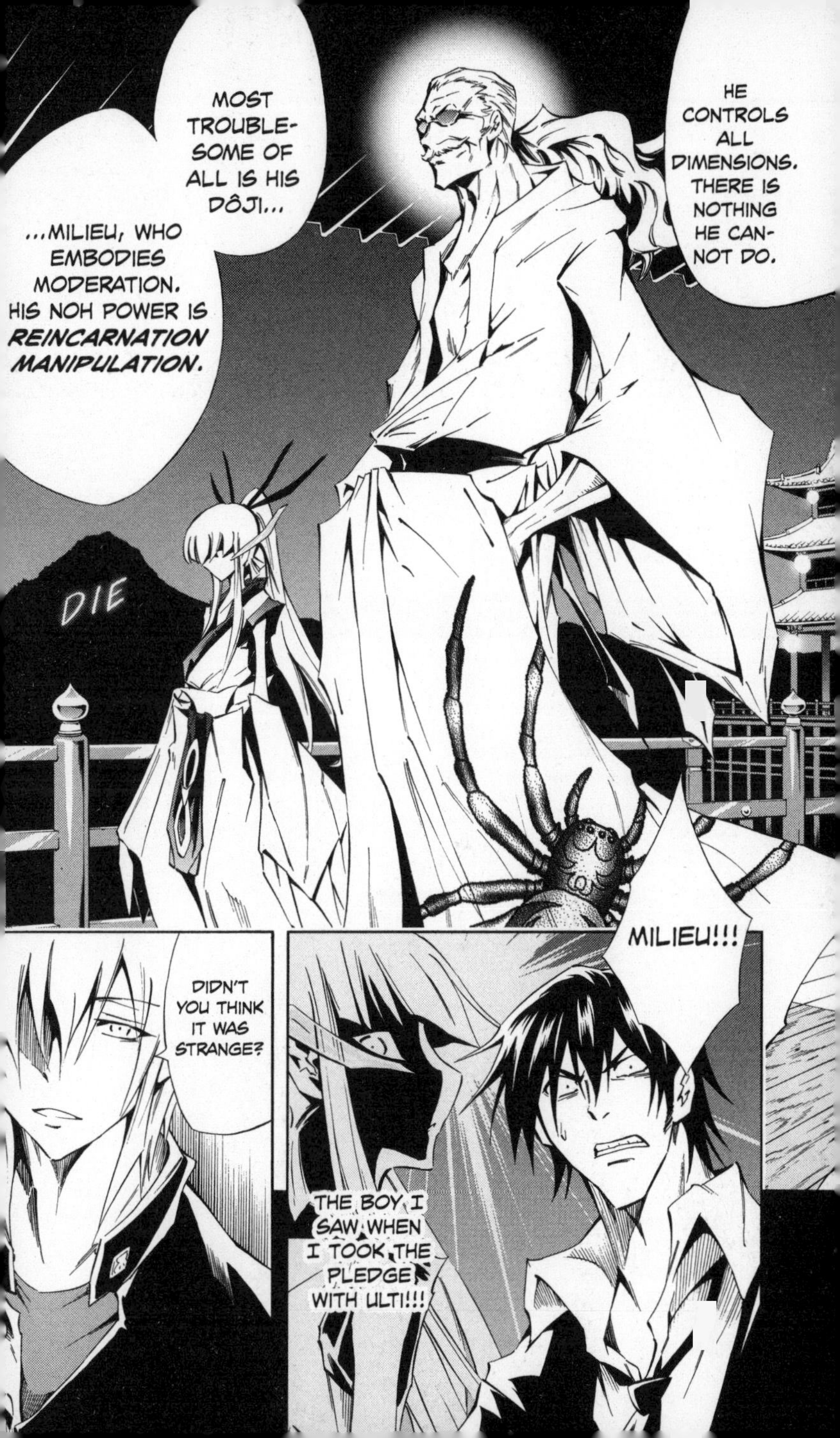
HE CONTROLS ALL DIMENSIONS. THERE IS NOTHING HE CAN-NOT DO.
MOST TROUBLE-SOME OF ALL IS HIS DÔJI...
...MILIEU, WHO EMBODIES MODERATION. HIS NOH POWER IS *REINCARNATION MANIPULATION*.
DIE
MILIEU!!!
THE BOY I SAW WHEN I TOOK THE PLEDGE WITH ULTI!!!
DIDN'T YOU THINK IT WAS STRANGE?

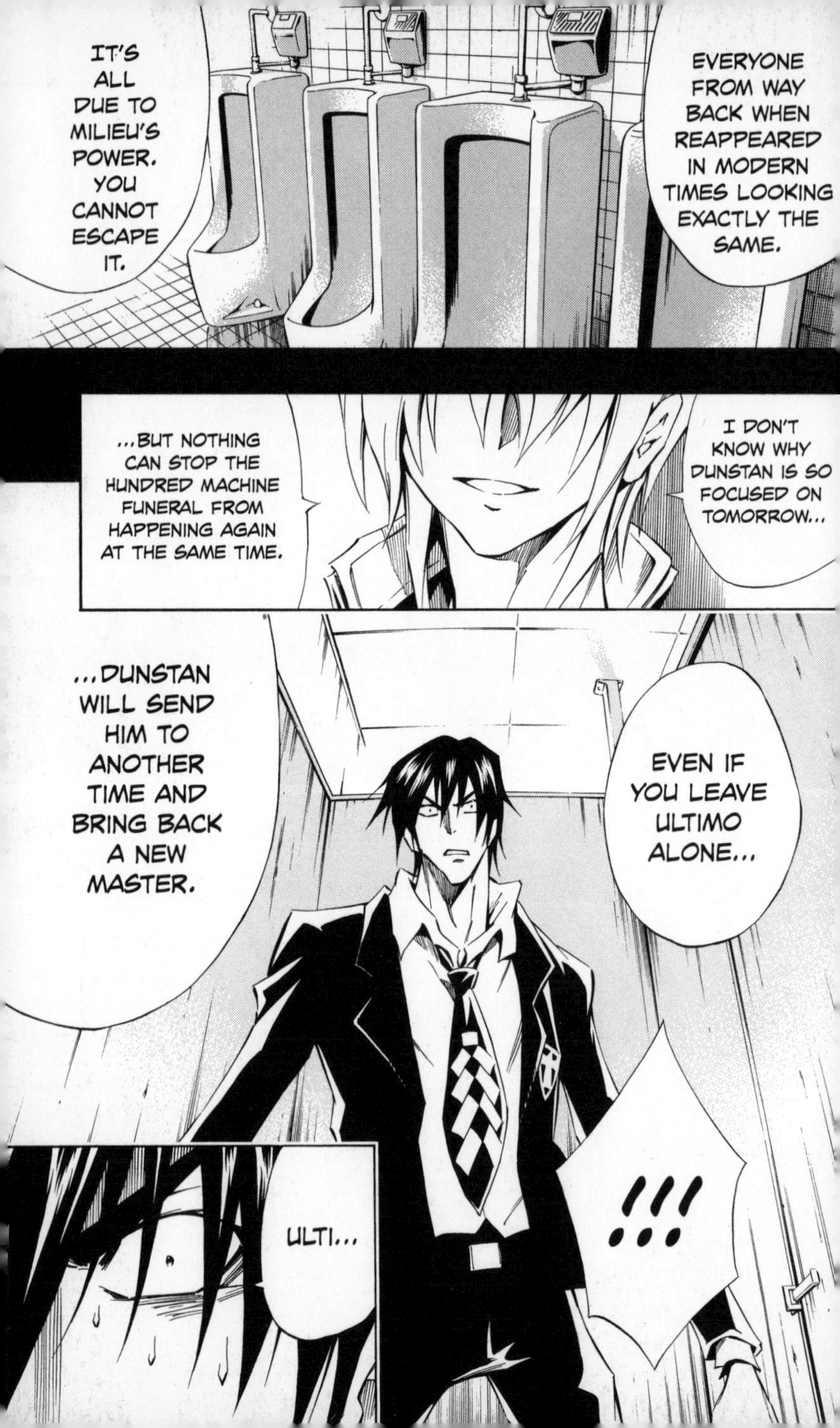
EVERYONE FROM WAY BACK WHEN REAPPEARED IN MODERN TIMES LOOKING EXACTLY THE SAME.
IT'S ALL DUE TO MILIEU'S POWER. YOU CANNOT ESCAPE IT.
I DON'T KNOW WHY DUNSTAN IS SO FOCUSED ON TOMORROW...
...BUT NOTHING CAN STOP THE HUNDRED MACHINE FUNERAL FROM HAPPENING AGAIN AT THE SAME TIME.
EVEN IF YOU LEAVE ULTIMO ALONE...
...DUNSTAN WILL SEND HIM TO ANOTHER TIME AND BRING BACK A NEW MASTER.
!!!
ULTI...

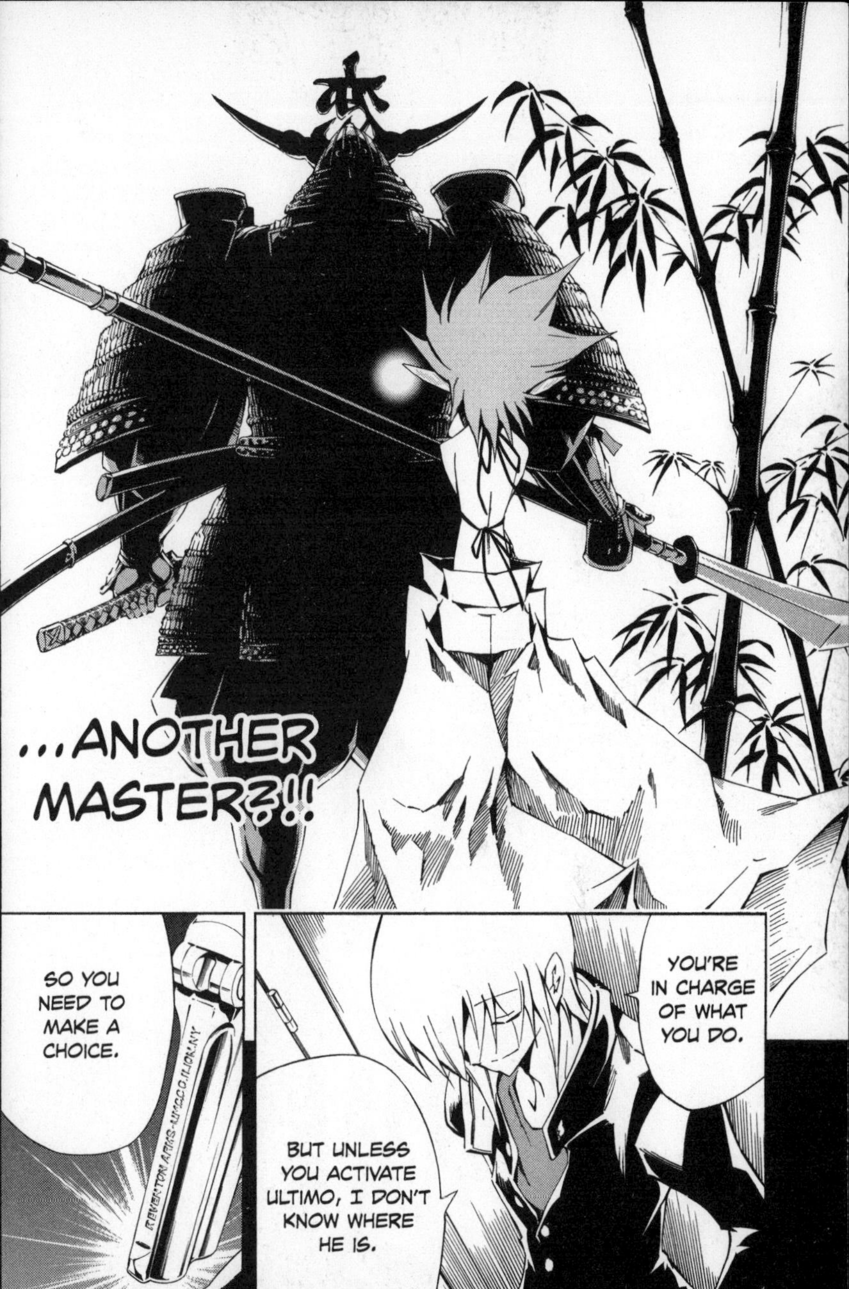
...ANOTHER MASTER?!!
YOU'RE IN CHARGE OF WHAT YOU DO.
BUT UNLESS YOU ACTIVATE ULTIMO, I DON'T KNOW WHERE HE IS.
SO YOU NEED TO MAKE A CHOICE.

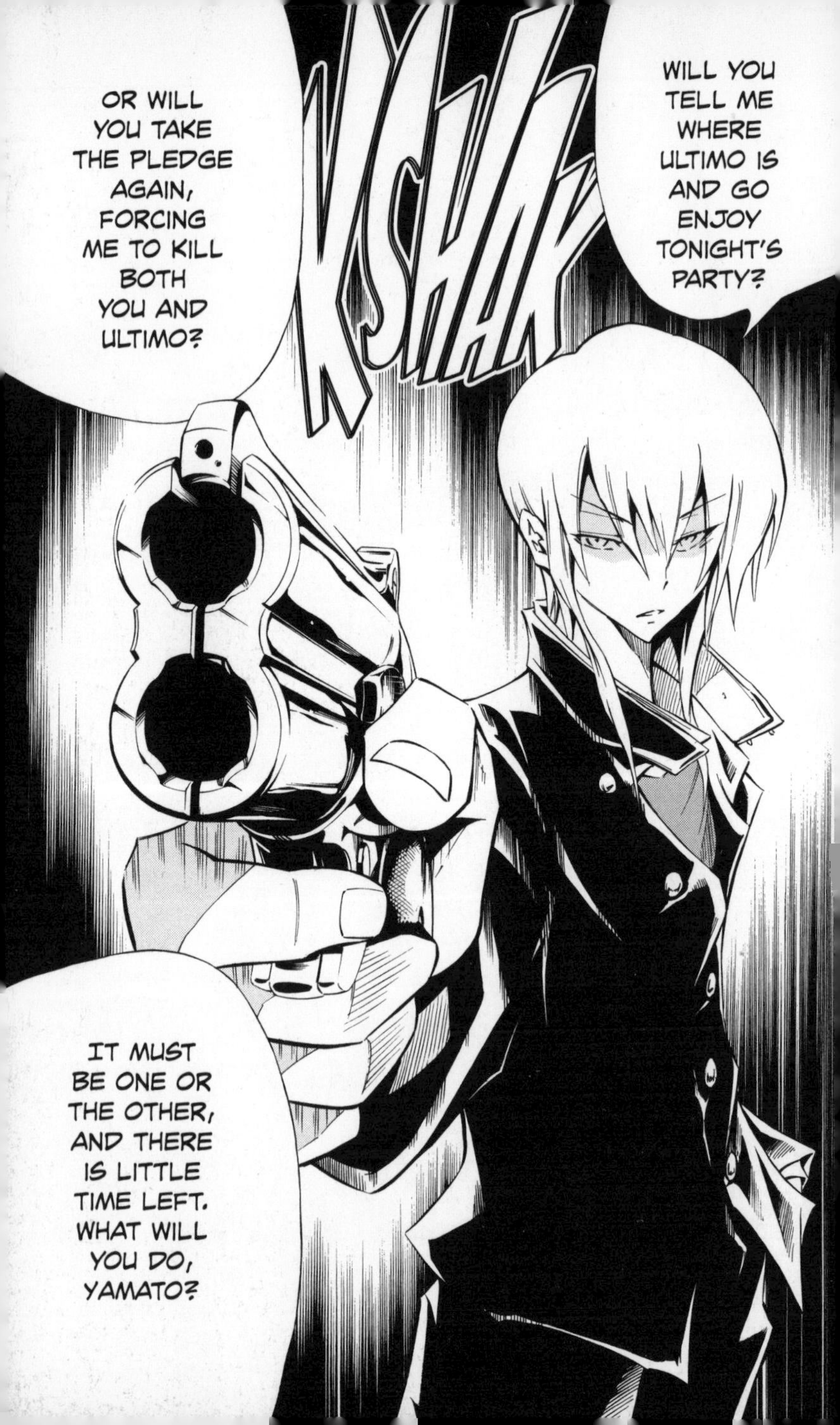
WILL YOU TELL ME WHERE ULTIMO IS AND GO ENJOY TONIGHT'S PARTY?
KSHAK
OR WILL YOU TAKE THE PLEDGE AGAIN, FORCING ME TO KILL BOTH YOU AND ULTIMO?
IT MUST BE ONE OR THE OTHER, AND THERE IS LITTLE TIME LEFT. WHAT WILL YOU DO, YAMATO?

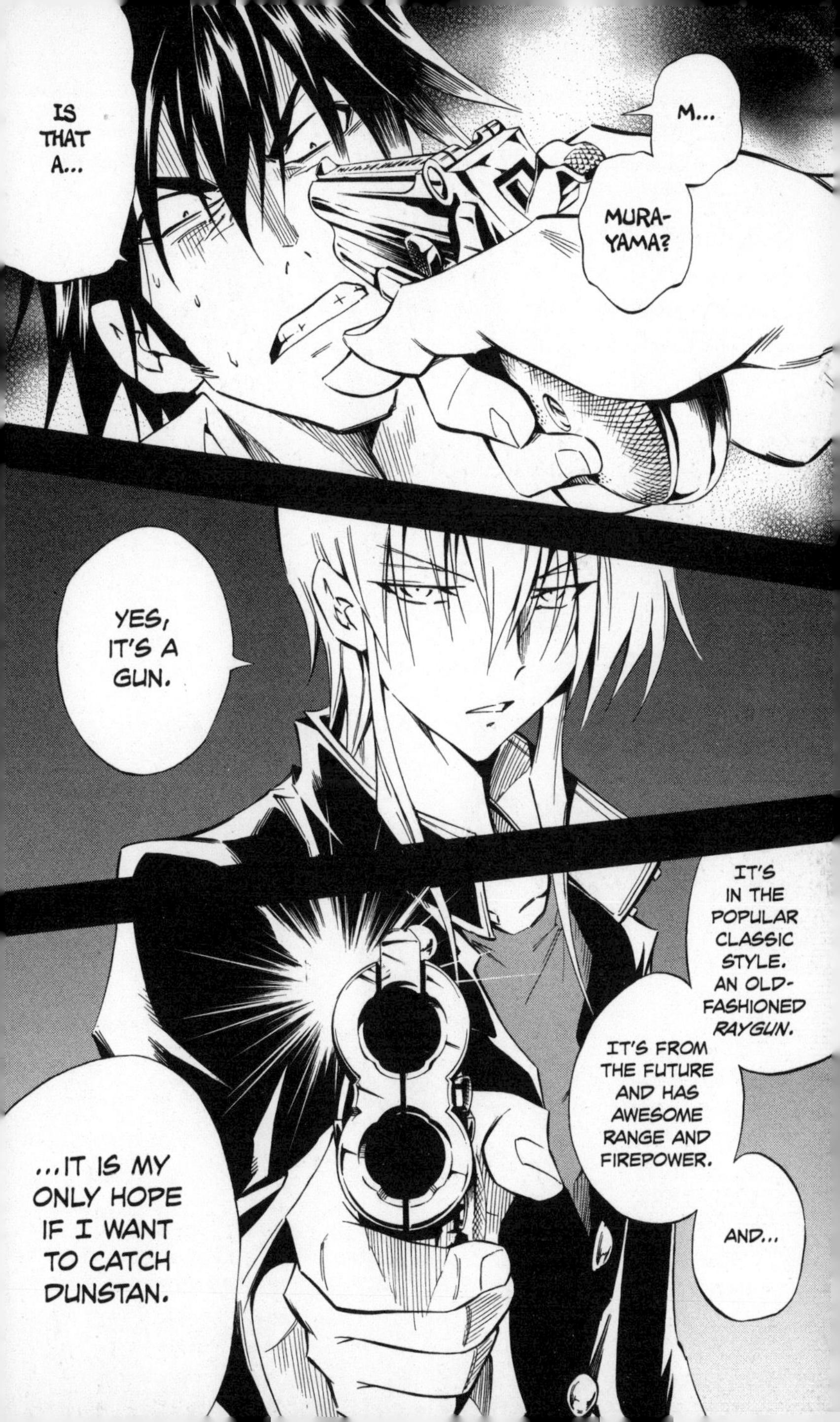
M...
MURA-YAMA?
IS THAT A...
YES, IT'S A GUN.
IT'S IN THE POPULAR CLASSIC STYLE. AN OLD-FASHIONED *RAYGUN*.
IT'S FROM THE FUTURE AND HAS AWESOME RANGE AND FIREPOWER.
AND...
...IT IS MY ONLY HOPE IF I WANT TO CATCH DUNSTAN.

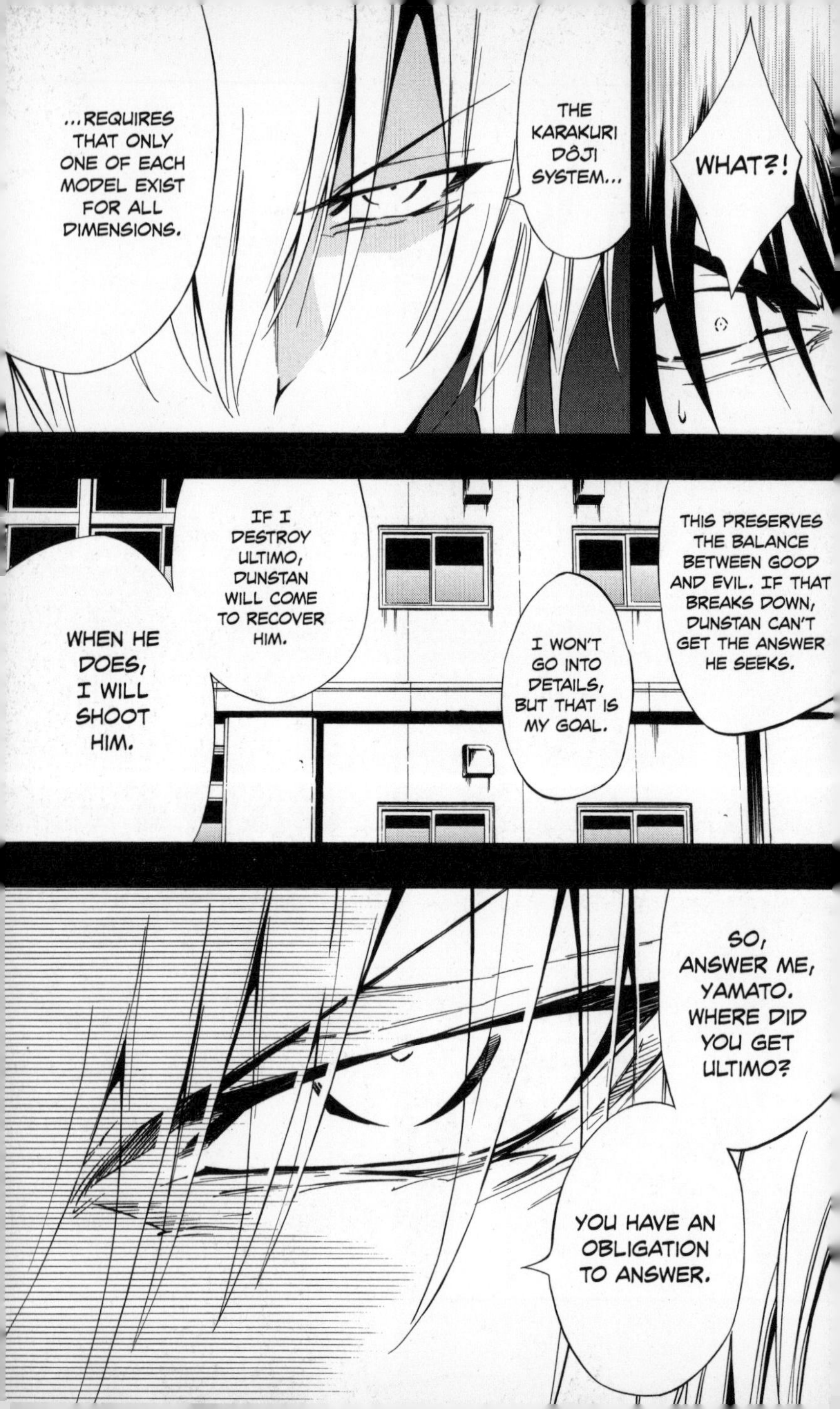
WHAT?!
THE KARAKURI DÔJI SYSTEM...
...REQUIRES THAT ONLY ONE OF EACH MODEL EXIST FOR ALL DIMENSIONS.
THIS PRESERVES THE BALANCE BETWEEN GOOD AND EVIL. IF THAT BREAKS DOWN, DUNSTAN CAN'T GET THE ANSWER HE SEEKS.
I WON'T GO INTO DETAILS, BUT THAT IS MY GOAL.
IF I DESTROY ULTIMO, DUNSTAN WILL COME TO RECOVER HIM.
WHEN HE DOES, I WILL SHOOT HIM.
SO, ANSWER ME, YAMATO. WHERE DID YOU GET ULTIMO?
YOU HAVE AN OBLIGATION TO ANSWER.

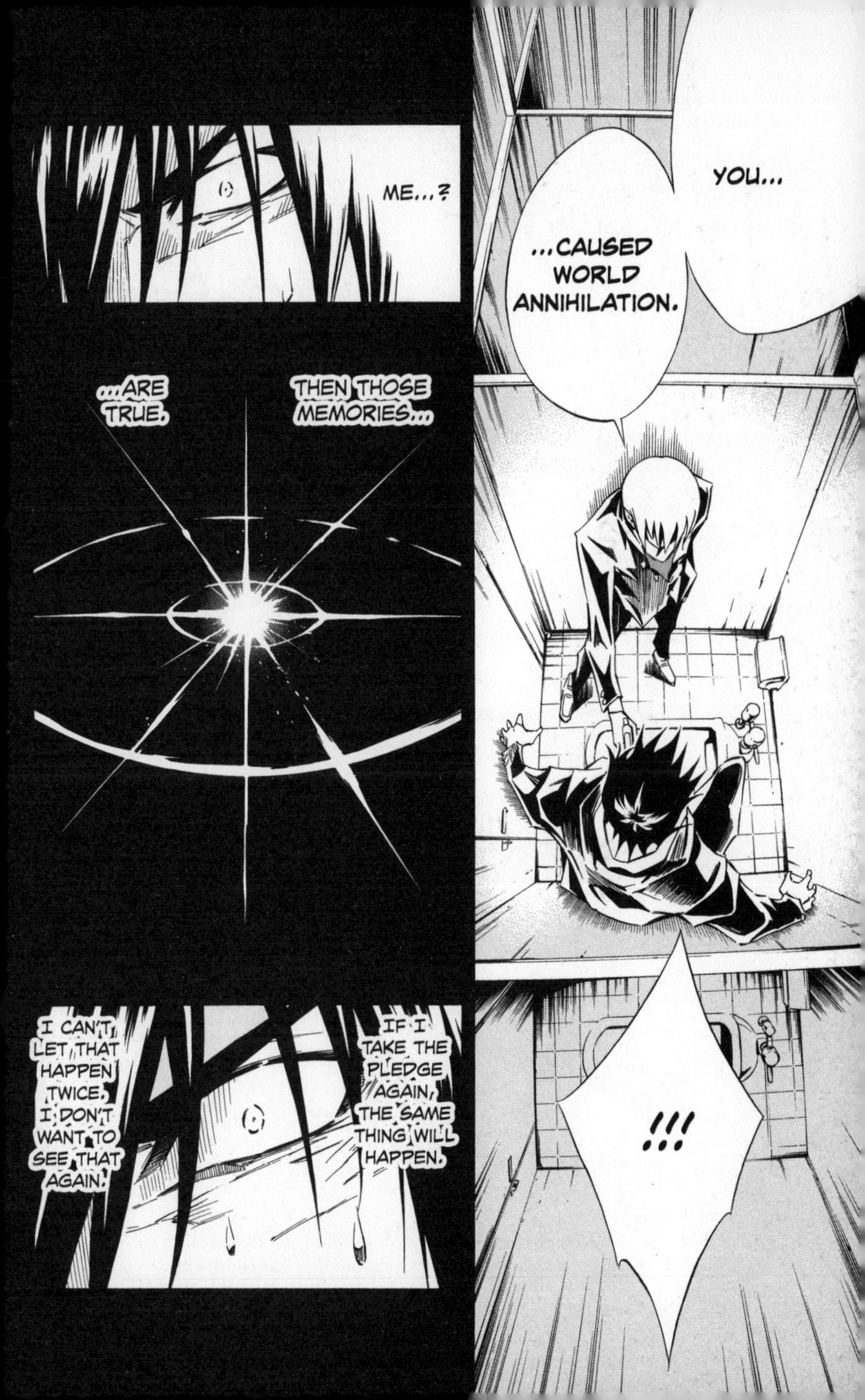
YOU...
...CAUSED WORLD ANNIHILATION.
!!!
ME...?
THEN THOSE MEMORIES...
...ARE TRUE.
IF I TAKE THE PLEDGE AGAIN, THE SAME THING WILL HAPPEN.
I CAN'T LET THAT HAPPEN TWICE. I DON'T WANT TO SEE THAT AGAIN.

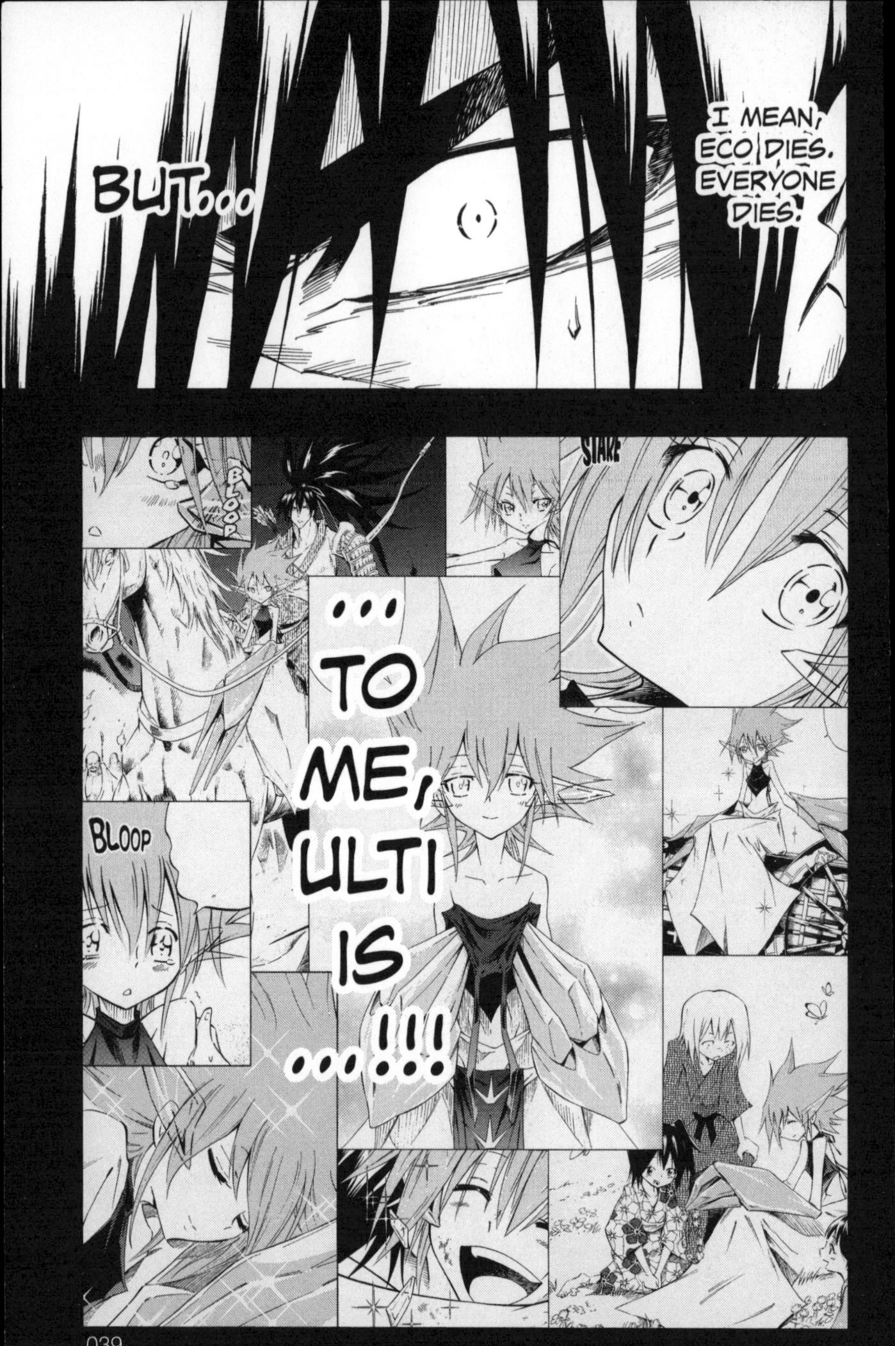
I MEAN, ECO DIES. EVERYONE DIES.
BUT...
STARE
BLOOP
...TO ME, ULTI IS ...!!!
BLOOP

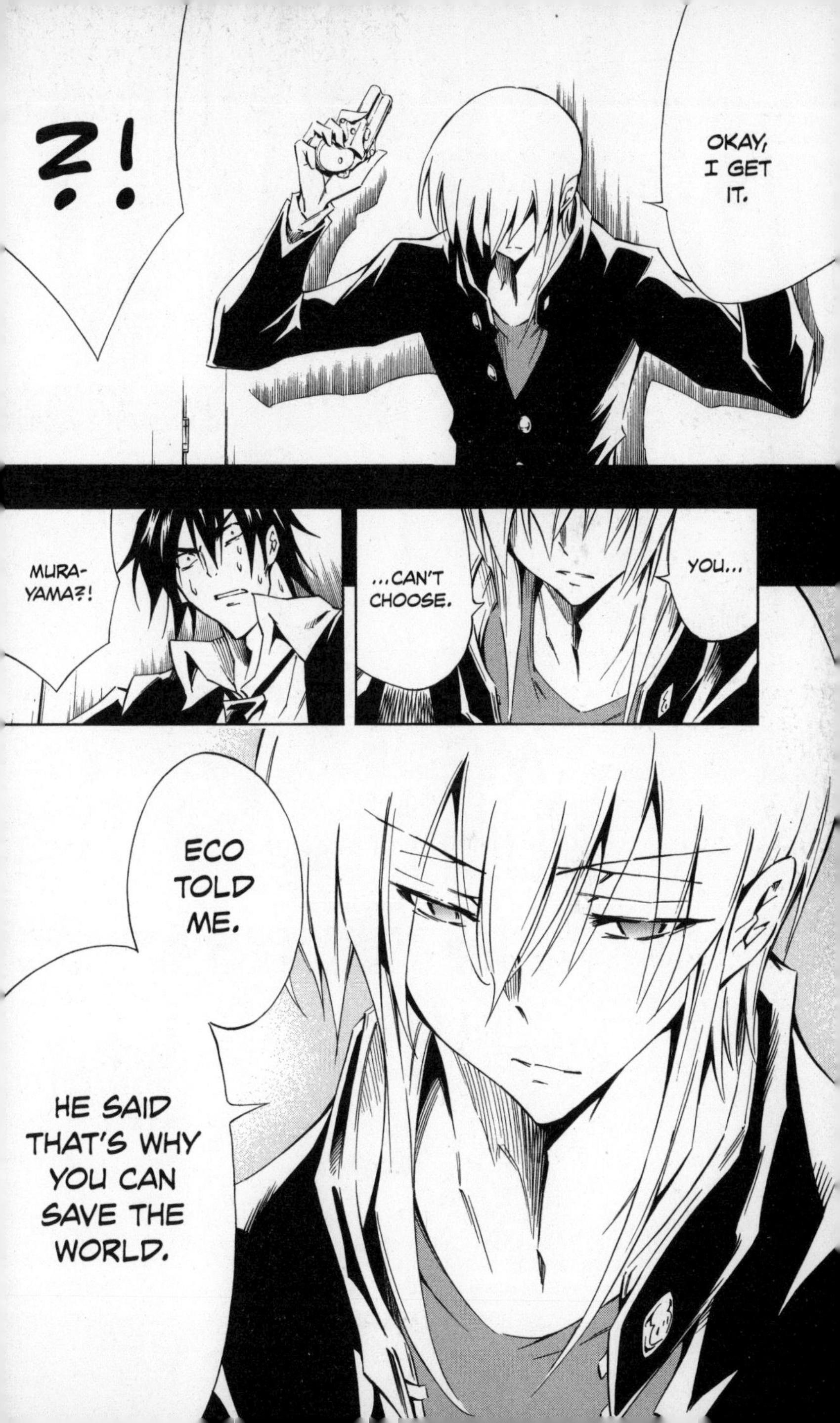
OKAY, I GET IT.
?!
YOU...
...CAN'T CHOOSE.
MURA-YAMA?!
ECO TOLD ME.
HE SAID THAT'S WHY YOU CAN SAVE THE WORLD.

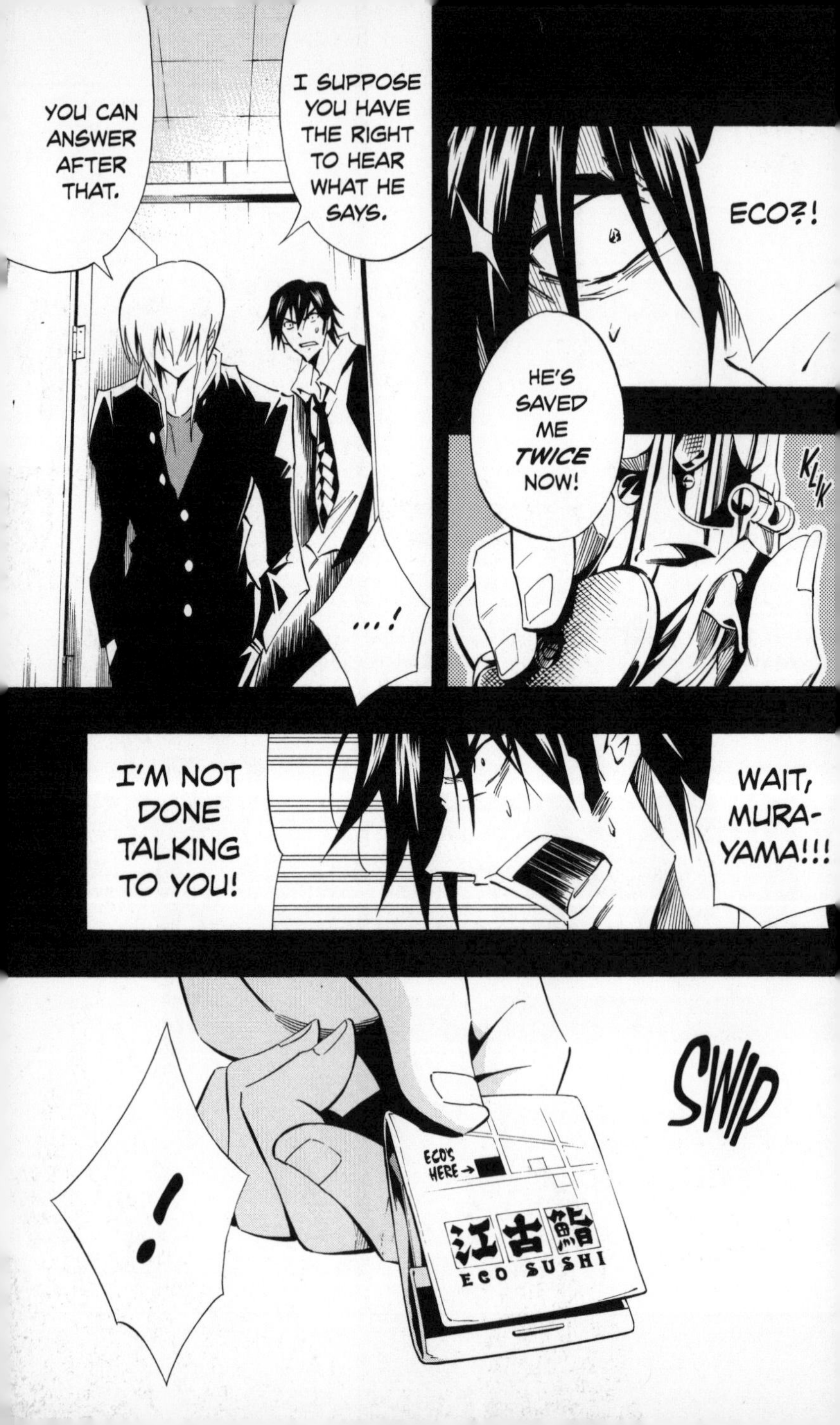
ECO?!
HE'S SAVED ME TWICE NOW!
KLIK
I SUPPOSE YOU HAVE THE RIGHT TO HEAR WHAT HE SAYS.
YOU CAN ANSWER AFTER THAT.
...!
WAIT, MURA-YAMA!!!
I'M NOT DONE TALKING TO YOU!
SWIP
ECO'S HERE →
江古鮨
ECO SUSHI
!

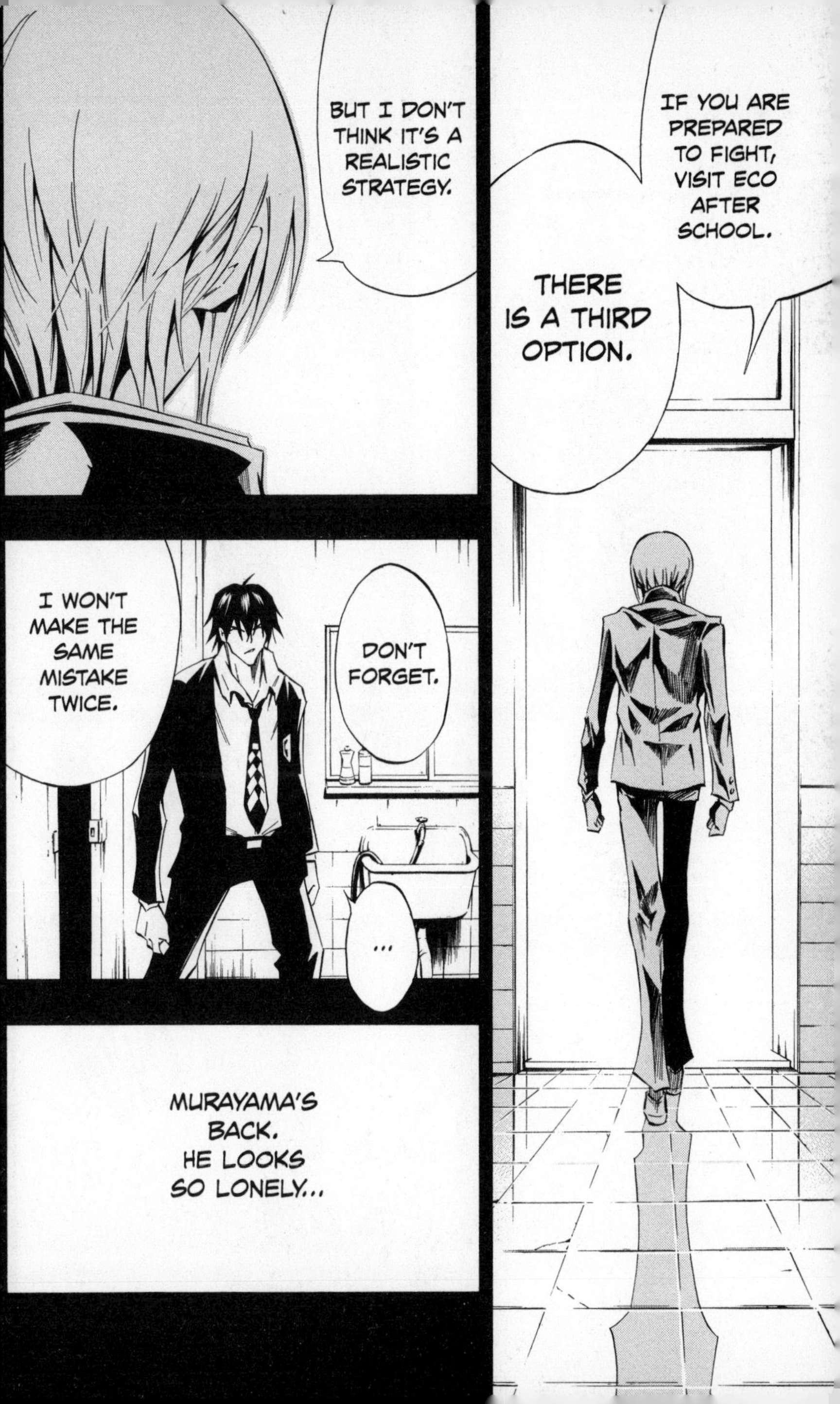
IF YOU ARE PREPARED TO FIGHT, VISIT ECO AFTER SCHOOL.
THERE IS A THIRD OPTION.
BUT I DON'T THINK IT'S A REALISTIC STRATEGY.
DON'T FORGET.
I WON'T MAKE THE SAME MISTAKE TWICE.
...
MURAYAMA'S BACK. HE LOOKS SO LONELY...

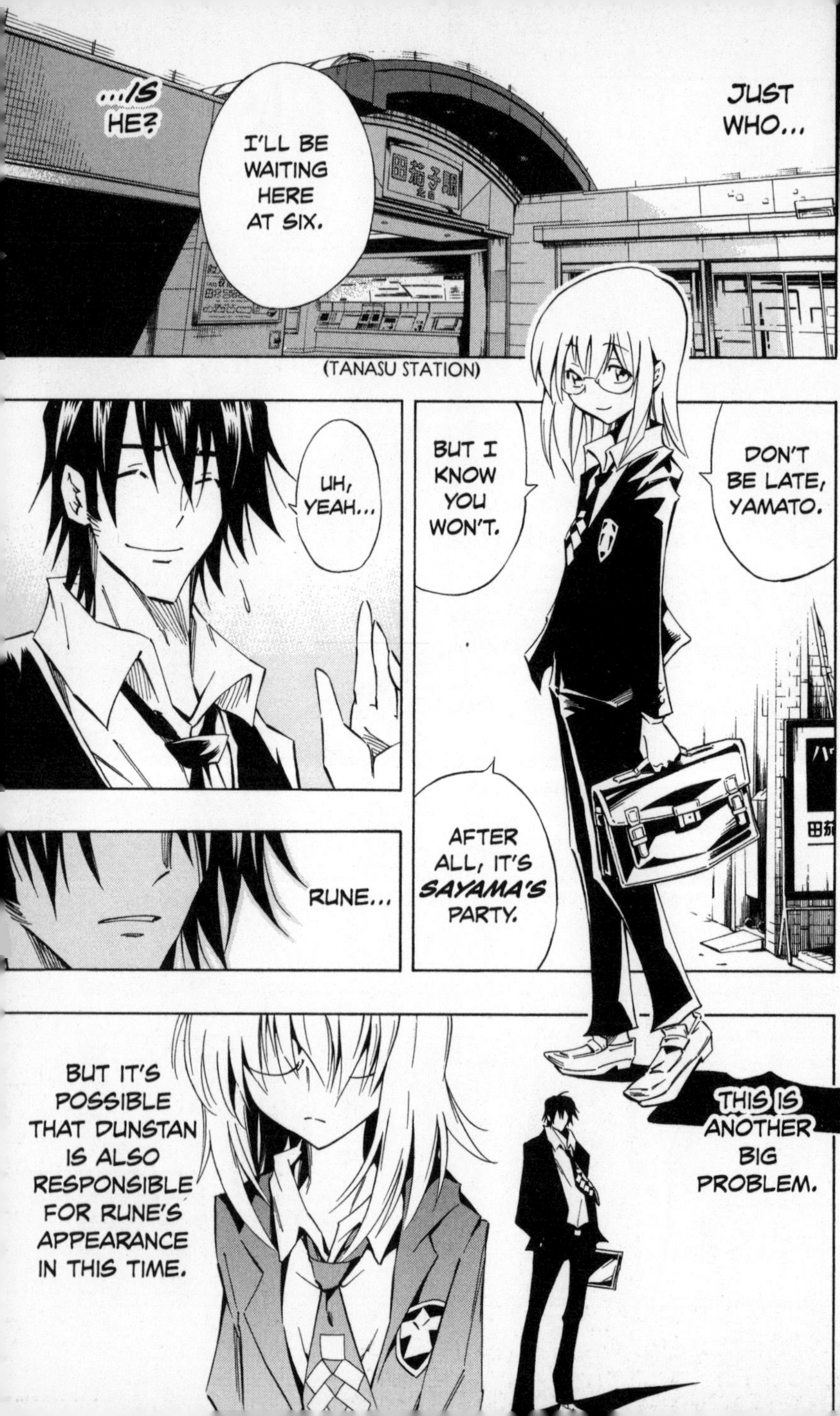
JUST WHO...
I'LL BE WAITING HERE AT SIX.
...IS HE?
(TANASU STATION)
DON'T BE LATE, YAMATO.
BUT I KNOW YOU WON'T.
AFTER ALL, IT'S *SAYAMA'S* PARTY.
UH, YEAH...
RUNE...
THIS IS ANOTHER BIG PROBLEM.
BUT IT'S POSSIBLE THAT DUNSTAN IS ALSO RESPONSIBLE FOR RUNE'S APPEARANCE IN THIS TIME.

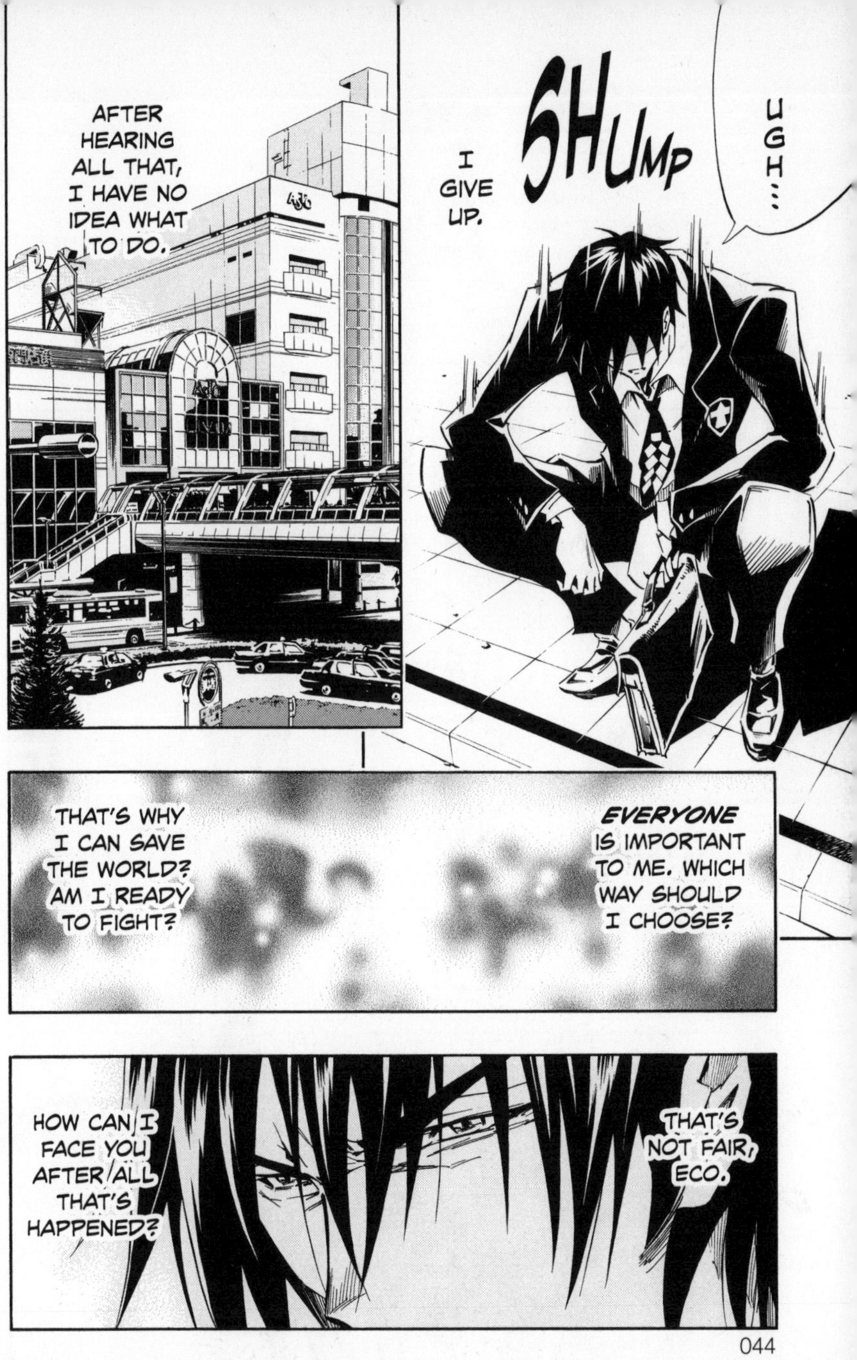
UGH...
SHUMP
I GIVE UP.
AFTER HEARING ALL THAT, I HAVE NO IDEA WHAT TO DO.
EVERYONE IS IMPORTANT TO ME. WHICH WAY SHOULD I CHOOSE?
THAT'S WHY I CAN SAVE THE WORLD? AM I READY TO FIGHT?
THAT'S NOT FAIR, ECO.
HOW CAN I FACE YOU AFTER ALL THAT'S HAPPENED?

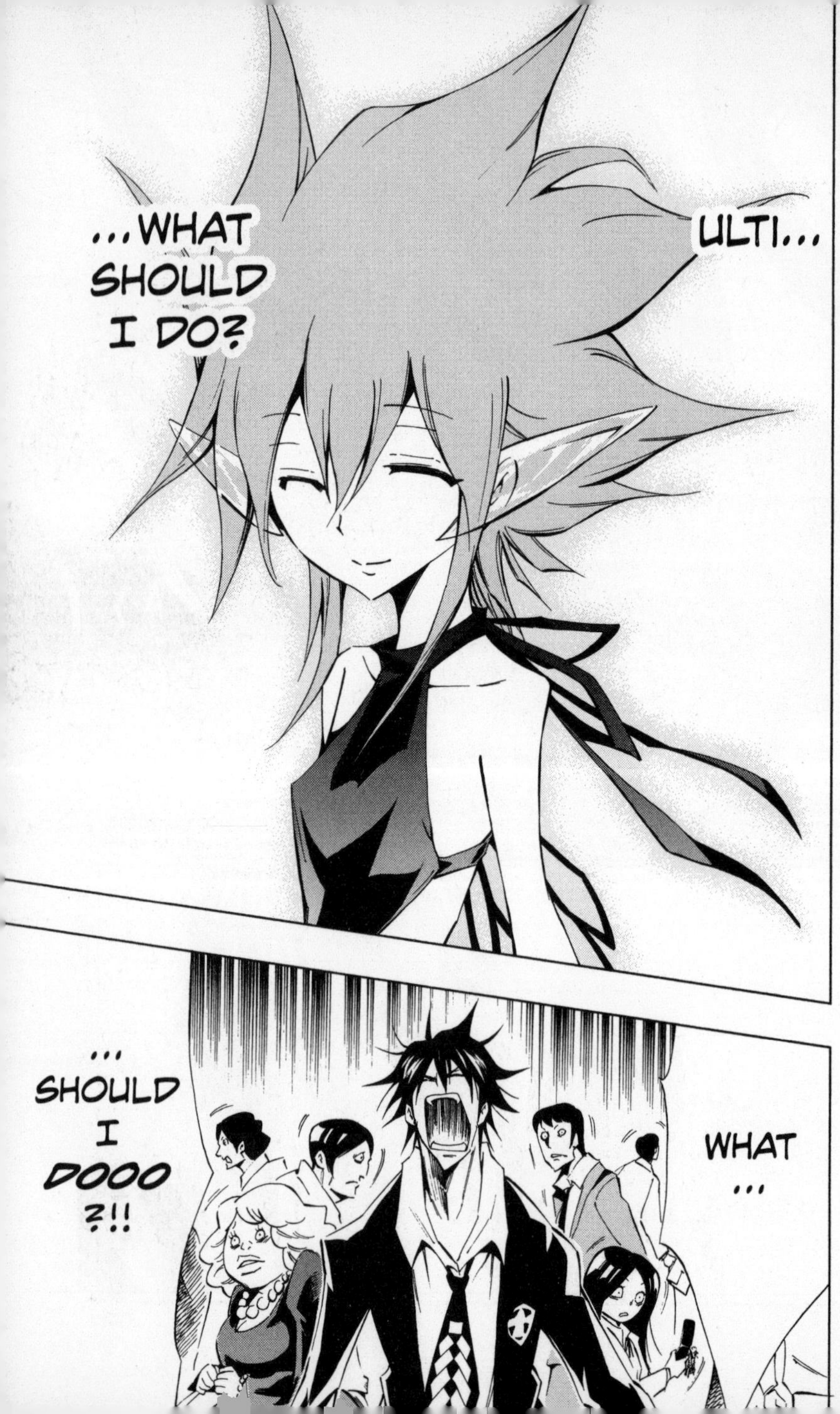
ULTI...
...WHAT SHOULD I DO?
WHAT ...
... SHOULD I DOOO ?!!

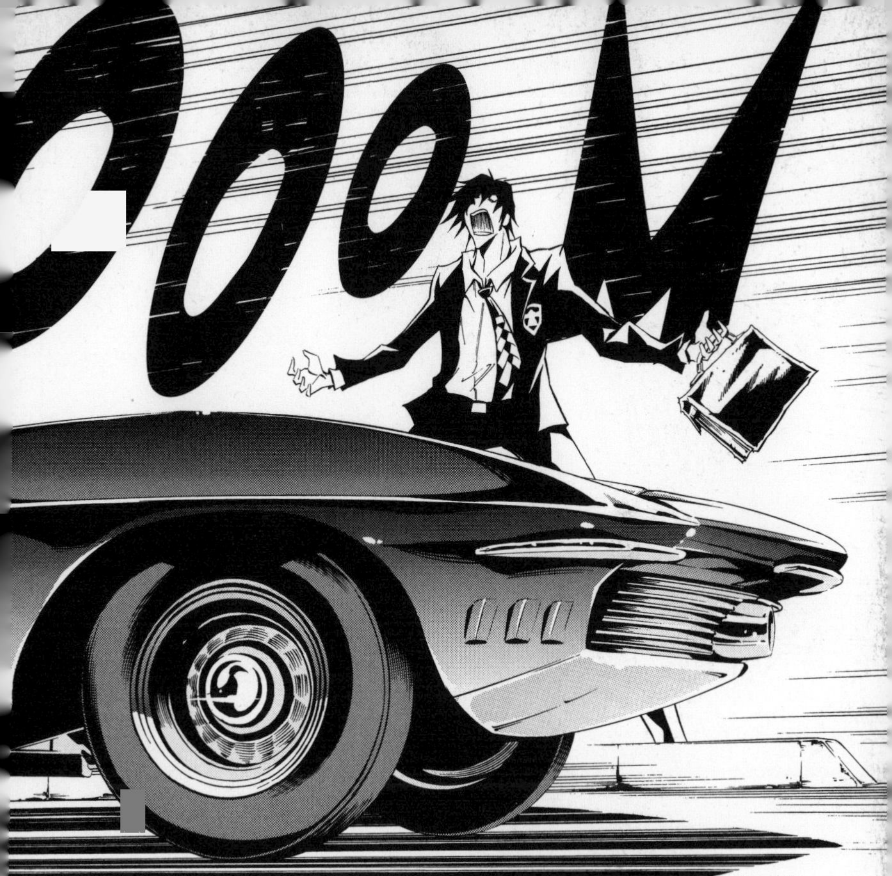

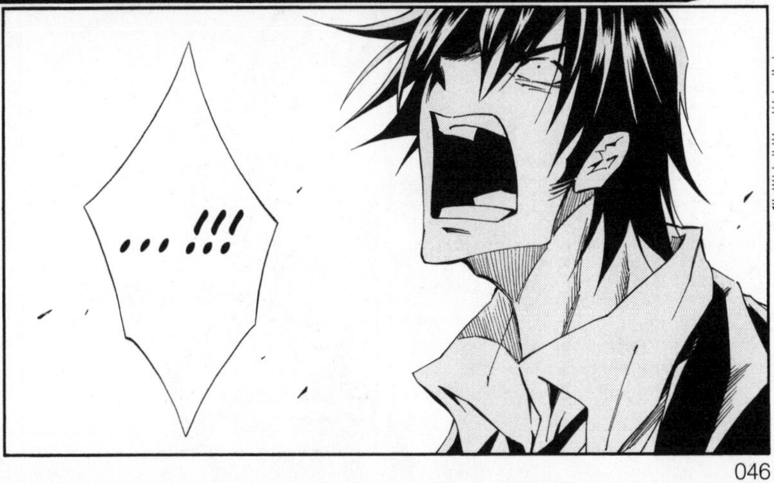
...!!!

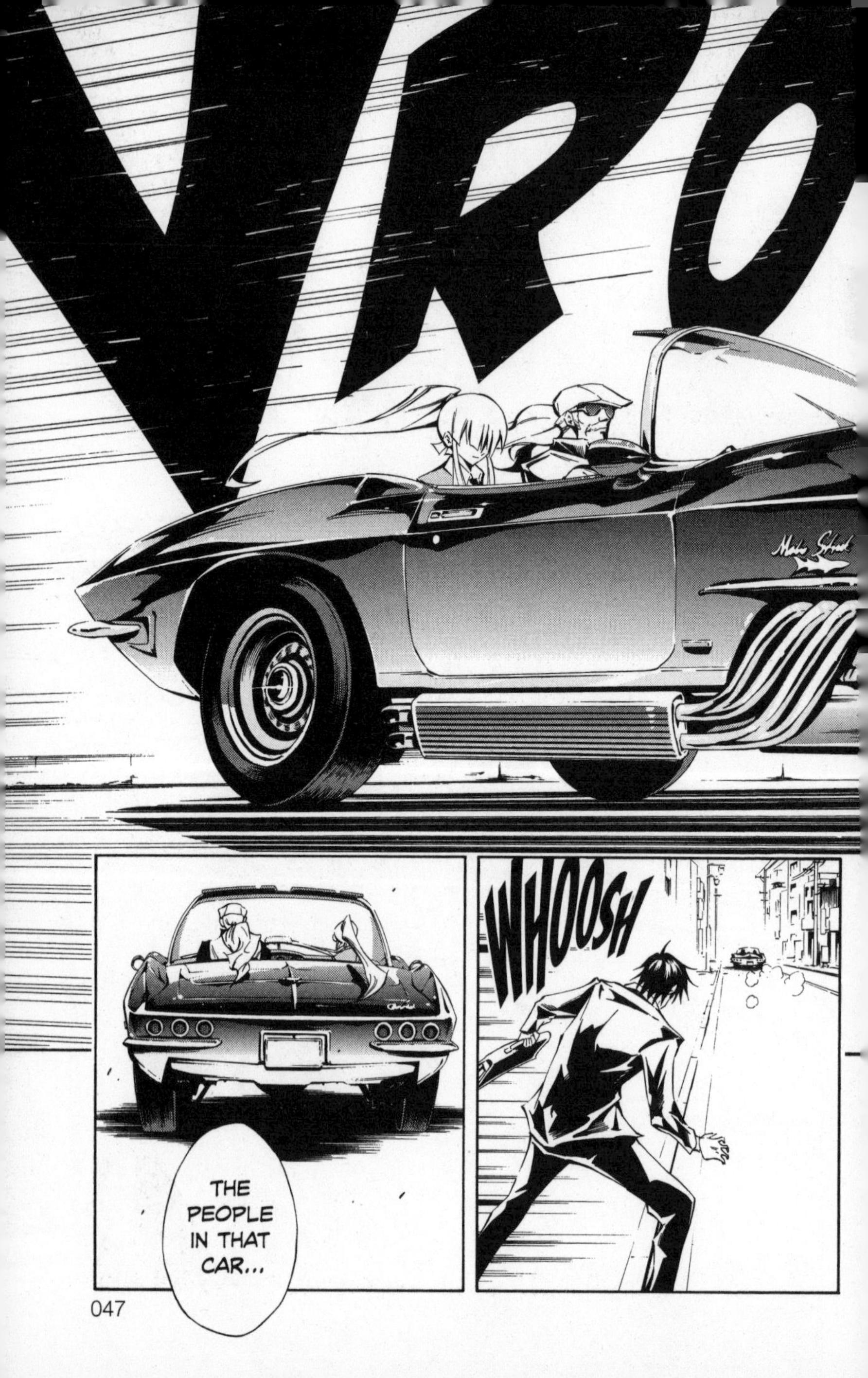
VRO
WHOOSH
THE PEOPLE IN THAT CAR...

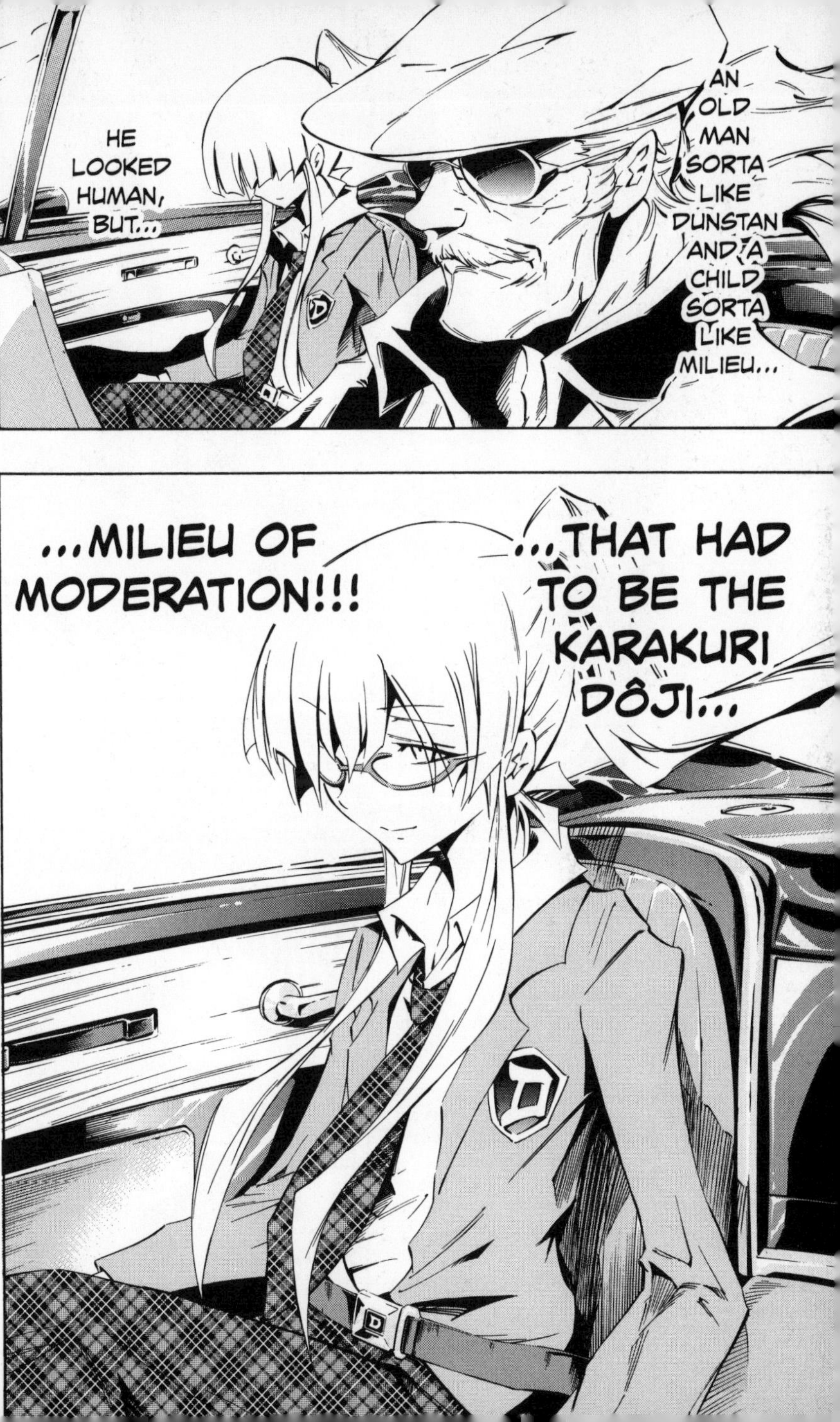
AN OLD MAN SORTA LIKE DUNSTAN AND A CHILD SORTA LIKE MILIEU...
HE LOOKED HUMAN, BUT...
...THAT HAD TO BE THE KARAKURI DÔJI...
...MILIEU OF MODERATION!!!

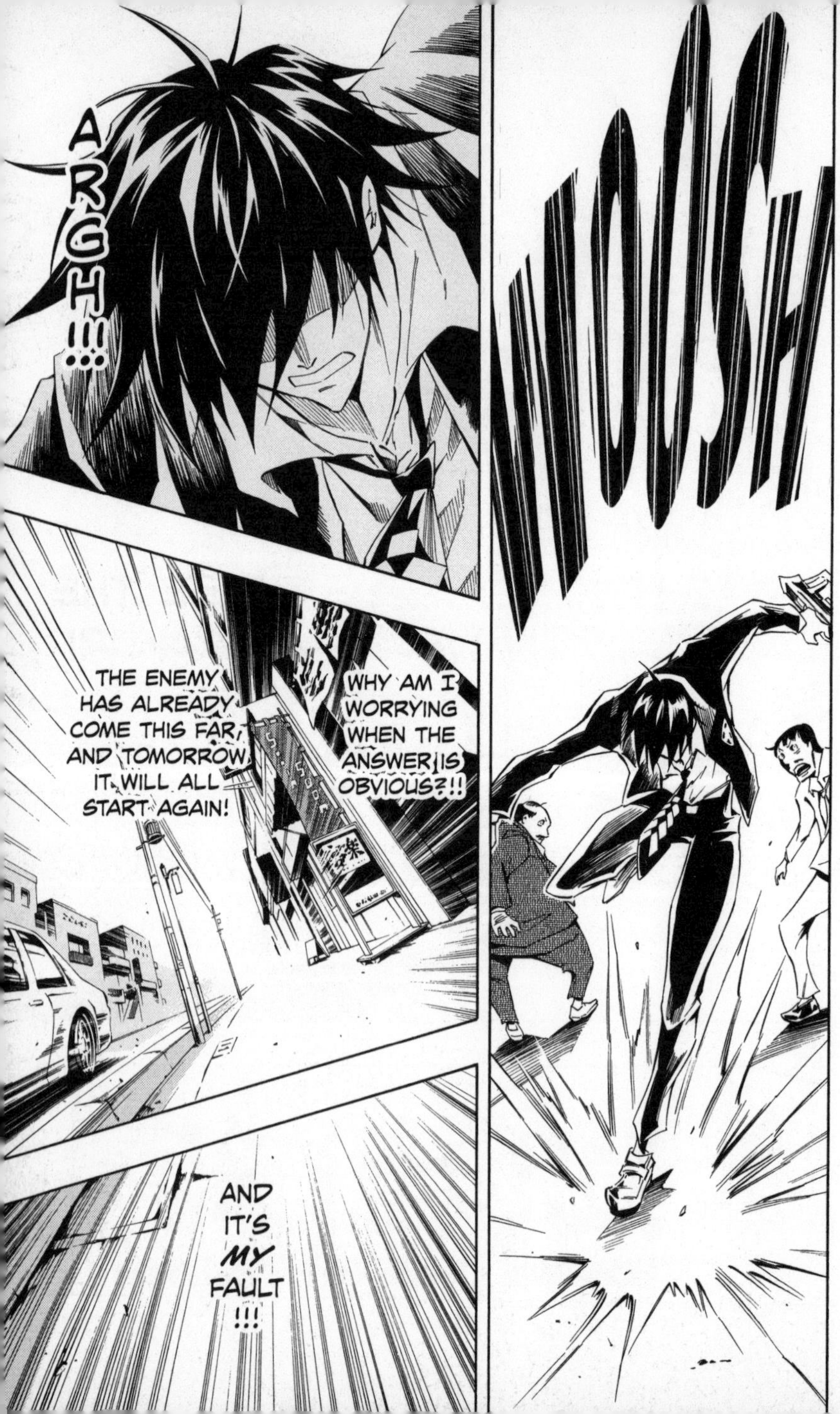
WHOOSH
ARGH!!!
WHY AM I WORRYING WHEN THE ANSWER IS OBVIOUS?!!
THE ENEMY HAS ALREADY COME THIS FAR, AND TOMORROW IT WILL ALL START AGAIN!
AND IT'S *MY* FAULT!!!

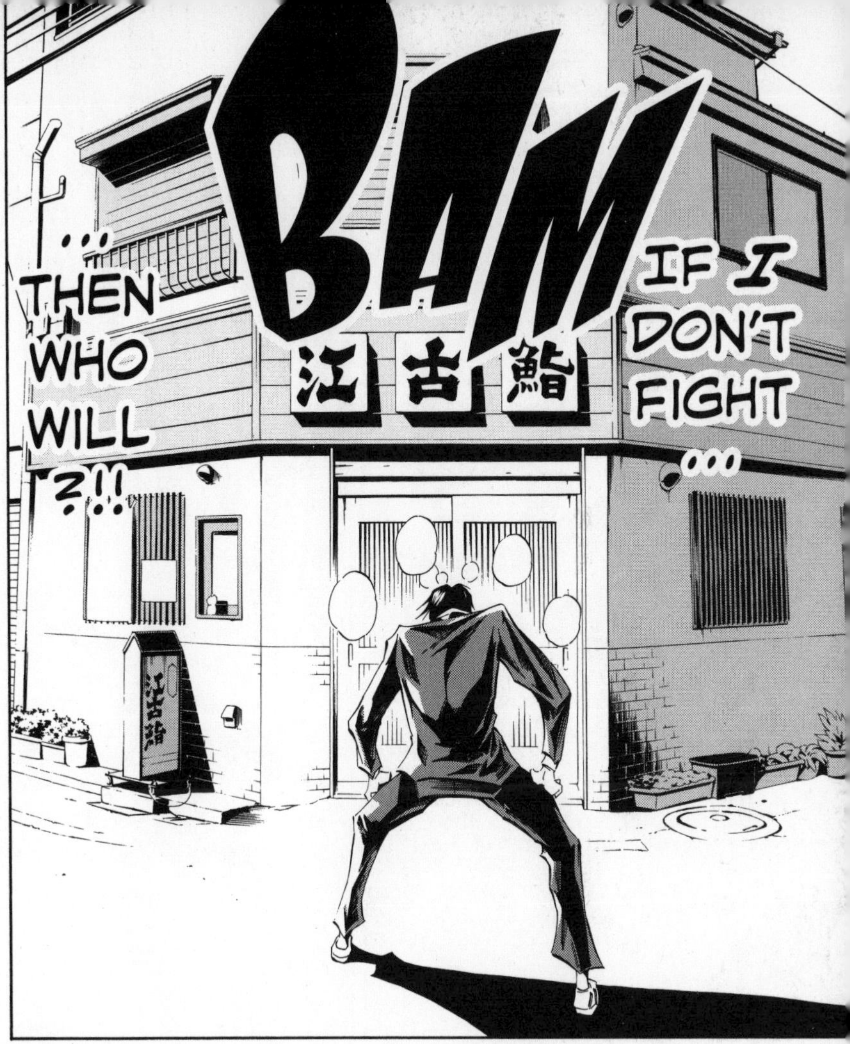
BAM
IF I DON'T FIGHT...
...THEN WHO WILL?!!
江古鮨

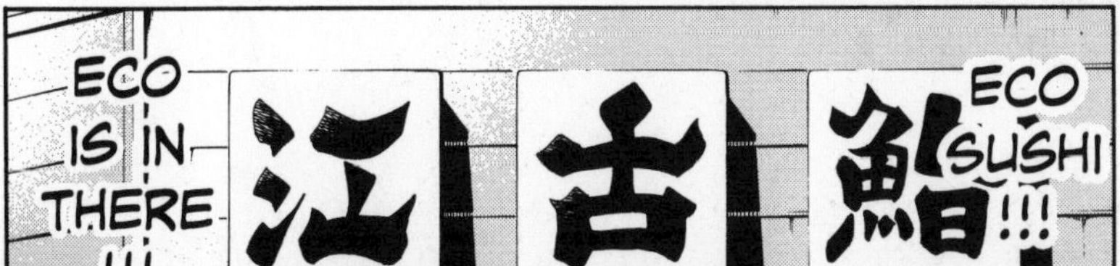
江古鮨
ECO SUSHI!!!
ECO IS IN THERE!!!

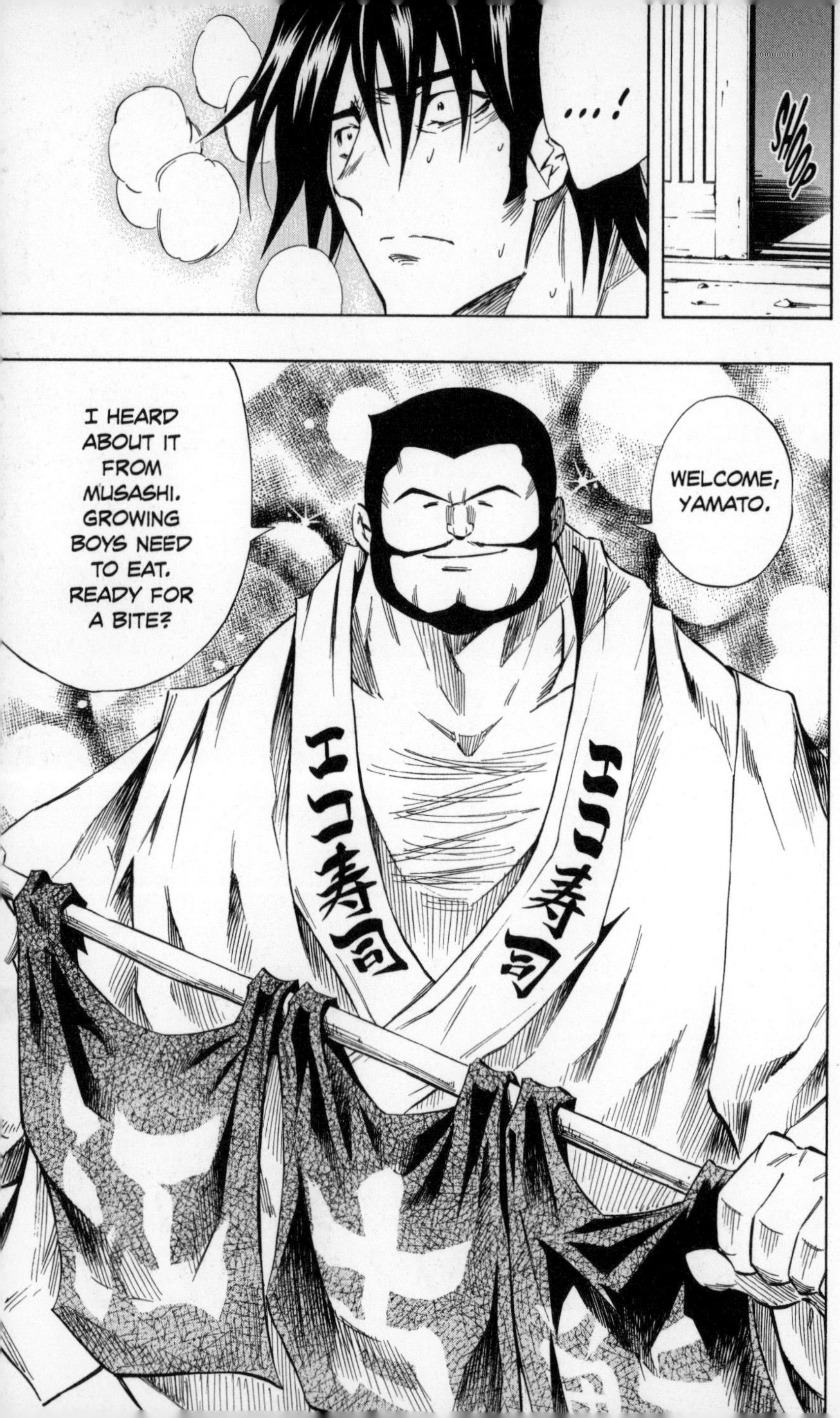
SHOOP
...!
WELCOME, YAMATO.
I HEARD ABOUT IT FROM MUSASHI. GROWING BOYS NEED TO EAT. READY FOR A BITE?
エコ寿司
エコ寿司

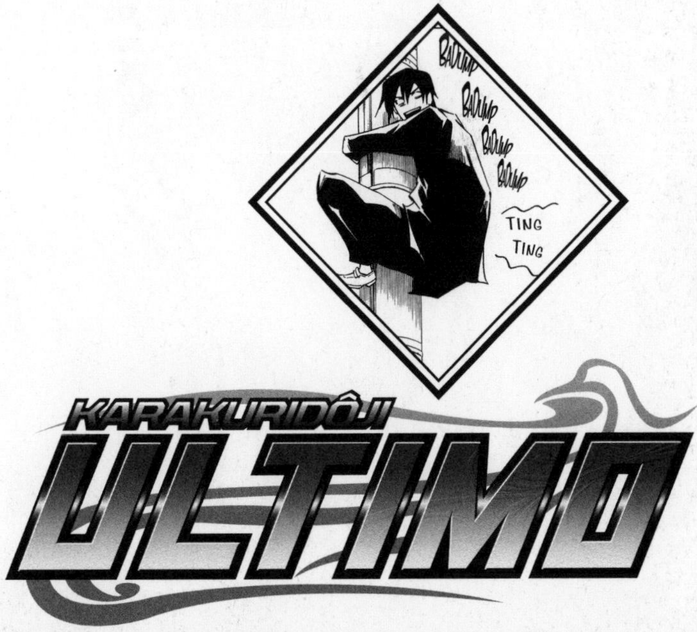
BADUMP
BADUMP
BADUMP
BADUMP
TING
TING

KARAKURIDÔJI

ULTIMO

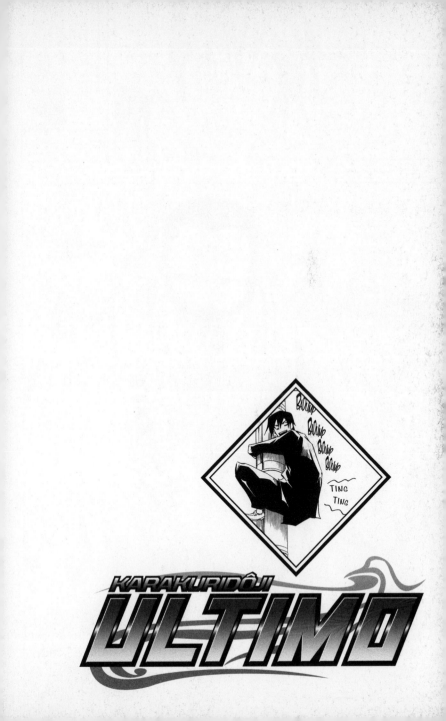

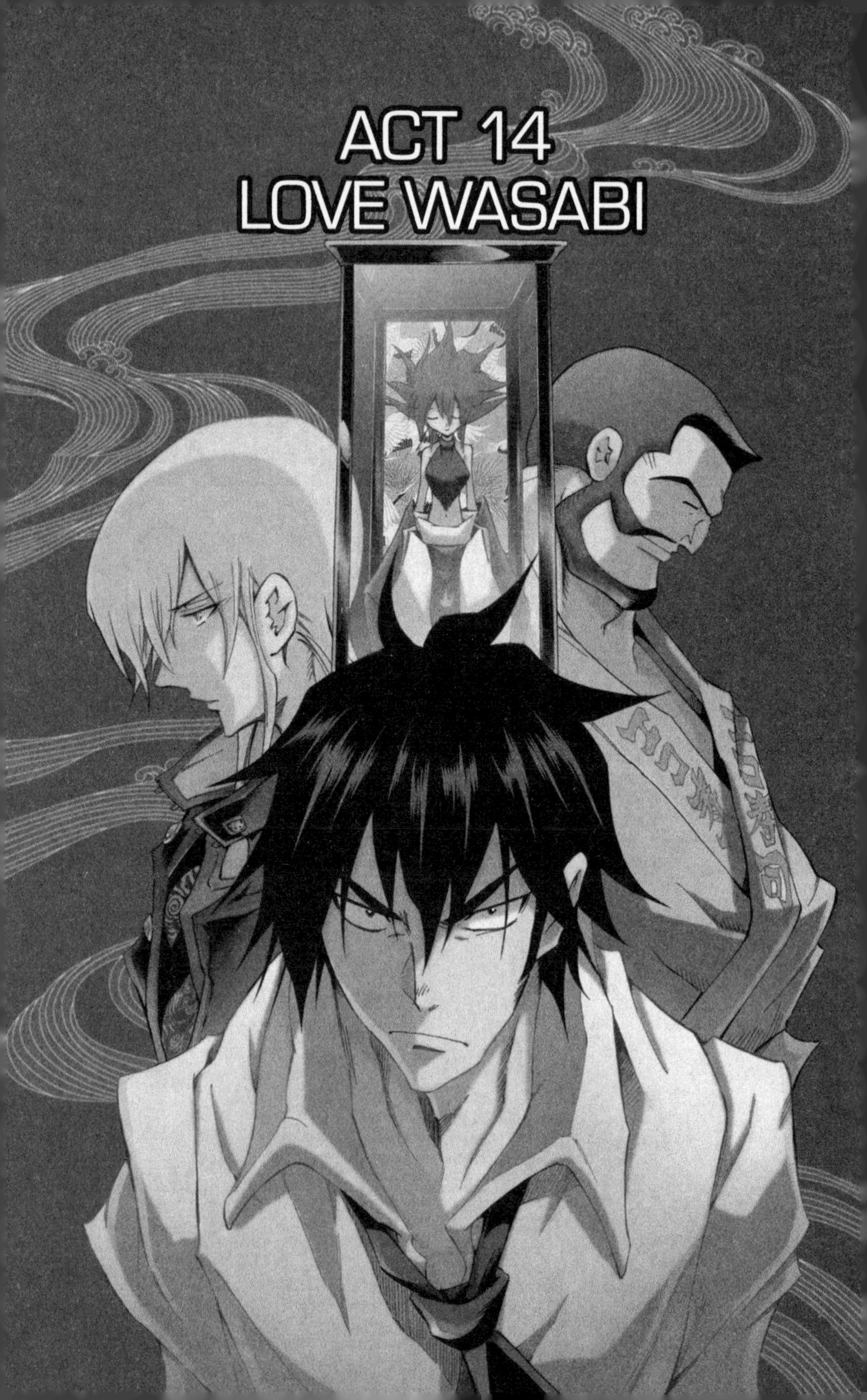
ACT 14
LOVE WASABI

KARAKURIDÔJI

ULTIMO

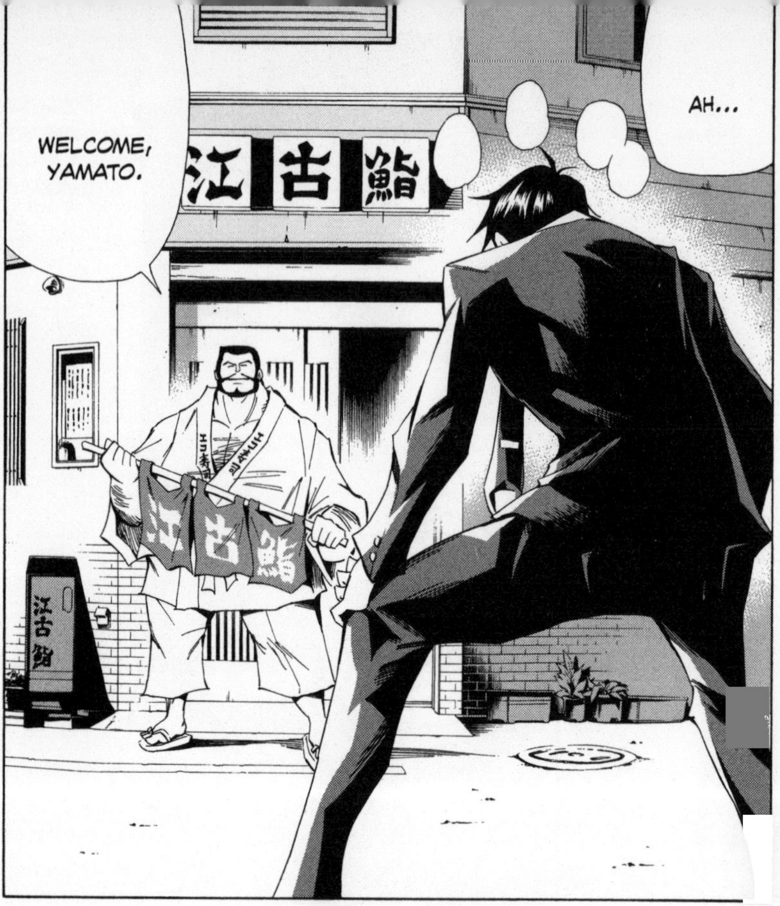
AH...
WELCOME, YAMATO.
江古鮨

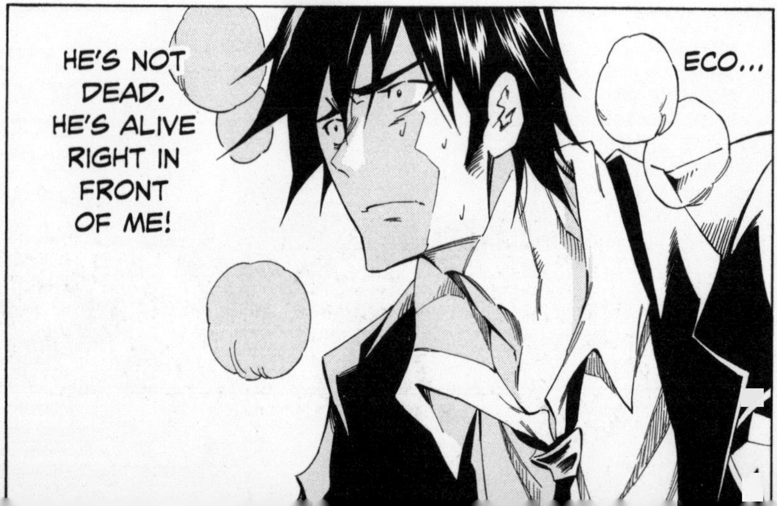
ECO...
HE'S NOT DEAD. HE'S ALIVE RIGHT IN FRONT OF ME!

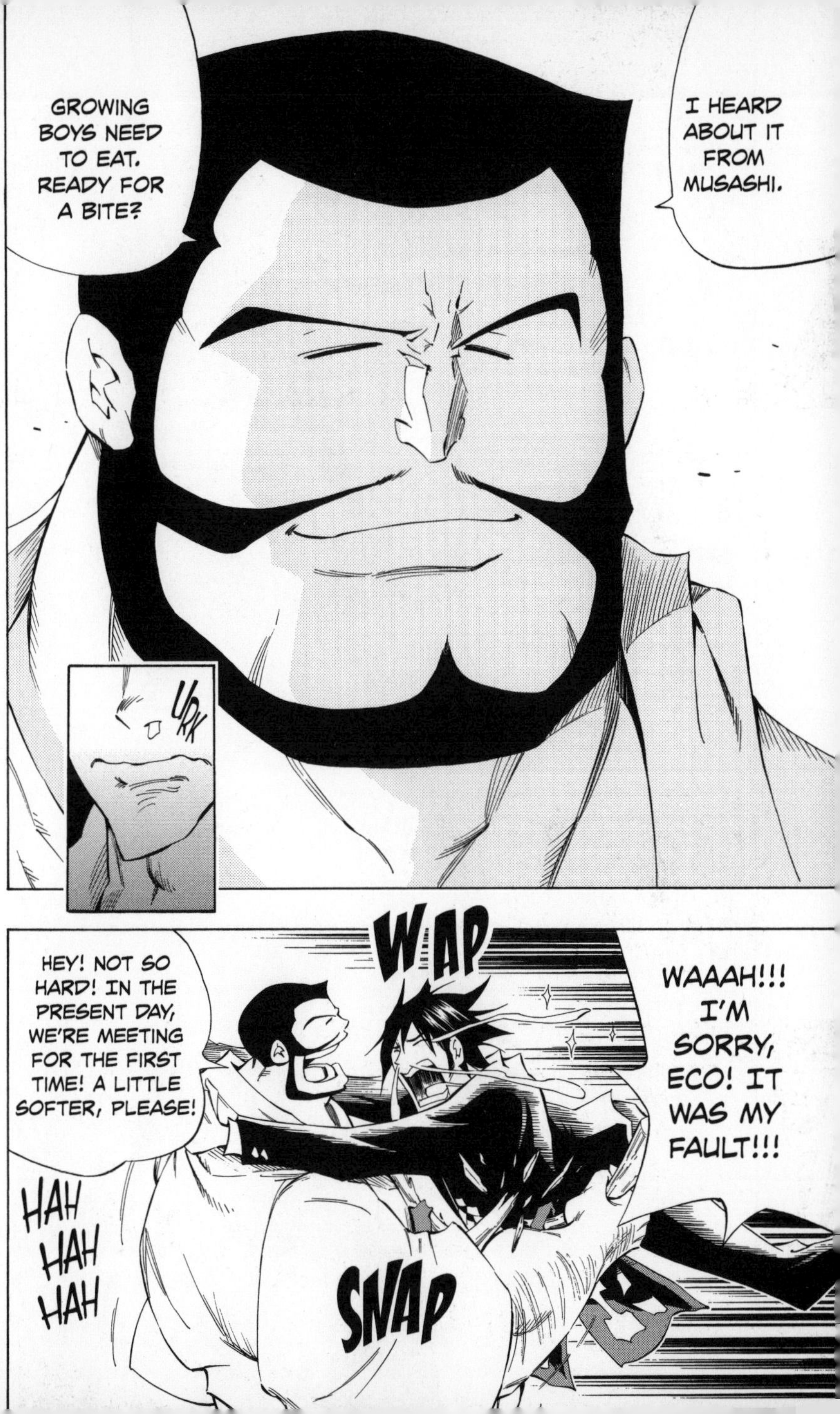
I HEARD ABOUT IT FROM MUSASHI.
GROWING BOYS NEED TO EAT. READY FOR A BITE?
URK
WAAAH!!! I'M SORRY, ECO! IT WAS MY FAULT!!!
WAP
HEY! NOT SO HARD! IN THE PRESENT DAY, WE'RE MEETING FOR THE FIRST TIME! A LITTLE SOFTER, PLEASE!
HAH HAH HAH
SNAP

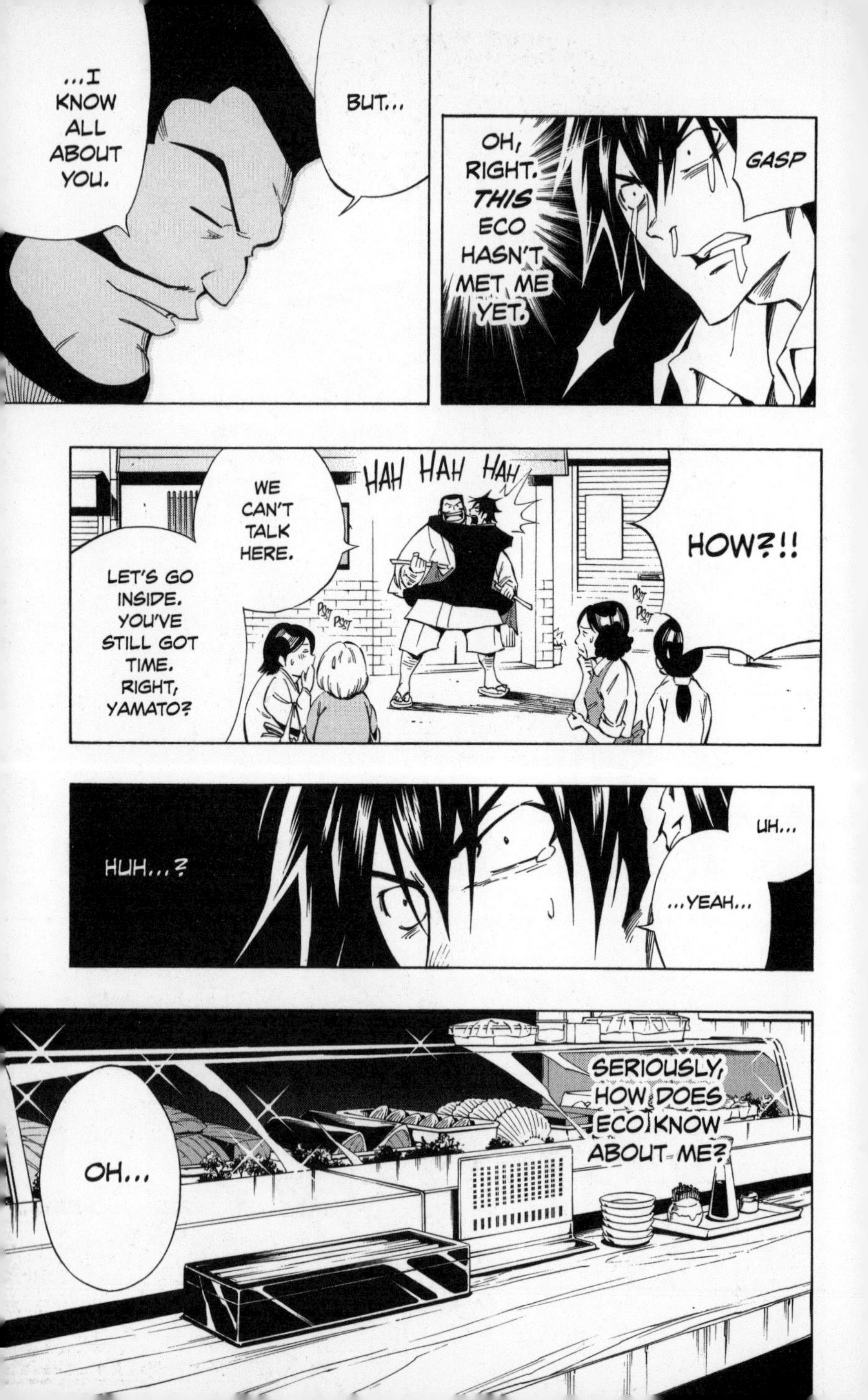
GASP
OH, RIGHT. *THIS* ECO HASN'T MET ME YET.
BUT...
...I KNOW ALL ABOUT YOU.
HOW?!!
PSST PSST
HAH HAH HAH
WE CAN'T TALK HERE.
LET'S GO INSIDE. YOU'VE STILL GOT TIME. RIGHT, YAMATO?
PSST PSST
UH...
...YEAH...
HUH...?
SERIOUSLY, HOW DOES ECO KNOW ABOUT ME?
OH...

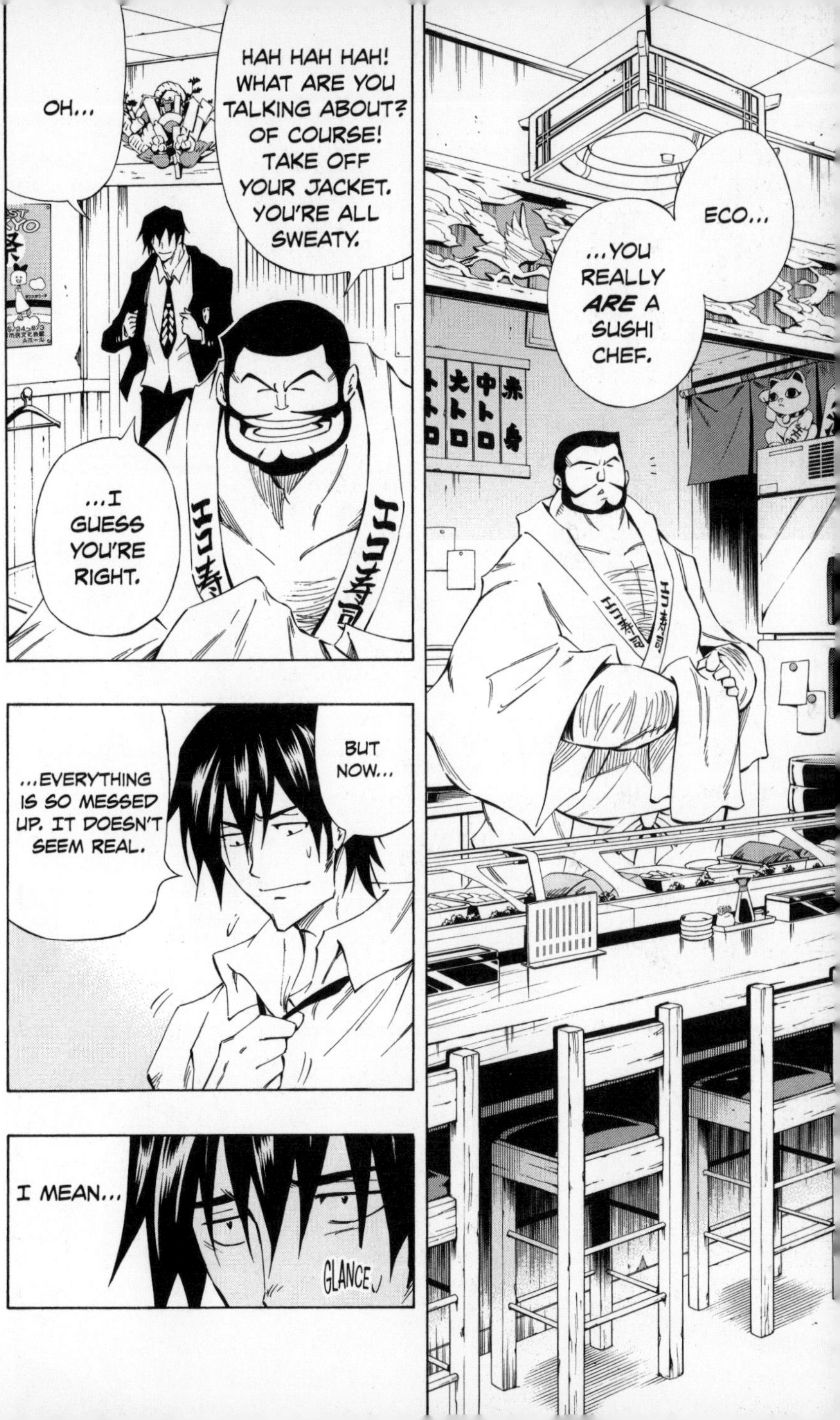
ECO...
...YOU REALLY ARE A SUSHI CHEF.
HAH HAH HAH! WHAT ARE YOU TALKING ABOUT? OF COURSE! TAKE OFF YOUR JACKET. YOU'RE ALL SWEATY.
OH...
...I GUESS YOU'RE RIGHT.
BUT NOW...
...EVERYTHING IS SO MESSED UP. IT DOESN'T SEEM REAL.
I MEAN...
GLANCE

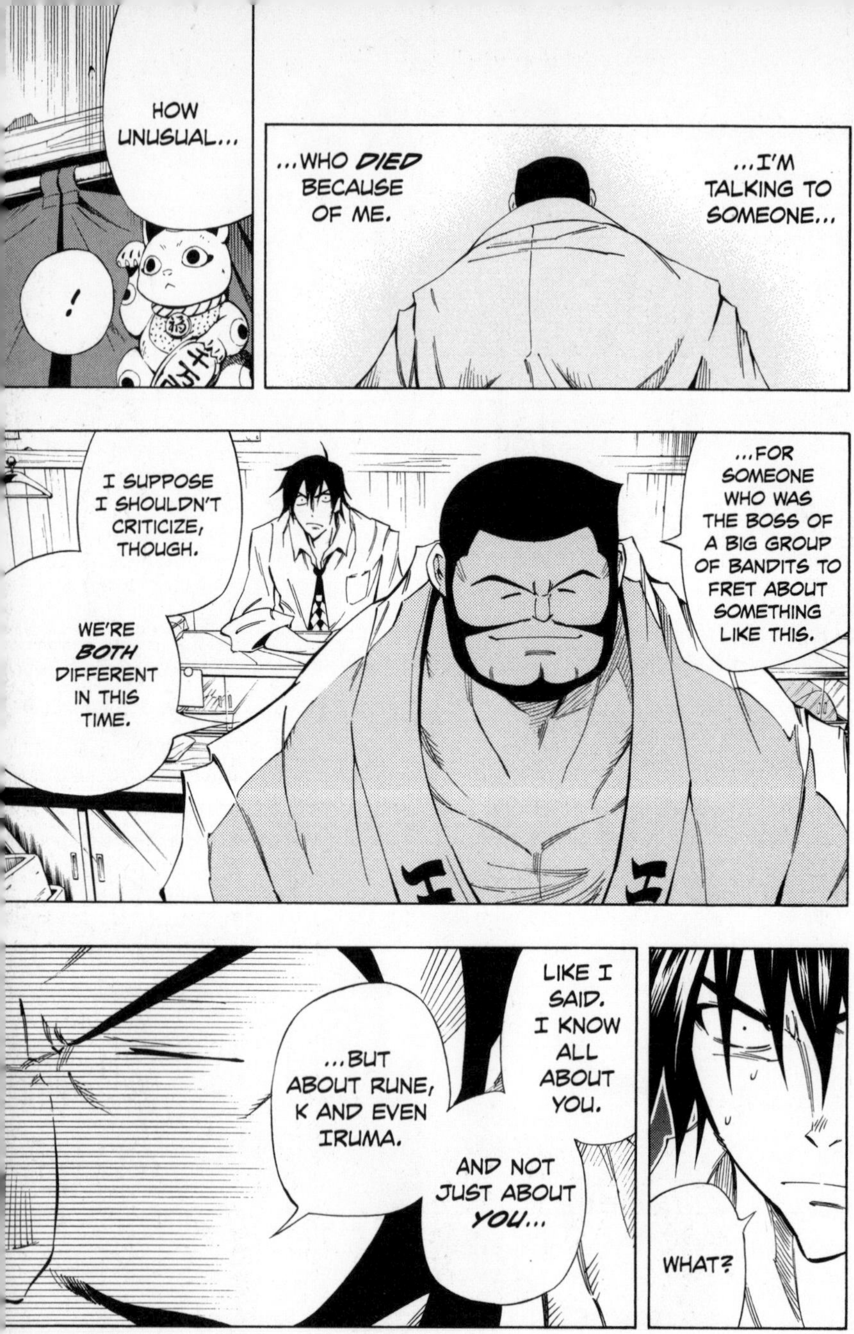
...I'M TALKING TO SOMEONE...
...WHO DIED BECAUSE OF ME.
HOW UNUSUAL...
!
...FOR SOMEONE WHO WAS THE BOSS OF A BIG GROUP OF BANDITS TO FRET ABOUT SOMETHING LIKE THIS.
I SUPPOSE I SHOULDN'T CRITICIZE, THOUGH.
WE'RE BOTH DIFFERENT IN THIS TIME.
WHAT?
LIKE I SAID. I KNOW ALL ABOUT YOU.
AND NOT JUST ABOUT YOU...
...BUT ABOUT RUNE, K AND EVEN IRUMA.

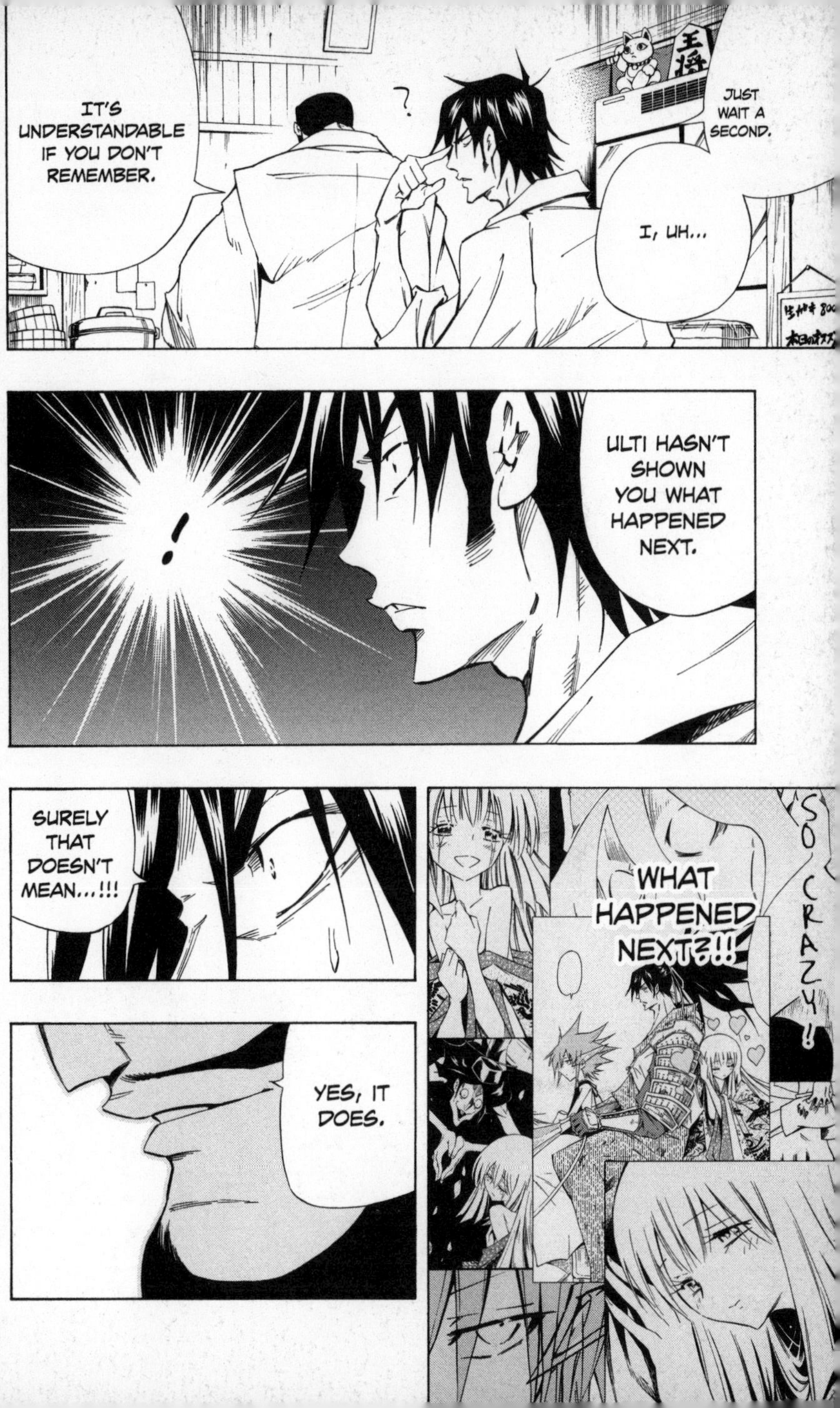
JUST WAIT A SECOND.
I, UH...
IT'S UNDERSTANDABLE IF YOU DON'T REMEMBER.
ULTI HASN'T SHOWN YOU WHAT HAPPENED NEXT.
SO CRAZY!
WHAT HAPPENED NEXT?!!
SURELY THAT DOESN'T MEAN...!!!
YES, IT DOES.

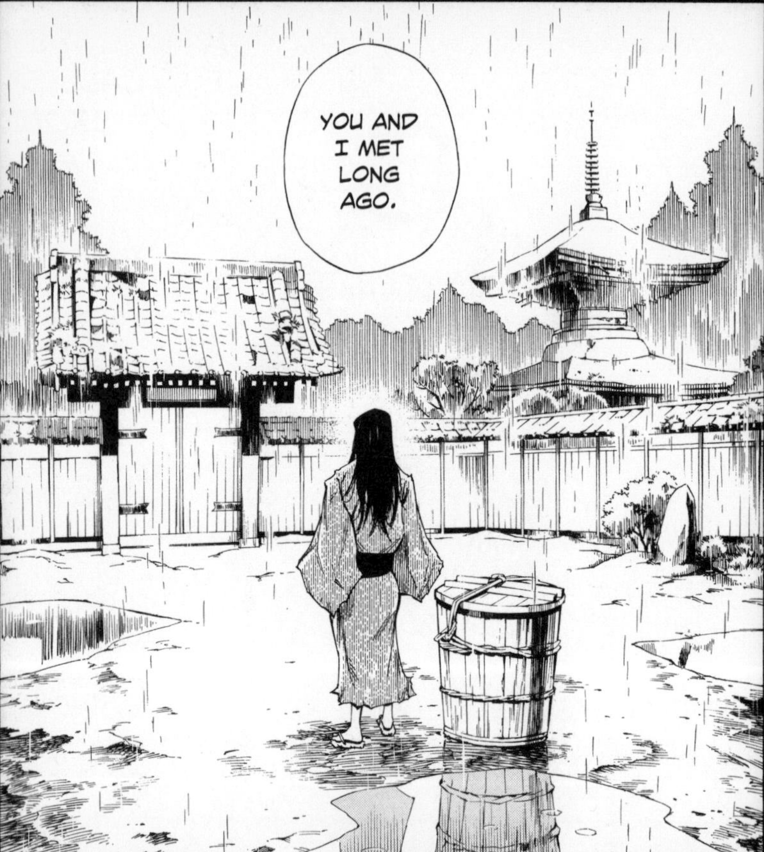
YOU AND I MET LONG AGO.

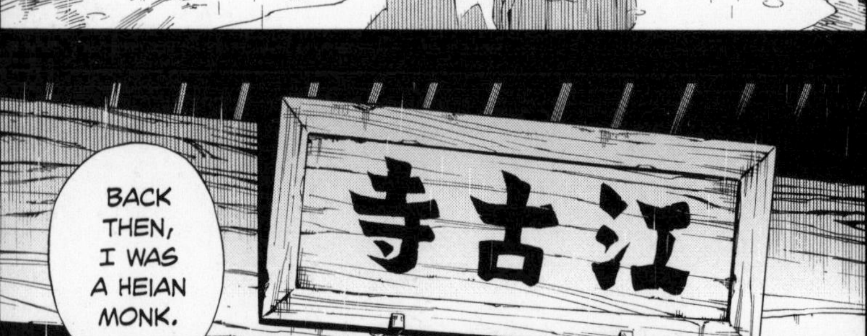
江古寺
BACK THEN, I WAS A HEIAN MONK.

(EKO TEMPLE)

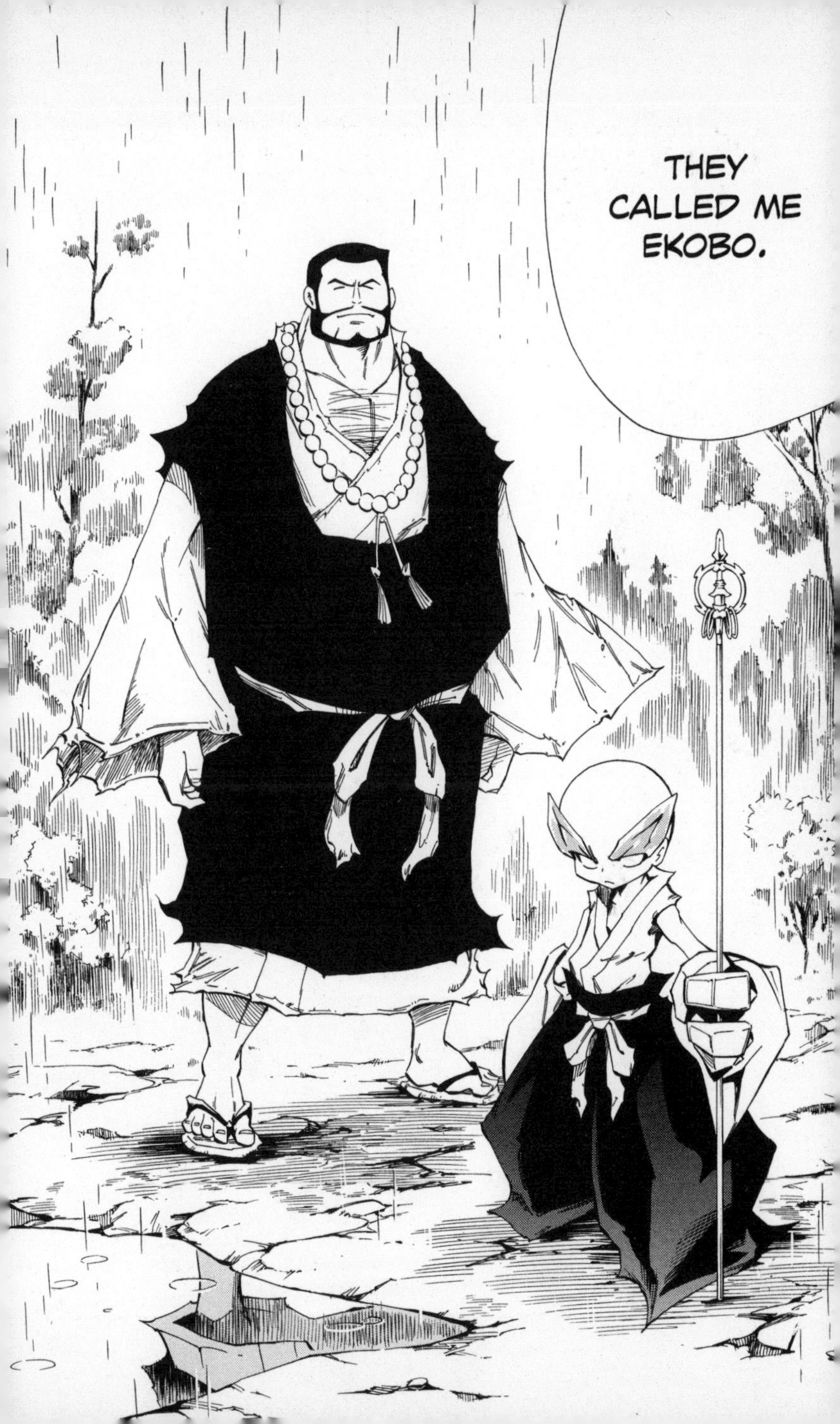
THEY CALLED ME EKOBO.

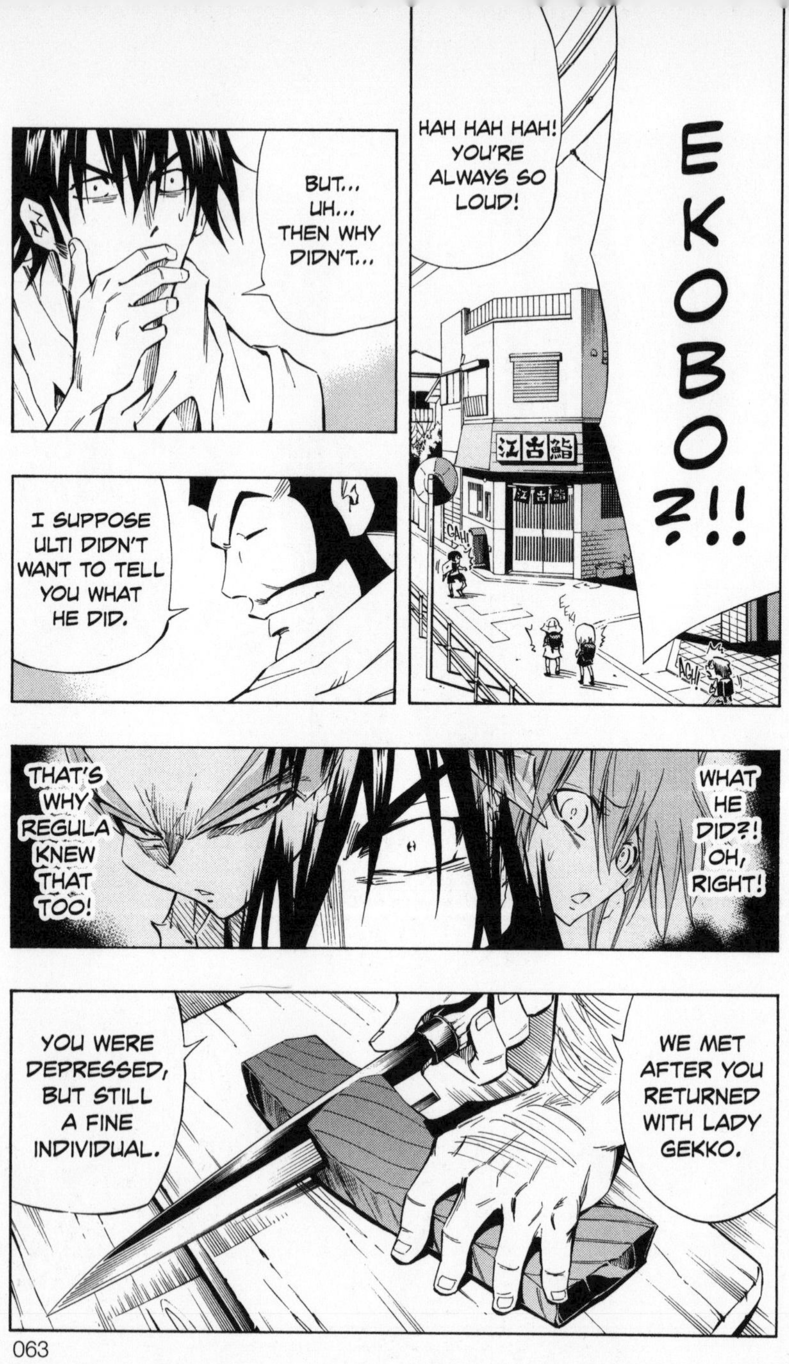
EKOBO?!!
HAH HAH HAH! YOU'RE ALWAYS SO LOUD!
GAH!
AGH!
BUT... UH... THEN WHY DIDN'T...
I SUPPOSE ULTI DIDN'T WANT TO TELL YOU WHAT HE DID.
WHAT HE DID?! OH, RIGHT!
THAT'S WHY REGULA KNEW THAT TOO!
WE MET AFTER YOU RETURNED WITH LADY GEKKO.
YOU WERE DEPRESSED, BUT STILL A FINE INDIVIDUAL.

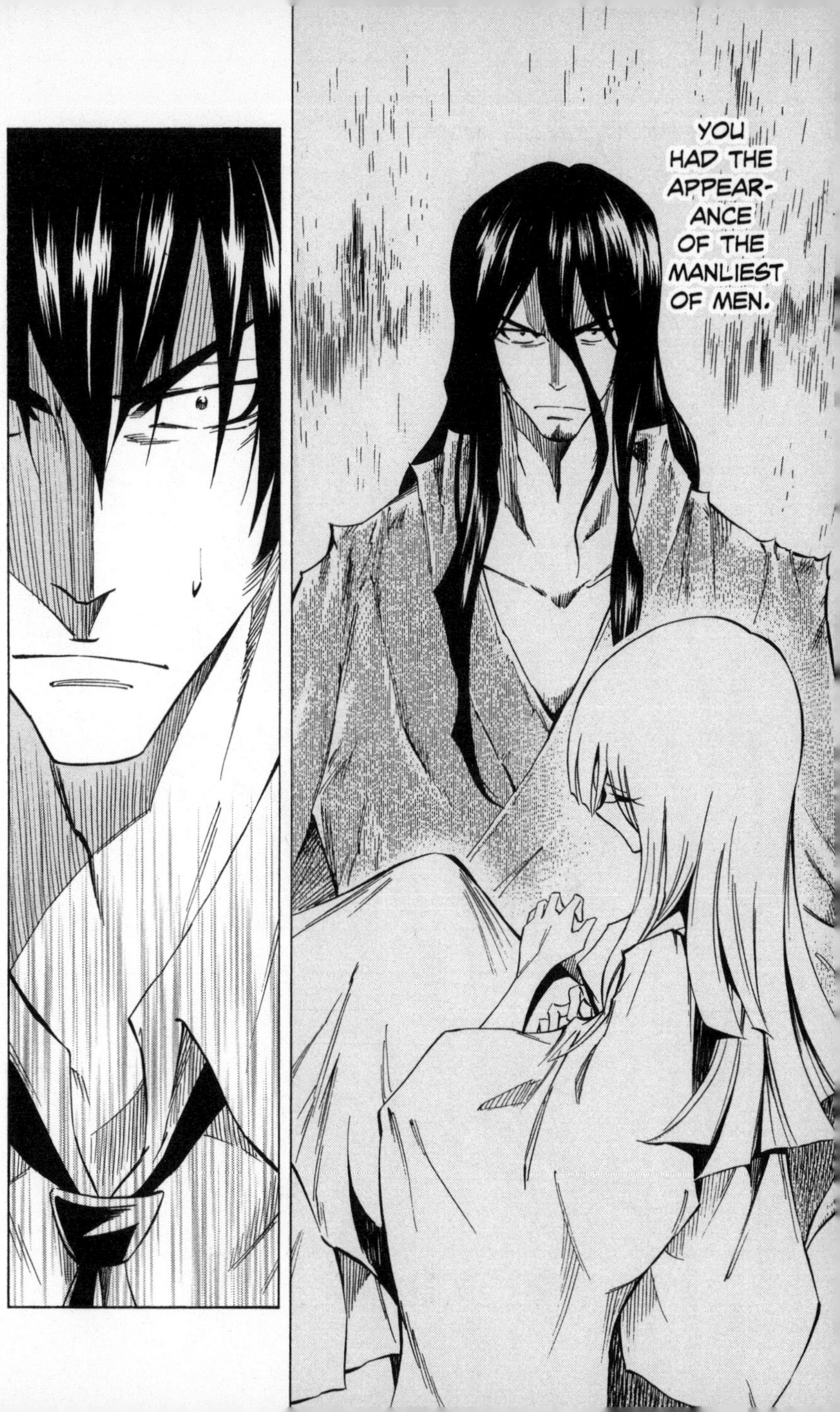
YOU HAD THE APPEAR-ANCE OF THE MANLIEST OF MEN.

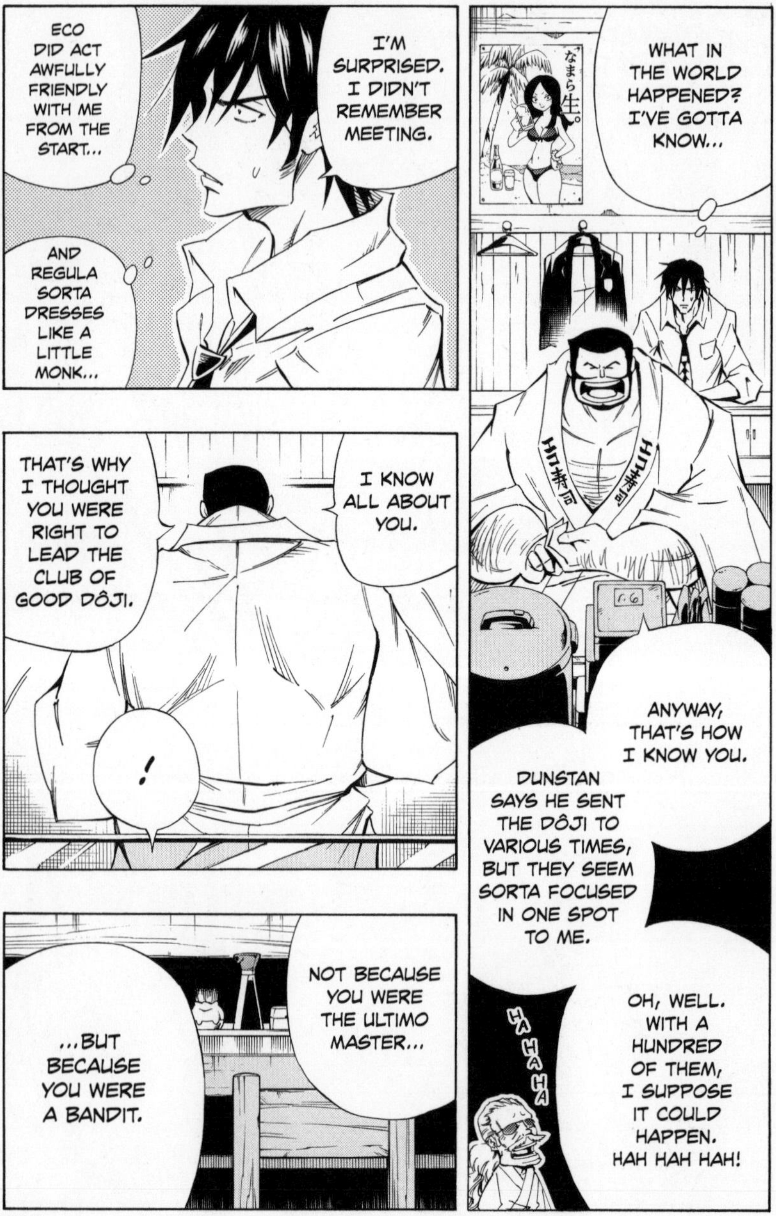

WHAT IN THE WORLD HAPPENED? I'VE GOTTA KNOW...
なまら生。
ANYWAY, THAT'S HOW I KNOW YOU.
DUNSTAN SAYS HE SENT THE DÔJI TO VARIOUS TIMES, BUT THEY SEEM SORTA FOCUSED IN ONE SPOT TO ME.
HA HA HA HA
OH, WELL. WITH A HUNDRED OF THEM, I SUPPOSE IT COULD HAPPEN. HAH HAH HAH!
I'M SURPRISED. I DIDN'T REMEMBER MEETING.
ECO DID ACT AWFULLY FRIENDLY WITH ME FROM THE START...
AND REGULA SORTA DRESSES LIKE A LITTLE MONK...
I KNOW ALL ABOUT YOU.
THAT'S WHY I THOUGHT YOU WERE RIGHT TO LEAD THE CLUB OF GOOD DÔJI.
!
NOT BECAUSE YOU WERE THE ULTIMO MASTER...
...BUT BECAUSE YOU WERE A BANDIT.

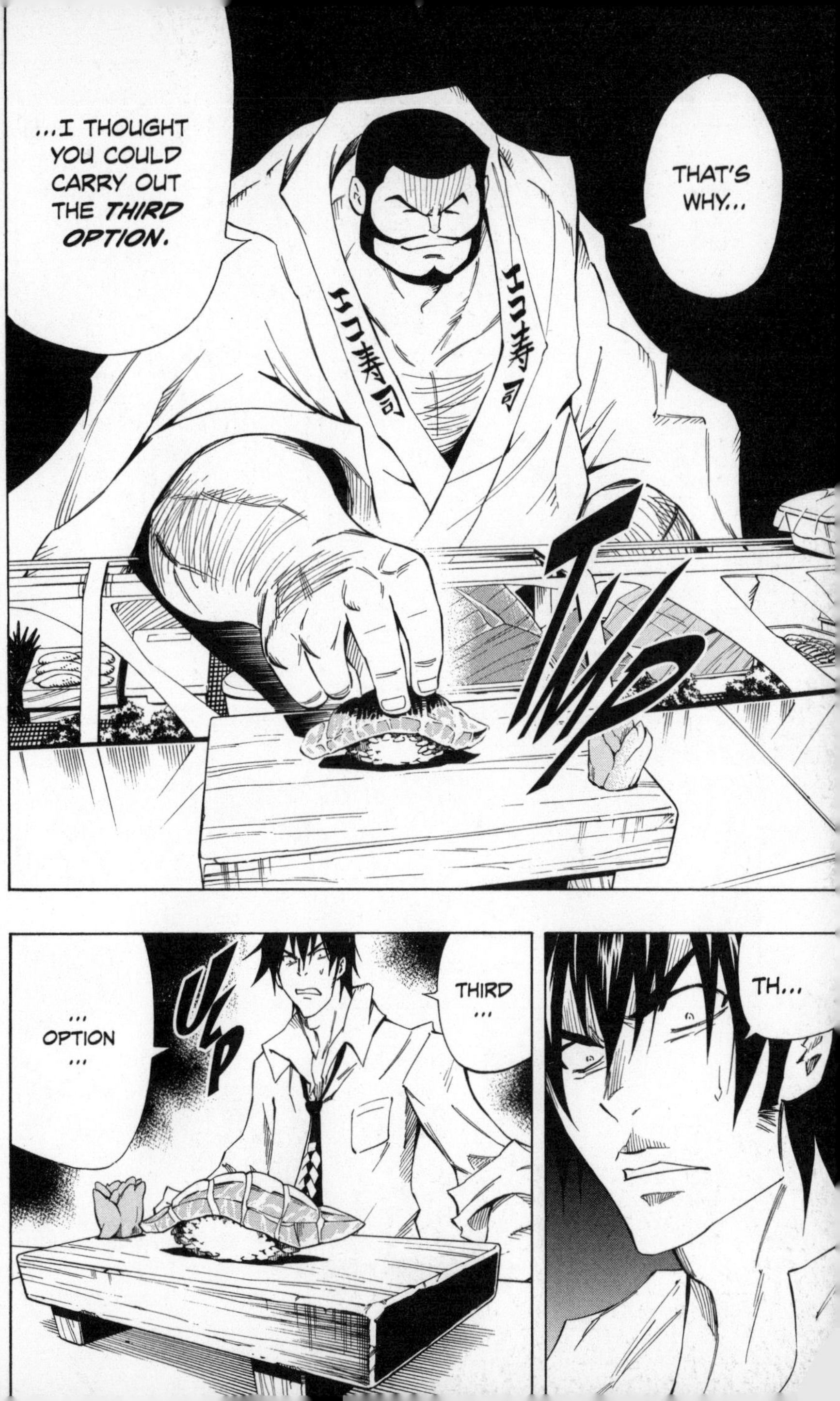
THAT'S WHY...
...I THOUGHT YOU COULD CARRY OUT THE *THIRD OPTION*.
エコ寿司
エコ寿司
TMP
TH...
THIRD ...
ULP
... OPTION ...

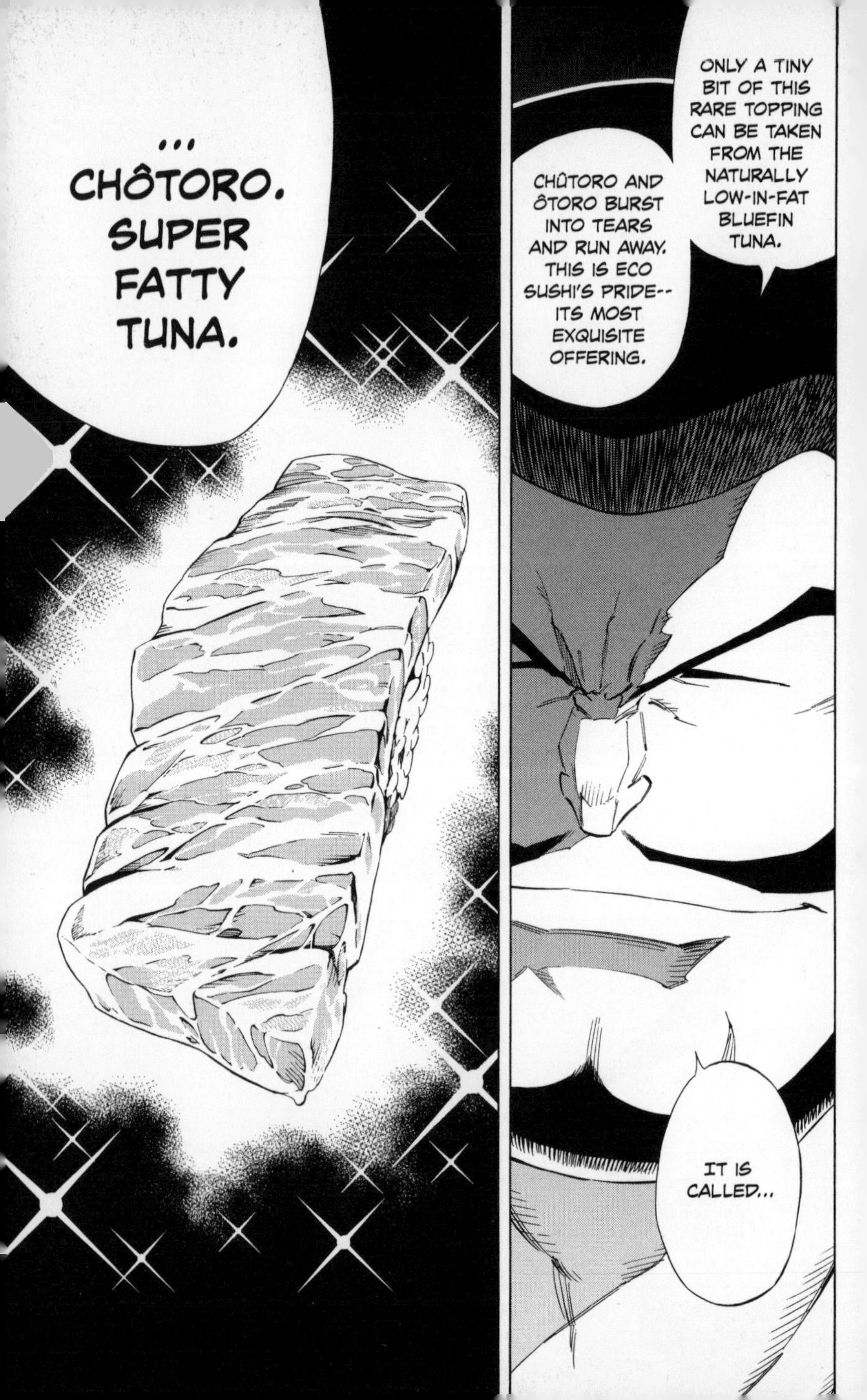
ONLY A TINY BIT OF THIS RARE TOPPING CAN BE TAKEN FROM THE NATURALLY LOW-IN-FAT BLUEFIN TUNA.
CHÛTORO AND ÔTORO BURST INTO TEARS AND RUN AWAY. THIS IS ECO SUSHI'S PRIDE-- ITS MOST EXQUISITE OFFERING.
IT IS CALLED...
... CHÔTORO. SUPER FATTY TUNA.

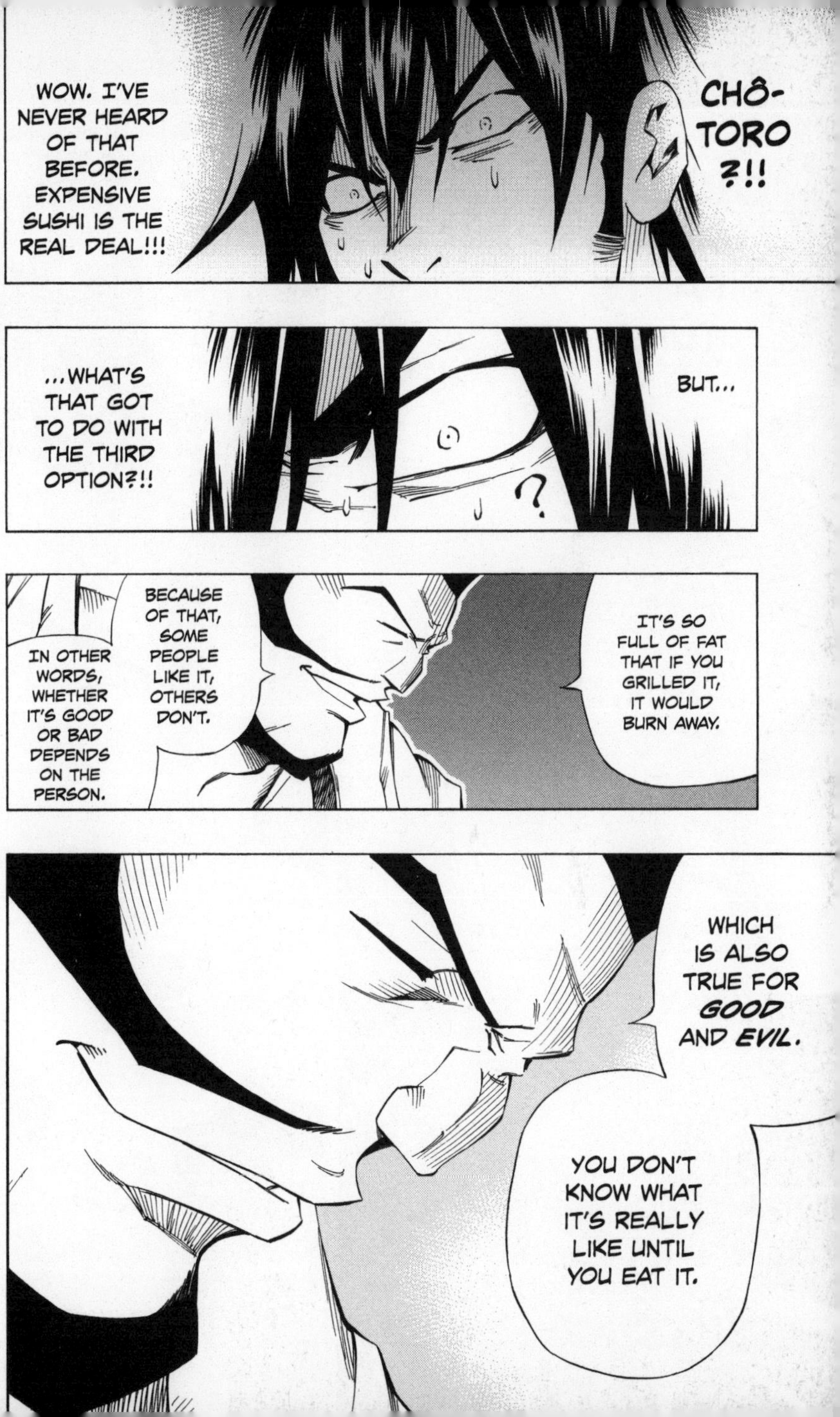
CHÔ-TORO ?!!
WOW. I'VE NEVER HEARD OF THAT BEFORE. EXPENSIVE SUSHI IS THE REAL DEAL!!!
BUT...
...WHAT'S THAT GOT TO DO WITH THE THIRD OPTION?!!
IT'S SO FULL OF FAT THAT IF YOU GRILLED IT, IT WOULD BURN AWAY.
BECAUSE OF THAT, SOME PEOPLE LIKE IT, OTHERS DON'T.
IN OTHER WORDS, WHETHER IT'S GOOD OR BAD DEPENDS ON THE PERSON.
WHICH IS ALSO TRUE FOR GOOD AND EVIL.
YOU DON'T KNOW WHAT IT'S REALLY LIKE UNTIL YOU EAT IT.

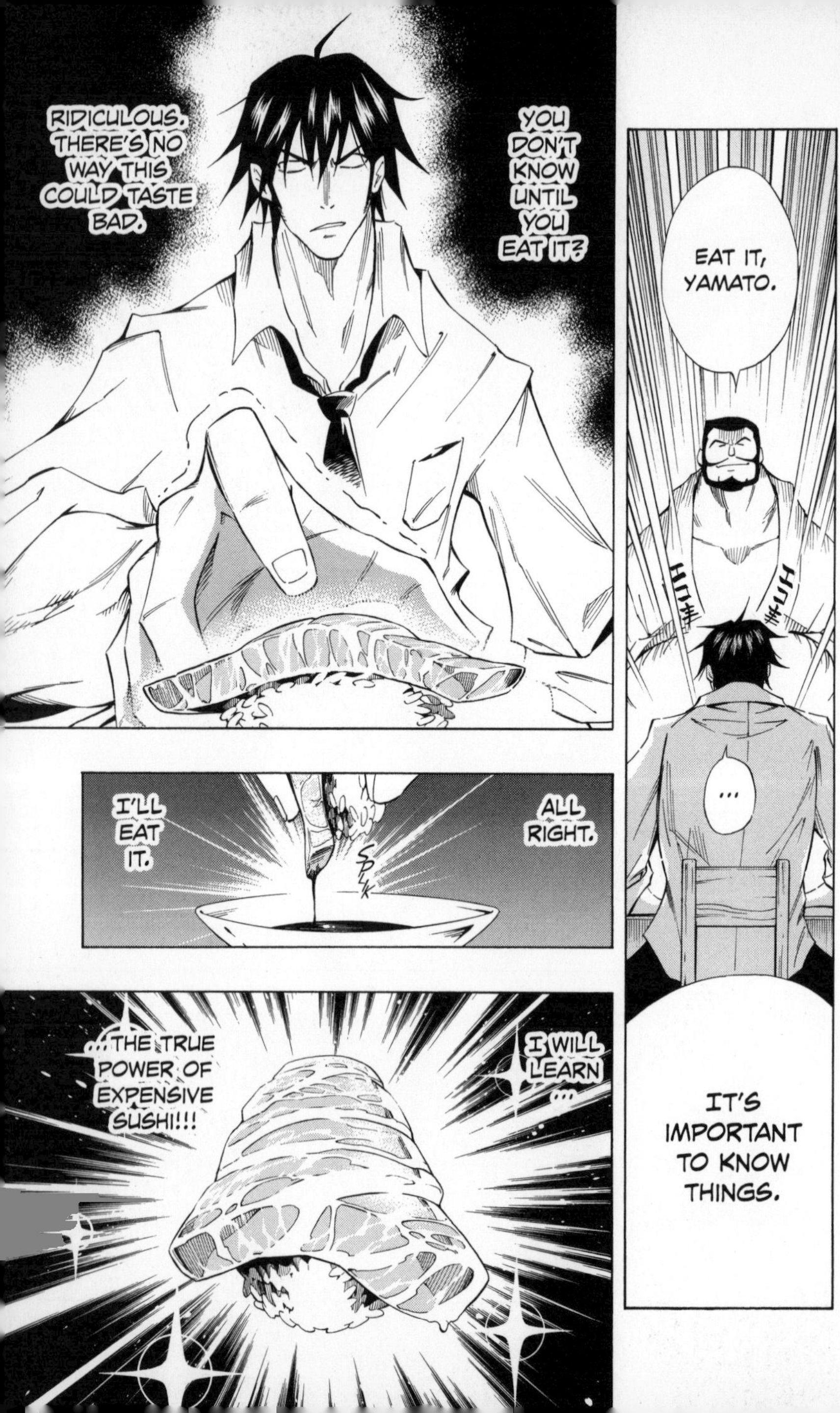
EAT IT, YAMATO.
...
IT'S IMPORTANT TO KNOW THINGS.
YOU DON'T KNOW UNTIL YOU EAT IT?
RIDICULOUS. THERE'S NO WAY THIS COULD TASTE BAD.
ALL RIGHT.
SPLK
I'LL EAT IT.
I WILL LEARN...
...THE TRUE POWER OF EXPENSIVE SUSHI!!!

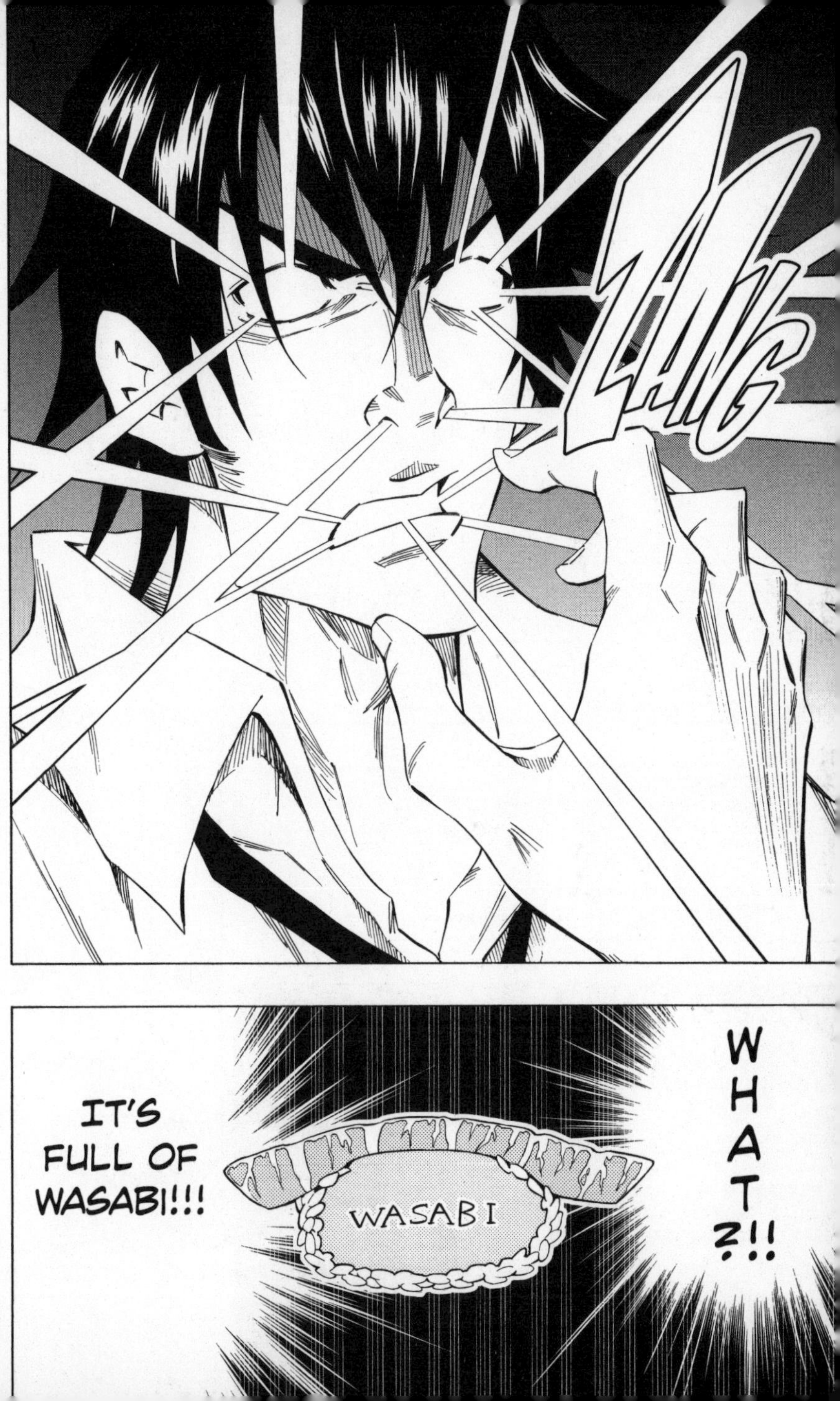
ZANG
WHAT?!!
WASABI
IT'S FULL OF WASABI!!!

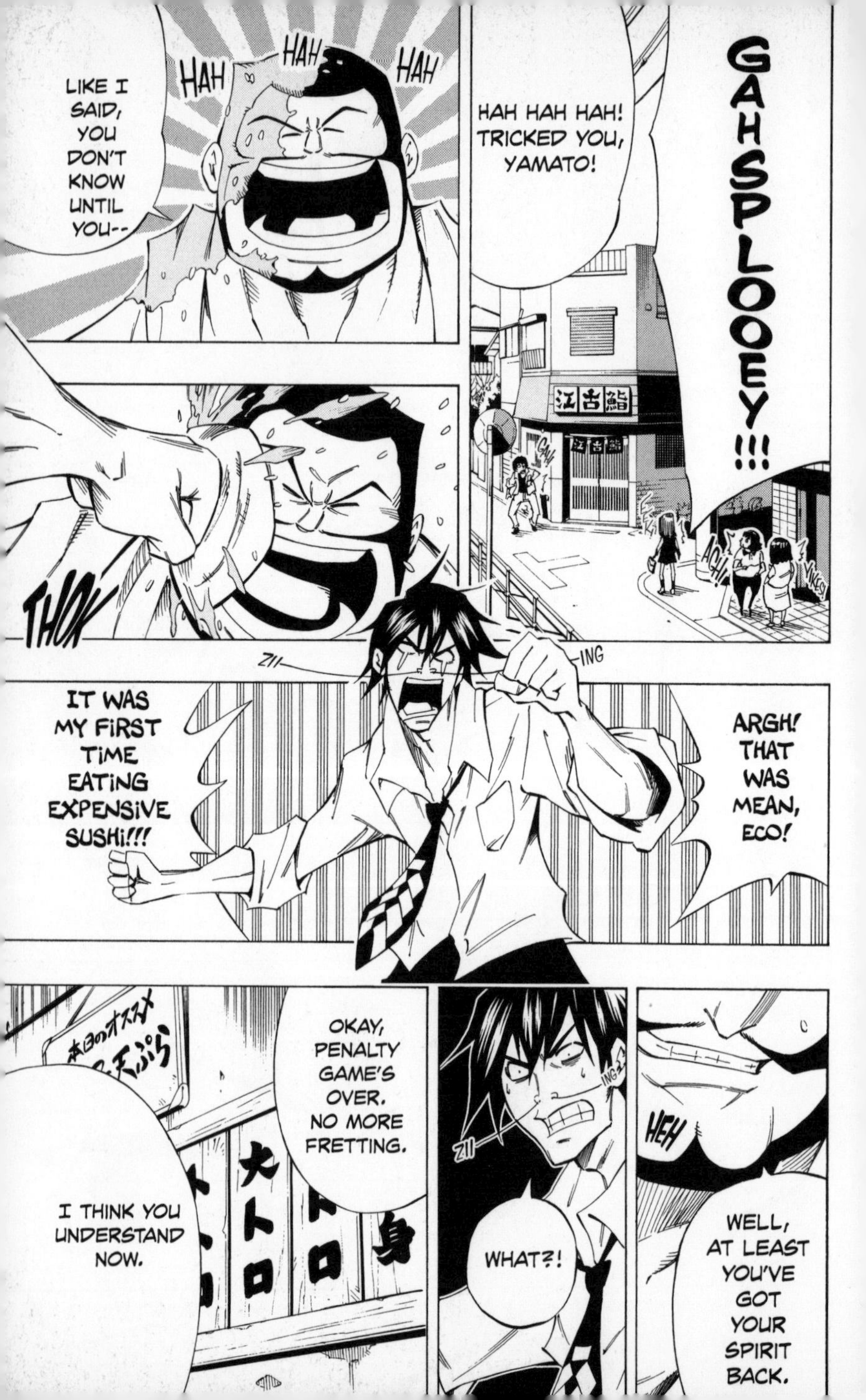
GAHSPLOOEY!!!
HAH HAH HAH! TRICKED YOU, YAMATO!
江古鮨
AGH!
YIKES!
HAH
HAH
HAH
LIKE I SAID, YOU DON'T KNOW UNTIL YOU--
THOK
ZII-ING
ARGH! THAT WAS MEAN, ECO!
IT WAS MY FIRST TIME EATING EXPENSIVE SUSHI!!!
HEH
WELL, AT LEAST YOU'VE GOT YOUR SPIRIT BACK.
ZII-ING
WHAT?!
OKAY, PENALTY GAME'S OVER. NO MORE FRETTING.
I THINK YOU UNDERSTAND NOW.

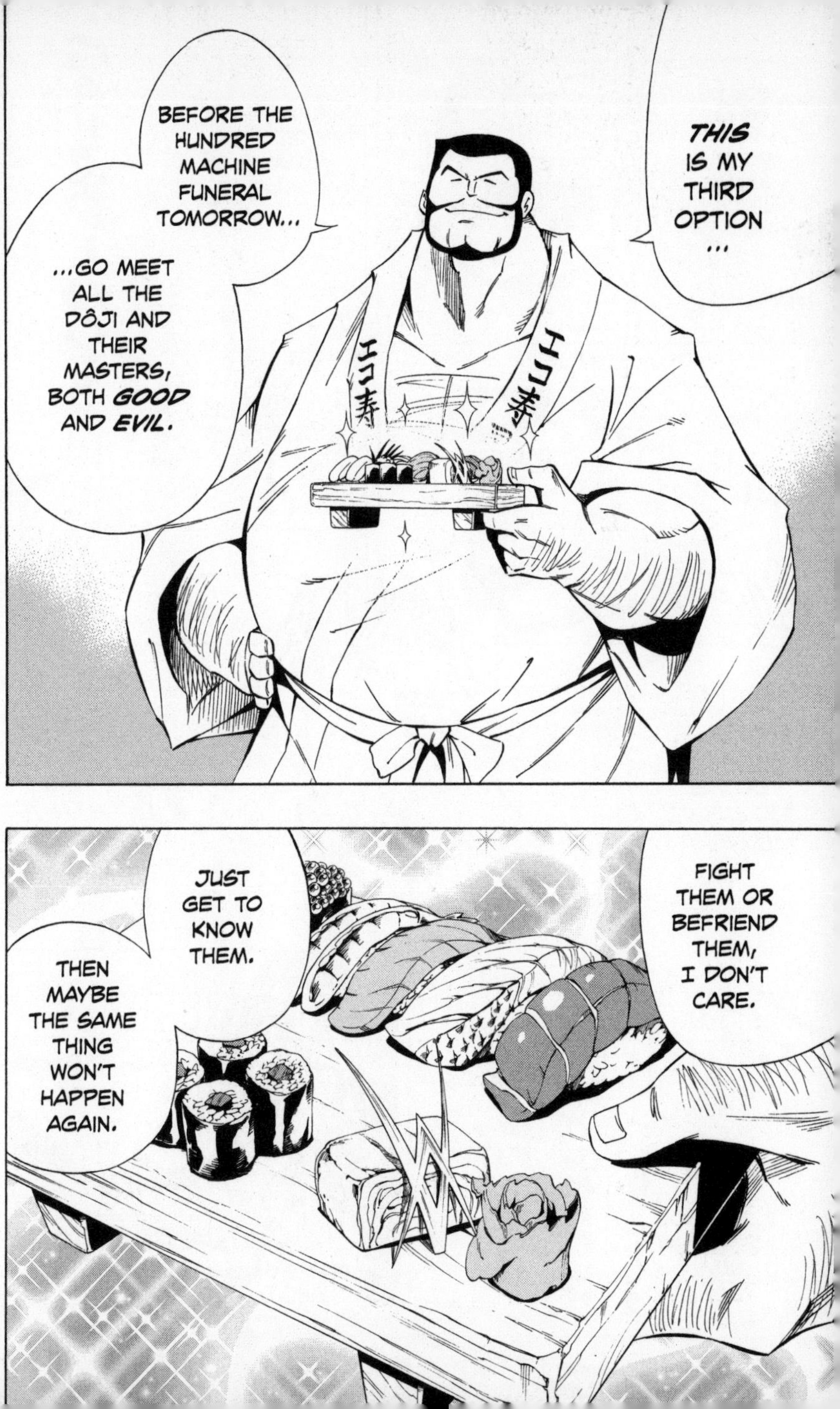
THIS IS MY THIRD OPTION...
BEFORE THE HUNDRED MACHINE FUNERAL TOMORROW...
...GO MEET ALL THE DÔJI AND THEIR MASTERS, BOTH GOOD AND EVIL.
エコ寿
FIGHT THEM OR BEFRIEND THEM, I DON'T CARE.
JUST GET TO KNOW THEM.
THEN MAYBE THE SAME THING WON'T HAPPEN AGAIN.

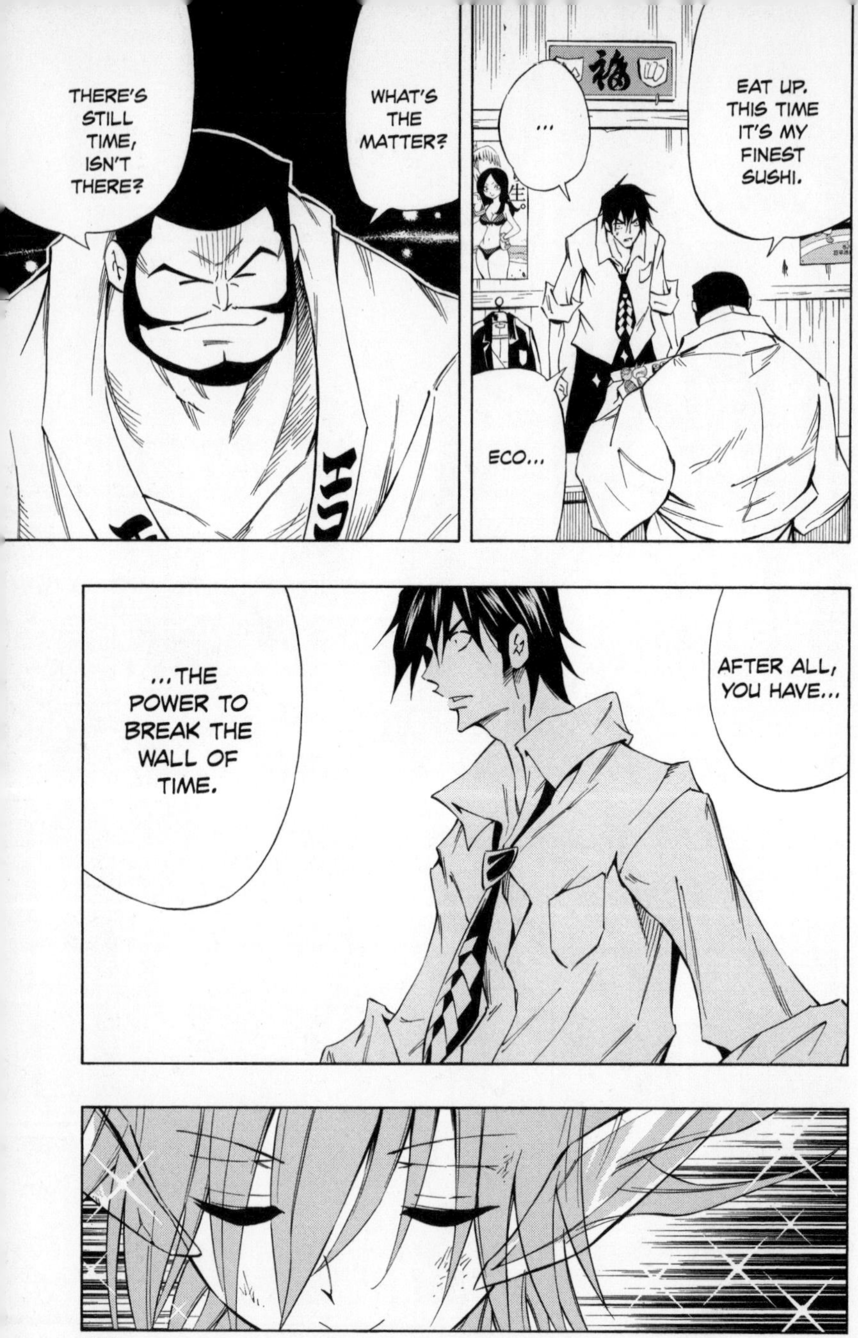
EAT UP. THIS TIME IT'S MY FINEST SUSHI.
...
ECO...
WHAT'S THE MATTER?
THERE'S STILL TIME, ISN'T THERE?
AFTER ALL, YOU HAVE...
...THE POWER TO BREAK THE WALL OF TIME.

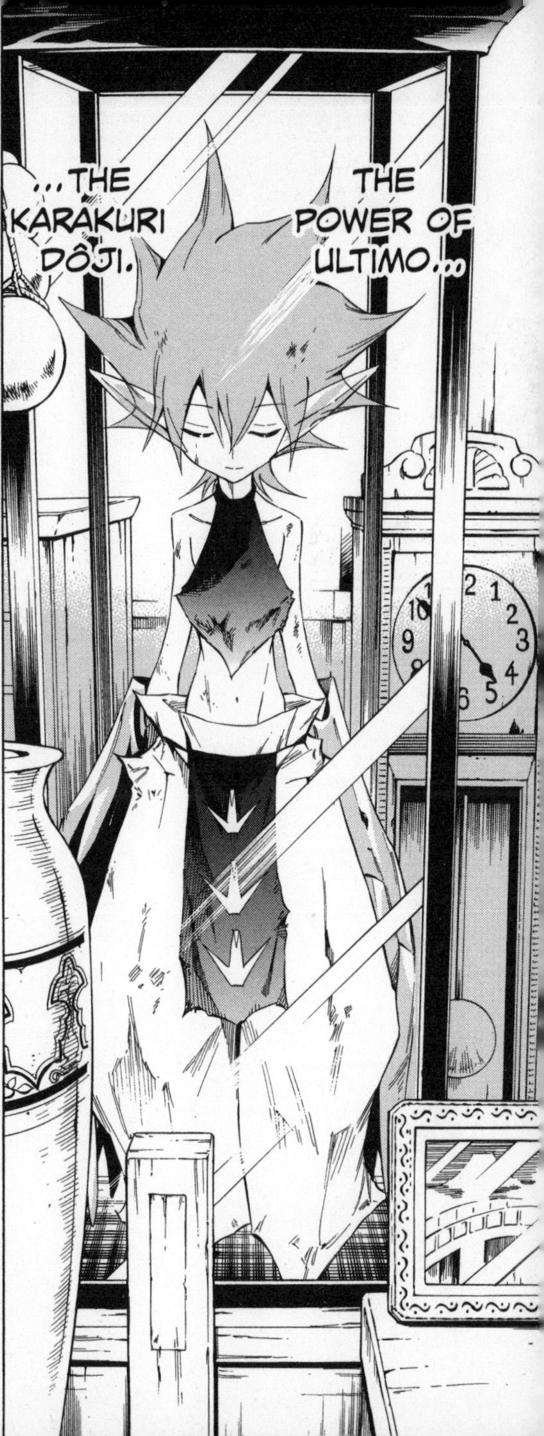
THE POWER OF ULTIMO...
...THE KARAKURI DÔJI.
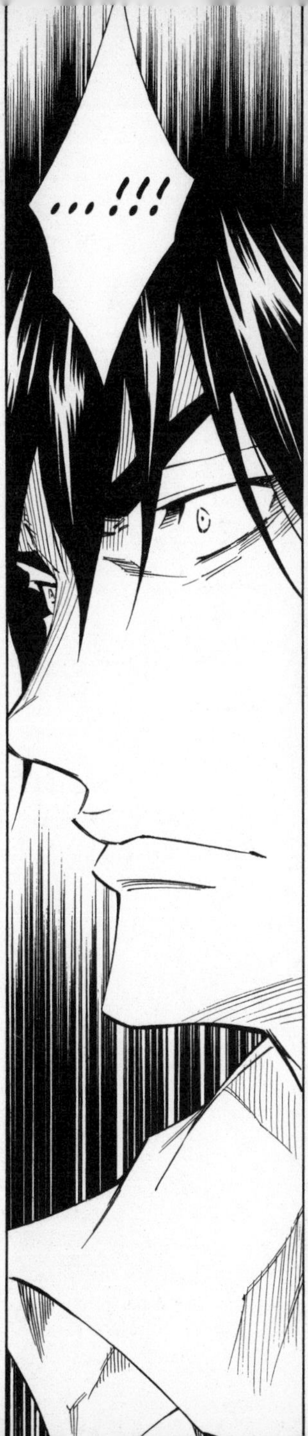
...!!!

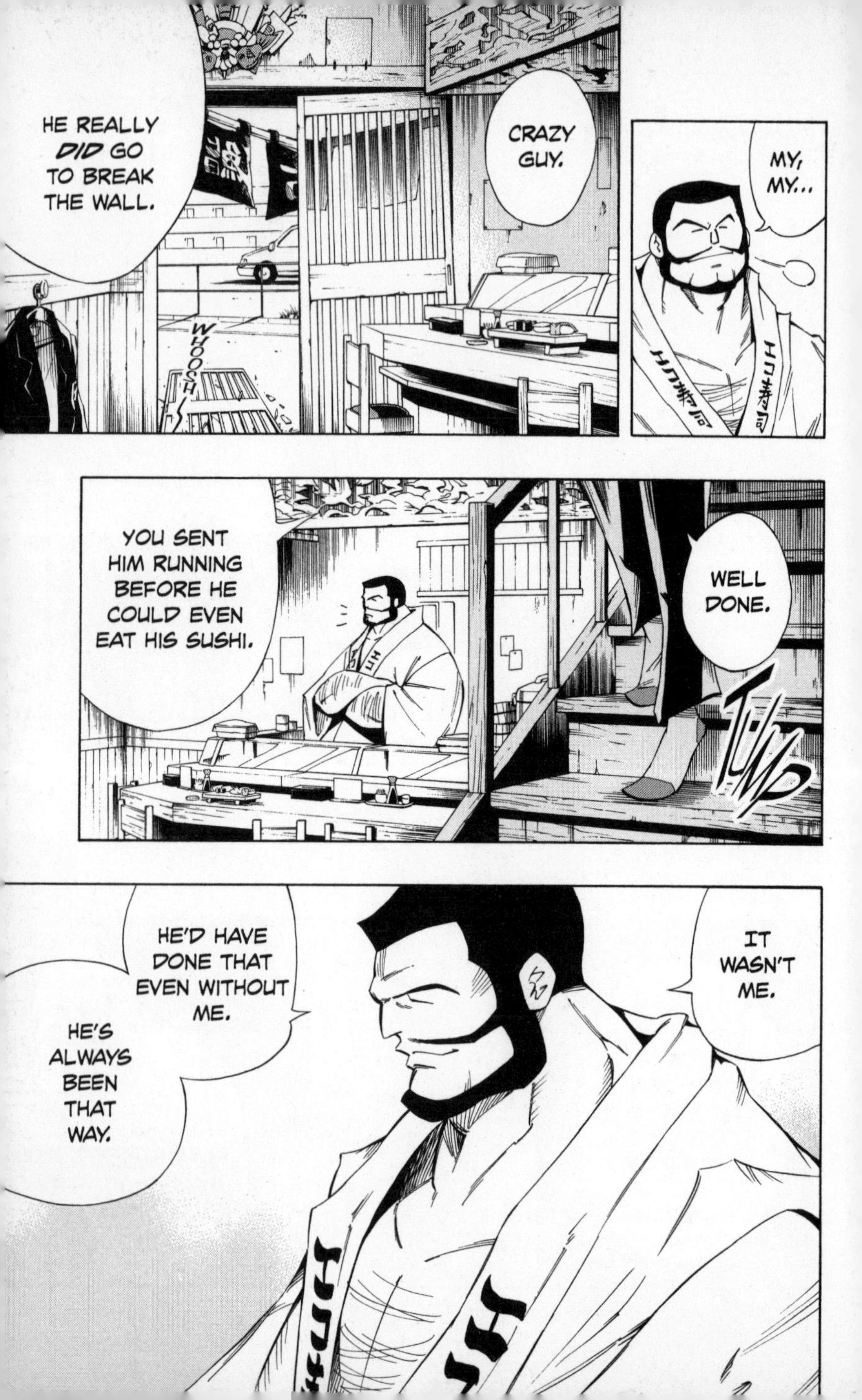
MY, MY...
CRAZY GUY.
HE REALLY *DID* GO TO BREAK THE WALL.
WHOOSH
WELL DONE.
YOU SENT HIM RUNNING BEFORE HE COULD EVEN EAT HIS SUSHI.
IT WASN'T ME.
HE'D HAVE DONE THAT EVEN WITHOUT ME.
HE'S ALWAYS BEEN THAT WAY.

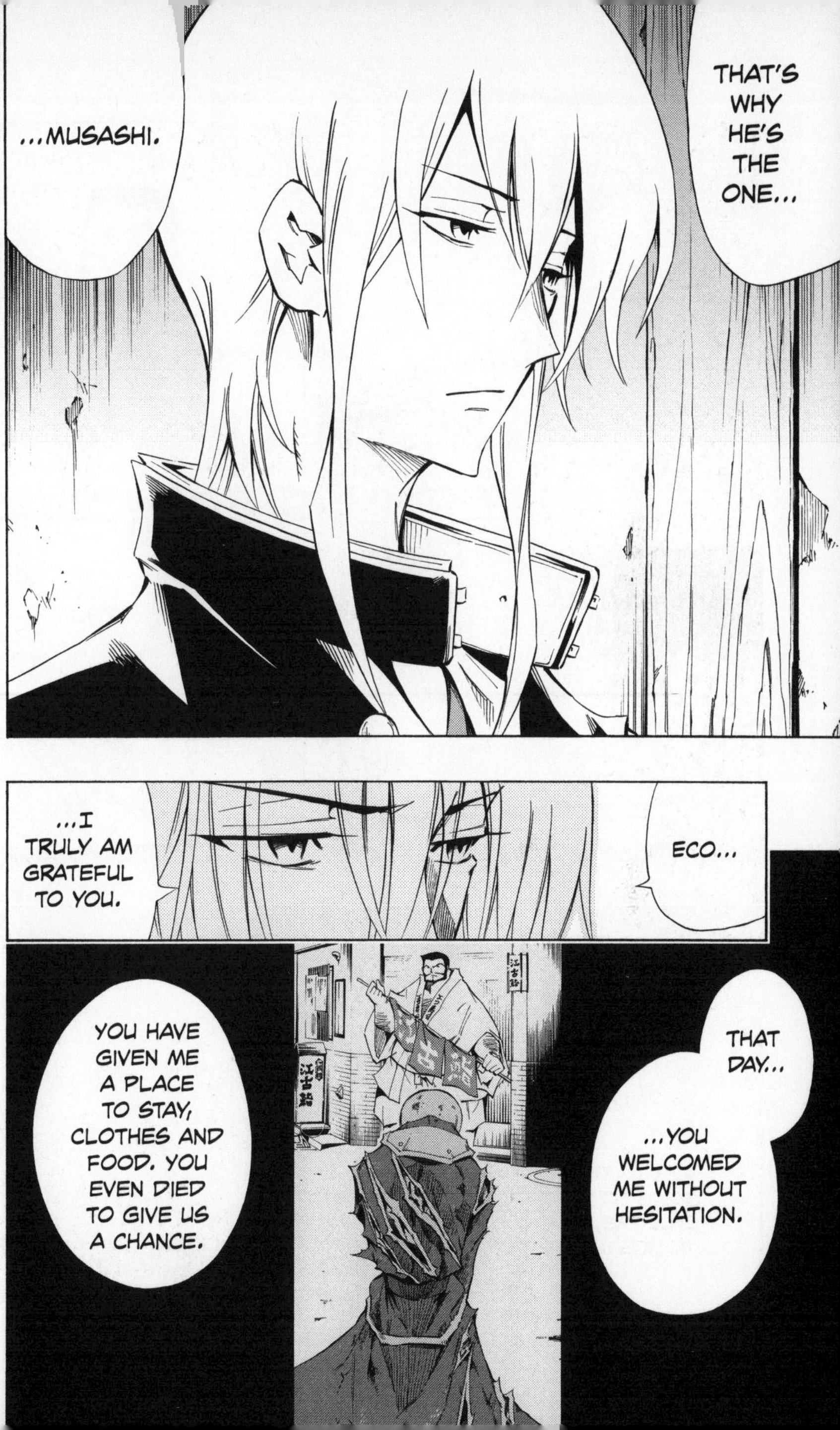
THAT'S WHY HE'S THE ONE...
...MUSASHI.
ECO...
...I TRULY AM GRATEFUL TO YOU.
THAT DAY...
...YOU WELCOMED ME WITHOUT HESITATION.
YOU HAVE GIVEN ME A PLACE TO STAY, CLOTHES AND FOOD. YOU EVEN DIED TO GIVE US A CHANCE.

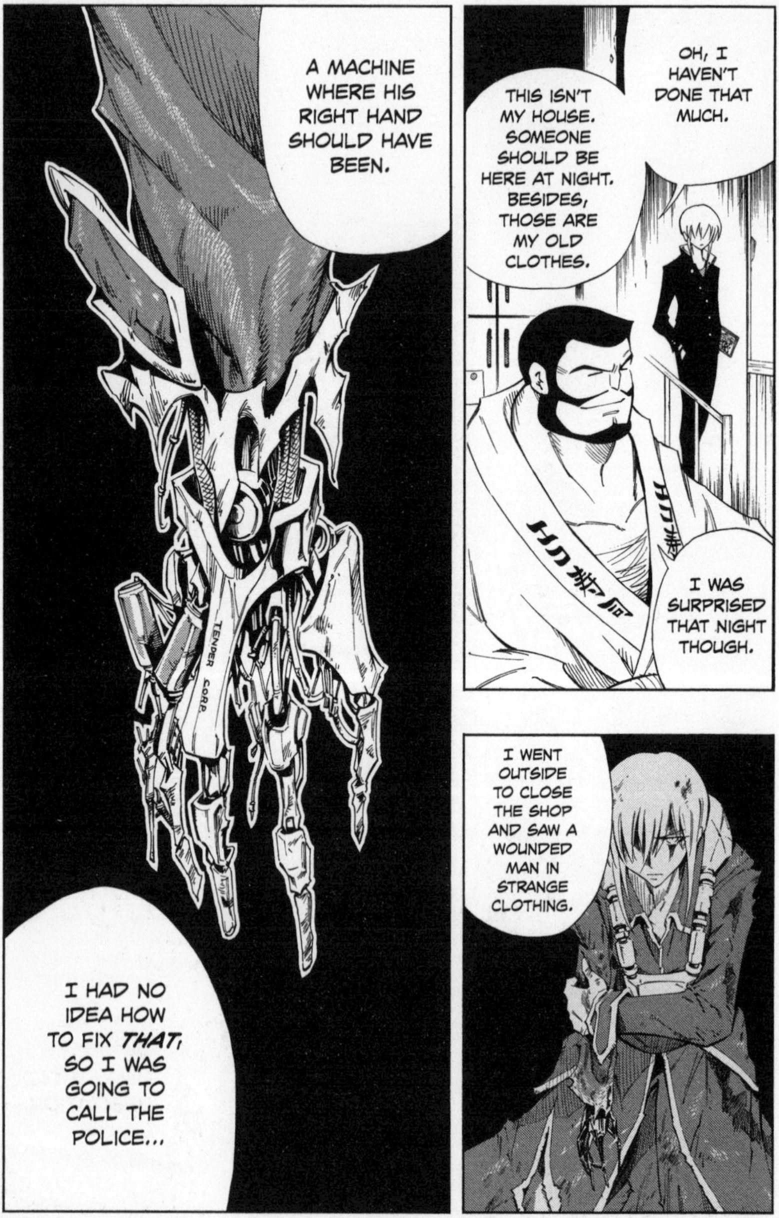
OH, I HAVEN'T DONE THAT MUCH.
THIS ISN'T MY HOUSE. SOMEONE SHOULD BE HERE AT NIGHT. BESIDES, THOSE ARE MY OLD CLOTHES.
I WAS SURPRISED THAT NIGHT THOUGH.
I WENT OUTSIDE TO CLOSE THE SHOP AND SAW A WOUNDED MAN IN STRANGE CLOTHING.
A MACHINE WHERE HIS RIGHT HAND SHOULD HAVE BEEN.
TENDER CORP.
I HAD NO IDEA HOW TO FIX *THAT*, SO I WAS GOING TO CALL THE POLICE...

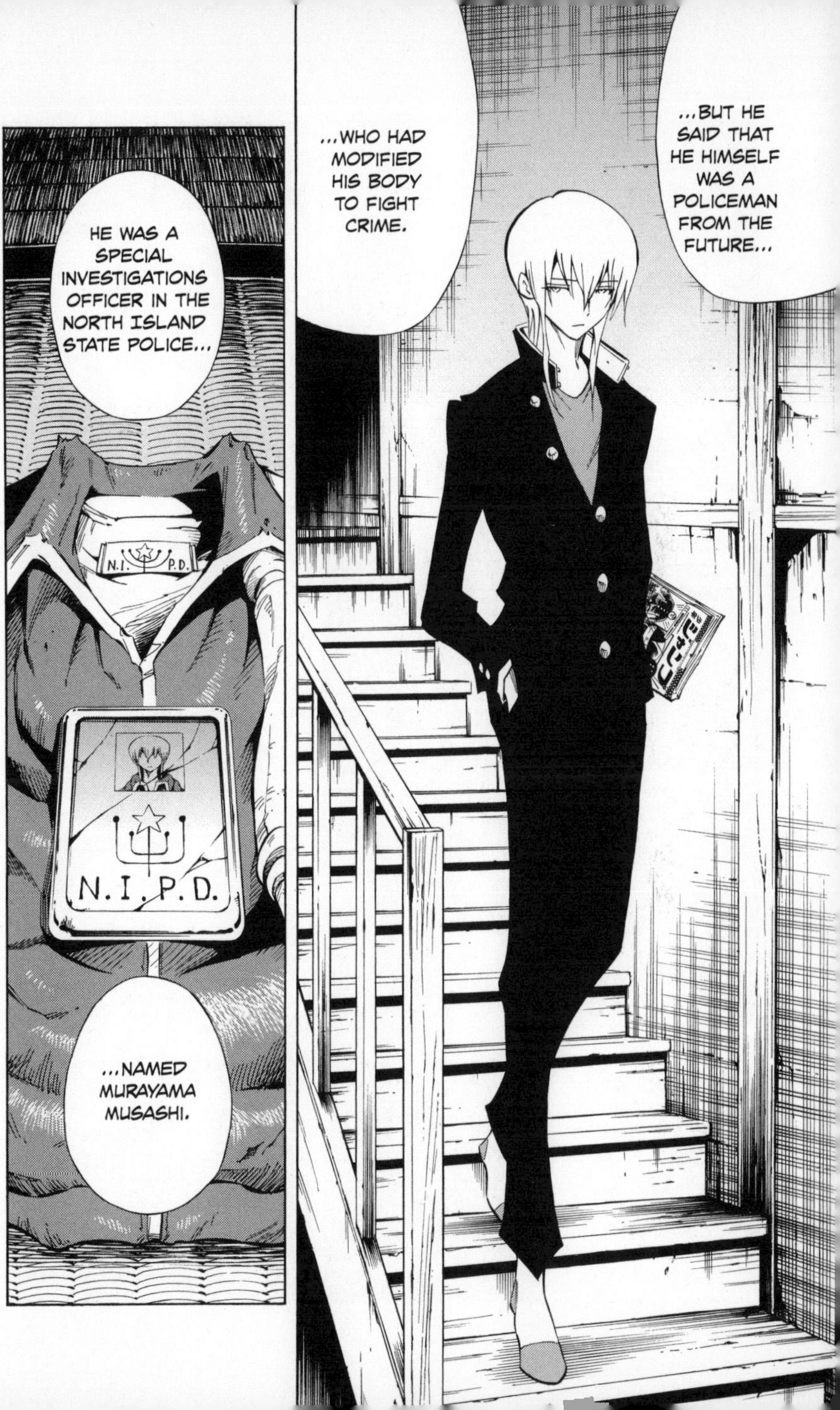
...BUT HE SAID THAT HE HIMSELF WAS A POLICEMAN FROM THE FUTURE...
...WHO HAD MODIFIED HIS BODY TO FIGHT CRIME.
HE WAS A SPECIAL INVESTIGATIONS OFFICER IN THE NORTH ISLAND STATE POLICE...
N.I. P.D.
N.I.P.D.
...NAMED MURAYAMA MUSASHI.

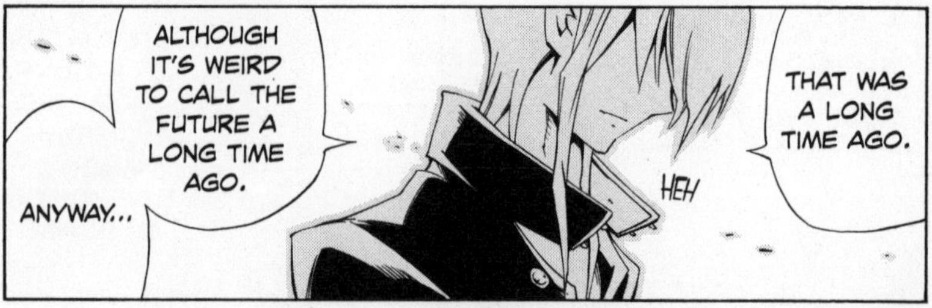
THAT WAS A LONG TIME AGO.
HEH
ALTHOUGH IT'S WEIRD TO CALL THE FUTURE A LONG TIME AGO.
ANYWAY...

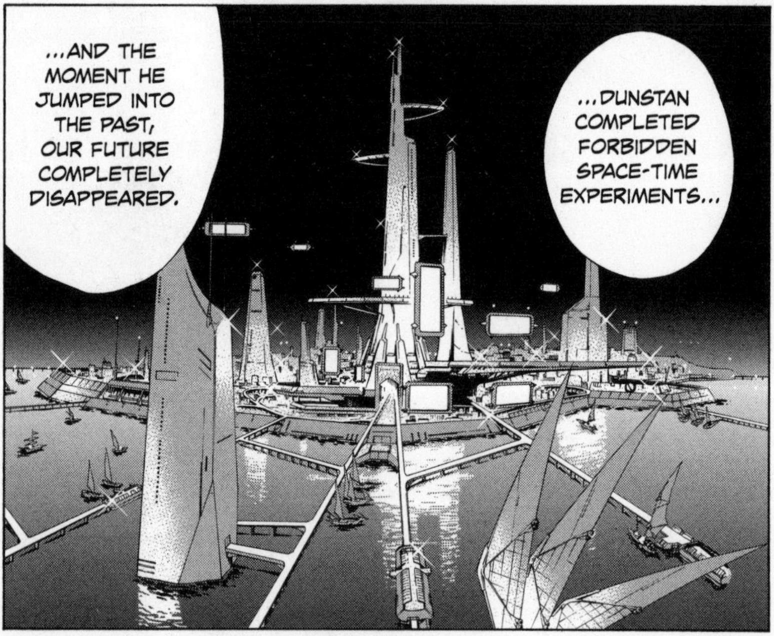
...DUNSTAN COMPLETED FORBIDDEN SPACE-TIME EXPERIMENTS...
...AND THE MOMENT HE JUMPED INTO THE PAST, OUR FUTURE COMPLETELY DISAPPEARED.

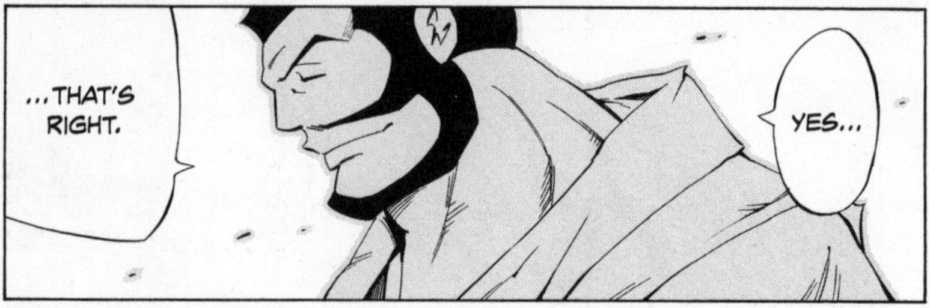
YES...
...THAT'S RIGHT.

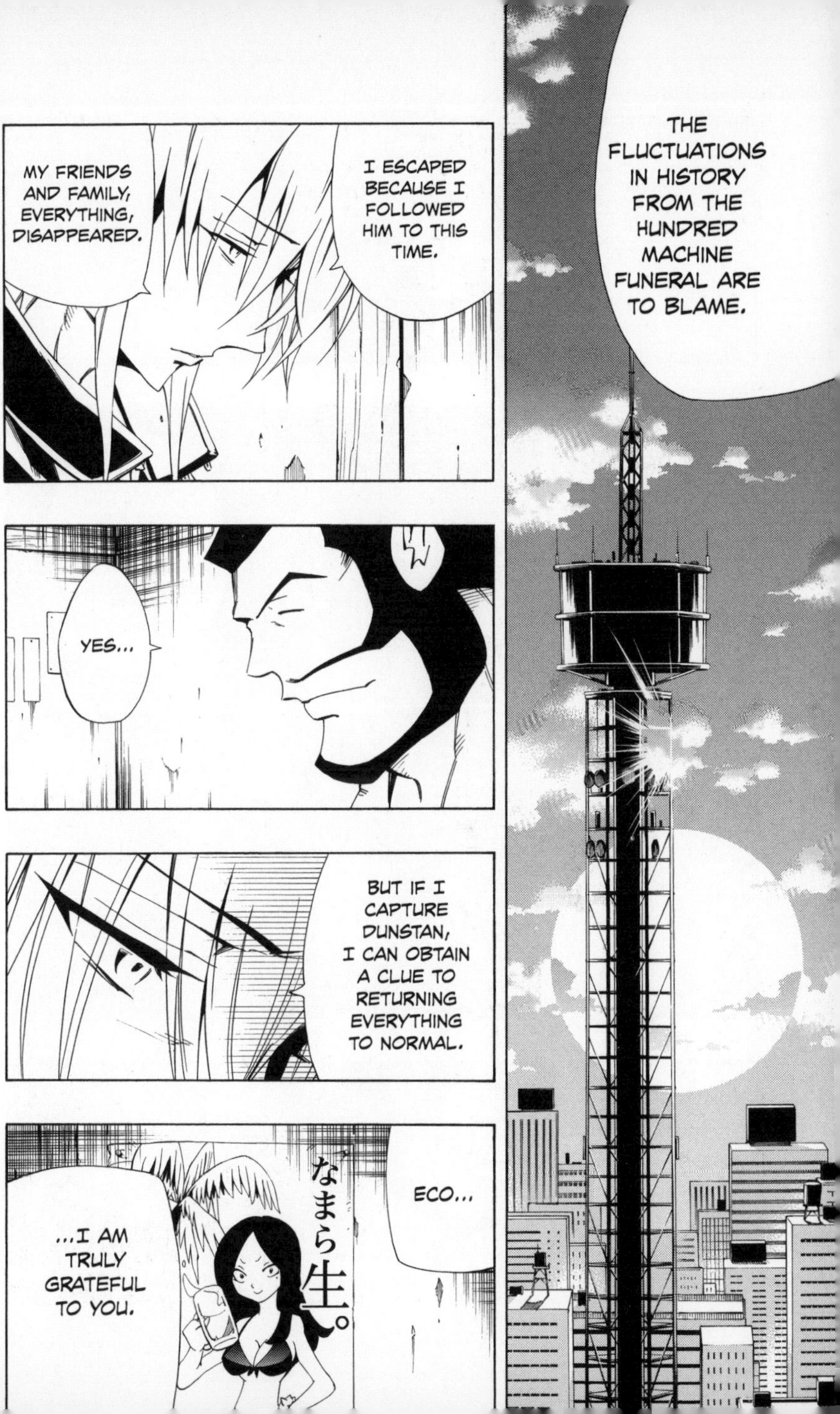
THE FLUCTUATIONS IN HISTORY FROM THE HUNDRED MACHINE FUNERAL ARE TO BLAME.
I ESCAPED BECAUSE I FOLLOWED HIM TO THIS TIME.
MY FRIENDS AND FAMILY, EVERYTHING, DISAPPEARED.
YES...
BUT IF I CAPTURE DUNSTAN, I CAN OBTAIN A CLUE TO RETURNING EVERYTHING TO NORMAL.
ECO...
なまら生。
...I AM TRULY GRATEFUL TO YOU.

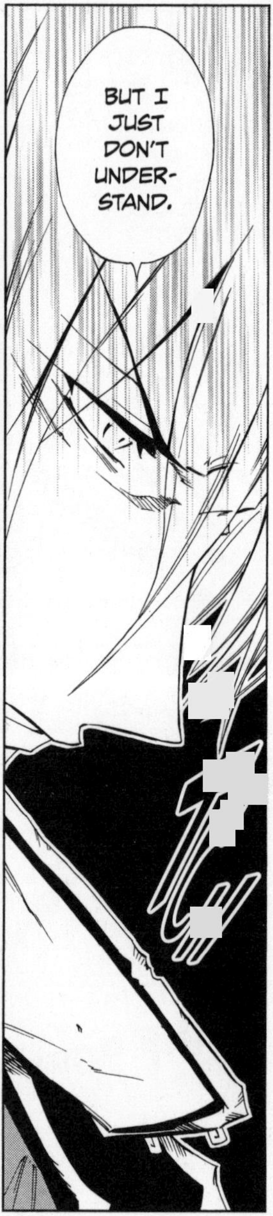
BUT I JUST DON'T UNDERSTAND.

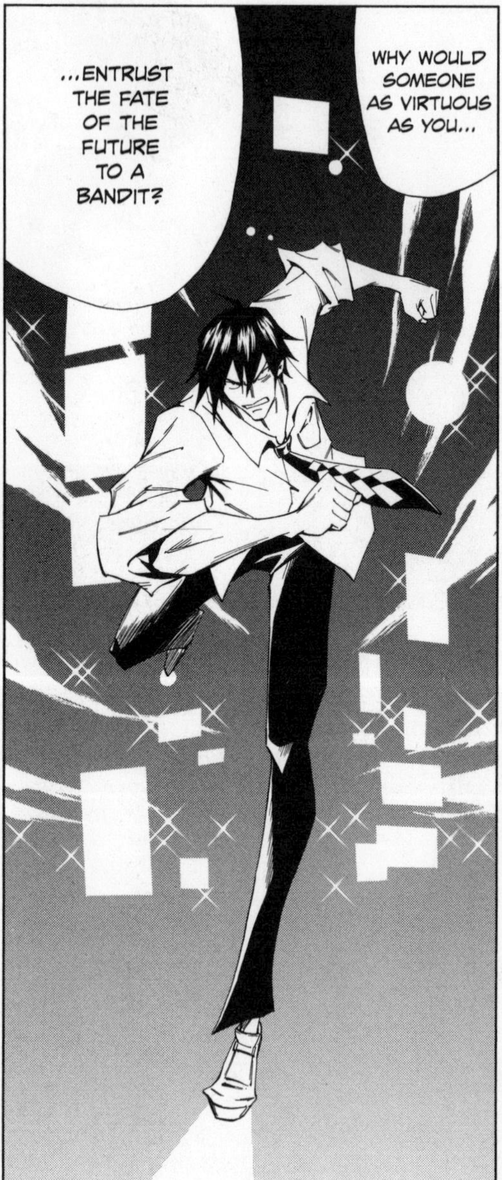
WHY WOULD SOMEONE AS VIRTUOUS AS YOU...
...ENTRUST THE FATE OF THE FUTURE TO A BANDIT?

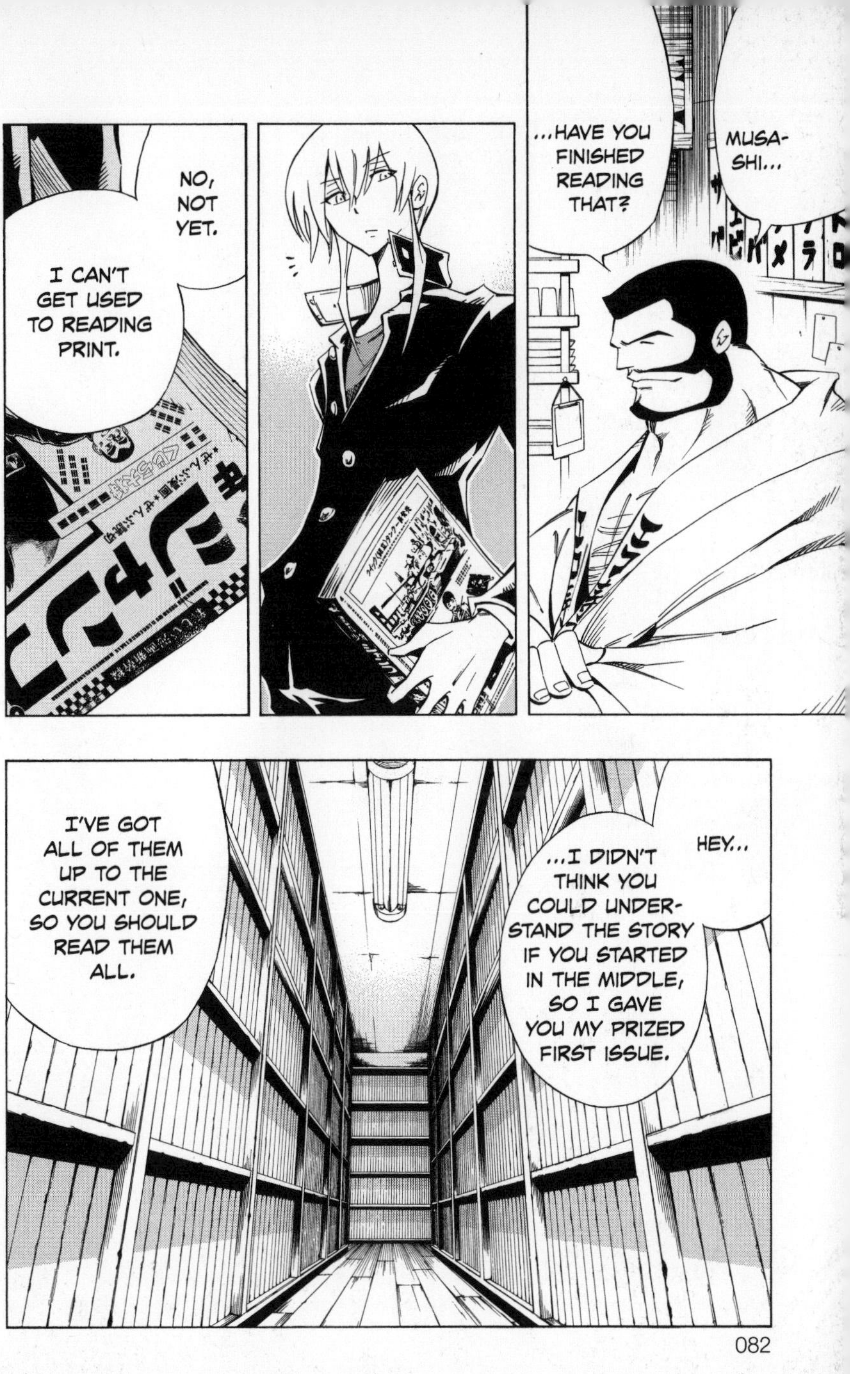
MUSA-SHI...
...HAVE YOU FINISHED READING THAT?
NO, NOT YET.
I CAN'T GET USED TO READING PRINT.
HEY...
...I DIDN'T THINK YOU COULD UNDER-STAND THE STORY IF YOU STARTED IN THE MIDDLE, SO I GAVE YOU MY PRIZED FIRST ISSUE.
I'VE GOT ALL OF THEM UP TO THE CURRENT ONE, SO YOU SHOULD READ THEM ALL.

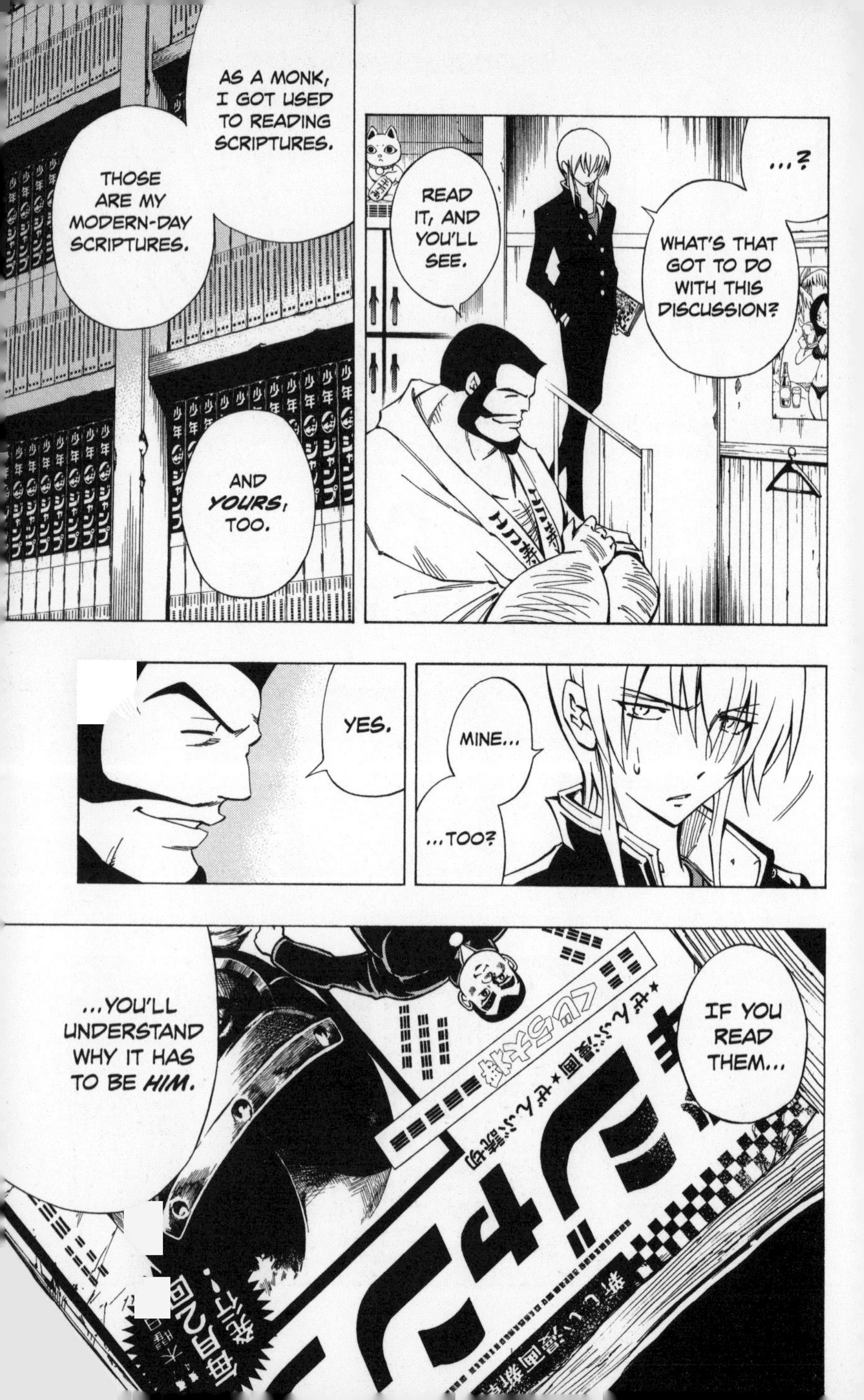
...?
WHAT'S THAT GOT TO DO WITH THIS DISCUSSION?
READ IT, AND YOU'LL SEE.
AS A MONK, I GOT USED TO READING SCRIPTURES.
THOSE ARE MY MODERN-DAY SCRIPTURES.
AND YOURS, TOO.
MINE...
...TOO?
YES.
IF YOU READ THEM...
...YOU'LL UNDERSTAND WHY IT HAS TO BE HIM.

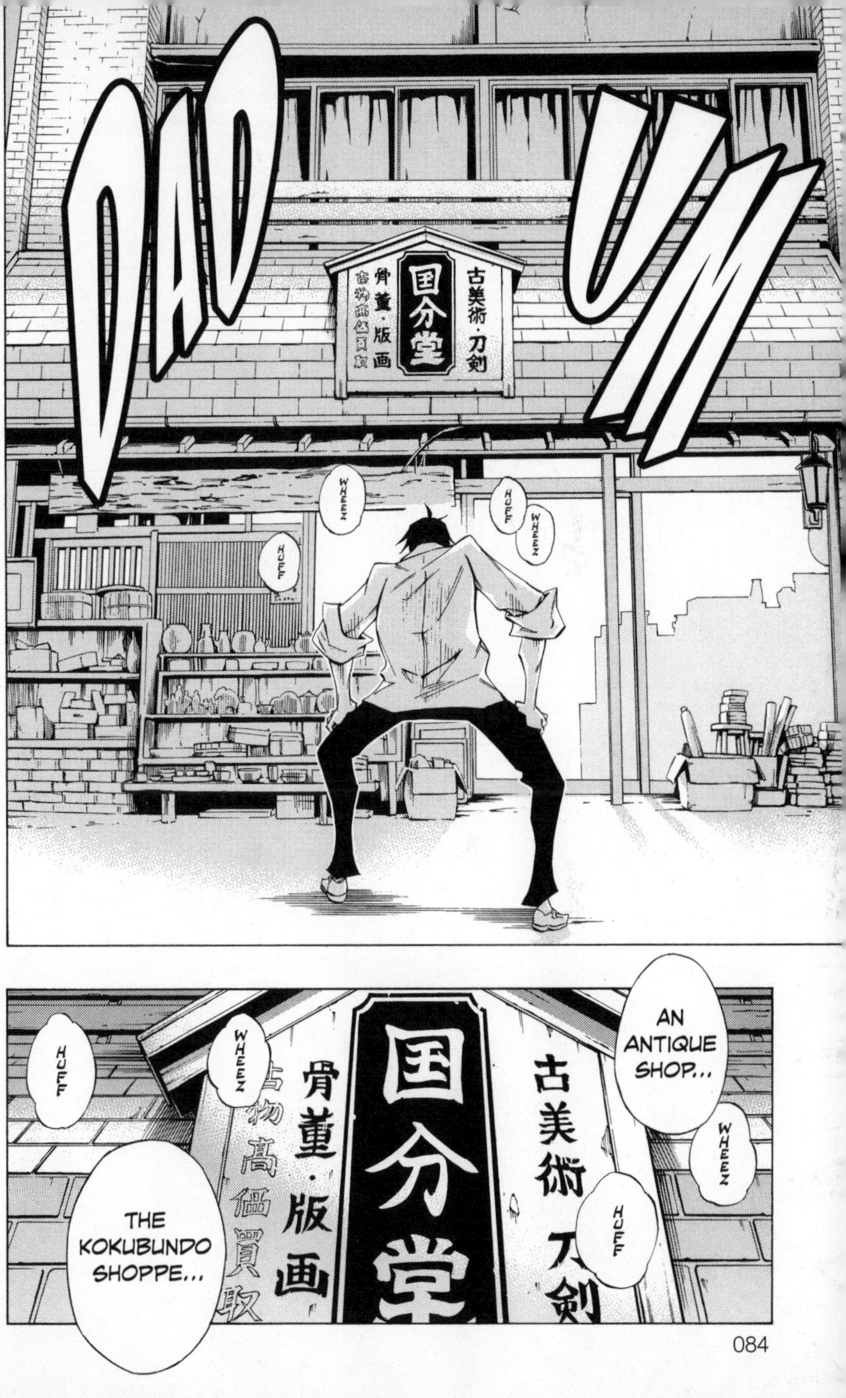
DAOUM
古美術・刀剣
国分堂
骨董・版画
古物高価買取
HUFF
WHEEZ
WHEEZ
HUFF
AN ANTIQUE SHOP...
WHEEZ
HUFF
THE KOKUBUNDO SHOPPE...
WHEEZ
HUFF

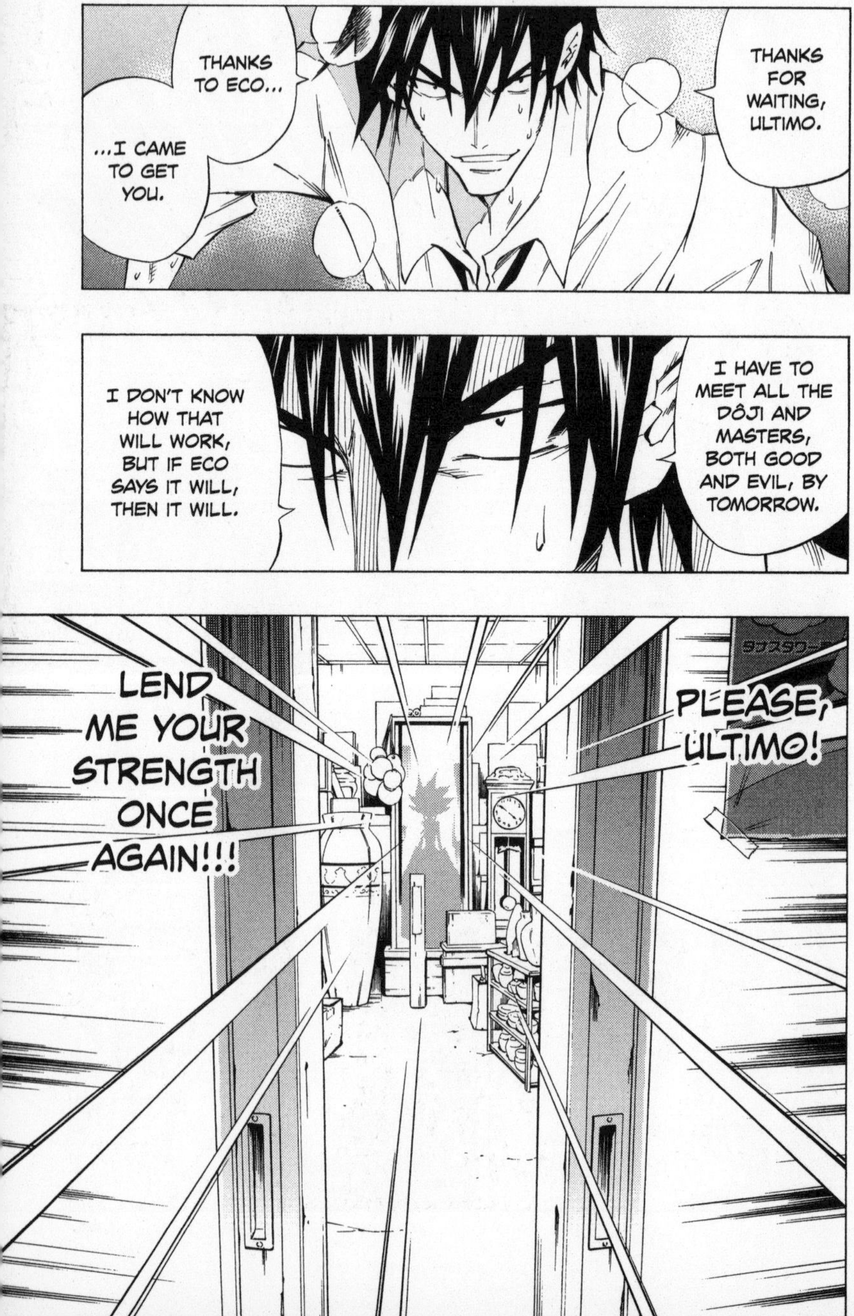
THANKS FOR WAITING, ULTIMO.
THANKS TO ECO...
...I CAME TO GET YOU.
I HAVE TO MEET ALL THE DÔJI AND MASTERS, BOTH GOOD AND EVIL, BY TOMORROW.
I DON'T KNOW HOW THAT WILL WORK, BUT IF ECO SAYS IT WILL, THEN IT WILL.
PLEASE, ULTIMO!
LEND ME YOUR STRENGTH ONCE AGAIN!!!

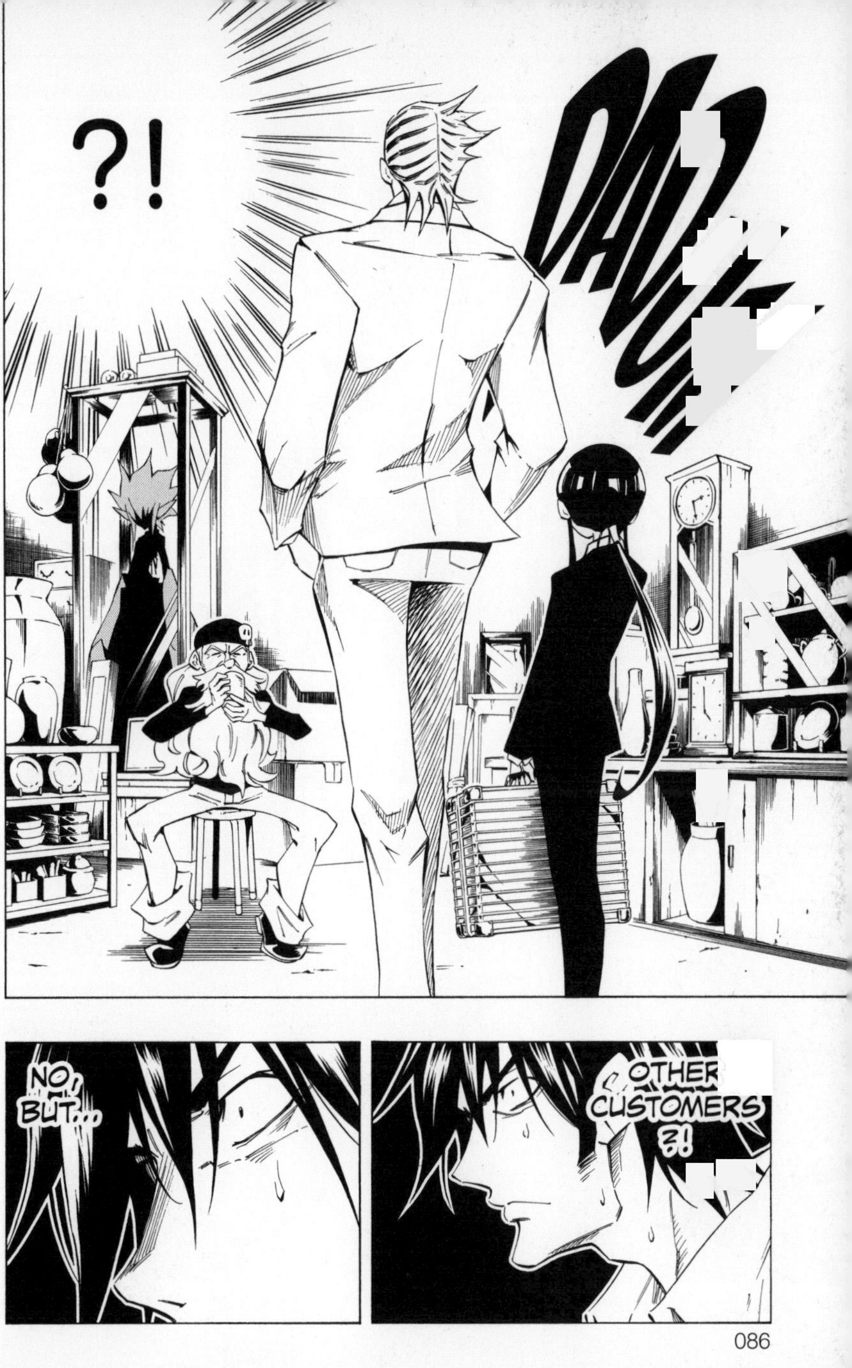
?!
OTHER CUSTOMERS?!
NO, BUT...

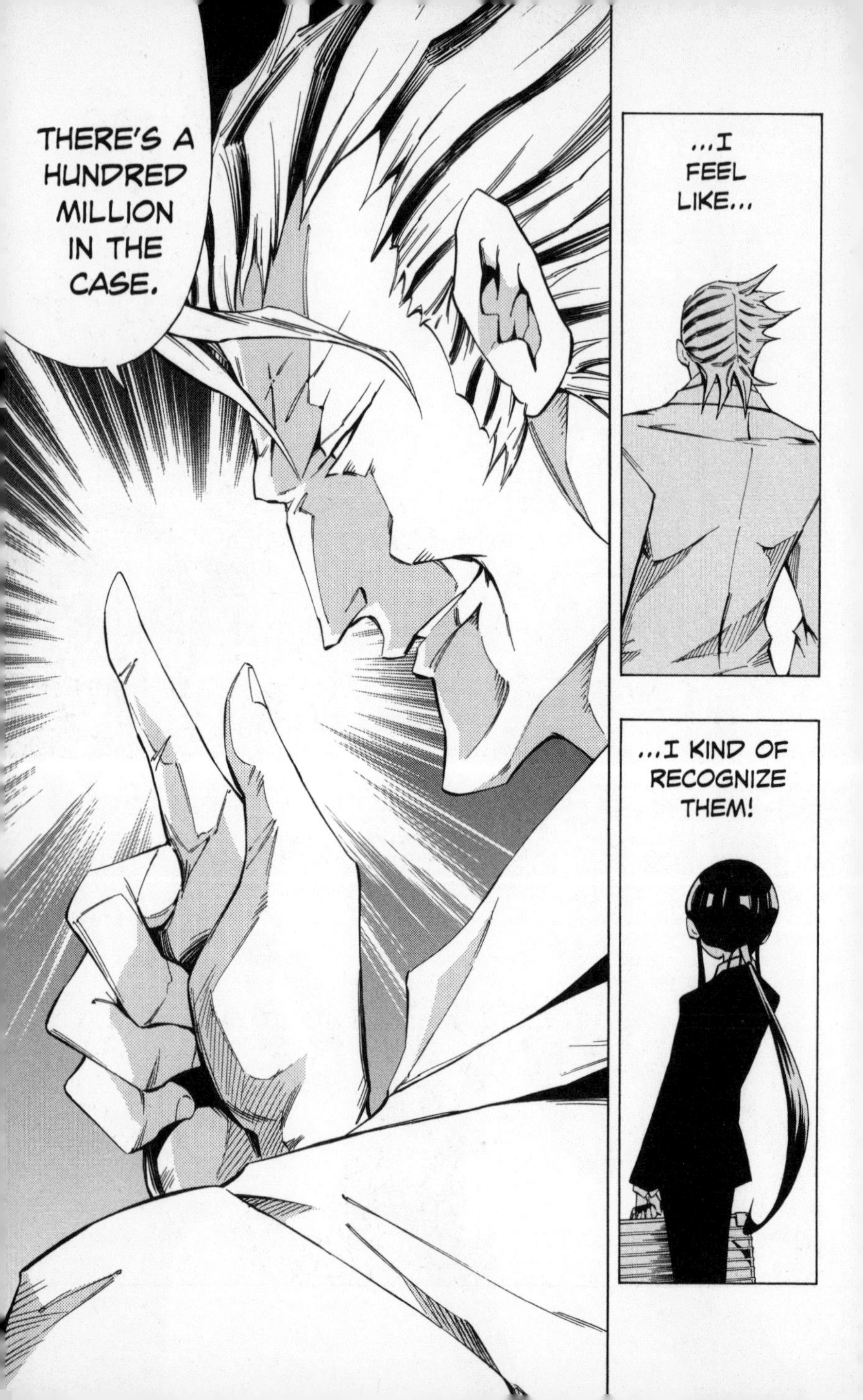
...I FEEL LIKE...
...I KIND OF RECOGNIZE THEM!
THERE'S A HUNDRED MILLION IN THE CASE.

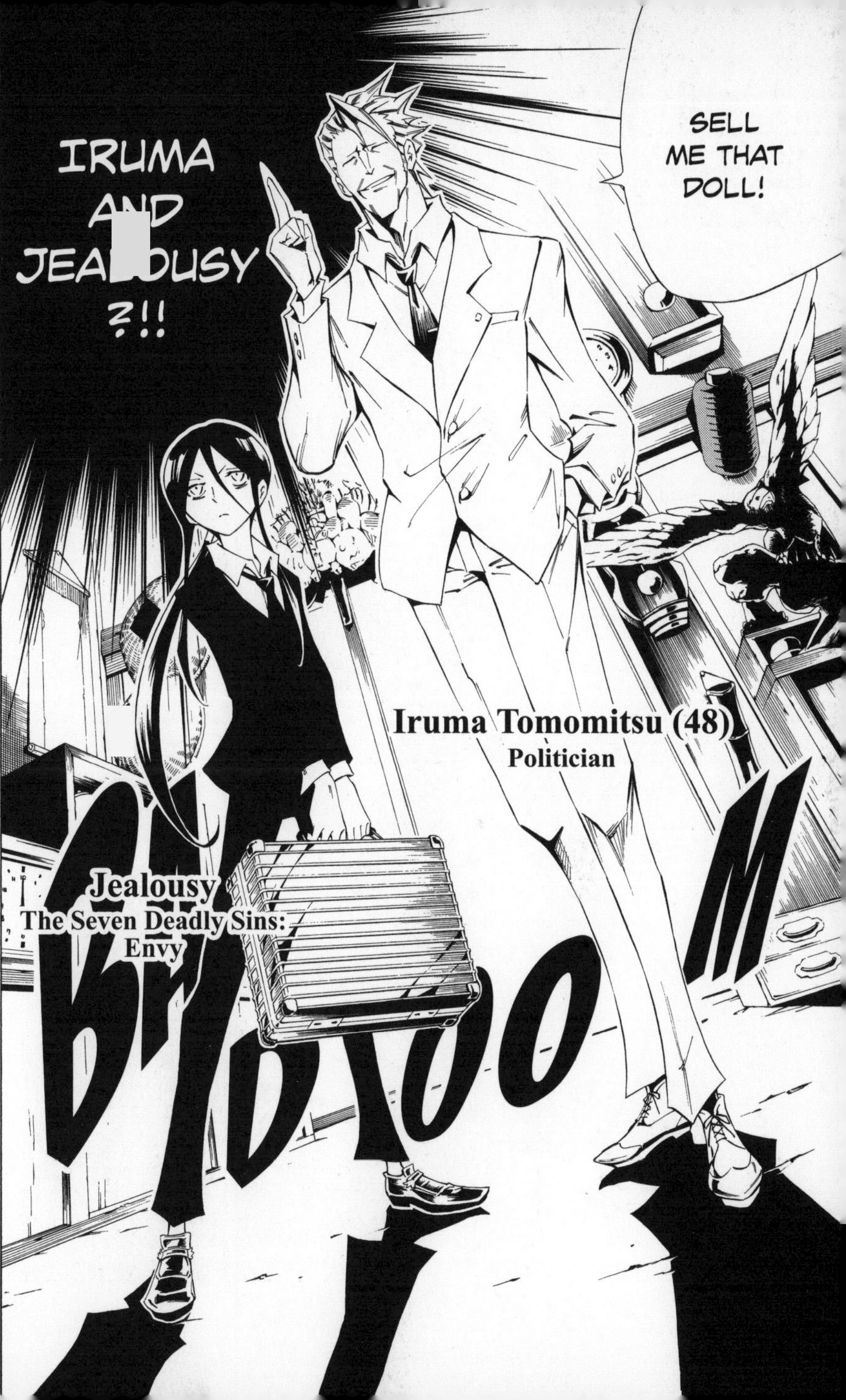
SELL ME THAT DOLL!
IRUMA AND JEALOUSY ?!!
Iruma Tomomitsu (48)
Politician
Jealousy
The Seven Deadly Sins:
Envy

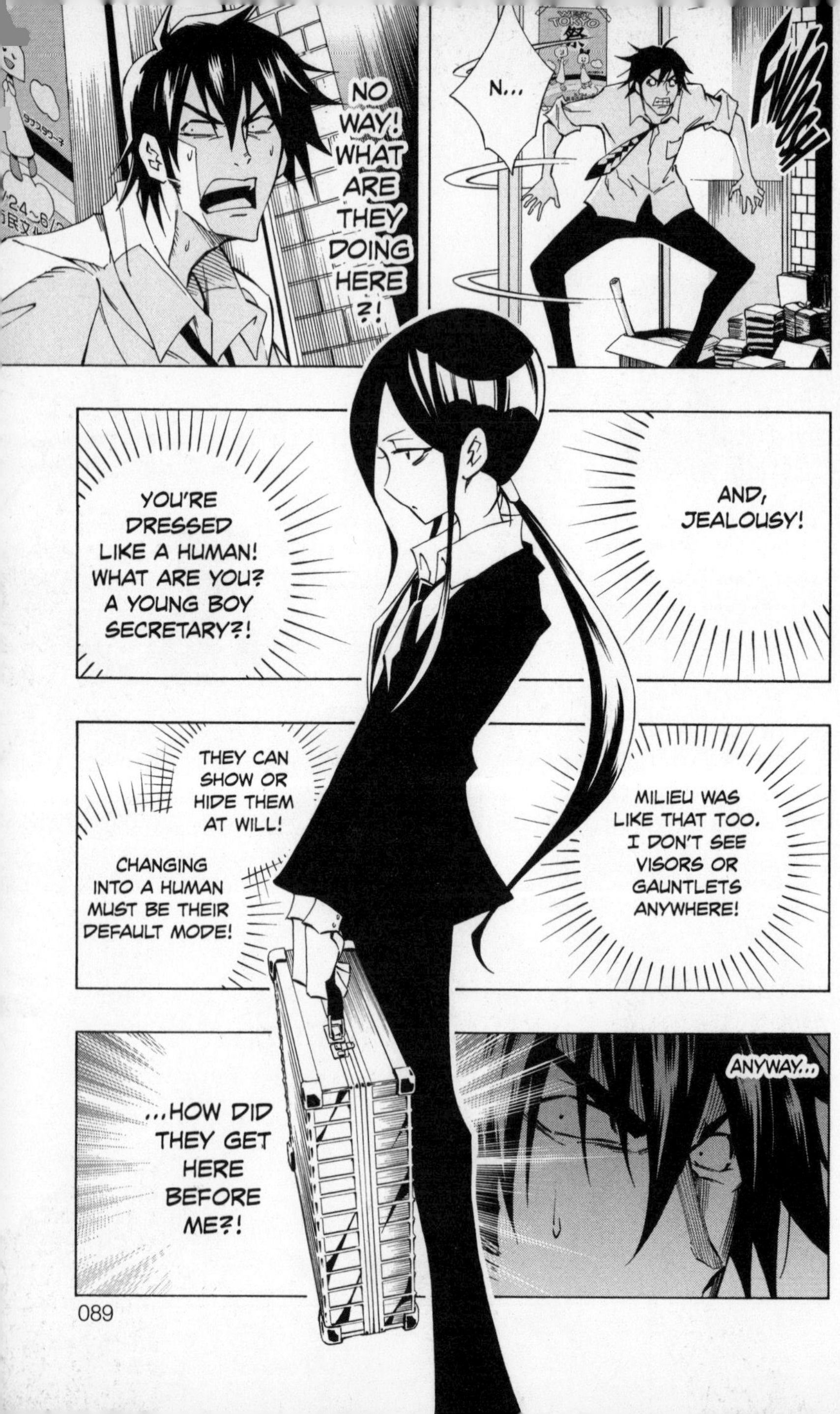
N...
NO WAY! WHAT ARE THEY DOING HERE?!
AND, JEALOUSY!
YOU'RE DRESSED LIKE A HUMAN! WHAT ARE YOU? A YOUNG BOY SECRETARY?!
MILIEU WAS LIKE THAT TOO. I DON'T SEE VISORS OR GAUNTLETS ANYWHERE!
THEY CAN SHOW OR HIDE THEM AT WILL!
CHANGING INTO A HUMAN MUST BE THEIR DEFAULT MODE!
ANYWAY...
...HOW DID THEY GET HERE BEFORE ME?!

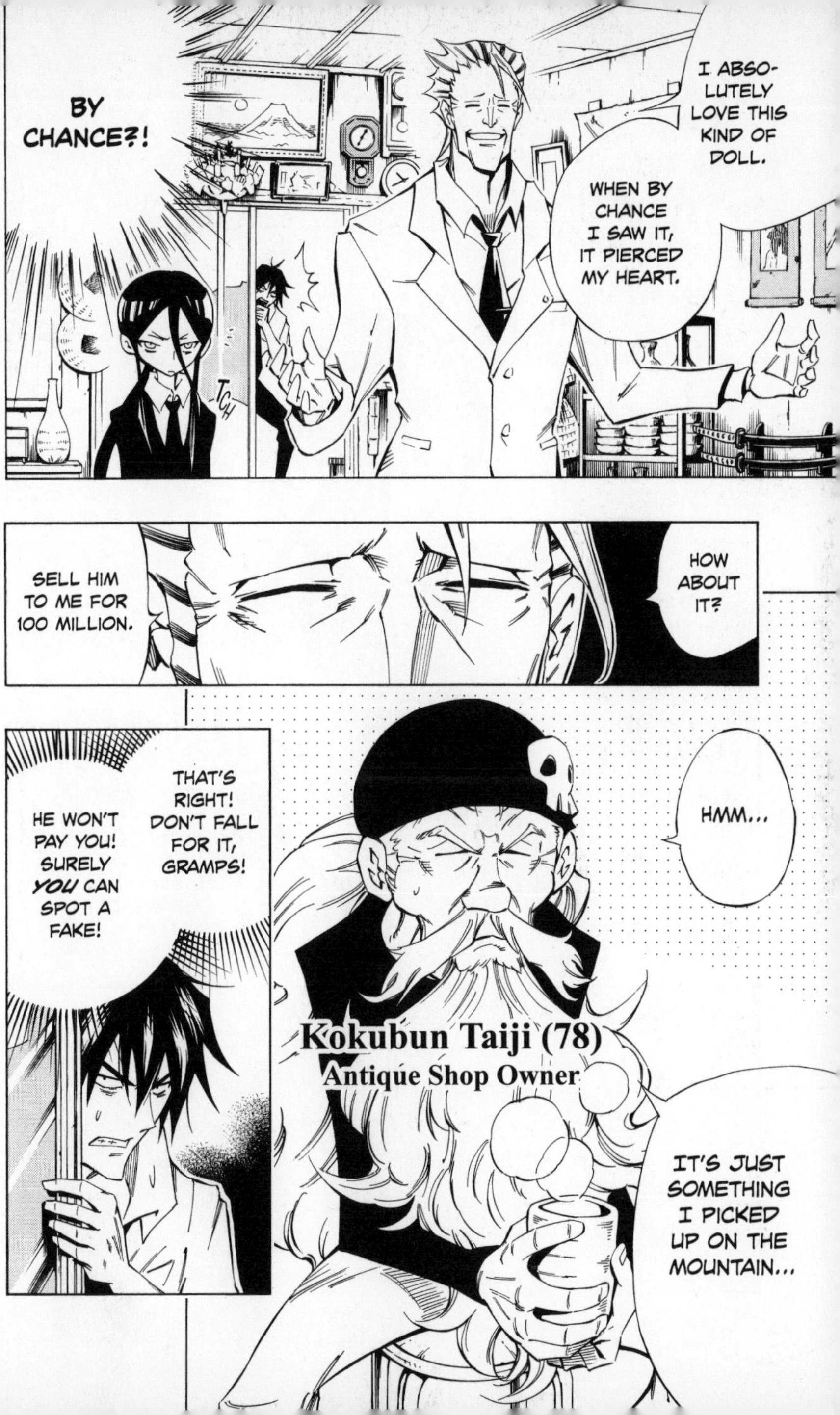
I ABSOLUTELY LOVE THIS KIND OF DOLL.
WHEN BY CHANCE I SAW IT, IT PIERCED MY HEART.
BY CHANCE?!
TCH
HOW ABOUT IT?
SELL HIM TO ME FOR 100 MILLION.
HMM...
Kokubun Taiji (78)
Antique Shop Owner
IT'S JUST SOMETHING I PICKED UP ON THE MOUNTAIN...
THAT'S RIGHT! DON'T FALL FOR IT, GRAMPS!
HE WON'T PAY YOU! SURELY *YOU* CAN SPOT A FAKE!

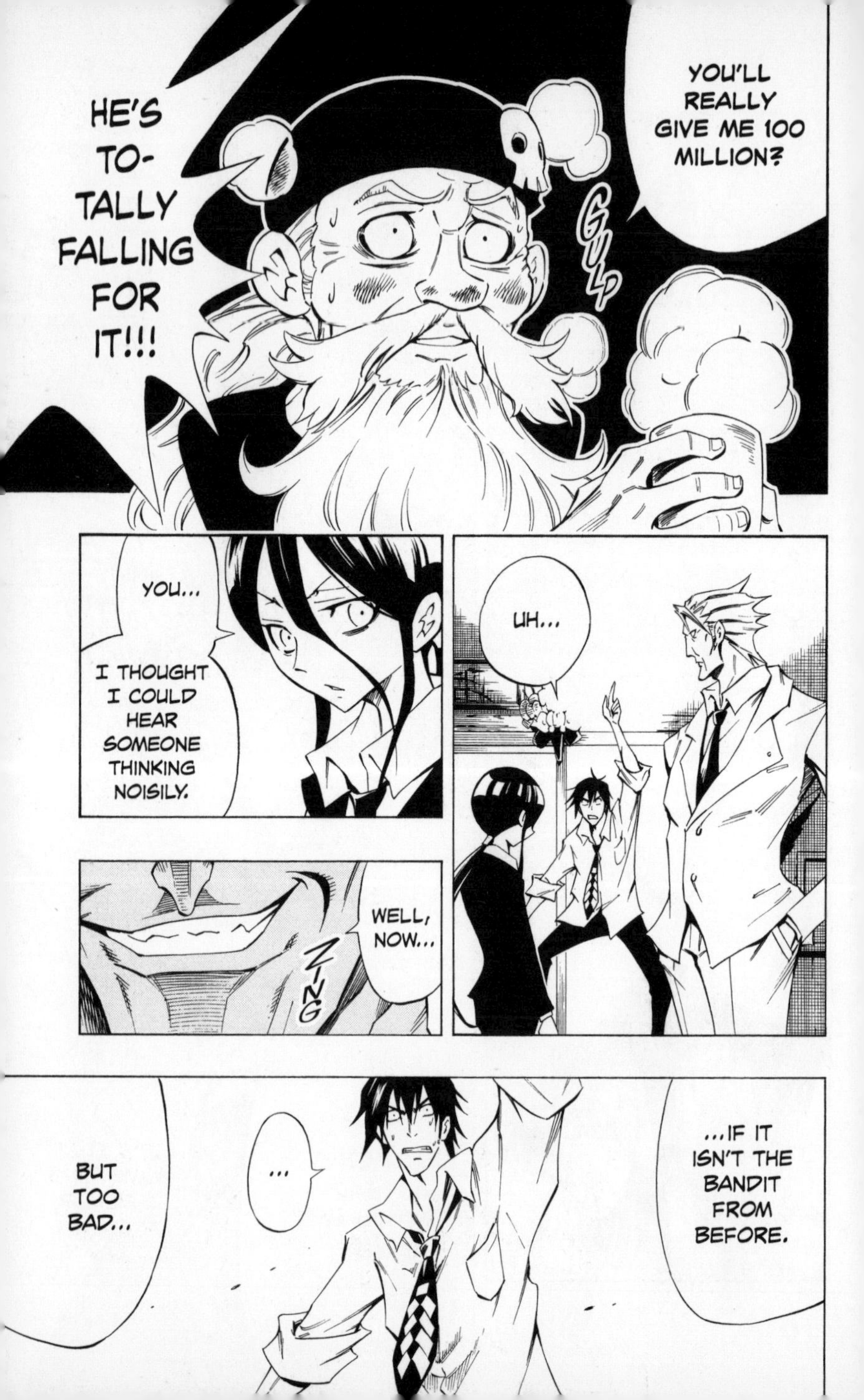
YOU'LL REALLY GIVE ME 100 MILLION?
GULP
HE'S TO-TALLY FALLING FOR IT!!!
UH...
YOU...
I THOUGHT I COULD HEAR SOMEONE THINKING NOISILY.
WELL, NOW...
ZING
...IF IT ISN'T THE BANDIT FROM BEFORE.
...
BUT TOO BAD...

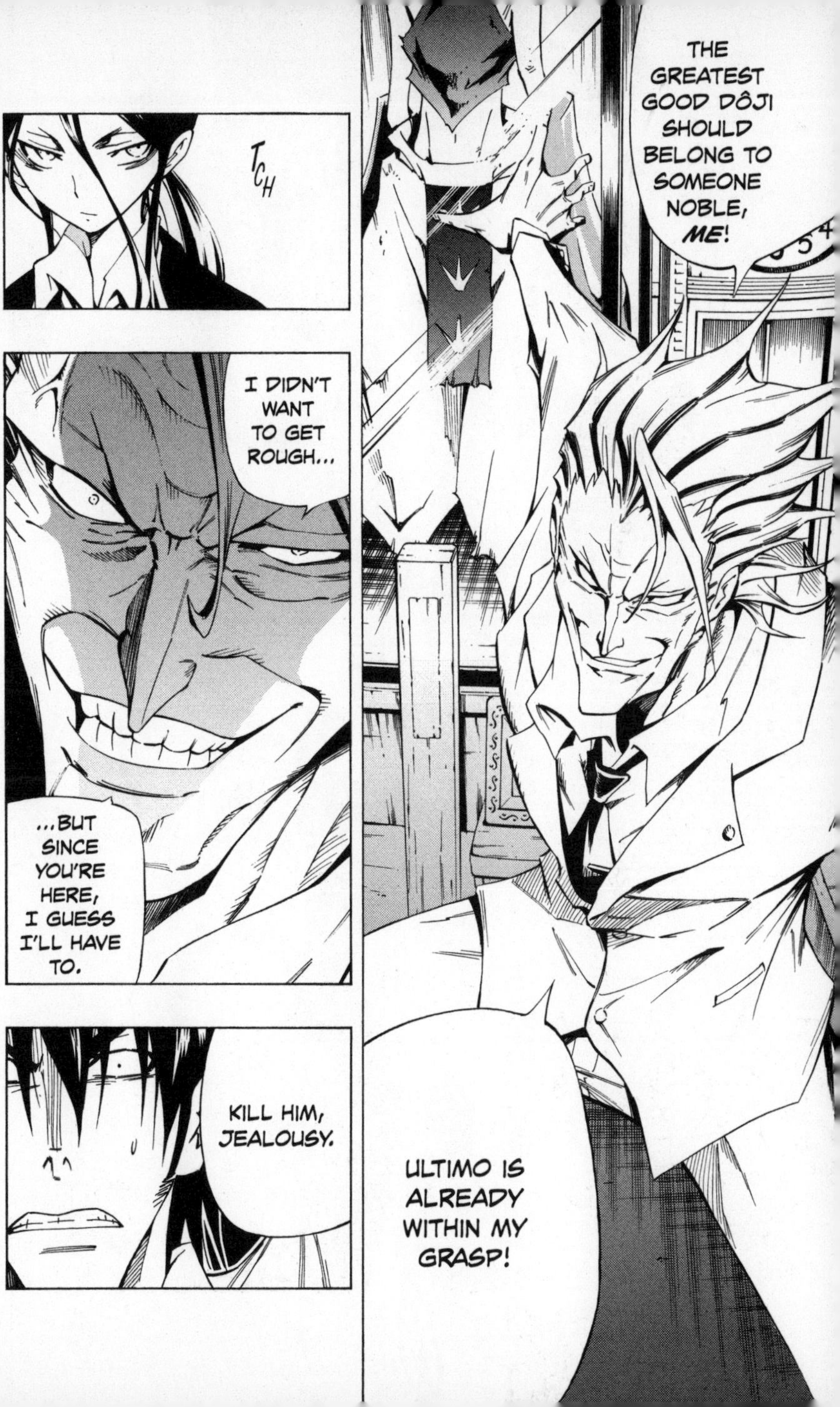
THE GREATEST GOOD DÔJI SHOULD BELONG TO SOMEONE NOBLE, ME!
ULTIMO IS ALREADY WITHIN MY GRASP!
TCH
I DIDN'T WANT TO GET ROUGH...
...BUT SINCE YOU'RE HERE, I GUESS I'LL HAVE TO.
KILL HIM, JEALOUSY.

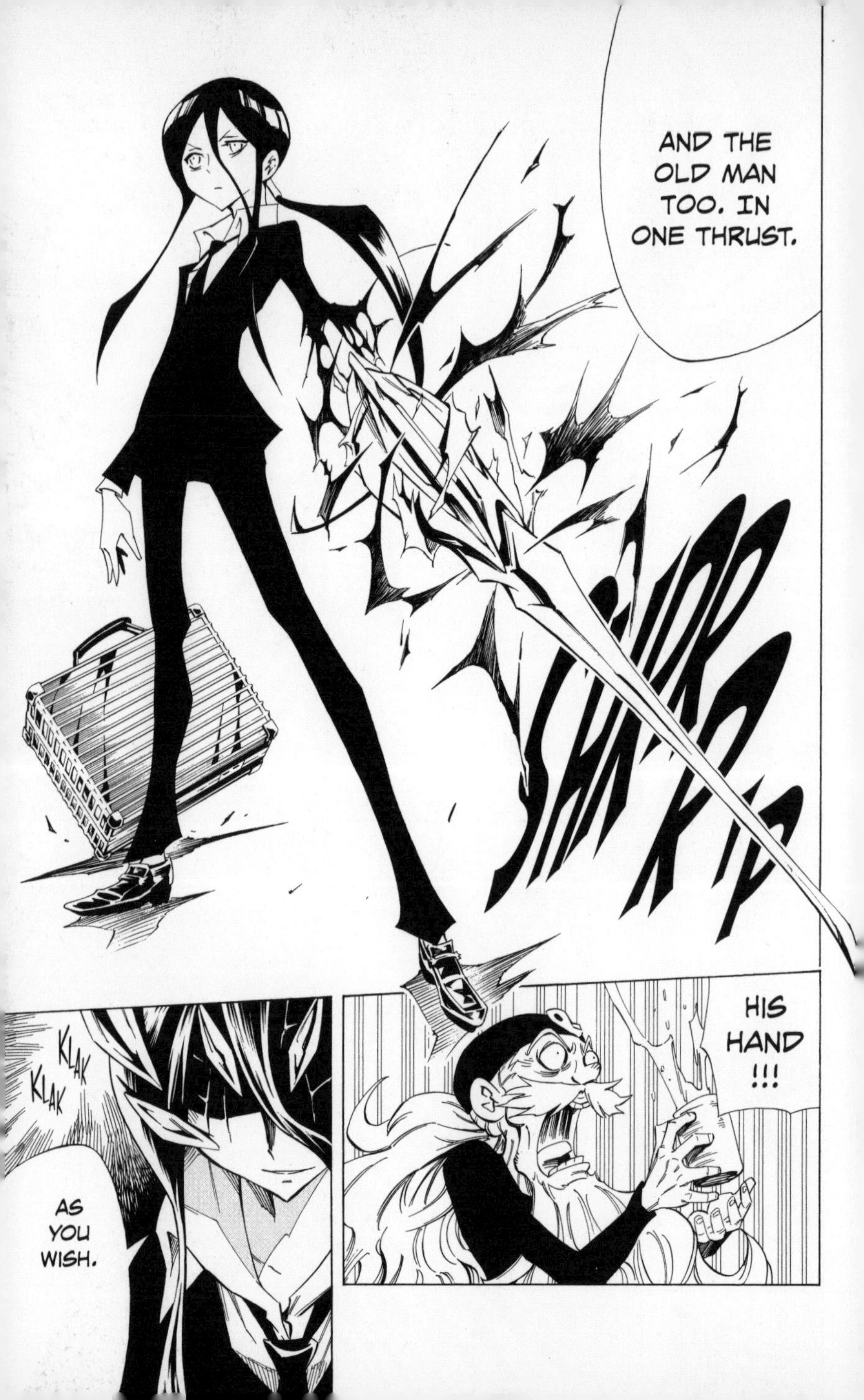
AND THE OLD MAN TOO. IN ONE THRUST.
HIS HAND !!!
KLAK KLAK
AS YOU WISH.

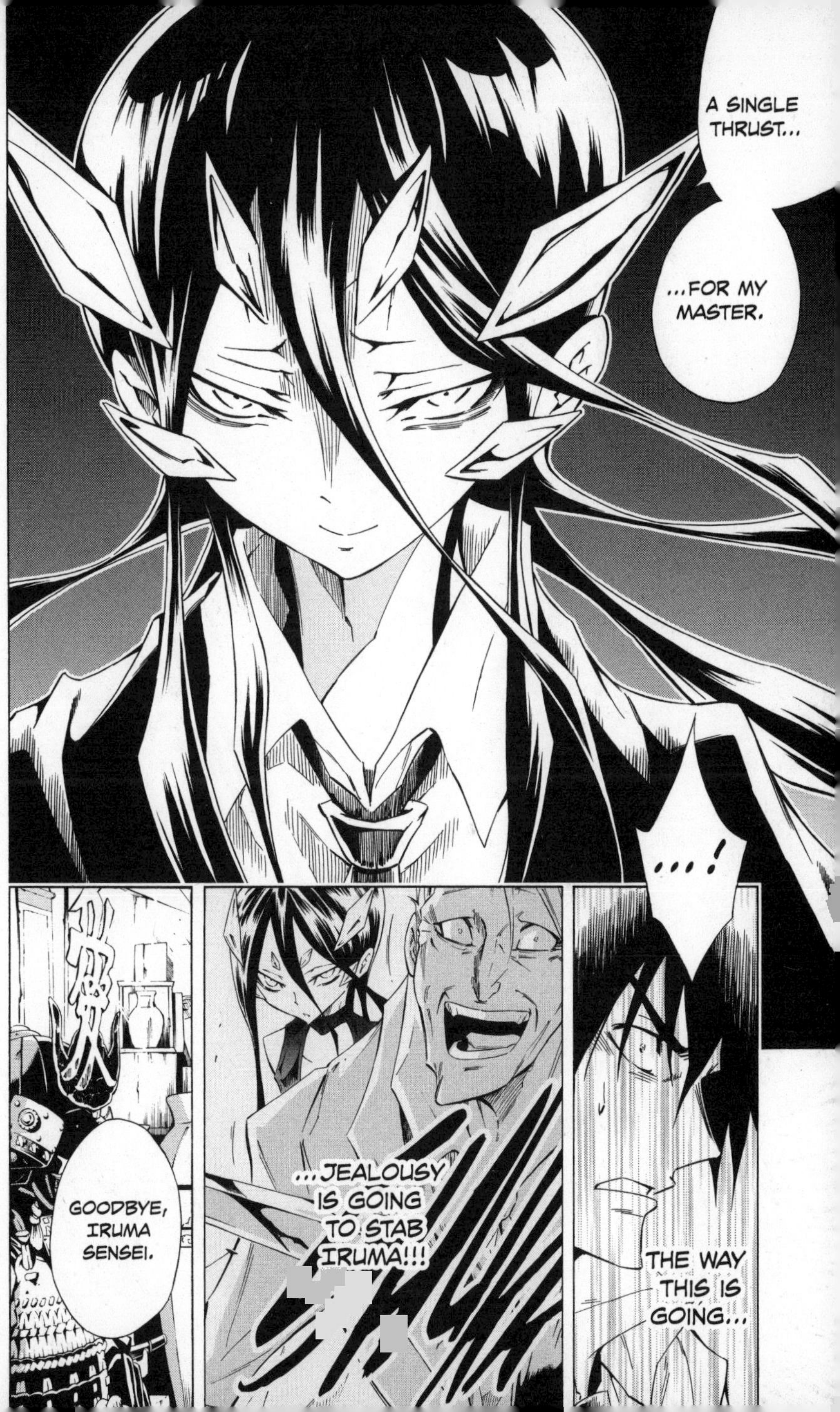
A SINGLE THRUST...
...FOR MY MASTER.
...!
THE WAY THIS IS GOING...
...JEALOUSY IS GOING TO STAB IRUMA!!!
GOODBYE, IRUMA SENSEI.

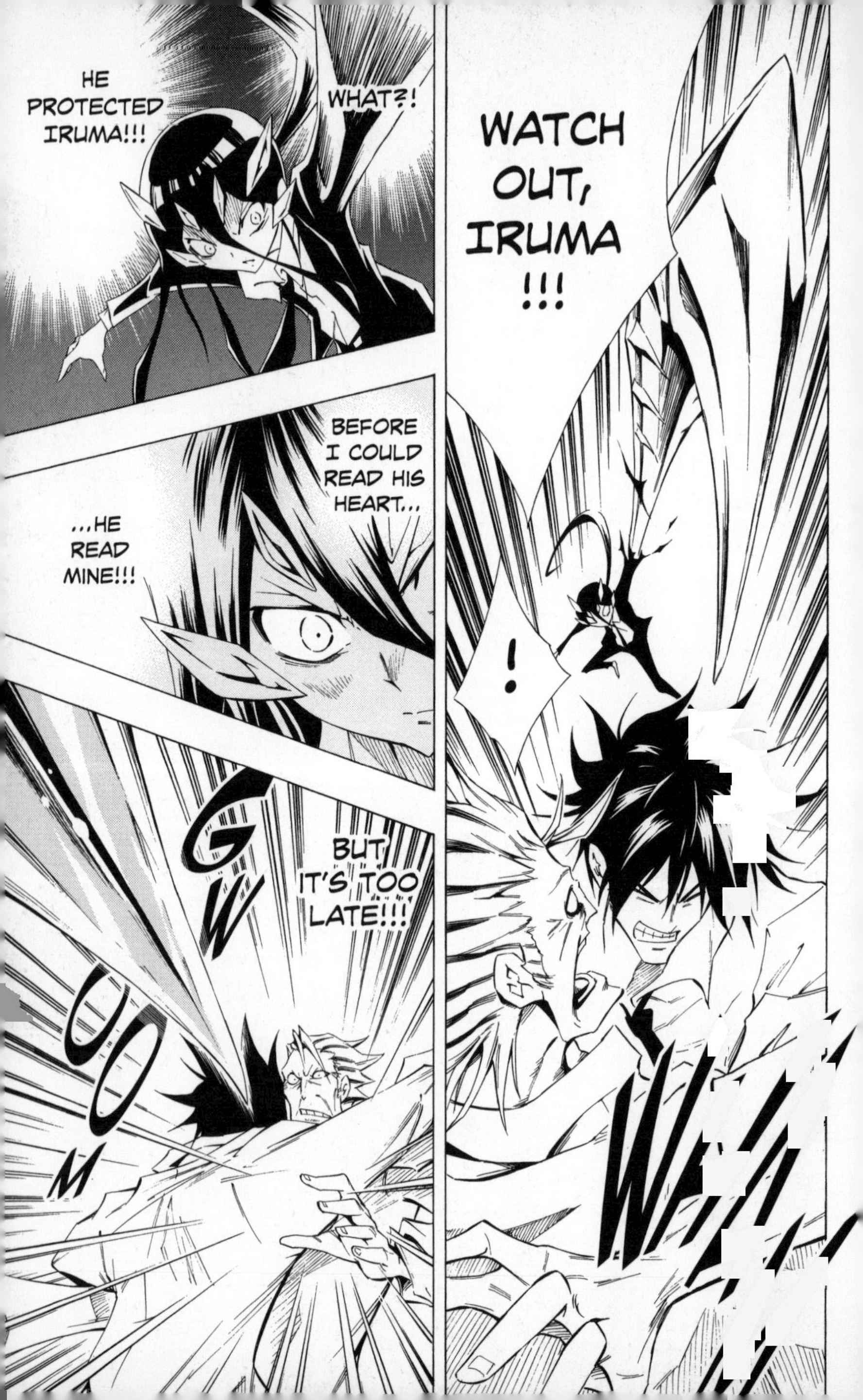
WATCH OUT, IRUMA!!!
!
WHAT?!
HE PROTECTED IRUMA!!!
BEFORE I COULD READ HIS HEART...
...HE READ MINE!!!
BUT IT'S TOO LATE!!!
GWOOM

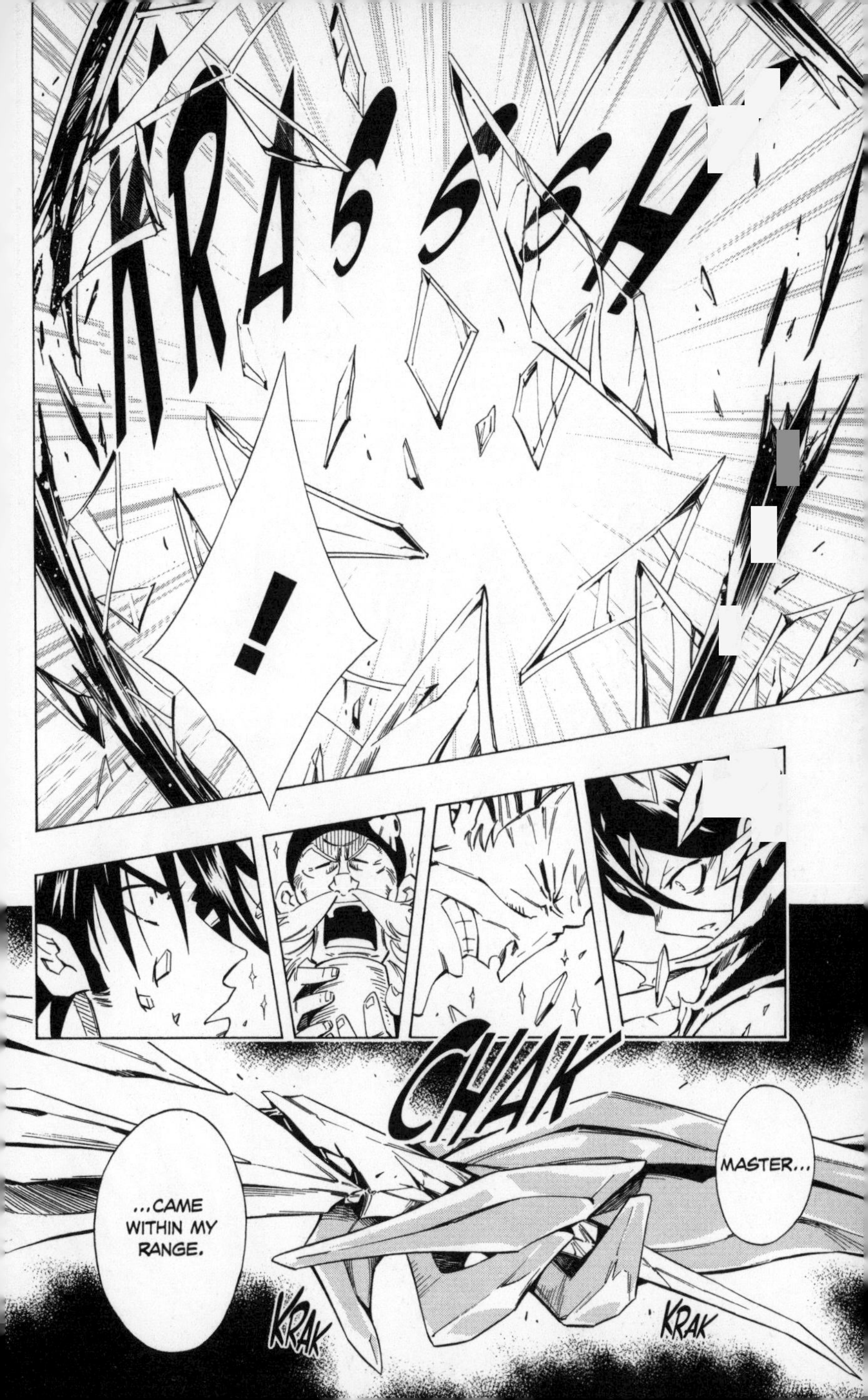
KRASSH
!
CHAK
MASTER...
...CAME WITHIN MY RANGE.
KRAK
KRAK

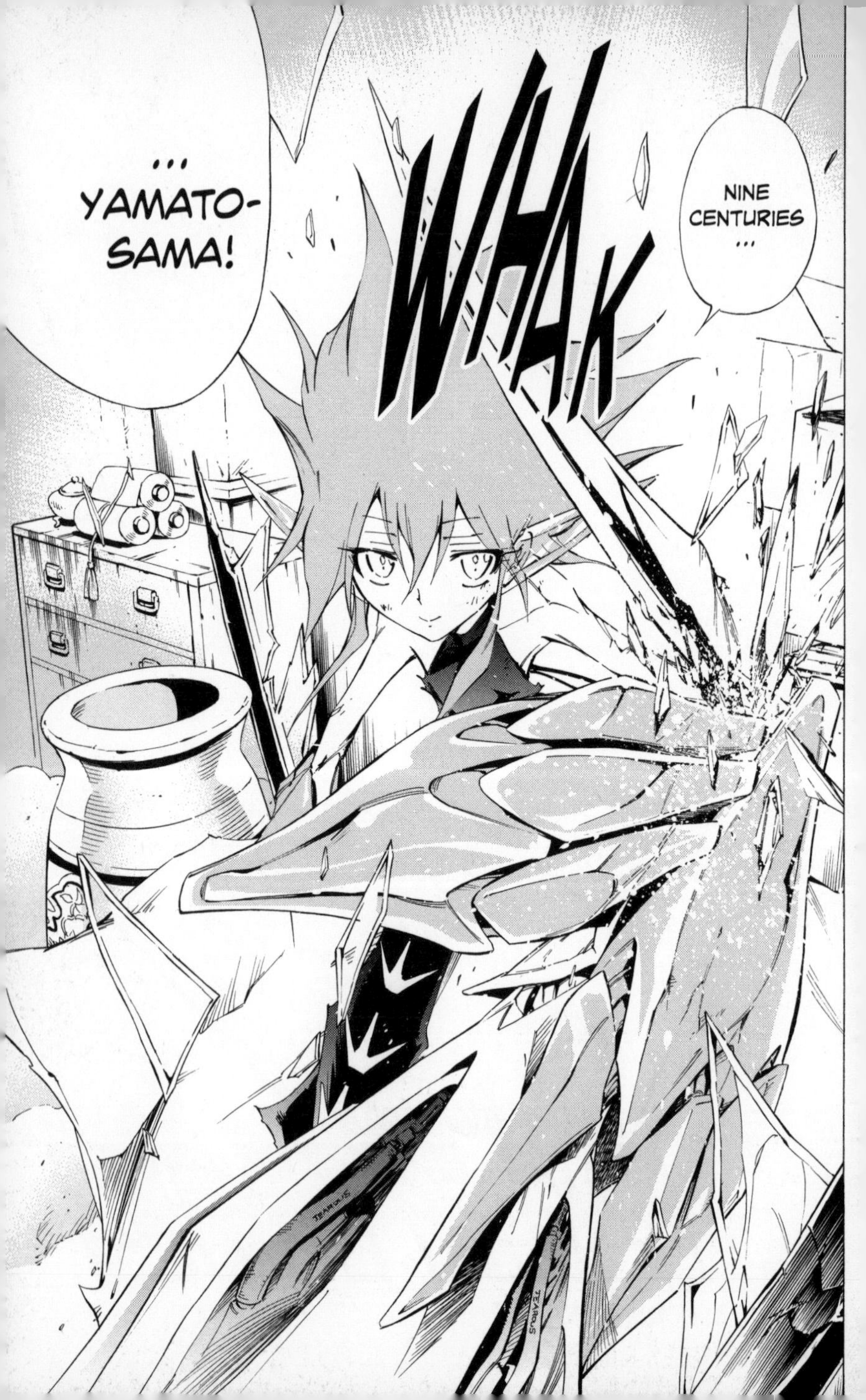
NINE CENTURIES ...
WHAK
... YAMATO-SAMA!

KARAKURIDÔJI ULTIMO

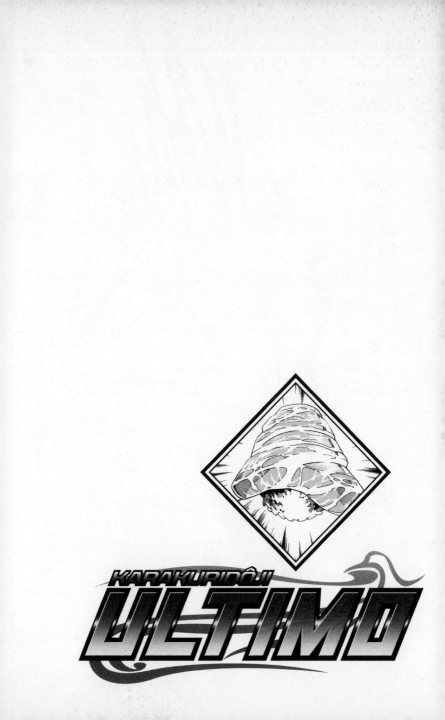

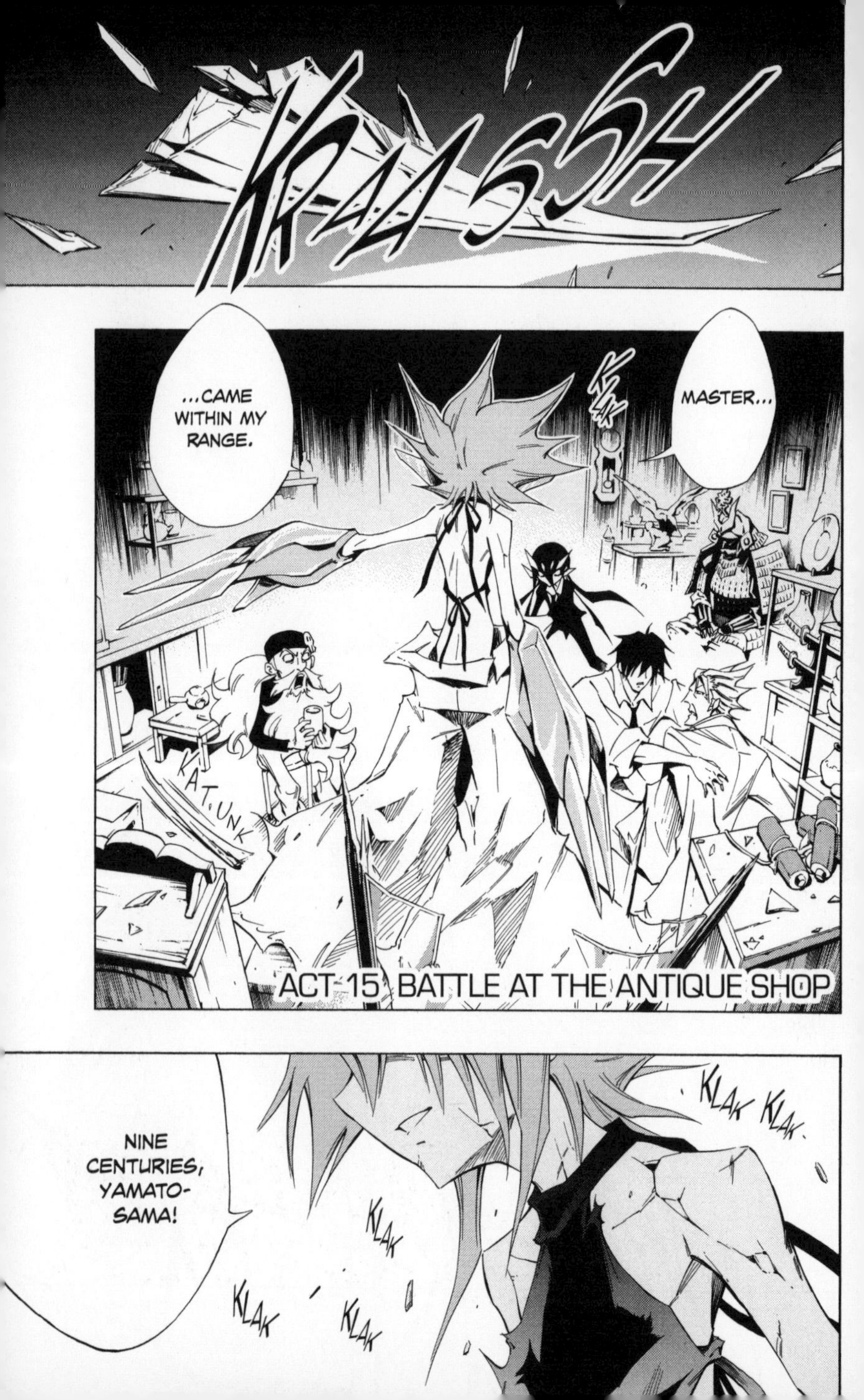
KRAASSH
MASTER...
KLAK
...CAME WITHIN MY RANGE.
KA-TUNK
ACT 15 BATTLE AT THE ANTIQUE SHOP
KLAK KLAK
NINE CENTURIES, YAMATO-SAMA!
KLAK
KLAK
KLAK

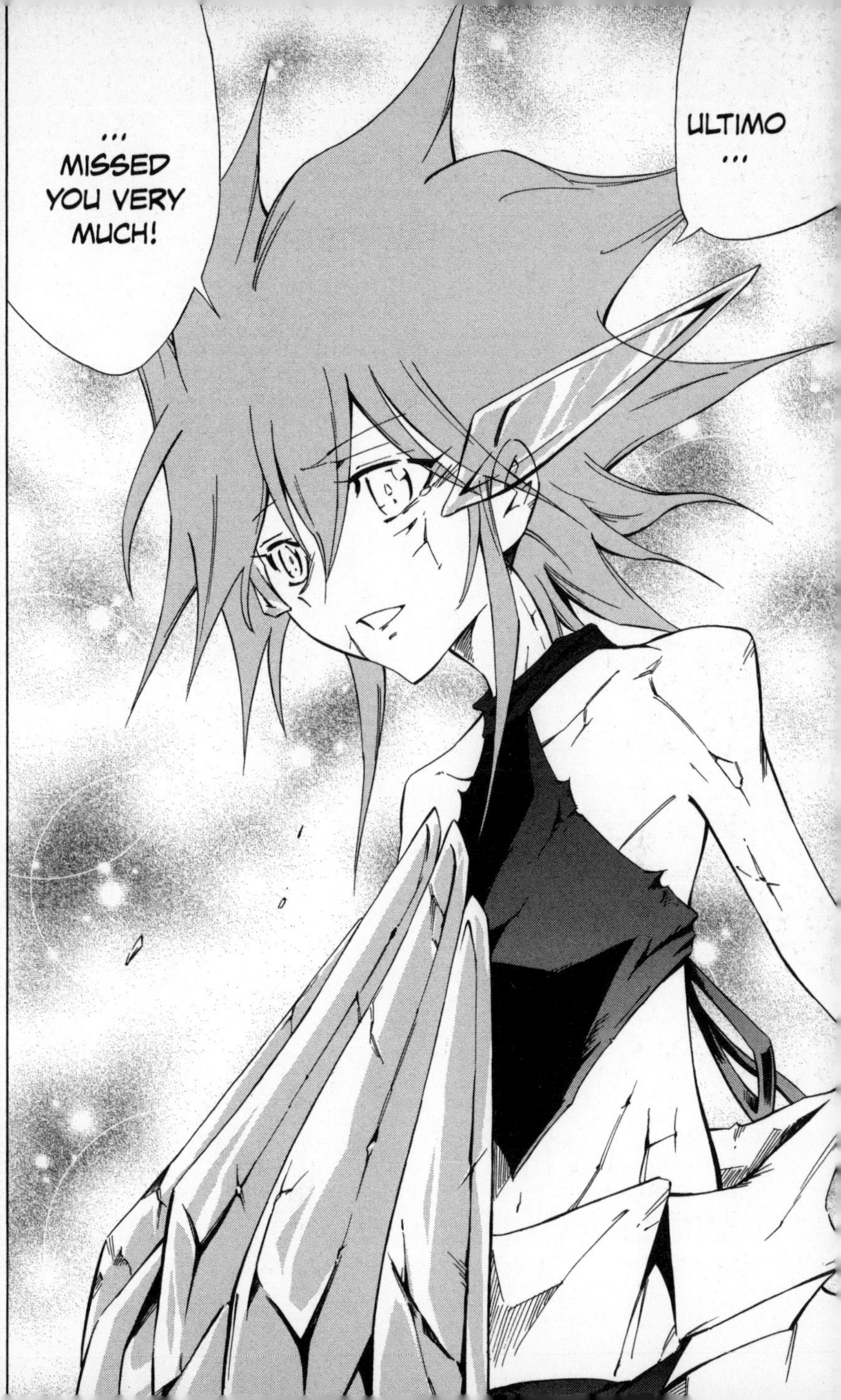
ULTIMO ...
... MISSED YOU VERY MUCH!

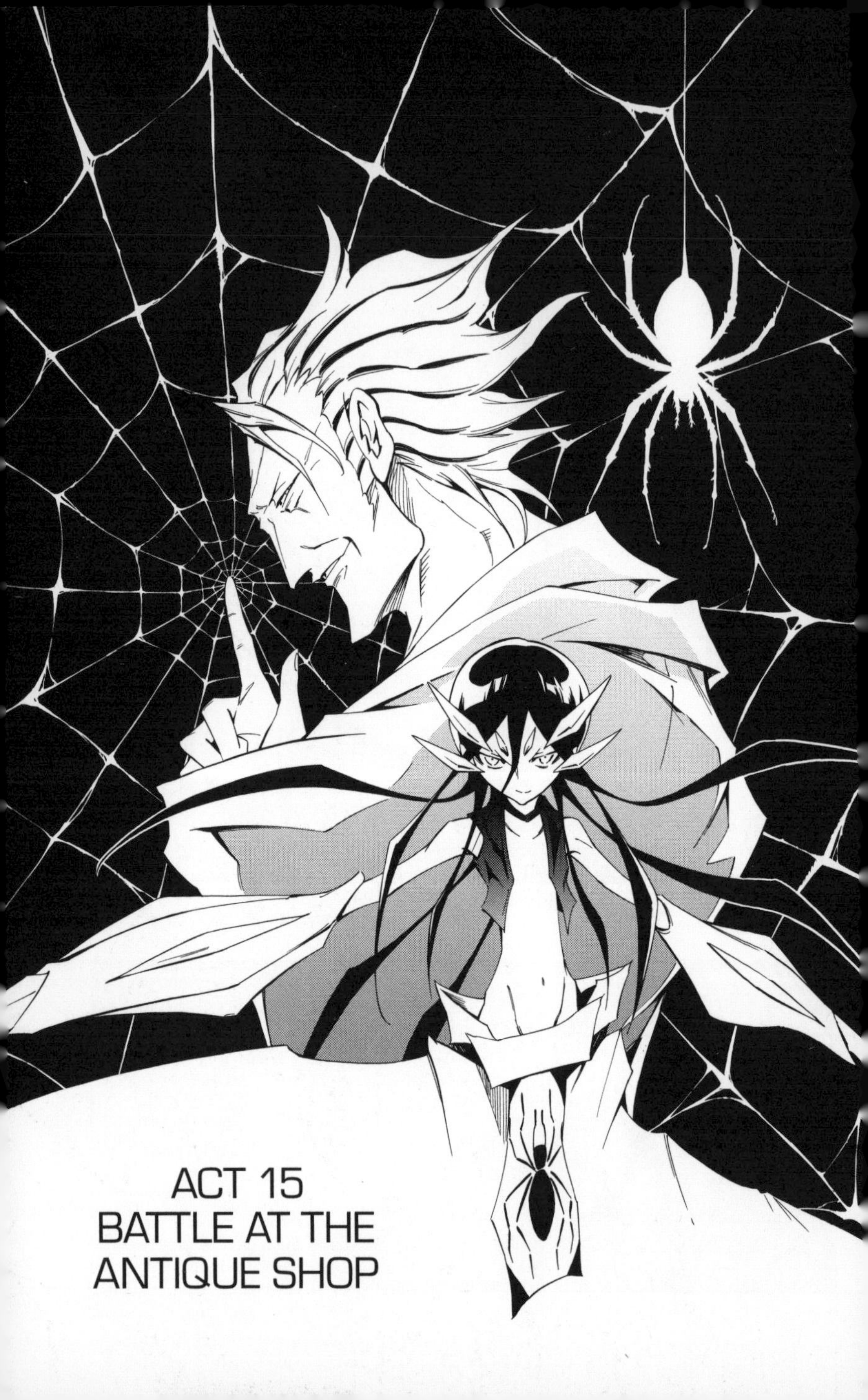
ACT 15
BATTLE AT THE
ANTIQUE SHOP

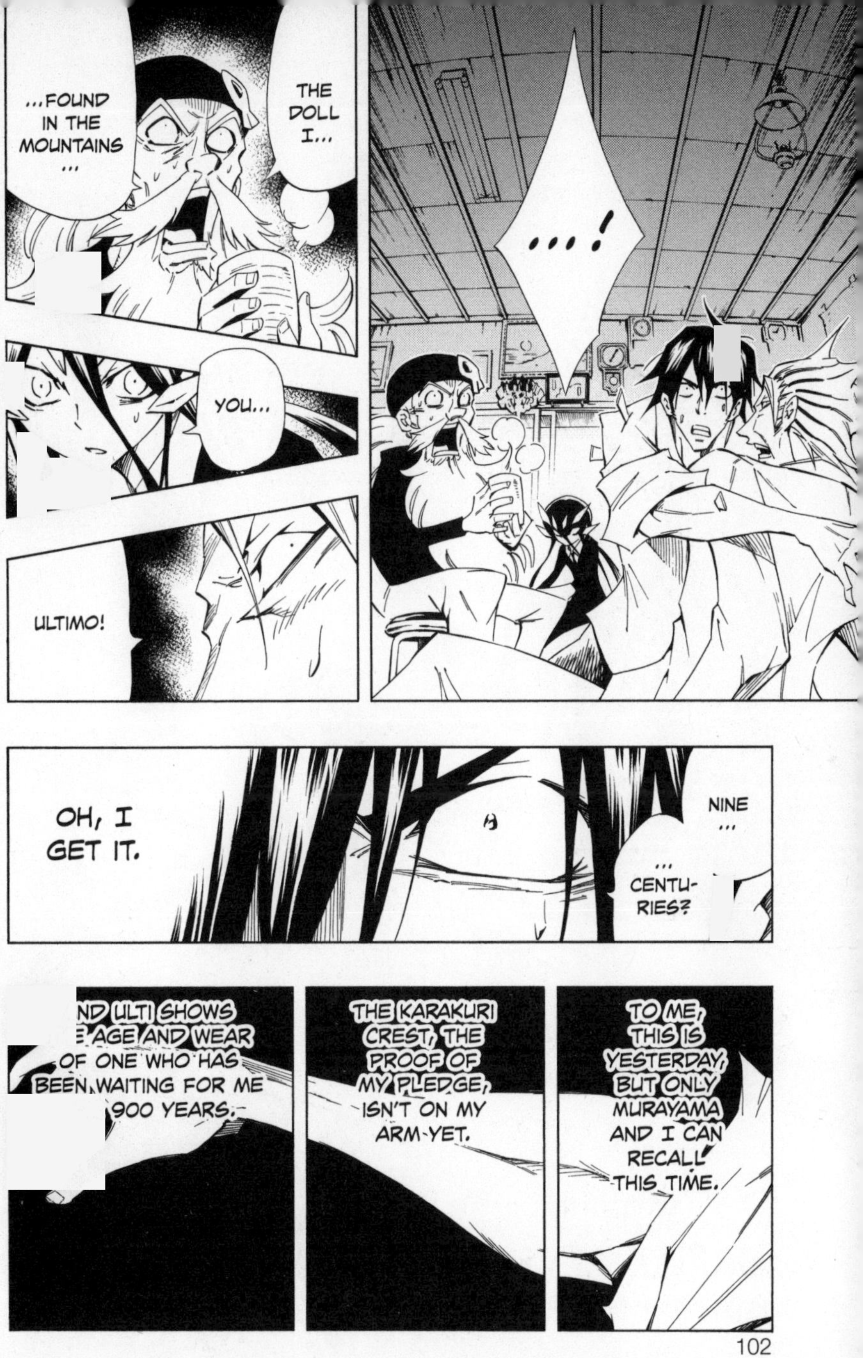
...!
THE DOLL I...
...FOUND IN THE MOUNTAINS...
YOU...
ULTIMO!
NINE...
...CENTURIES?
OH, I GET IT.
TO ME, THIS IS YESTERDAY, BUT ONLY MURAYAMA AND I CAN RECALL THIS TIME.
THE KARAKURI CREST, THE PROOF OF MY PLEDGE, ISN'T ON MY ARM YET.
ND ULTI SHOWS E AGE AND WEAR OF ONE WHO HAS BEEN WAITING FOR ME 900 YEARS.

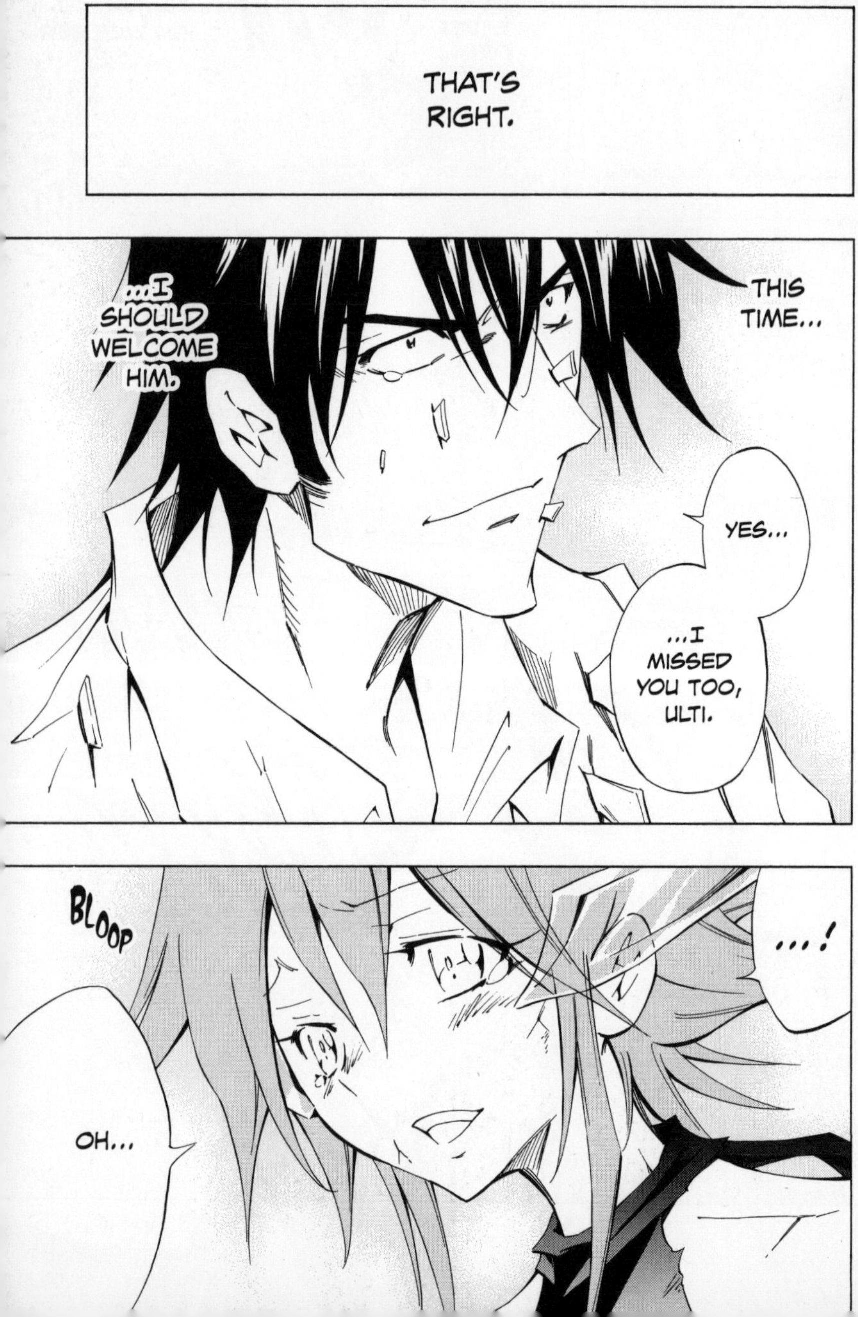
THAT'S RIGHT.
THIS TIME...
...I SHOULD WELCOME HIM.
YES...
...I MISSED YOU TOO, ULTI.
...!
BLOOP
OH...

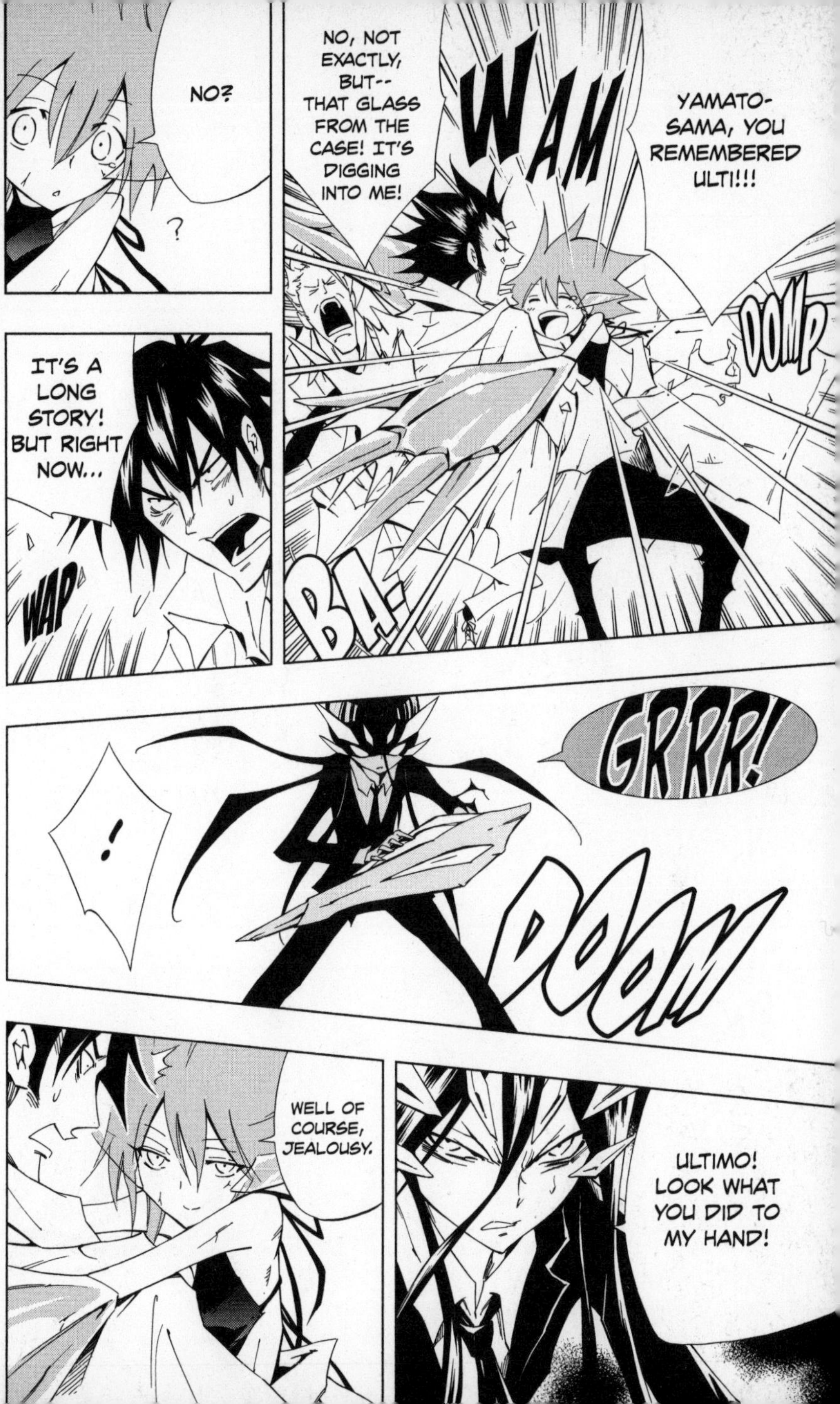
YAMATO-SAMA, YOU REMEMBERED ULTI!!!
WAM
NO, NOT EXACTLY, BUT-- THAT GLASS FROM THE CASE! IT'S DIGGING INTO ME!
DOMP
BA
NO?
?
IT'S A LONG STORY! BUT RIGHT NOW...
WAP
GRRR!
!
DOON
ULTIMO! LOOK WHAT YOU DID TO MY HAND!
WELL OF COURSE, JEALOUSY.

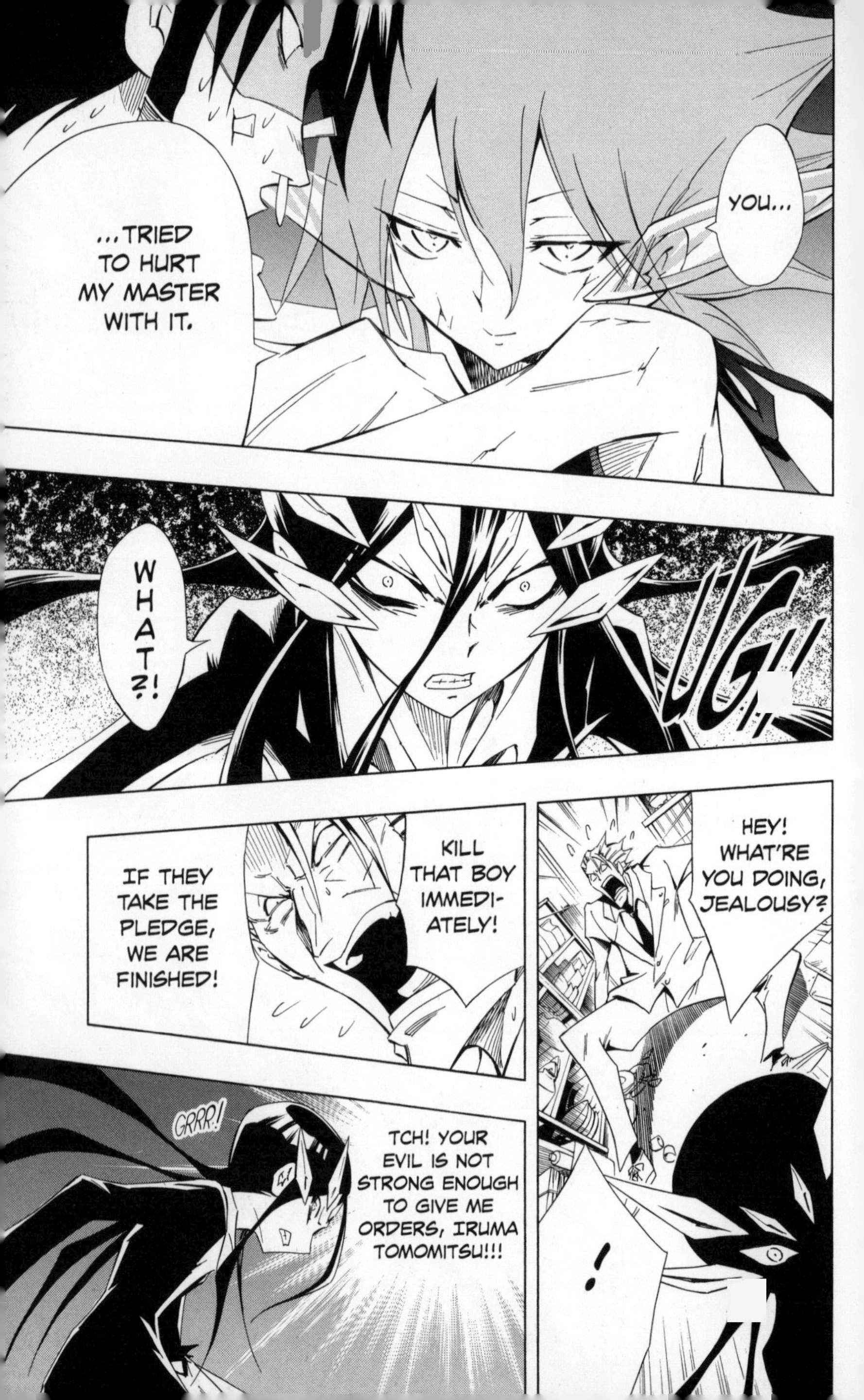
YOU...
...TRIED TO HURT MY MASTER WITH IT.
UGH
WHAT?!
HEY! WHAT'RE YOU DOING, JEALOUSY?
!
KILL THAT BOY IMMEDI-ATELY!
IF THEY TAKE THE PLEDGE, WE ARE FINISHED!
GRRR!
TCH! YOUR EVIL IS NOT STRONG ENOUGH TO GIVE ME ORDERS, IRUMA TOMOMITSU!!!

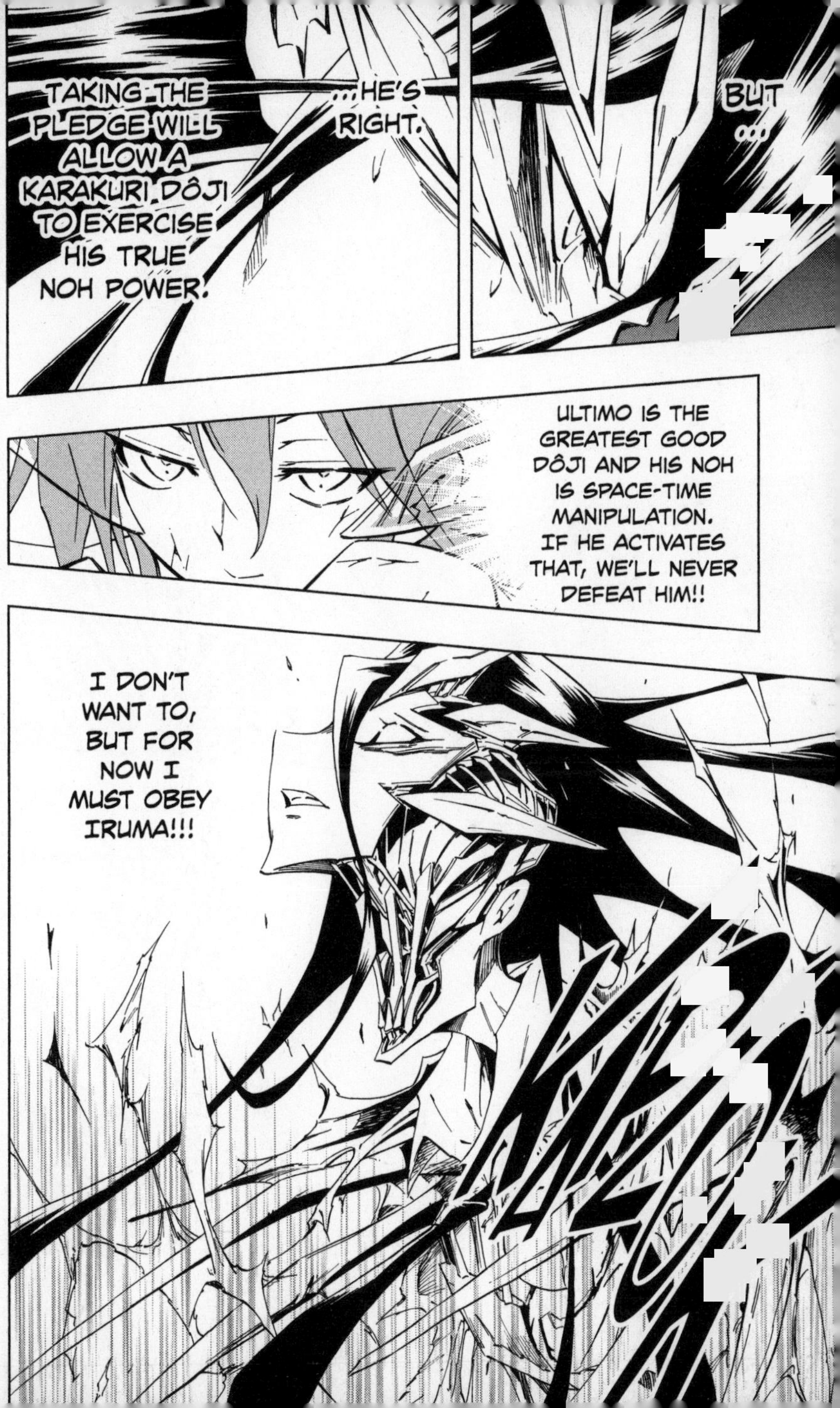
BUT ...
...HE'S RIGHT.
TAKING THE PLEDGE WILL ALLOW A KARAKURI DÔJI TO EXERCISE HIS TRUE NOH POWER.
ULTIMO IS THE GREATEST GOOD DÔJI AND HIS NOH IS SPACE-TIME MANIPULATION. IF HE ACTIVATES THAT, WE'LL NEVER DEFEAT HIM!!
I DON'T WANT TO, BUT FOR NOW I MUST OBEY IRUMA!!!

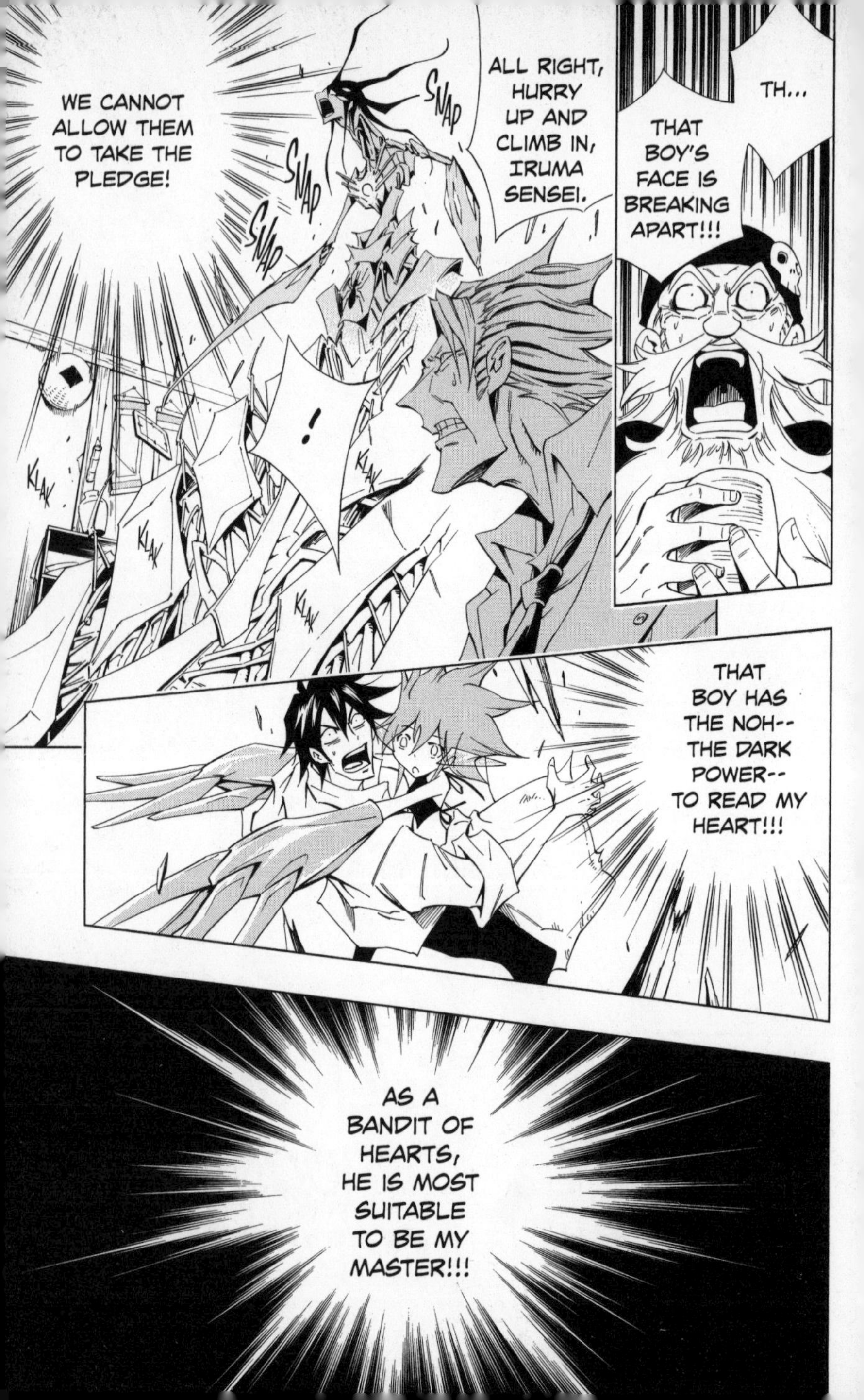
TH...
THAT BOY'S FACE IS BREAKING APART!!!
ALL RIGHT, HURRY UP AND CLIMB IN, IRUMA SENSEI.
SNAP
SNAP
SNAP
WE CANNOT ALLOW THEM TO TAKE THE PLEDGE!
!
KLAK
KLAK
KLAK
KLAK
THAT BOY HAS THE NOH--THE DARK POWER--TO READ MY HEART!!!
AS A BANDIT OF HEARTS, HE IS MOST SUITABLE TO BE MY MASTER!!!

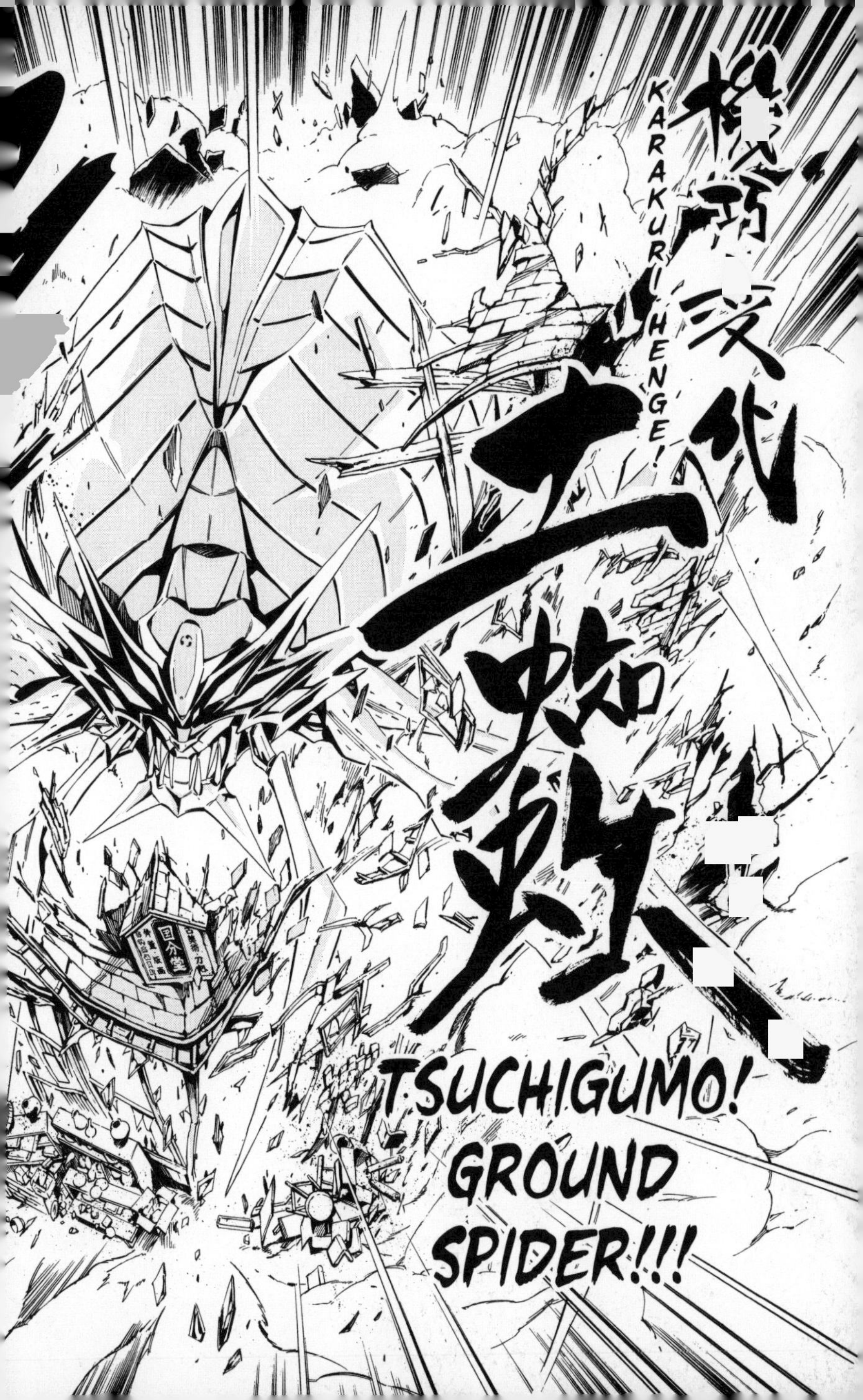
KARAKURI HENGE!
TSUCHIGUMO! GROUND SPIDER!!!

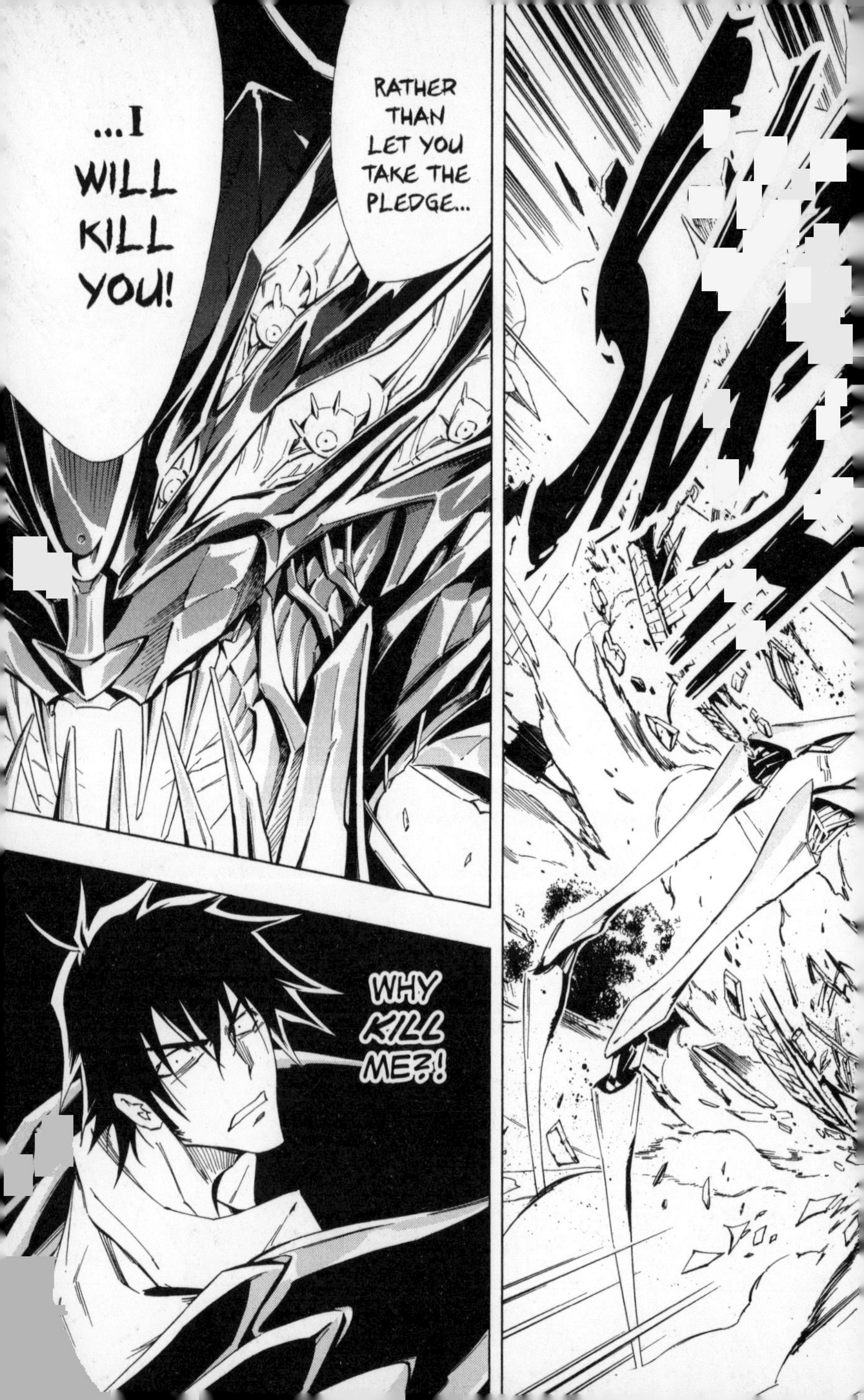
RATHER THAN LET YOU TAKE THE PLEDGE...
...I WILL KILL YOU!
WHY KILL ME?!

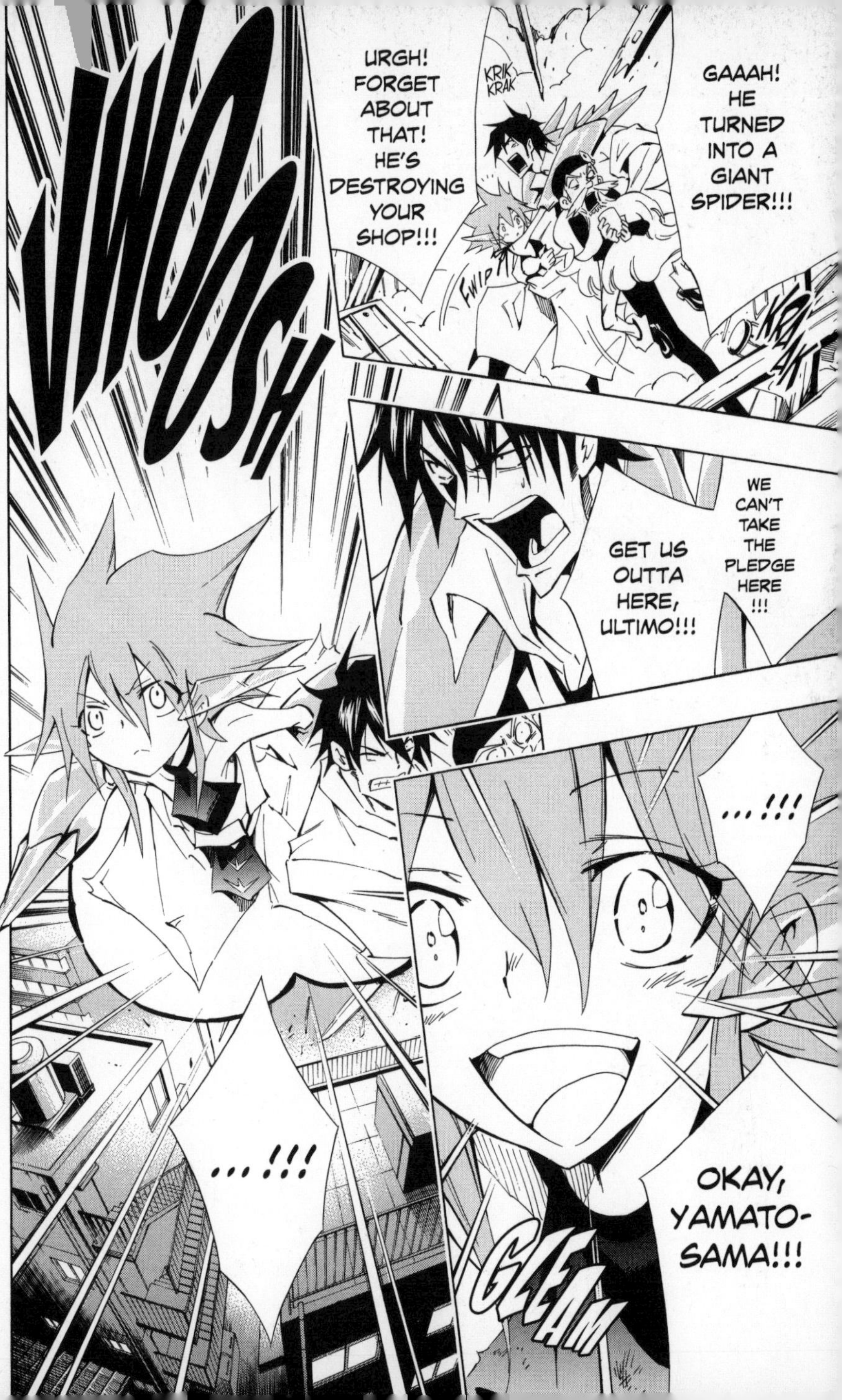
GAAAH! HE TURNED INTO A GIANT SPIDER!!!
KRIK KRAK
URGH! FORGET ABOUT THAT! HE'S DESTROYING YOUR SHOP!!!
FWIP
WE CAN'T TAKE THE PLEDGE HERE!!!
GET US OUTTA HERE, ULTIMO!!!
...!!!
OKAY, YAMATO-SAMA!!!
GLEAM
VWOOSH
...!!!

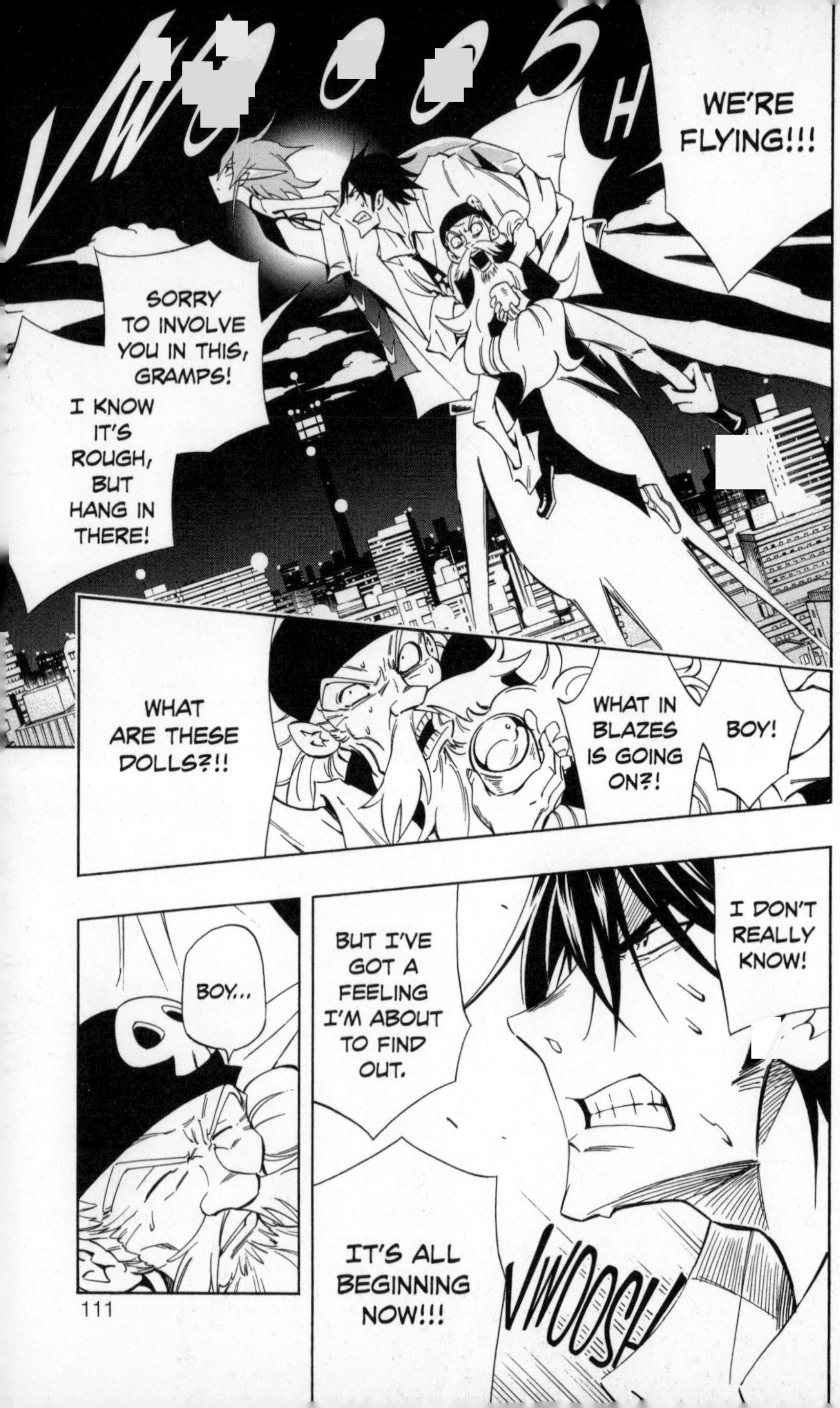
VWOOOSH
WE'RE FLYING!!!
SORRY TO INVOLVE YOU IN THIS, GRAMPS!
I KNOW IT'S ROUGH, BUT HANG IN THERE!
BOY!
WHAT IN BLAZES IS GOING ON?!
WHAT ARE THESE DOLLS?!!
I DON'T REALLY KNOW!
BUT I'VE GOT A FEELING I'M ABOUT TO FIND OUT.
IT'S ALL BEGINNING NOW!!!
VWOOSH
BOY...

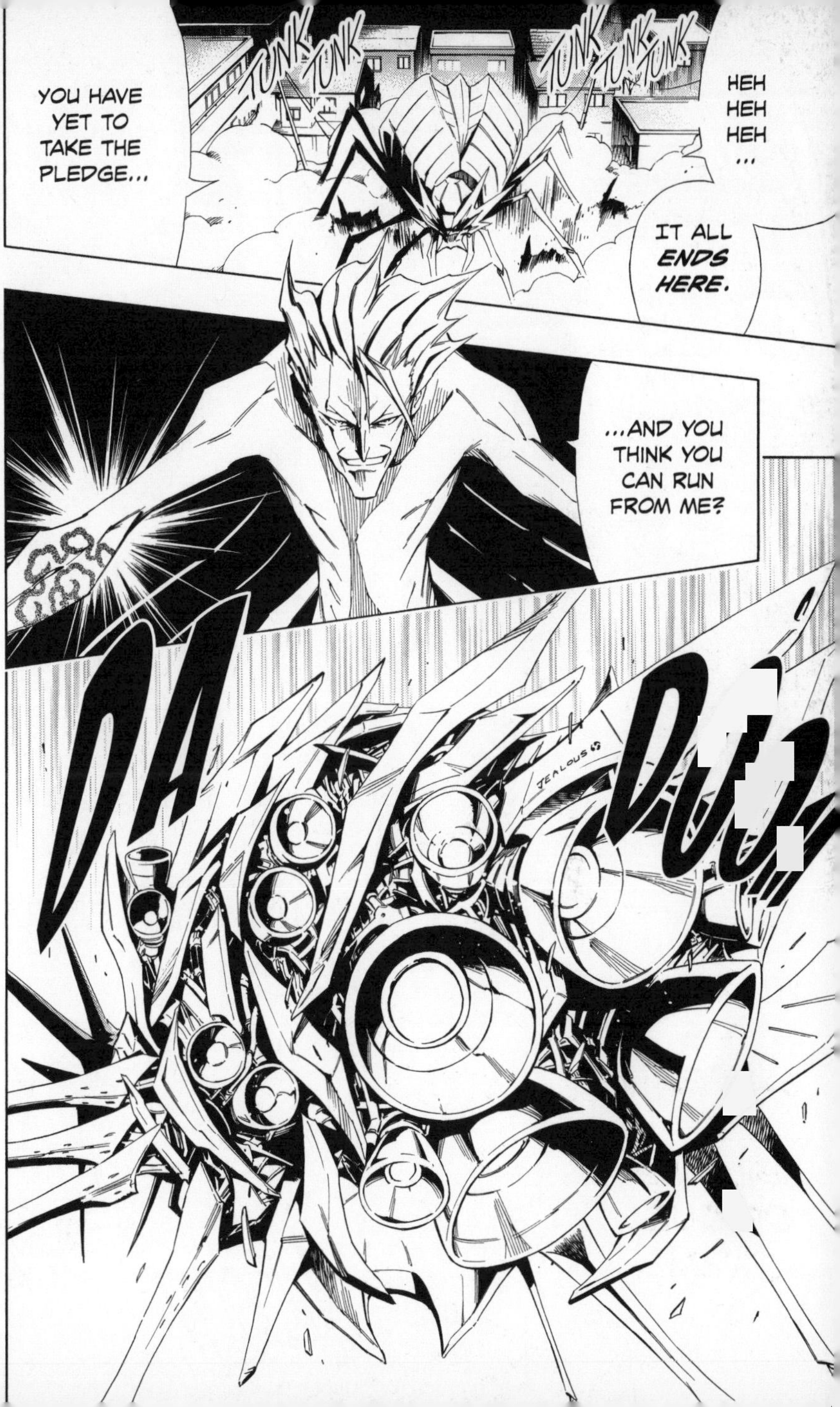
TUNK TUNK TUNK
HEH HEH HEH ...
IT ALL ENDS HERE.
TUNK TUNK
YOU HAVE YET TO TAKE THE PLEDGE...
...AND YOU THINK YOU CAN RUN FROM ME?

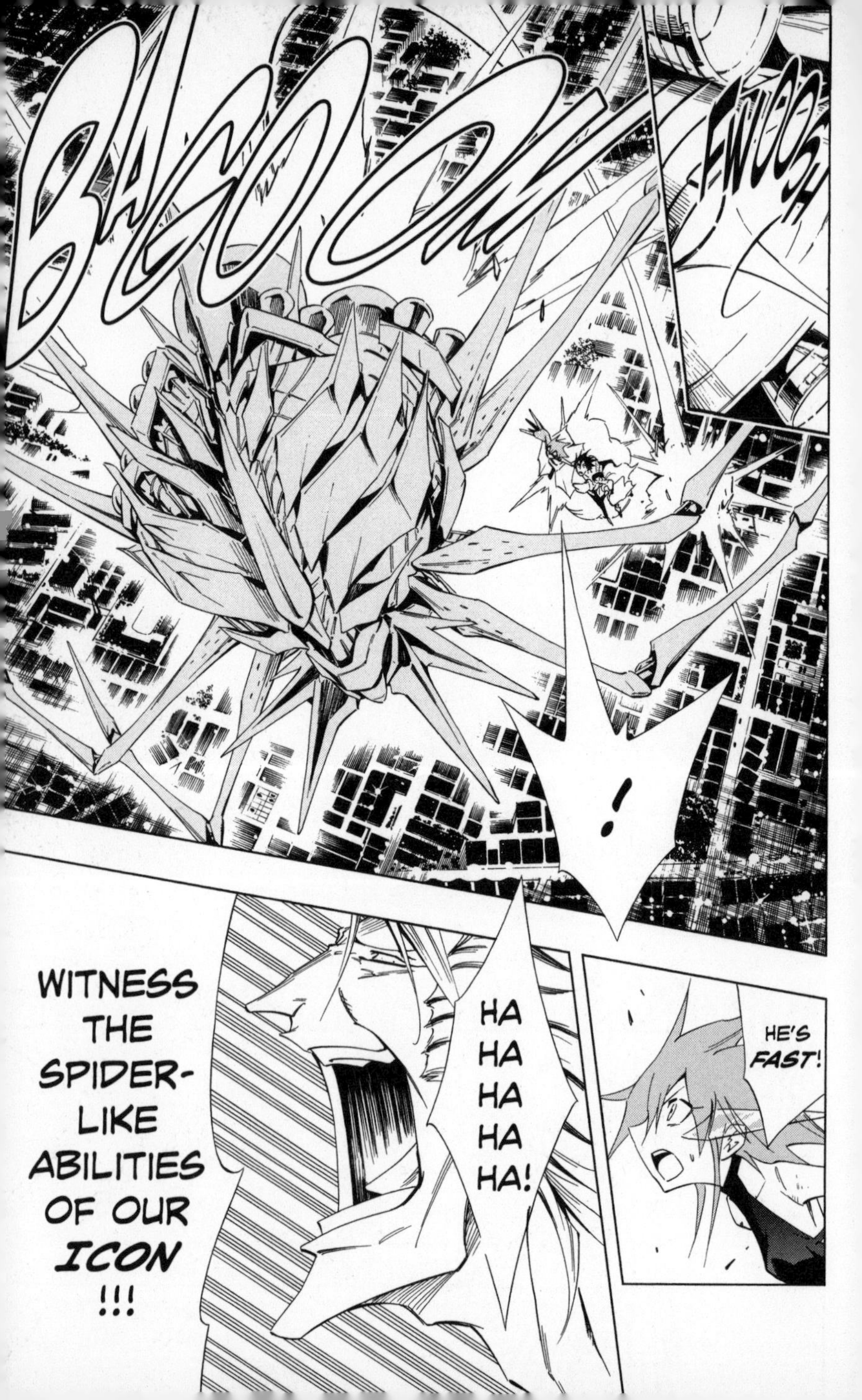
FWOOSH
BAZOOM
!
HE'S FAST!
HA HA HA HA HA HA!
WITNESS THE SPIDER-LIKE ABILITIES OF OUR ICON!!!

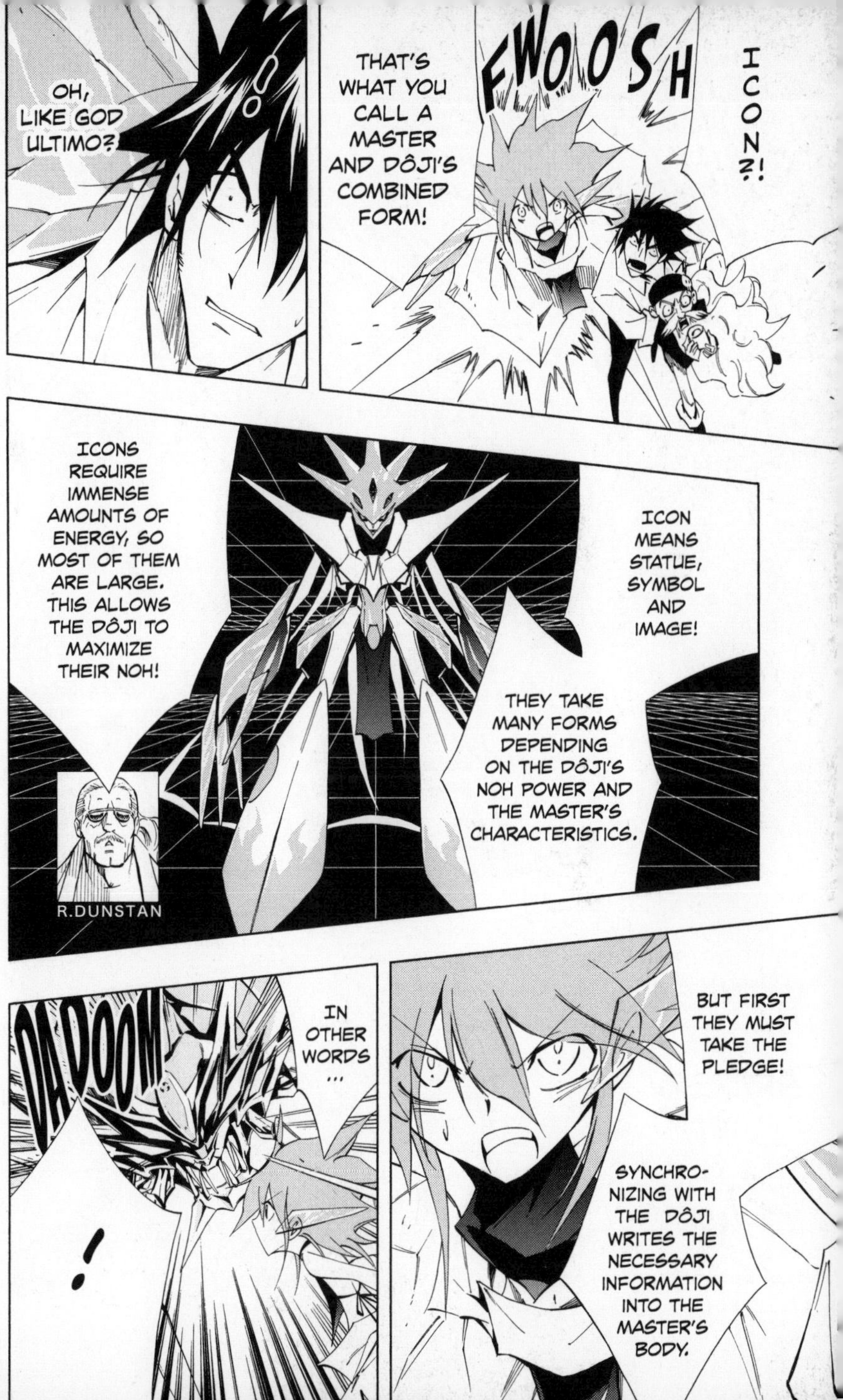
ICON?!
FWOOSH
THAT'S WHAT YOU CALL A MASTER AND DÔJI'S COMBINED FORM!
OH, LIKE GOD ULTIMO?
ICON MEANS STATUE, SYMBOL AND IMAGE!
THEY TAKE MANY FORMS DEPENDING ON THE DÔJI'S NOH POWER AND THE MASTER'S CHARACTERISTICS.
ICONS REQUIRE IMMENSE AMOUNTS OF ENERGY, SO MOST OF THEM ARE LARGE. THIS ALLOWS THE DÔJI TO MAXIMIZE THEIR NOH!
R.DUNSTAN
BUT FIRST THEY MUST TAKE THE PLEDGE!
SYNCHRO-NIZING WITH THE DÔJI WRITES THE NECESSARY INFORMATION INTO THE MASTER'S BODY.
IN OTHER WORDS...
DADOOM
!

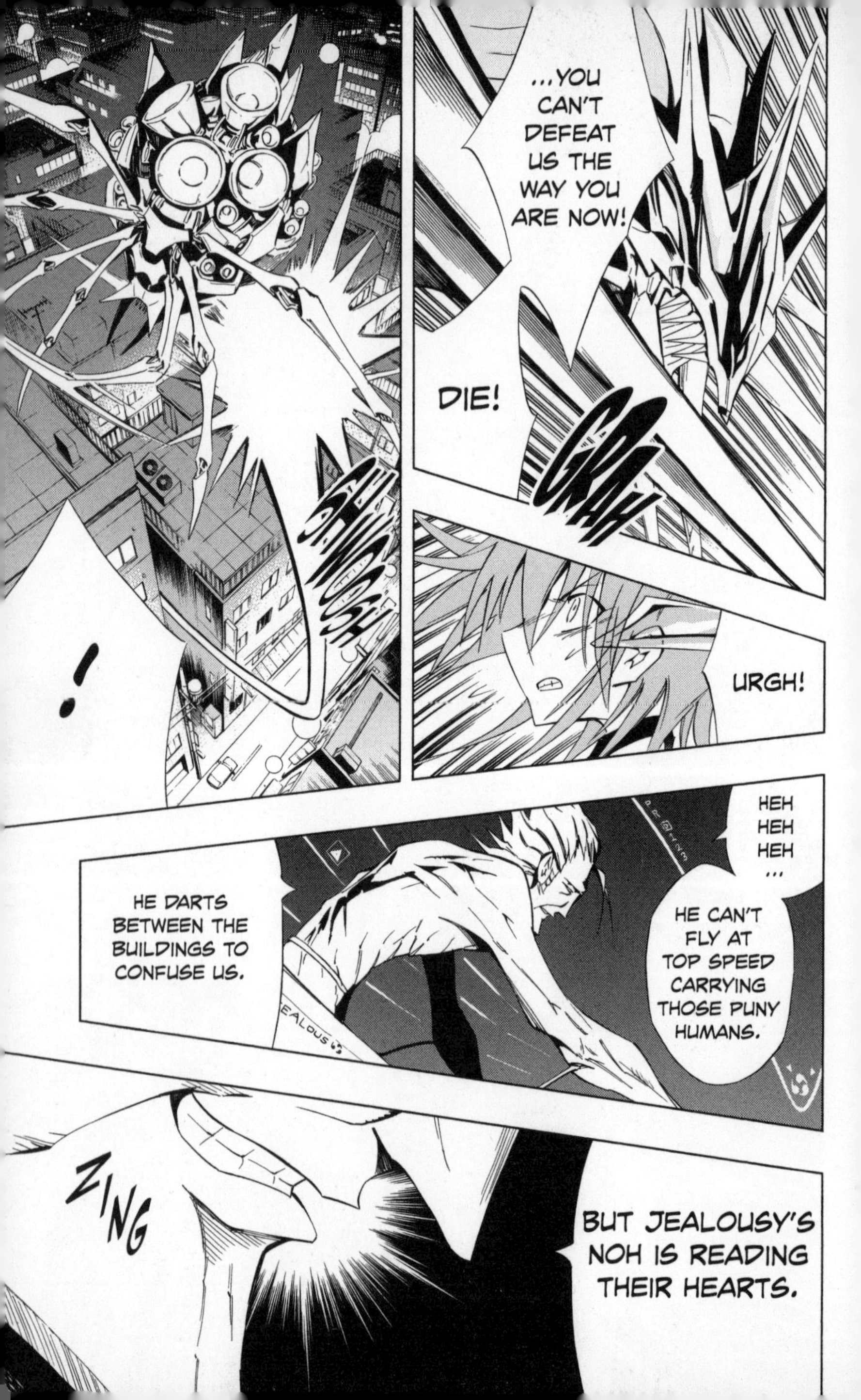
...YOU CAN'T DEFEAT US THE WAY YOU ARE NOW!
DIE!
URGH!
SHWOOSH
!
HEH HEH HEH...
HE CAN'T FLY AT TOP SPEED CARRYING THOSE PUNY HUMANS.
HE DARTS BETWEEN THE BUILDINGS TO CONFUSE US.
BUT JEALOUSY'S NOH IS READING THEIR HEARTS.
ZING

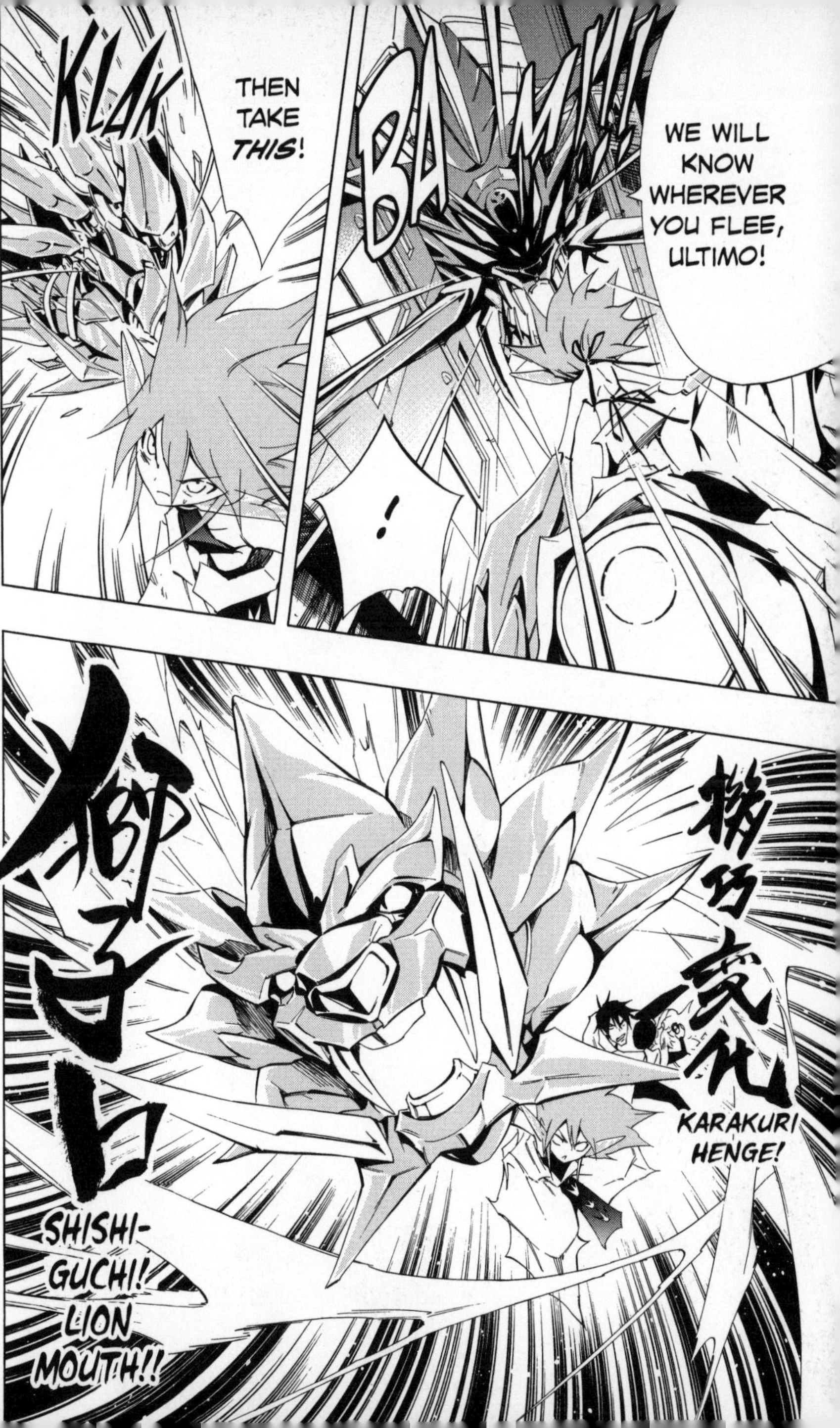
BAMM!!
WE WILL KNOW WHEREVER YOU FLEE, ULTIMO!
KLAK
THEN TAKE THIS!
!
機巧変化
KARAKURI HENGE!
獅子口
SHISHI-GUCHI! LION MOUTH!!

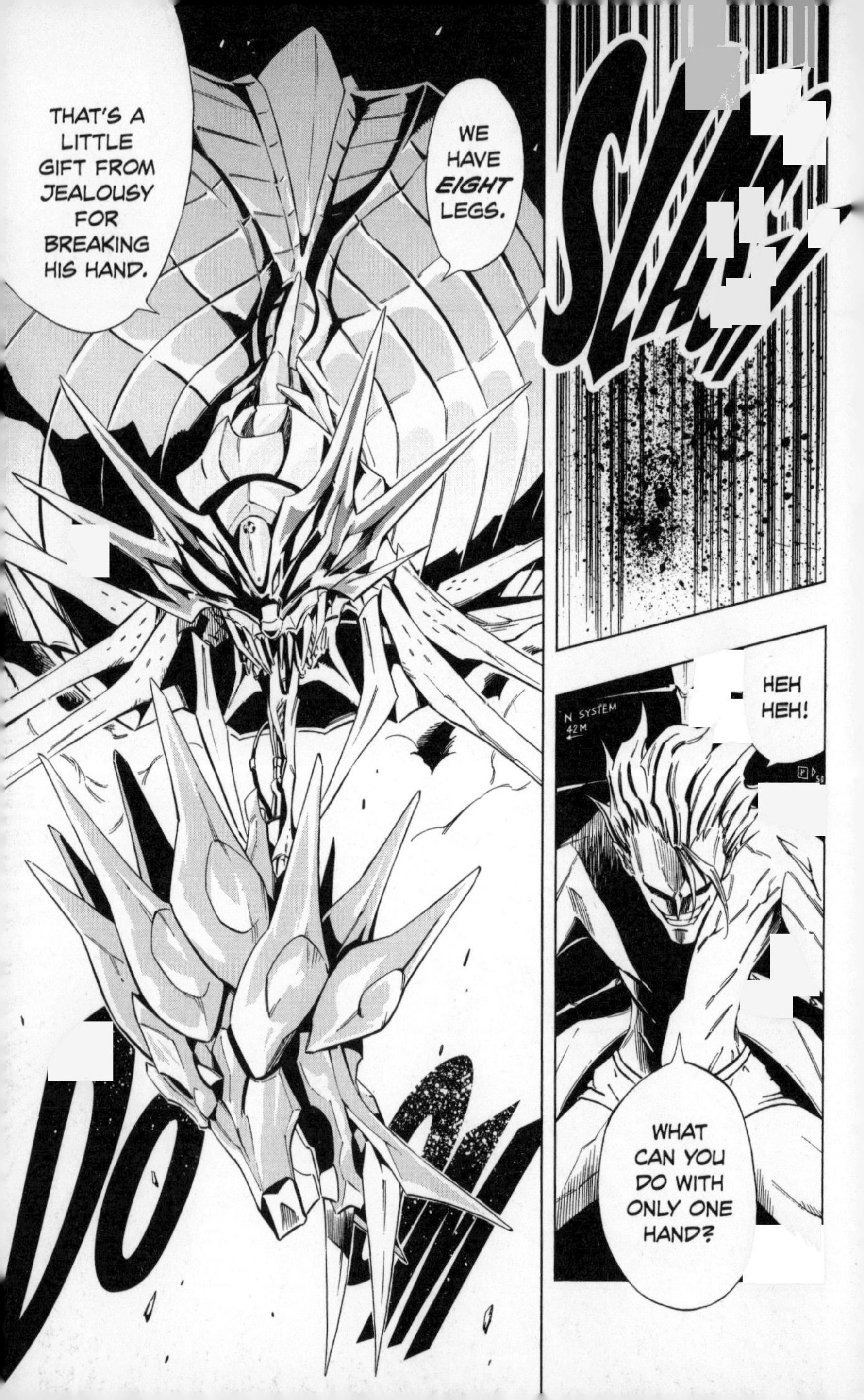
HEH HEH!
N SYSTEM 42M
WHAT CAN YOU DO WITH ONLY ONE HAND?
WE HAVE EIGHT LEGS.
THAT'S A LITTLE GIFT FROM JEALOUSY FOR BREAKING HIS HAND.

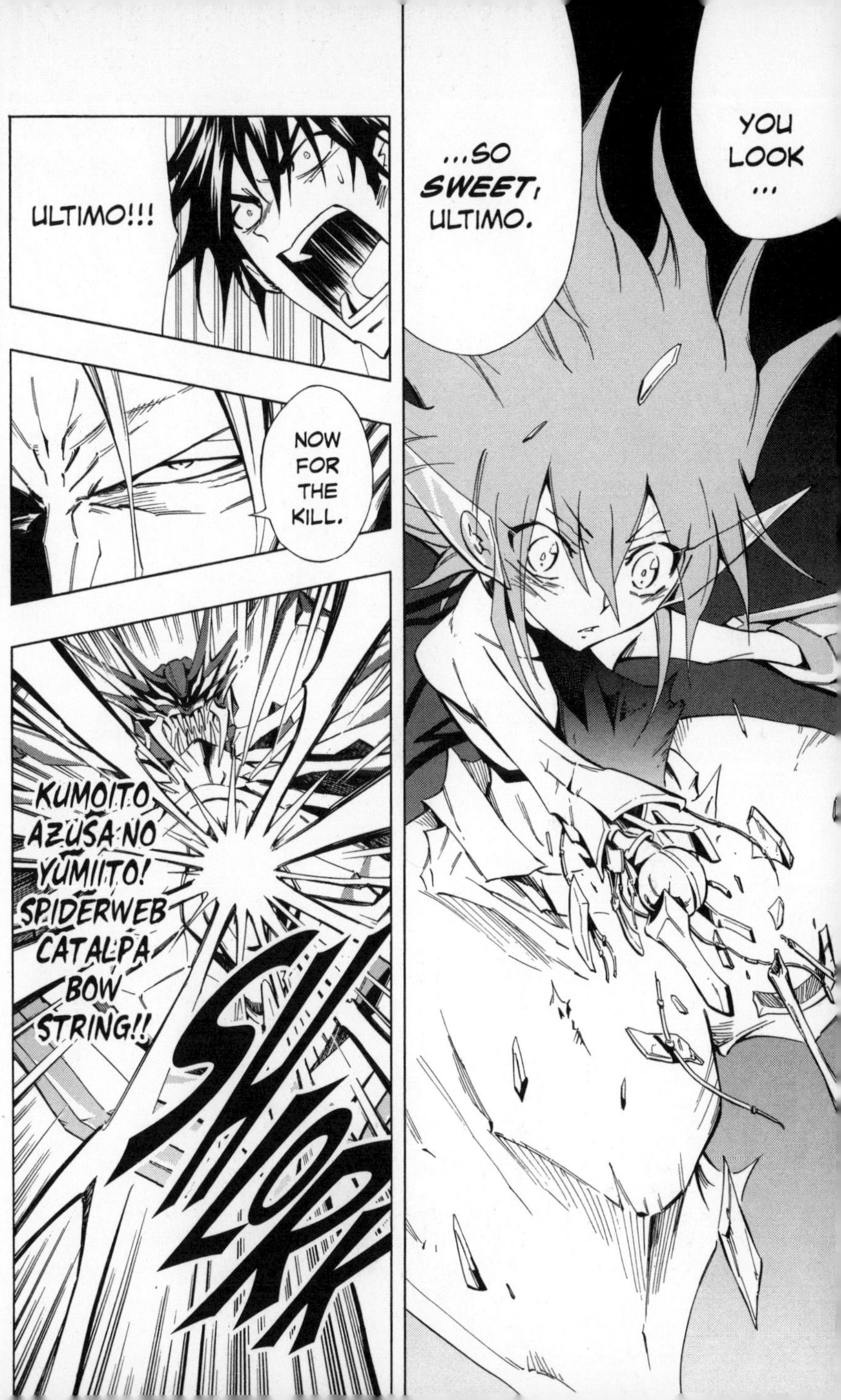
YOU LOOK ...
...SO SWEET, ULTIMO.
ULTIMO!!!
NOW FOR THE KILL.
KUMOITO AZUSA NO YUMIITO! SPIDERWEB CATALPA BOW STRING!!
SHLOK

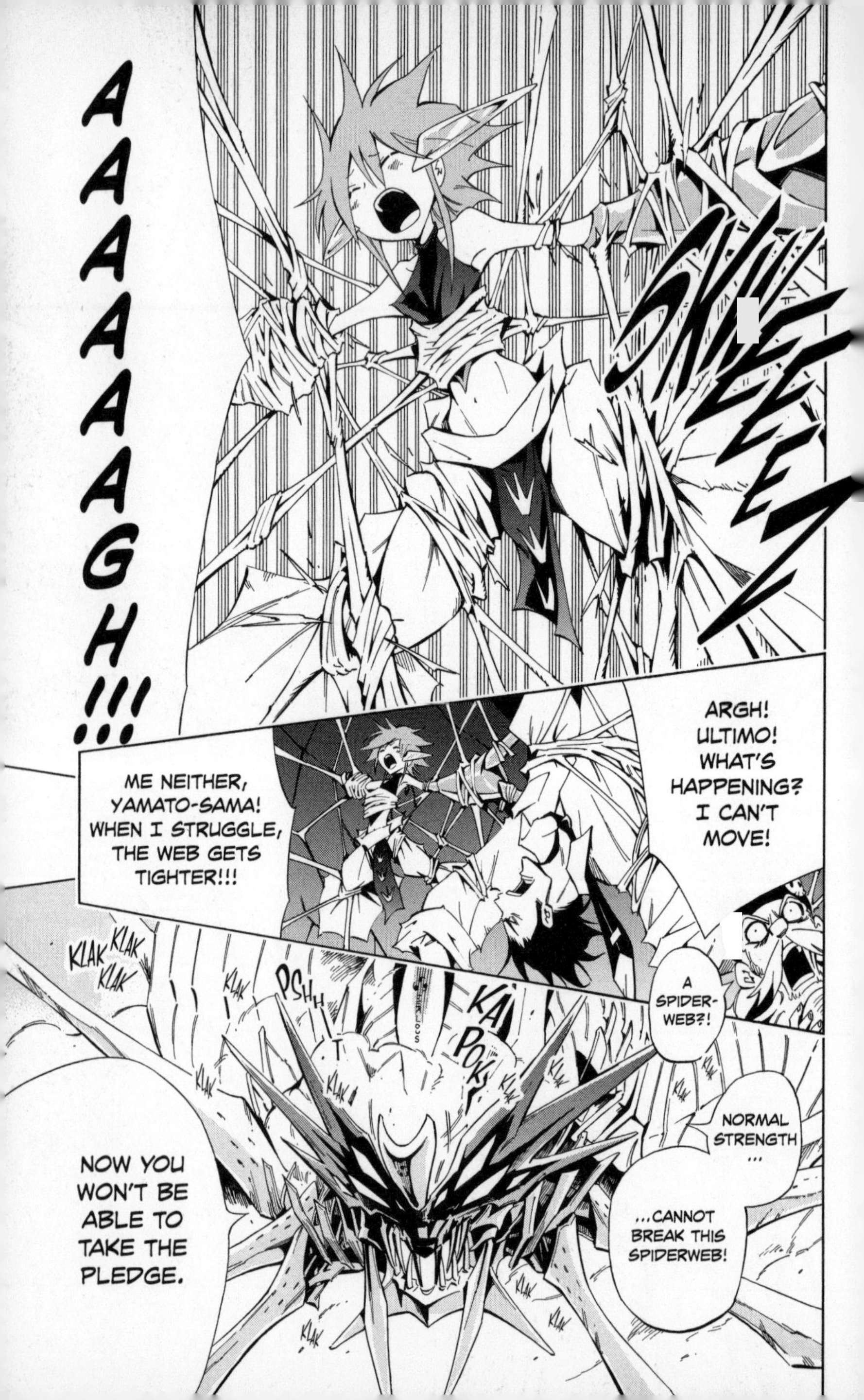
AAAAAAAGH!!!
ARGH! ULTIMO! WHAT'S HAPPENING? I CAN'T MOVE!
ME NEITHER, YAMATO-SAMA! WHEN I STRUGGLE, THE WEB GETS TIGHTER!!!
A SPIDER-WEB?!
NORMAL STRENGTH ...
...CANNOT BREAK THIS SPIDERWEB!
KA POK
PSHH
KLAK KLAK KLAK KLAK
NOW YOU WON'T BE ABLE TO TAKE THE PLEDGE.

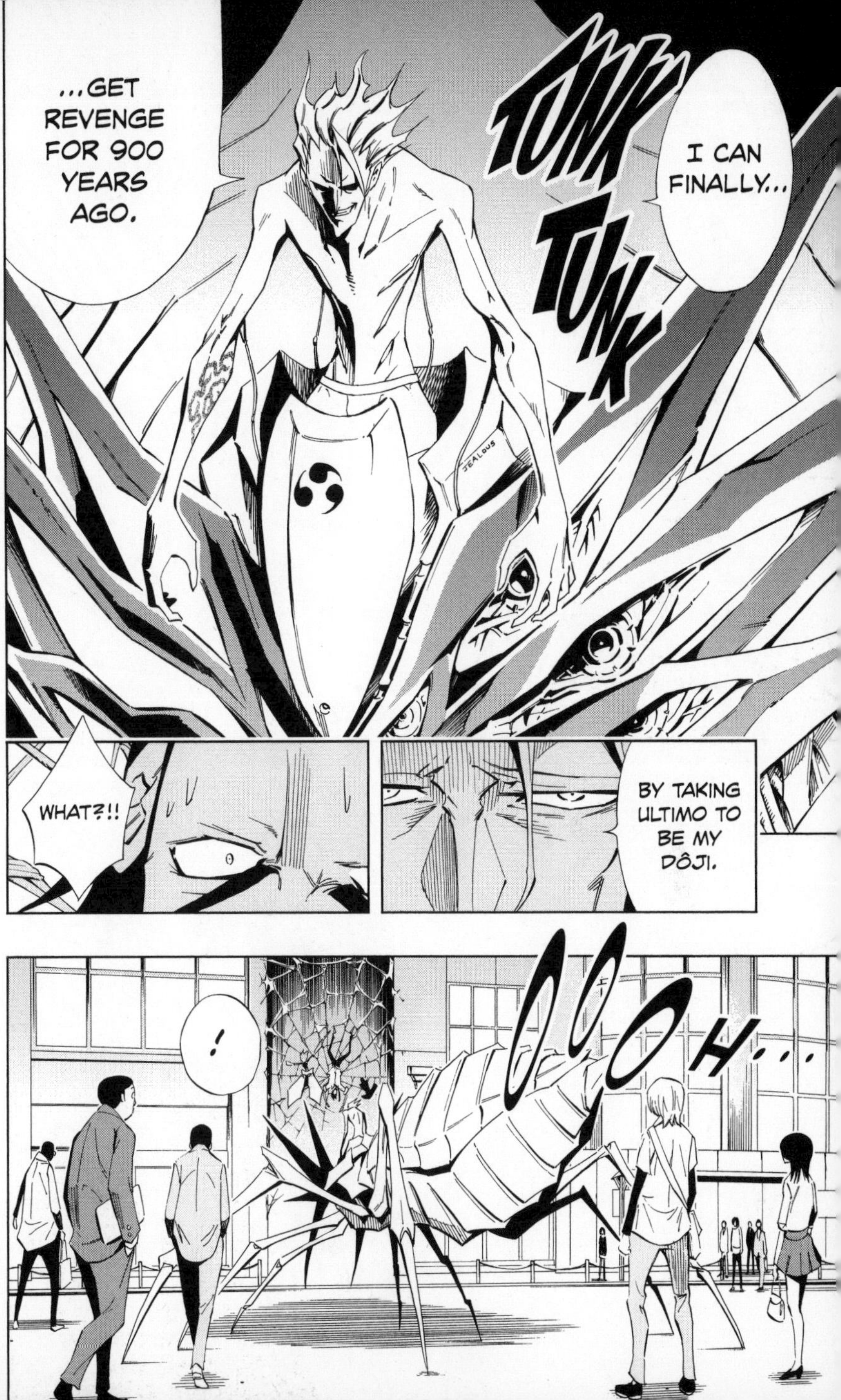
I CAN FINALLY...
TUNK TUNK
...GET REVENGE FOR 900 YEARS AGO.
JEALOUS
BY TAKING ULTIMO TO BE MY DÔJI.
WHAT?!!
OOOH...
!

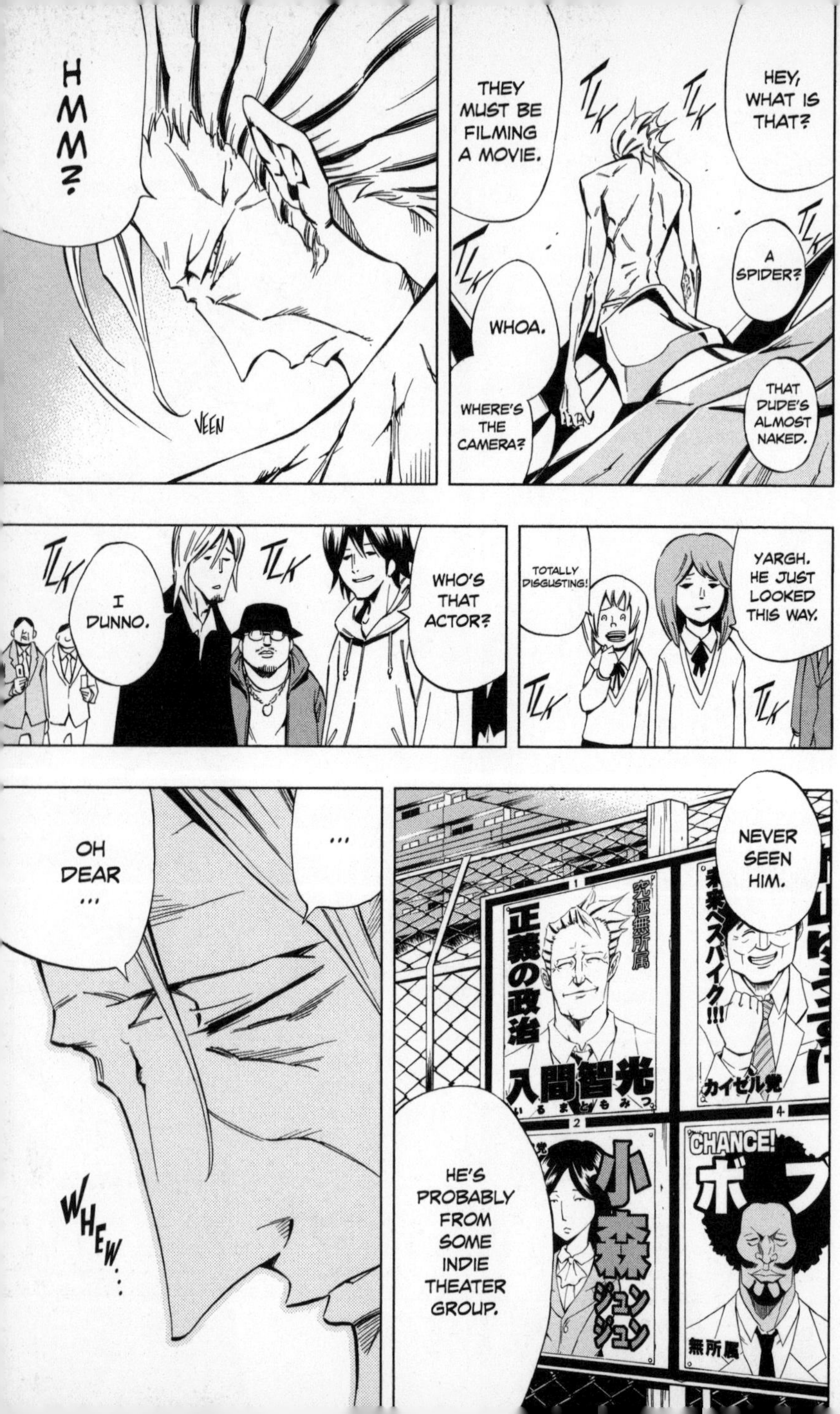

HEY, WHAT IS THAT?
TLK
TLK
A SPIDER?
THEY MUST BE FILMING A MOVIE.
TLK
WHOA.
WHERE'S THE CAMERA?
THAT DUDE'S ALMOST NAKED.
HMMM?
VEEN
YARGH. HE JUST LOOKED THIS WAY.
TOTALLY DISGUSTING!
TLK
TLK
WHO'S THAT ACTOR?
TLK
I DUNNO.
TLK
NEVER SEEN HIM.
HE'S PROBABLY FROM SOME INDIE THEATER GROUP.
未来へスパイク!!!
カイゼル党
究極無所属
正義の政治
入間智光
いるまともみつ
CHANCE!
ボブ
無所属
小森ジュンジュン
...
OH DEAR...
WHEW...

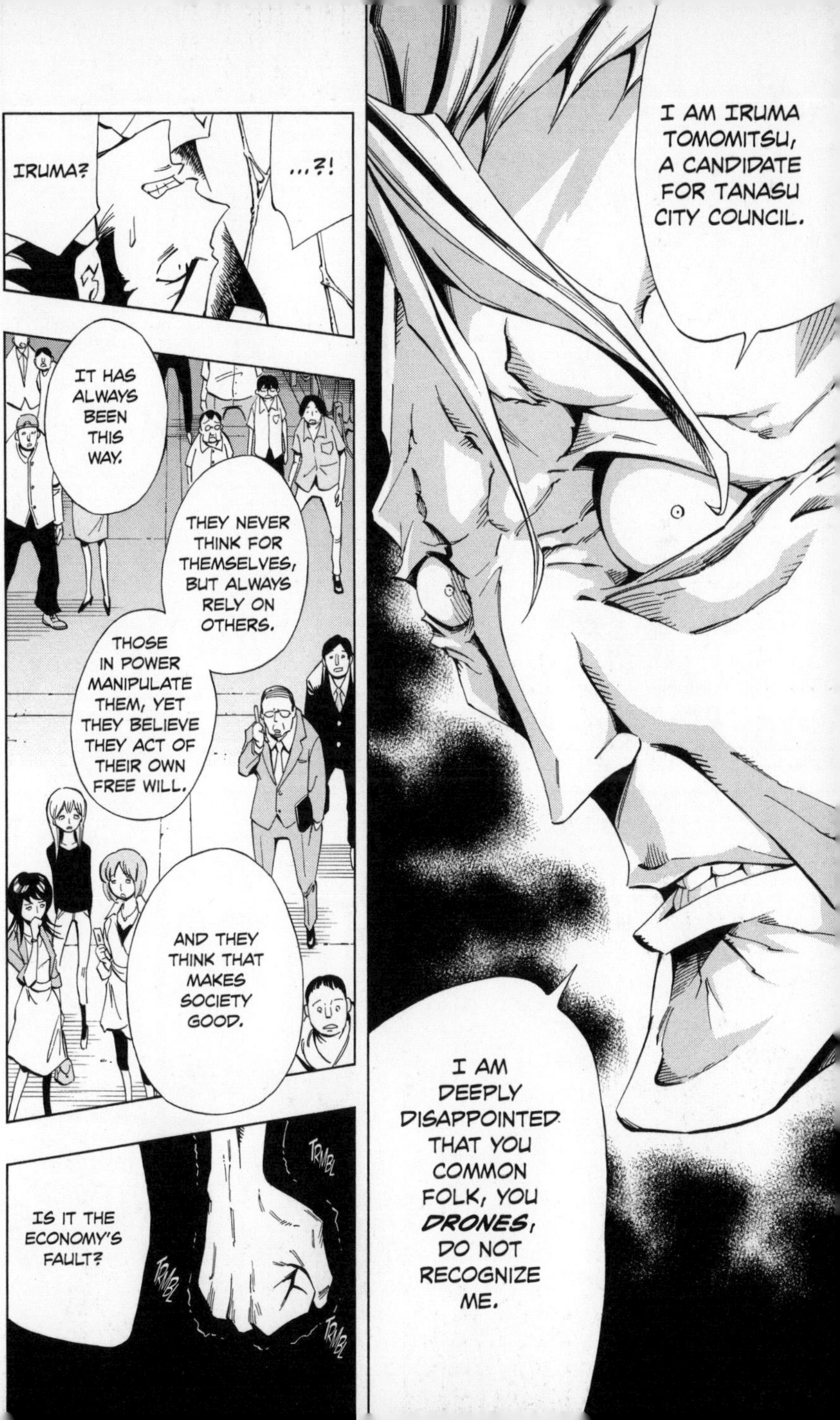
I AM IRUMA TOMOMITSU, A CANDIDATE FOR TANASU CITY COUNCIL.
I AM DEEPLY DISAPPOINTED THAT YOU COMMON FOLK, YOU *DRONES*, DO NOT RECOGNIZE ME.
...?!
IRUMA?
IT HAS ALWAYS BEEN THIS WAY.
THEY NEVER THINK FOR THEMSELVES, BUT ALWAYS RELY ON OTHERS.
THOSE IN POWER MANIPULATE THEM, YET THEY BELIEVE THEY ACT OF THEIR OWN FREE WILL.
AND THEY THINK THAT MAKES SOCIETY GOOD.
TRMBL
TRMBL
TRMBL
IS IT THE ECONOMY'S FAULT?

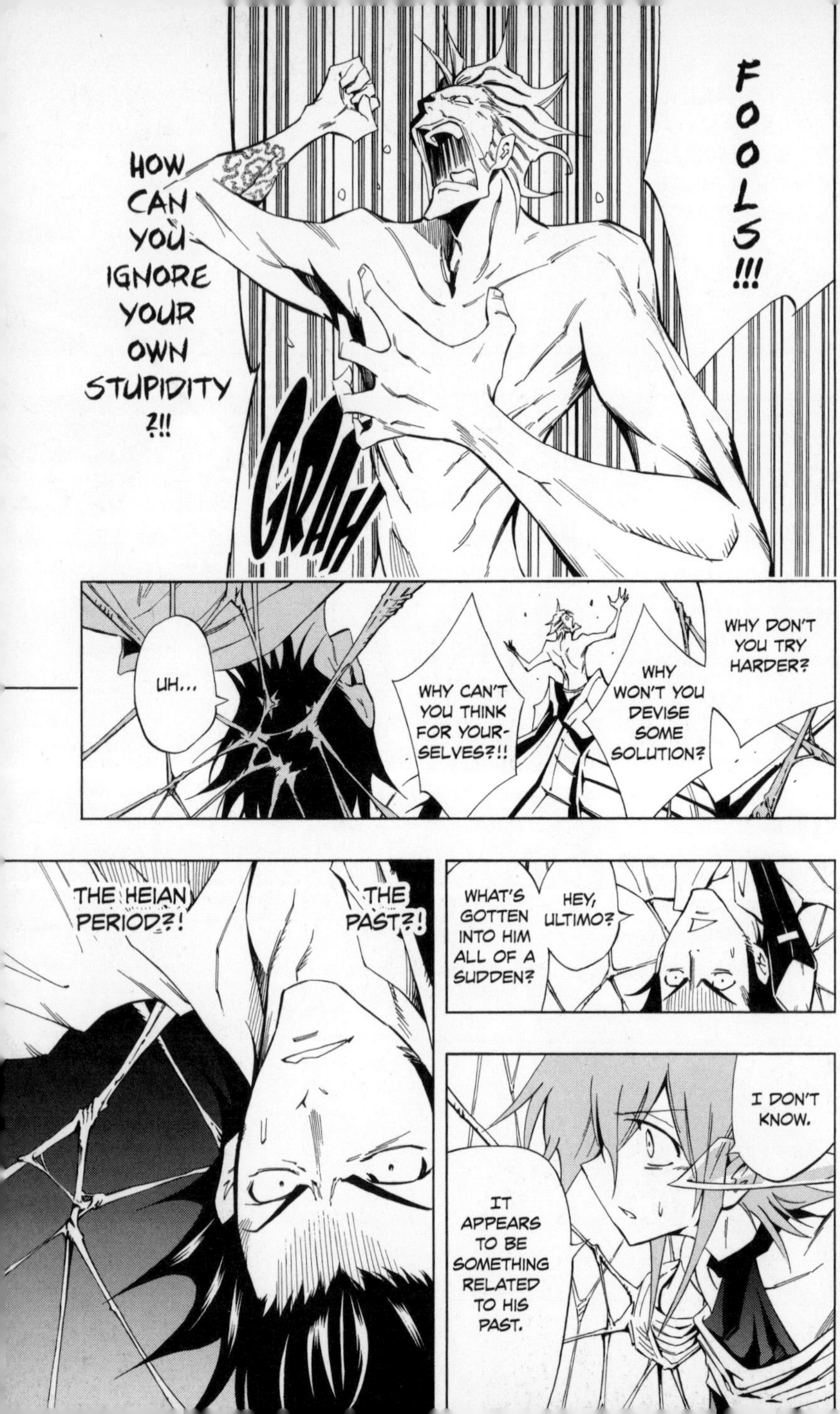
FOOLS!!!
HOW CAN YOU IGNORE YOUR OWN STUPIDITY ?!!
GRAH
WHY DON'T YOU TRY HARDER?
WHY WON'T YOU DEVISE SOME SOLUTION?
WHY CAN'T YOU THINK FOR YOUR-SELVES?!!
UH...
HEY, ULTIMO?
WHAT'S GOTTEN INTO HIM ALL OF A SUDDEN?
I DON'T KNOW.
IT APPEARS TO BE SOMETHING RELATED TO HIS PAST.
THE PAST?!
THE HEIAN PERIOD?!

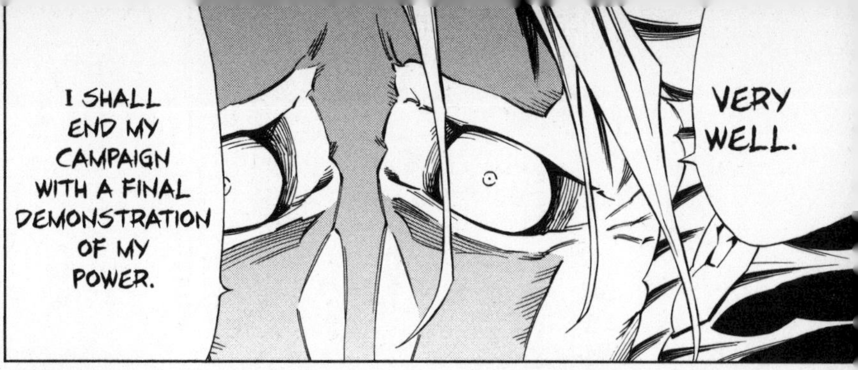
VERY WELL.
I SHALL END MY CAMPAIGN WITH A FINAL DEMONSTRATION OF MY POWER.

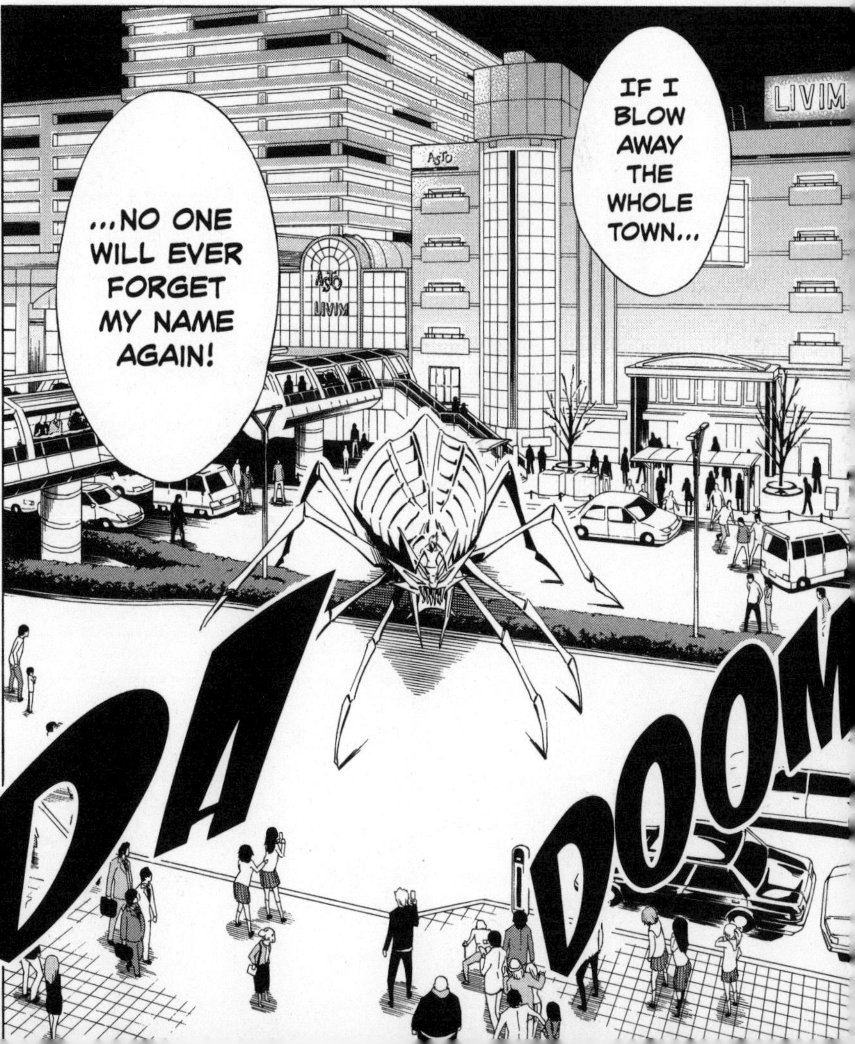
LIVIM
IF I BLOW AWAY THE WHOLE TOWN...
...NO ONE WILL EVER FORGET MY NAME AGAIN!
DA DOOM

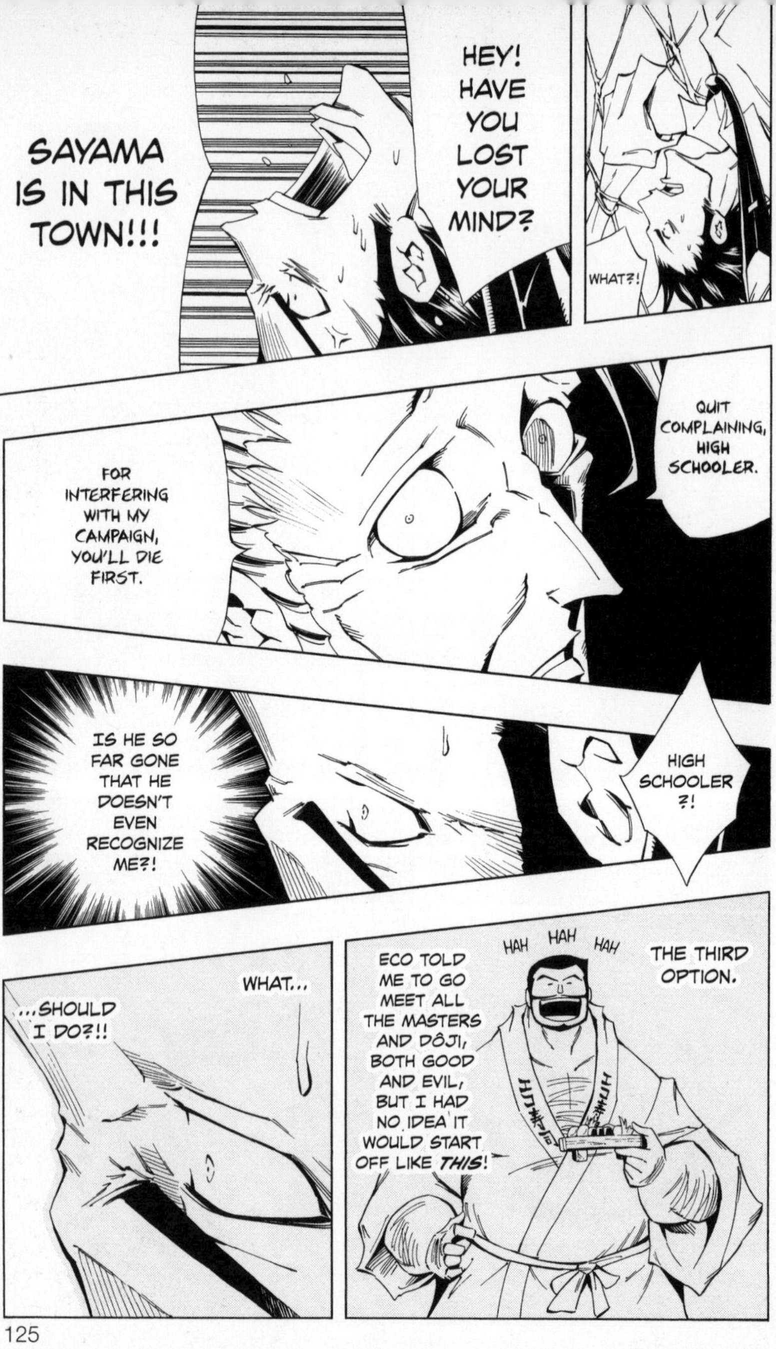
WHAT?!
HEY! HAVE YOU LOST YOUR MIND?
SAYAMA IS IN THIS TOWN!!!
QUIT COMPLAINING, HIGH SCHOOLER.
FOR INTERFERING WITH MY CAMPAIGN, YOU'LL DIE FIRST.
HIGH SCHOOLER?!
IS HE SO FAR GONE THAT HE DOESN'T EVEN RECOGNIZE ME?!
THE THIRD OPTION.
HAH HAH HAH
ECO TOLD ME TO GO MEET ALL THE MASTERS AND DÔJI, BOTH GOOD AND EVIL, BUT I HAD NO IDEA IT WOULD START OFF LIKE *THIS*!
WHAT...
...SHOULD I DO?!!

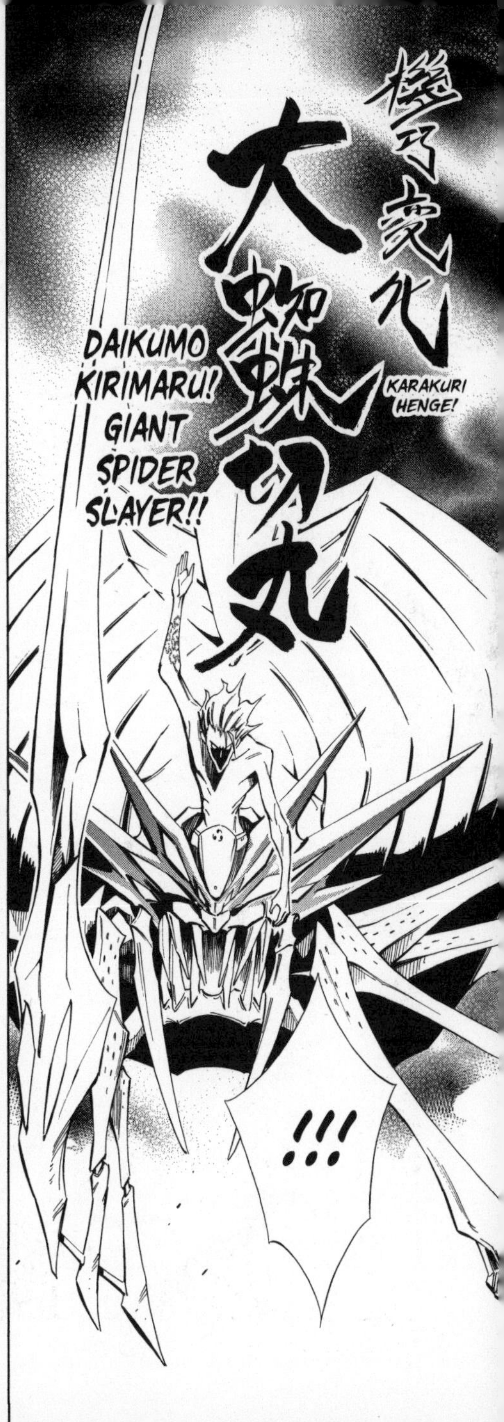
機巧変化
KARAKURI HENGE!
大蜘蛛切丸
DAIKUMO KIRIMARU! GIANT SPIDER SLAYER!!
!!!
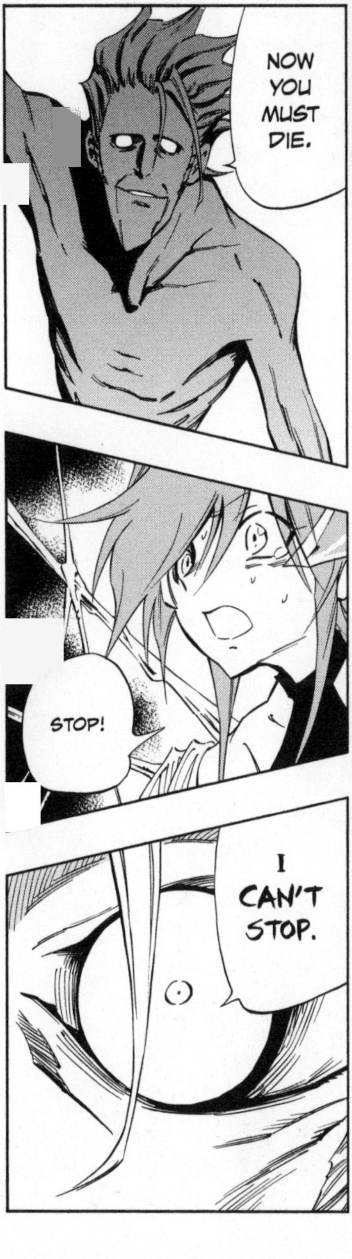
NOW YOU MUST DIE.
STOP!
I CAN'T STOP.

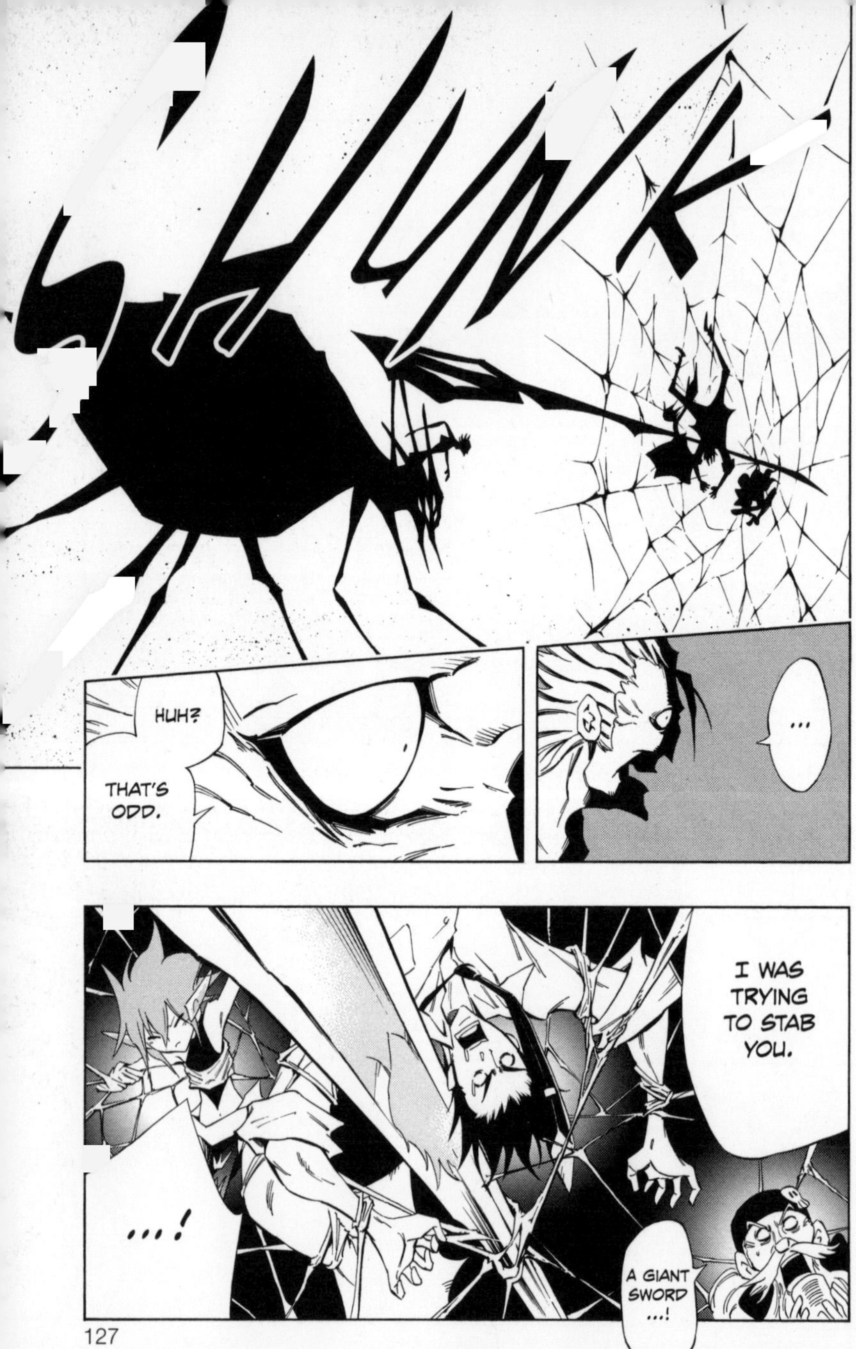
SHUNK
...
HUH? THAT'S ODD.
I WAS TRYING TO STAB YOU.
A GIANT SWORD ...!
...!

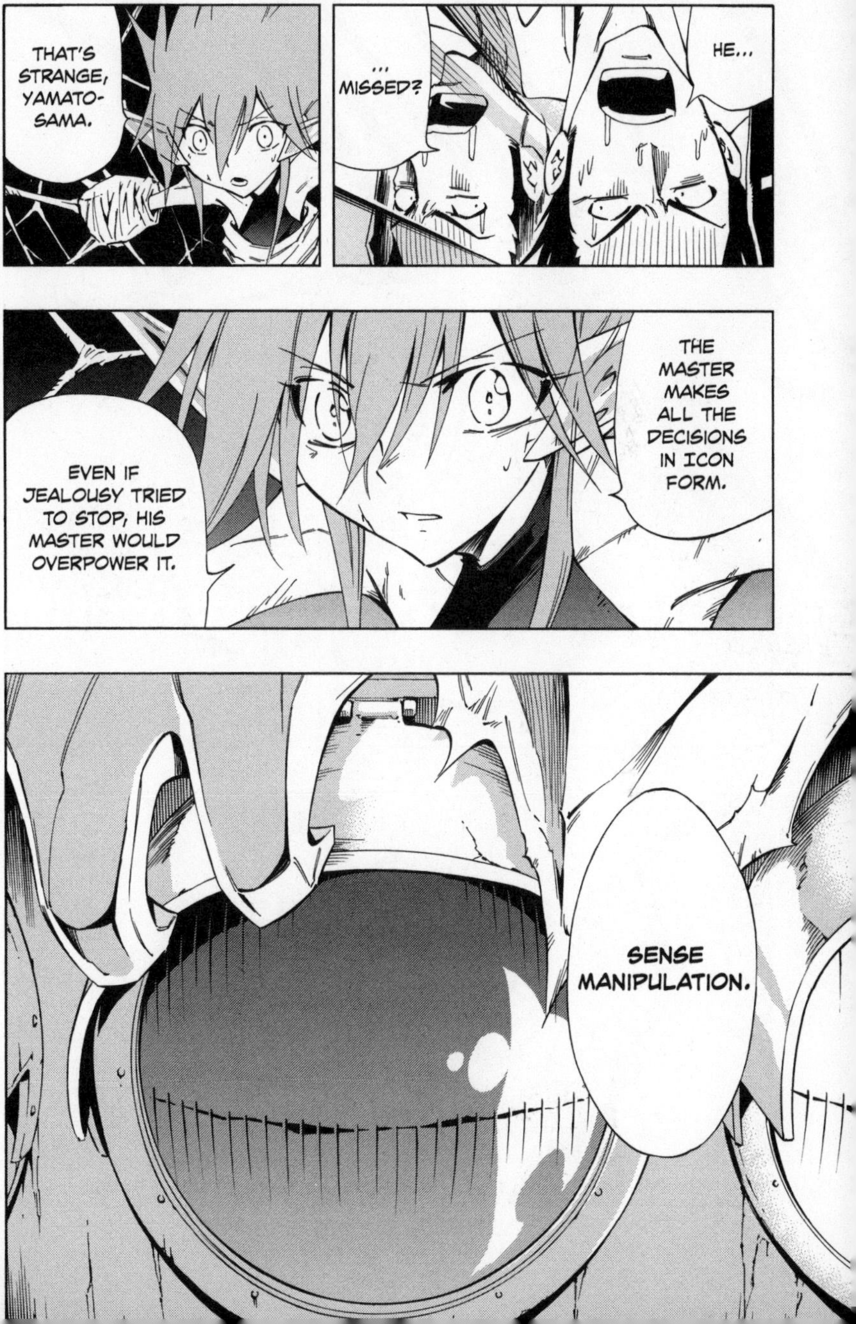
HE...
...MISSED?
THAT'S STRANGE, YAMATO-SAMA.
THE MASTER MAKES ALL THE DECISIONS IN ICON FORM.
EVEN IF JEALOUSY TRIED TO STOP, HIS MASTER WOULD OVERPOWER IT.
SENSE MANIPULATION.

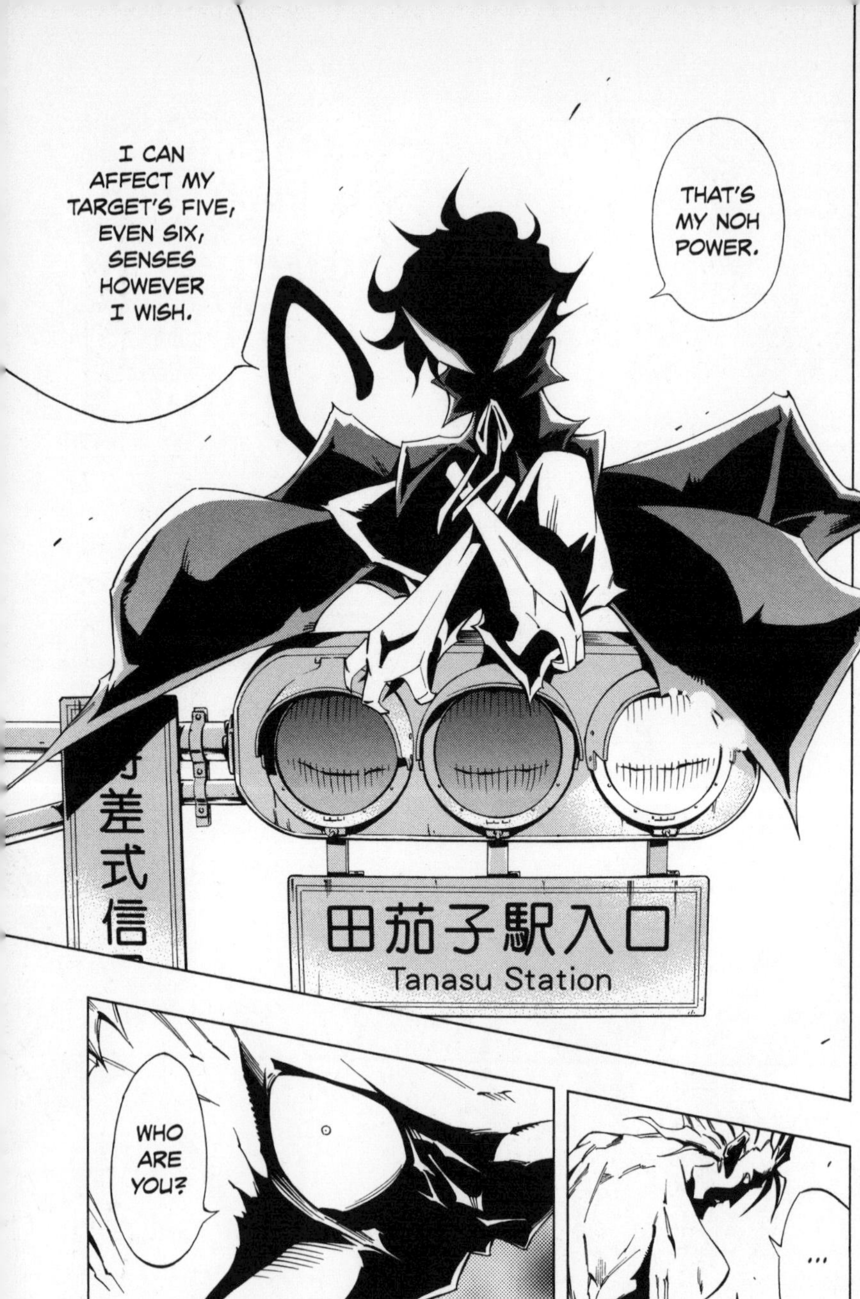
I CAN AFFECT MY TARGET'S FIVE, EVEN SIX, SENSES HOWEVER I WISH.
THAT'S MY NOH POWER.
差式信
田茄子駅入口
Tanasu Station
...
WHO ARE YOU?

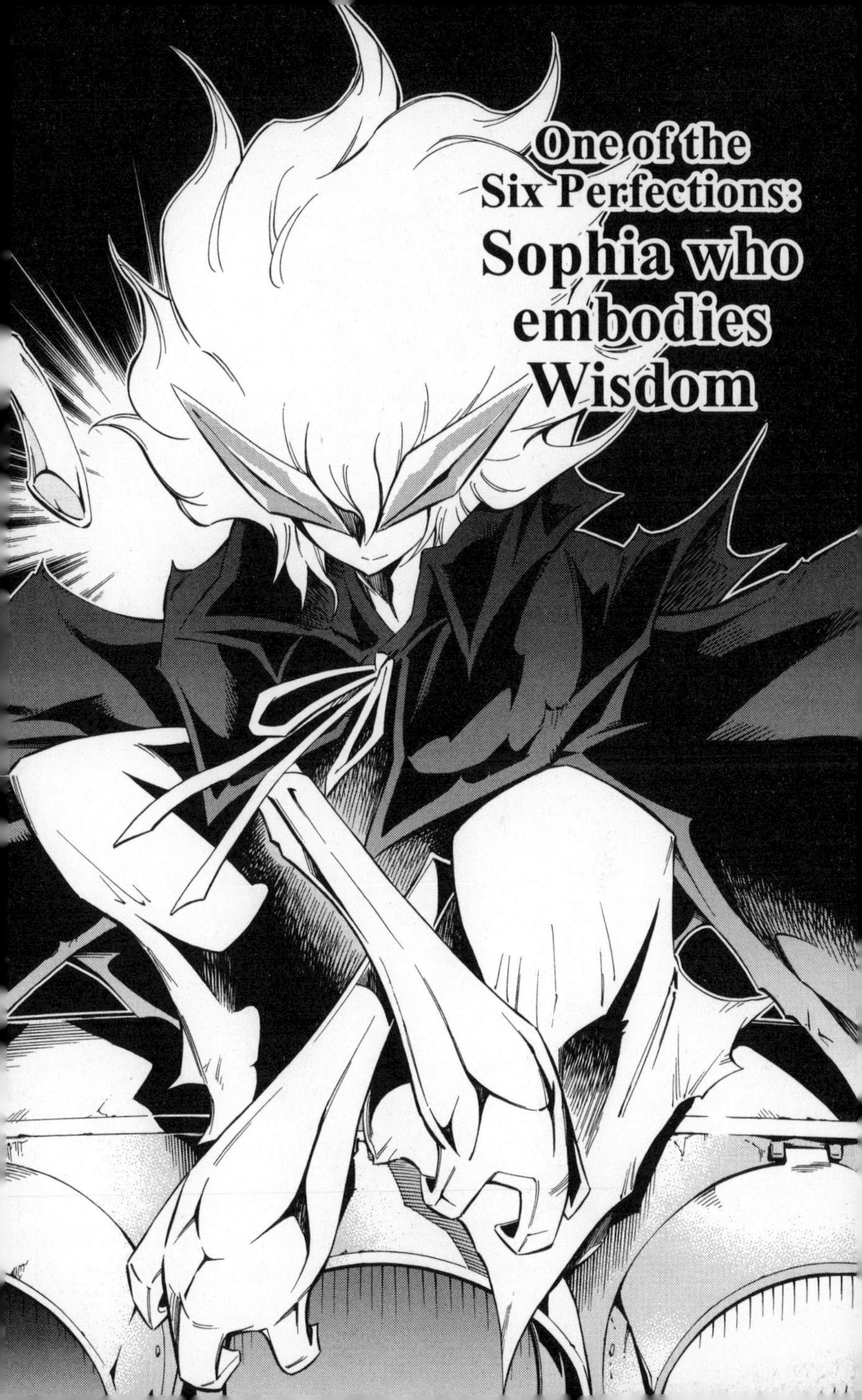
One of the Six Perfections:
Sophia who embodies Wisdom

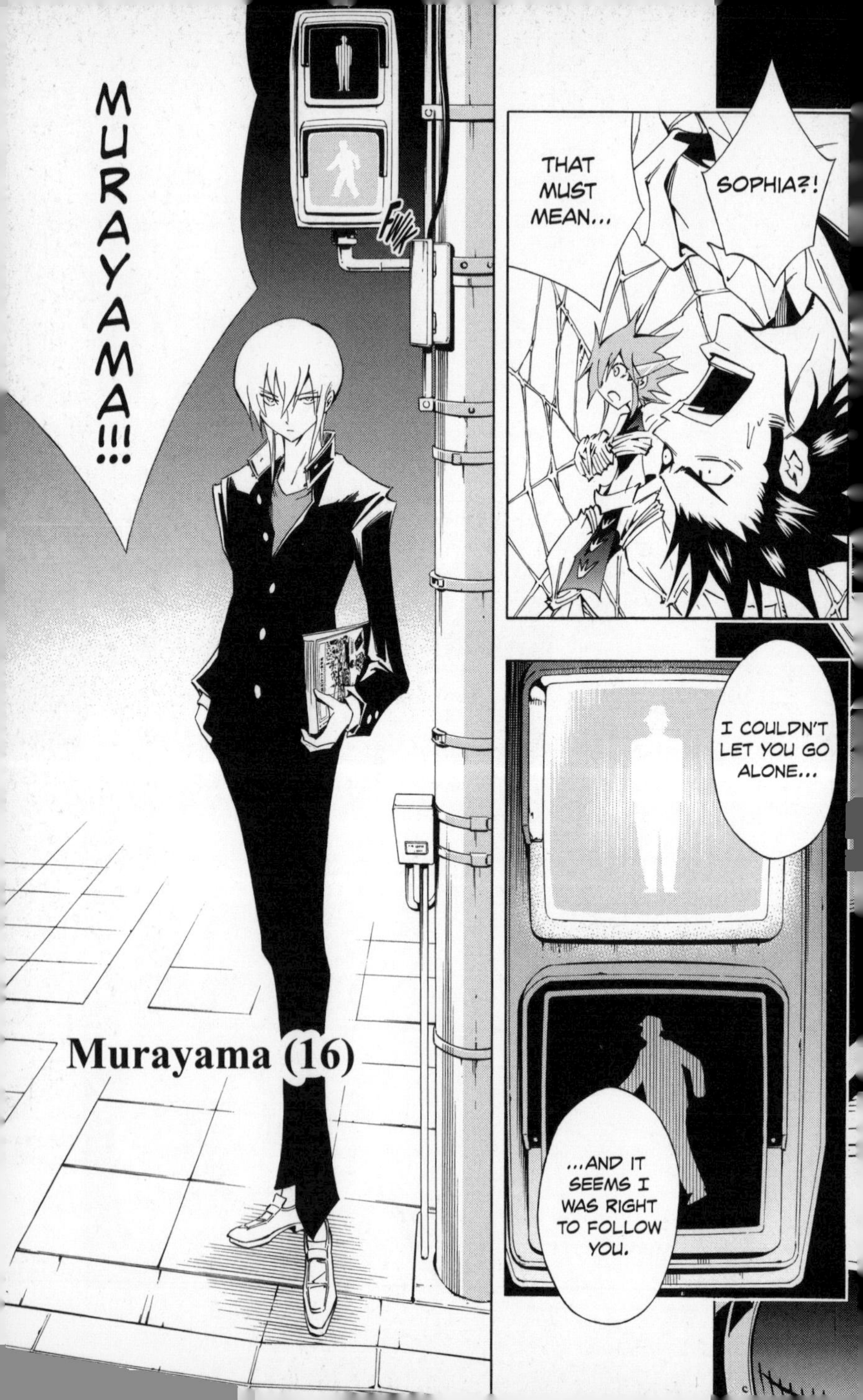
SOPHIA?!
THAT MUST MEAN...
I COULDN'T LET YOU GO ALONE...
...AND IT SEEMS I WAS RIGHT TO FOLLOW YOU.
MURAYAMA!!!
Murayama (16)

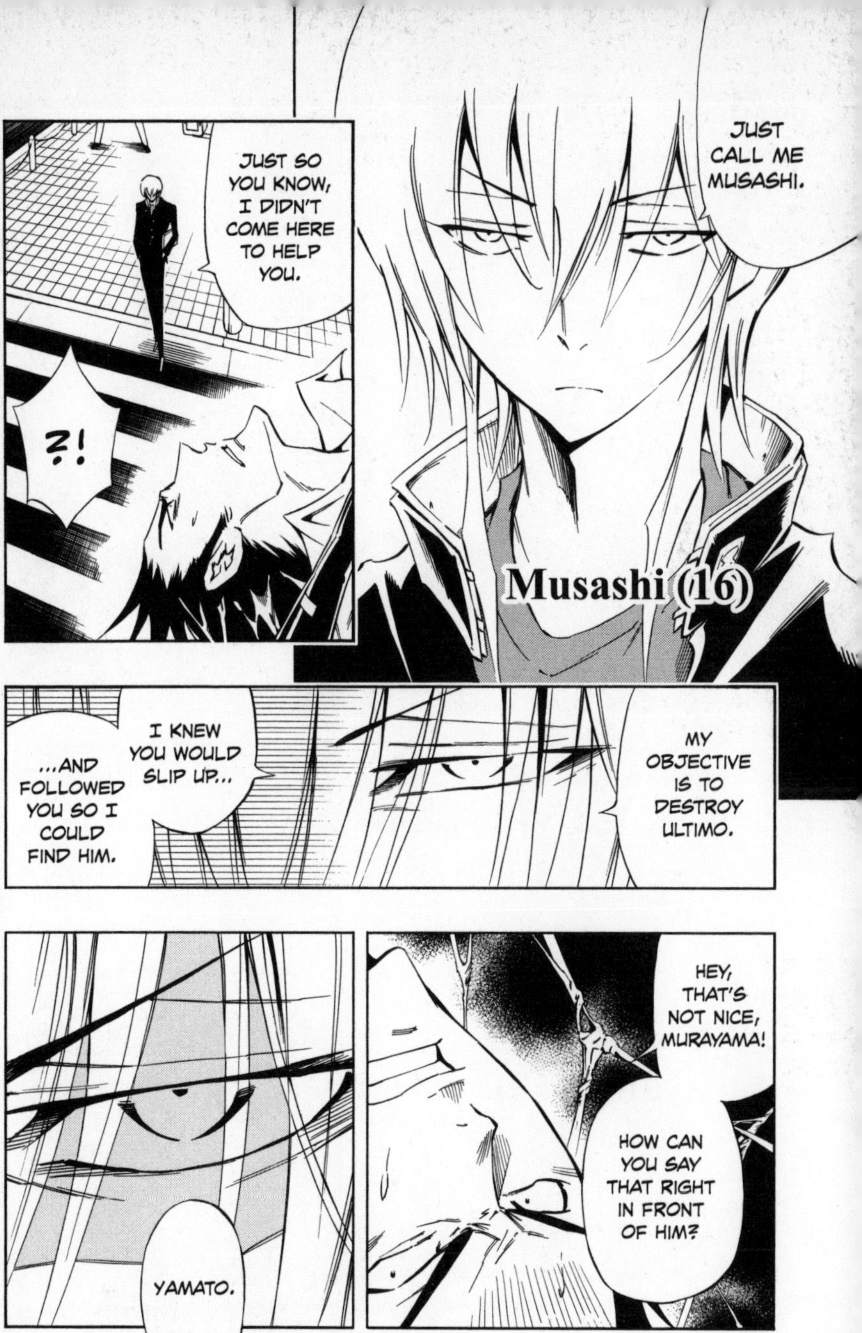
JUST CALL ME MUSASHI.
Musashi (16)
JUST SO YOU KNOW, I DIDN'T COME HERE TO HELP YOU.
?!
MY OBJECTIVE IS TO DESTROY ULTIMO.
I KNEW YOU WOULD SLIP UP...
...AND FOLLOWED YOU SO I COULD FIND HIM.
HEY, THAT'S NOT NICE, MURAYAMA!
HOW CAN YOU SAY THAT RIGHT IN FRONT OF HIM?
YAMATO.

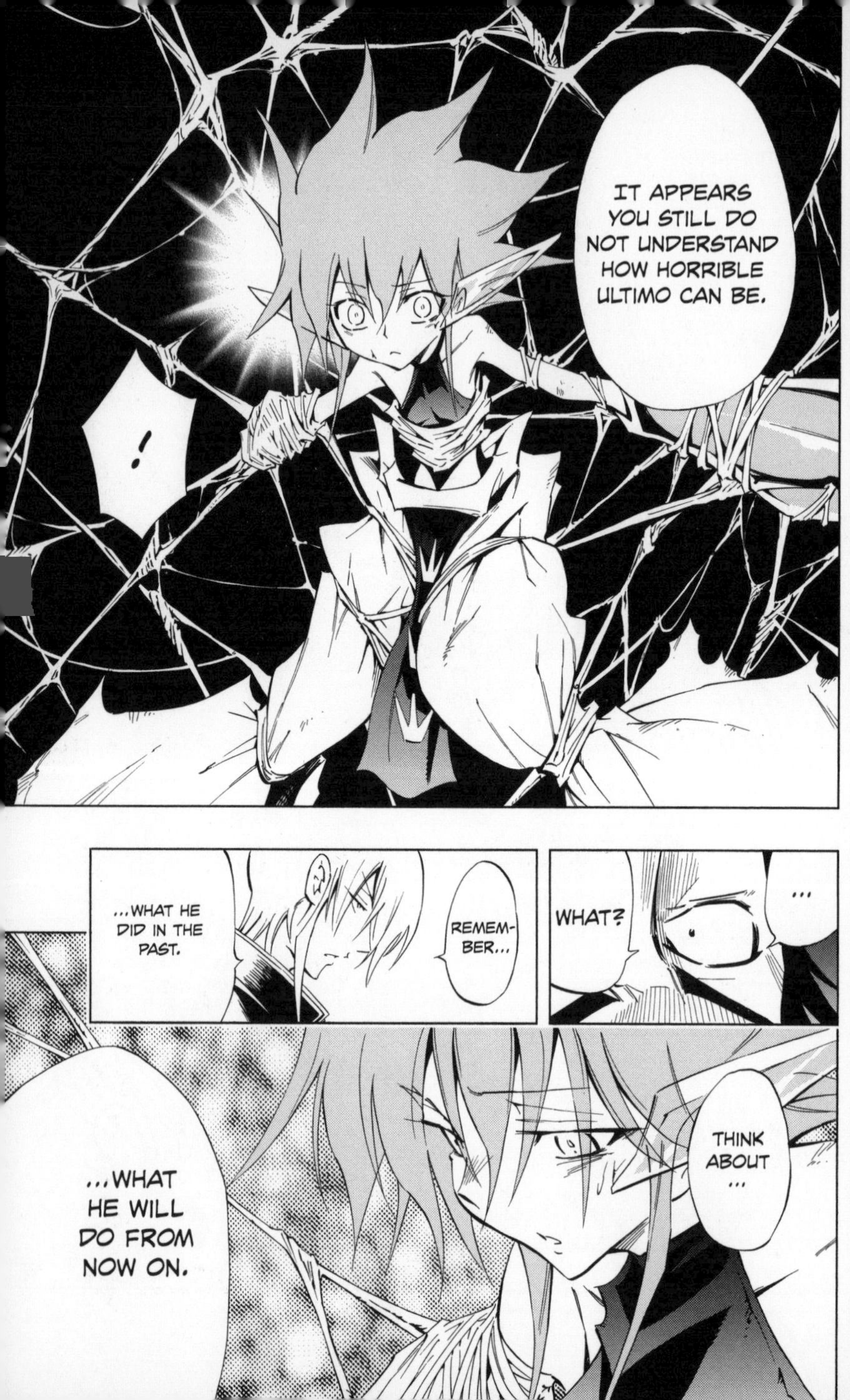
IT APPEARS YOU STILL DO NOT UNDERSTAND HOW HORRIBLE ULTIMO CAN BE.
!
...
WHAT?
REMEMBER...
...WHAT HE DID IN THE PAST.
THINK ABOUT ...
...WHAT HE WILL DO FROM NOW ON.

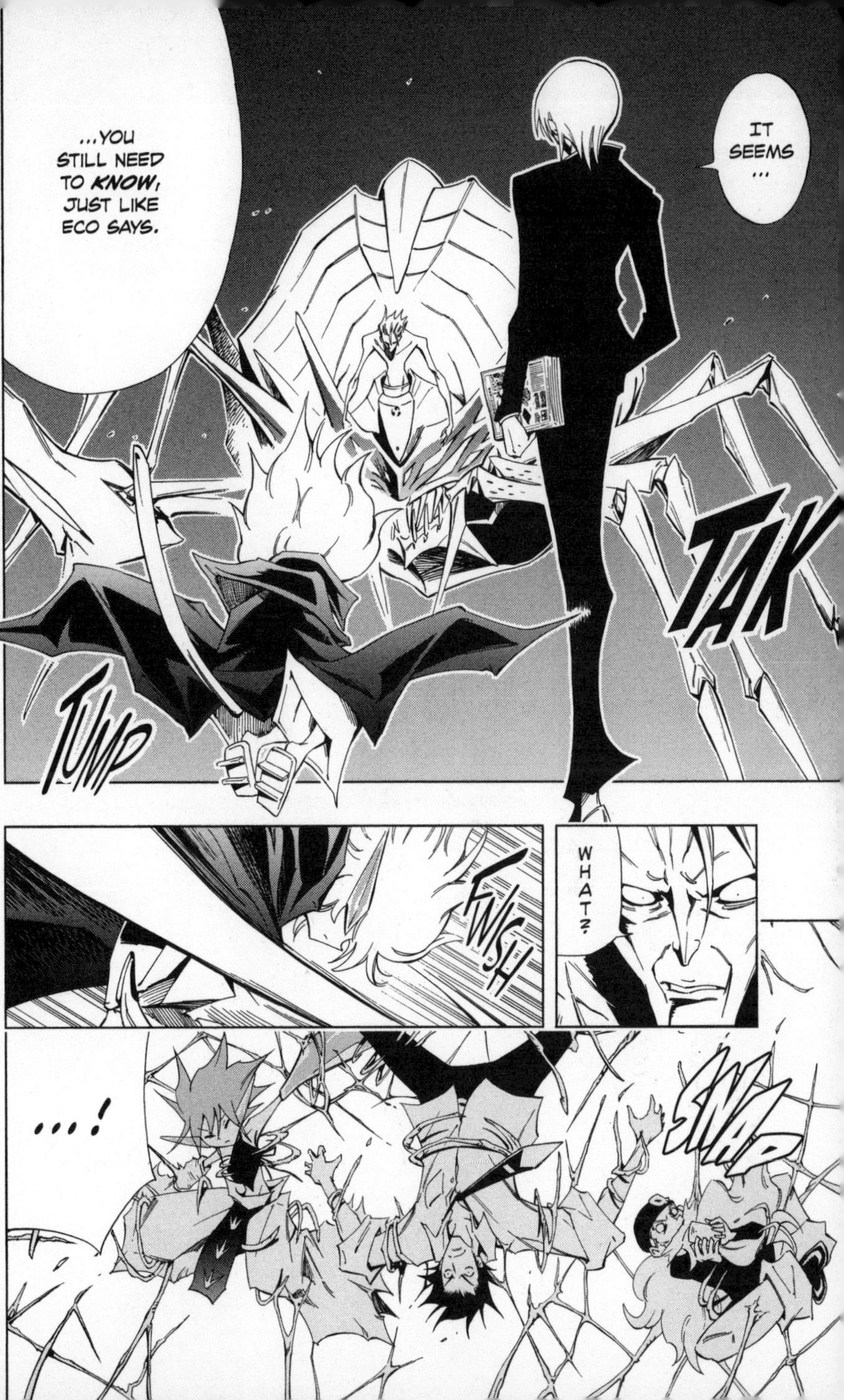
IT SEEMS...
...YOU STILL NEED TO KNOW, JUST LIKE ECO SAYS.
TAK
TUMP
WHAT?
FWISH
SNAP
...!

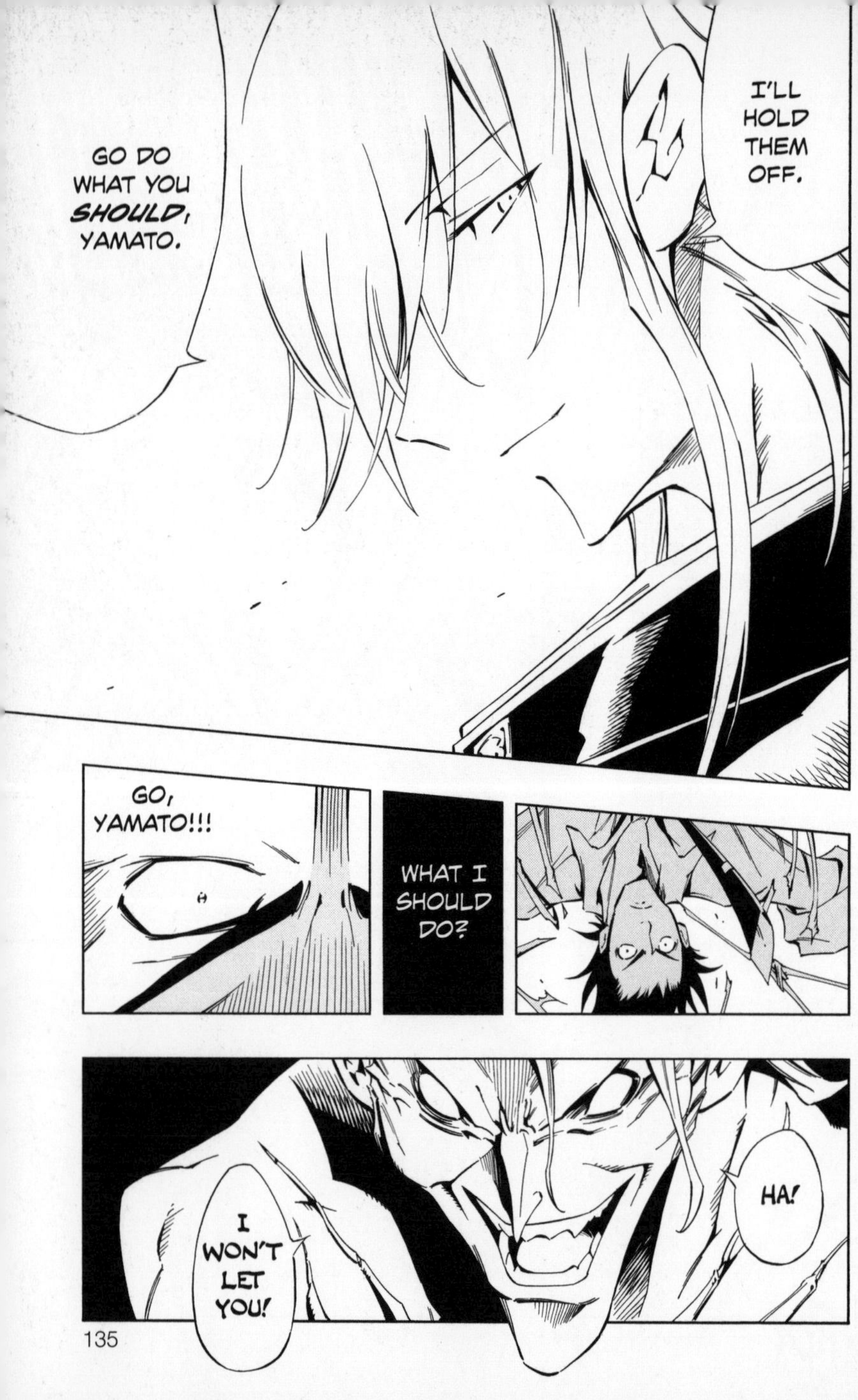
I'LL HOLD THEM OFF.
GO DO WHAT YOU *SHOULD*, YAMATO.
WHAT I SHOULD DO?
GO, YAMATO!!!
HA!
I WON'T LET YOU!

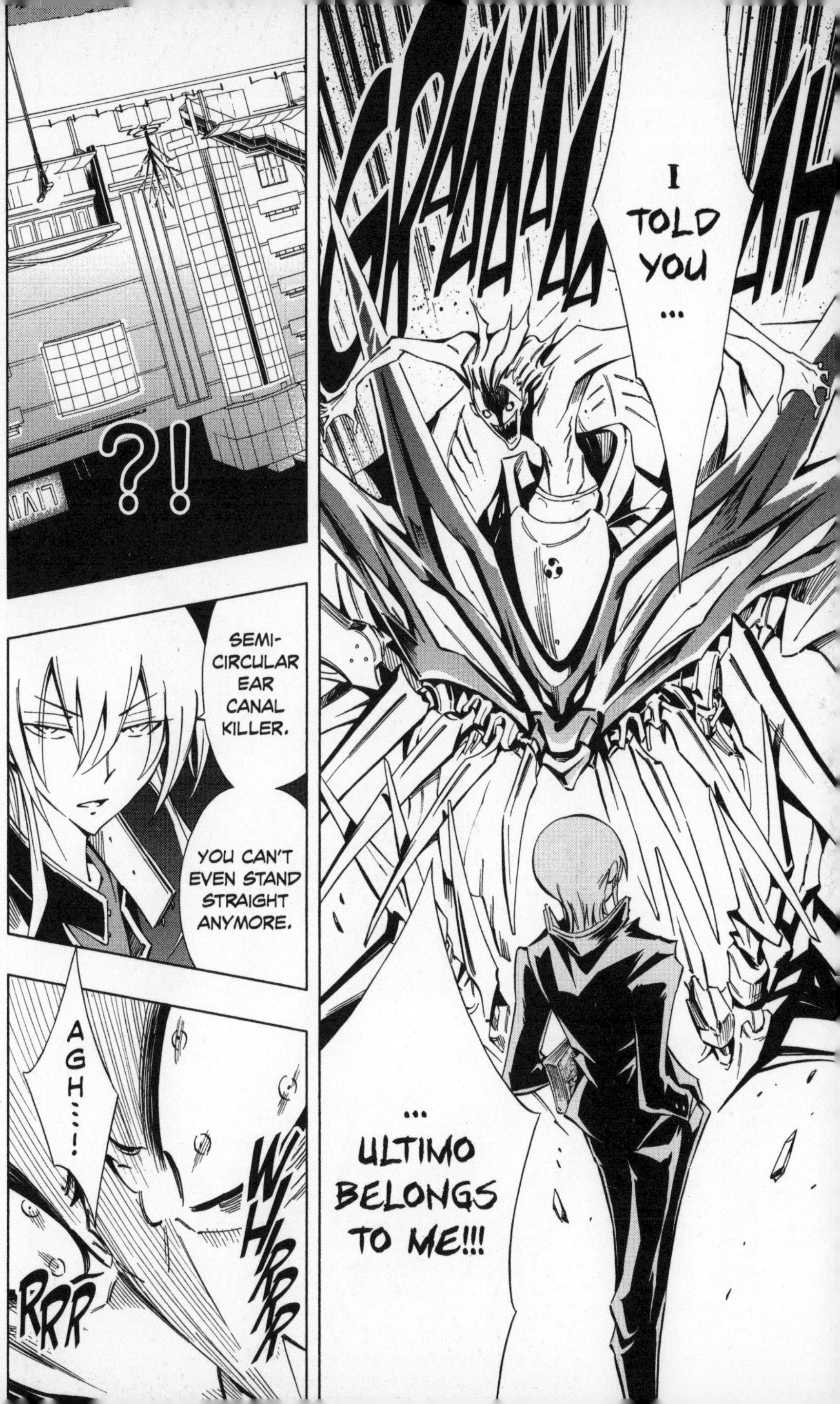
I TOLD YOU ...
... ULTIMO BELONGS TO ME!!!
?!
SEMI-CIRCULAR EAR CANAL KILLER.
YOU CAN'T EVEN STAND STRAIGHT ANYMORE.
AGH...!
WHRRRR
RRR

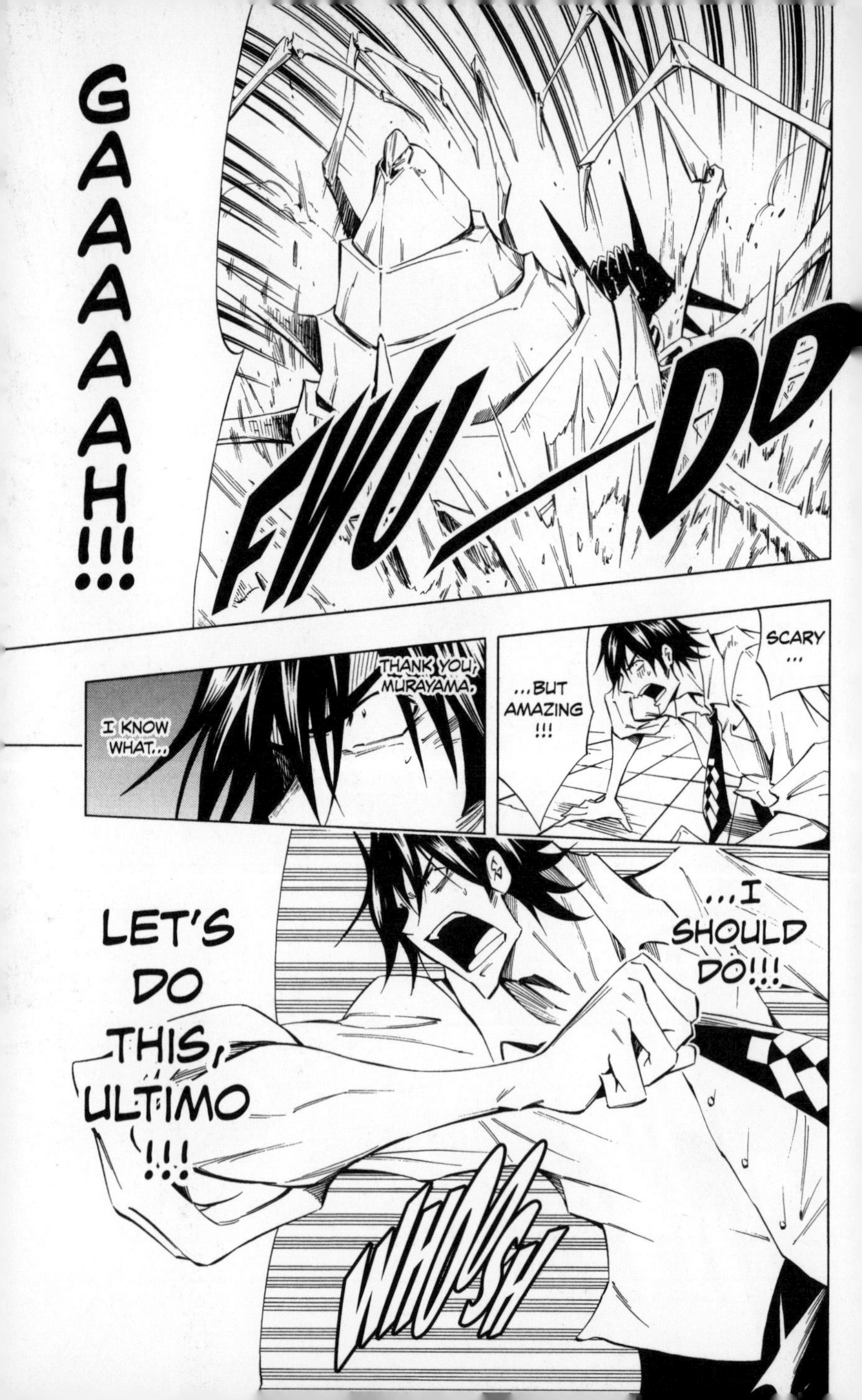
FWU-DD
GAAAAAH!!!
SCARY...
...BUT AMAZING!!!
THANK YOU, MURAYAMA.
I KNOW WHAT...
...I SHOULD DO!!!
LET'S DO THIS, ULTIMO!!!

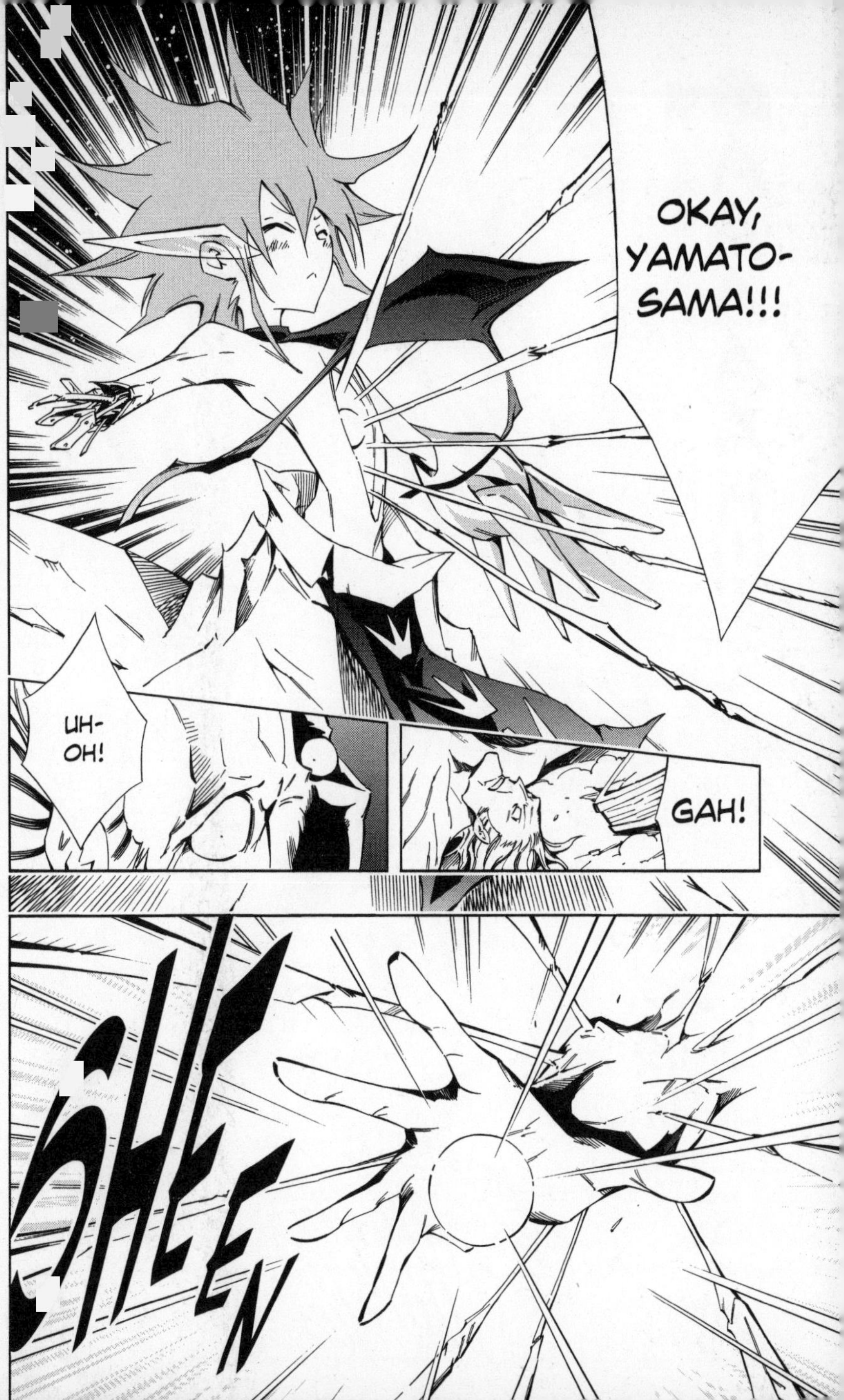
OKAY, YAMATO-SAMA!!!
GAH!
UH-OH!
SHEEN

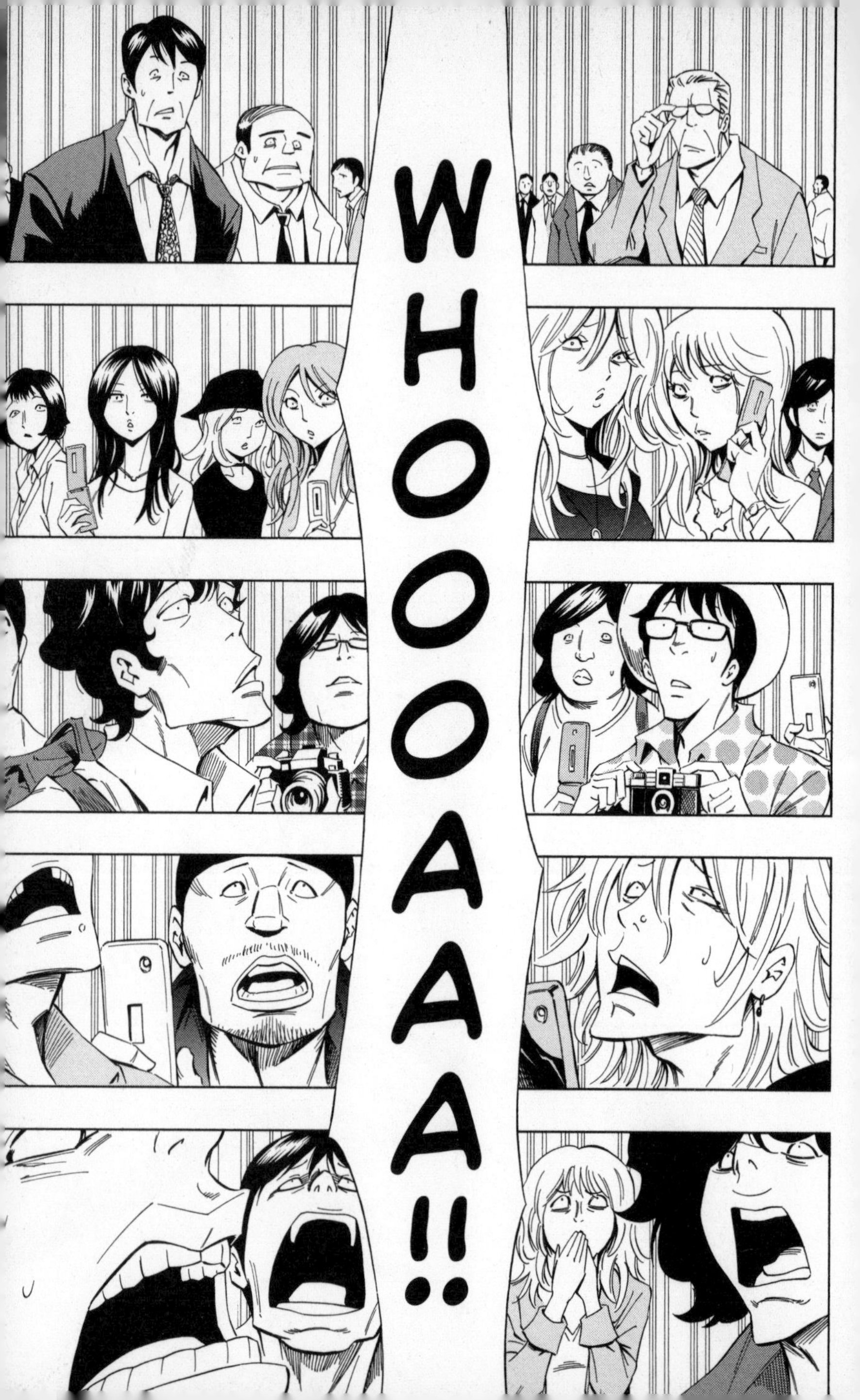
WHOOOAAA!!

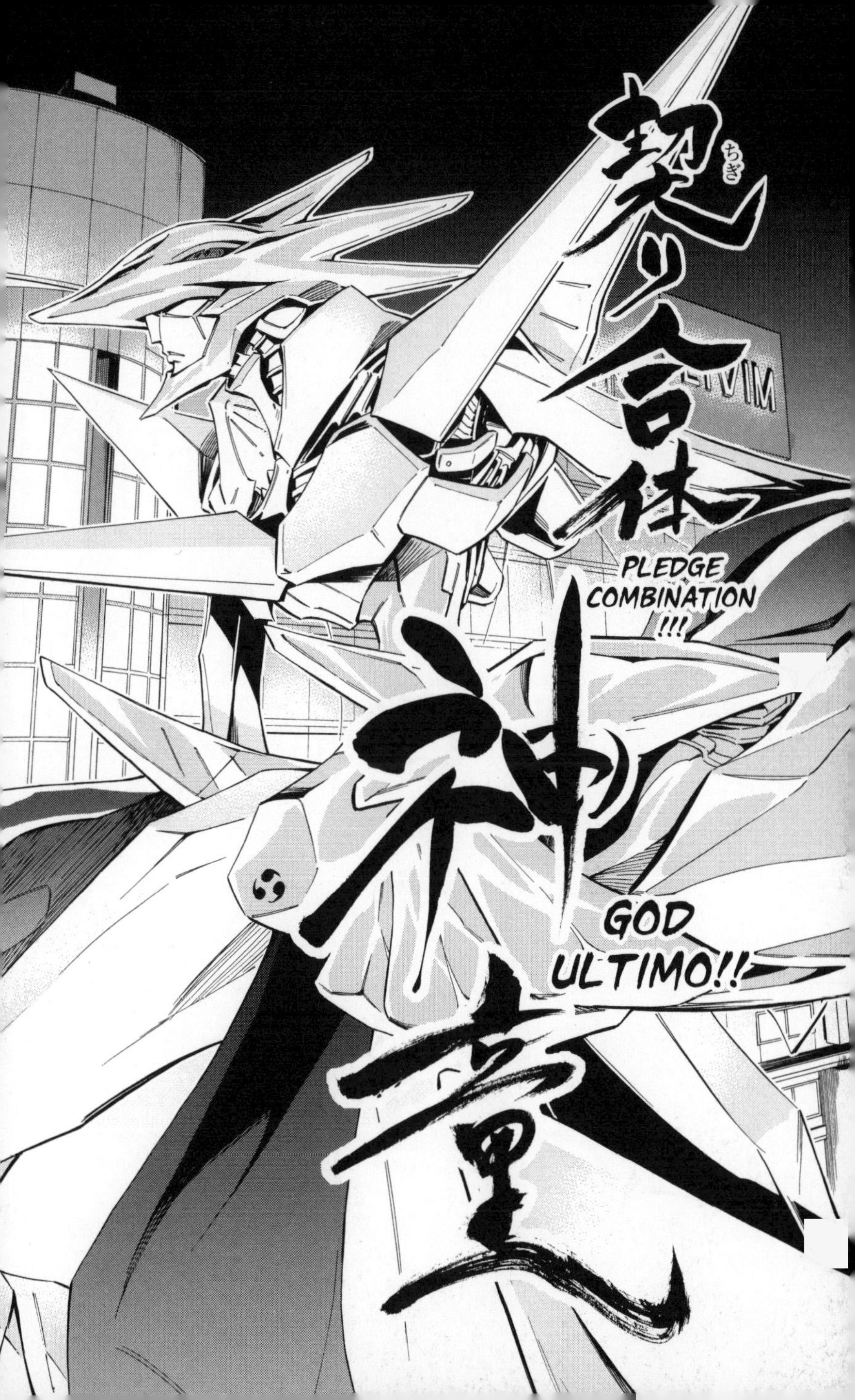
契り合体
PLEDGE COMBINATION!!!
GOD ULTIMO!!

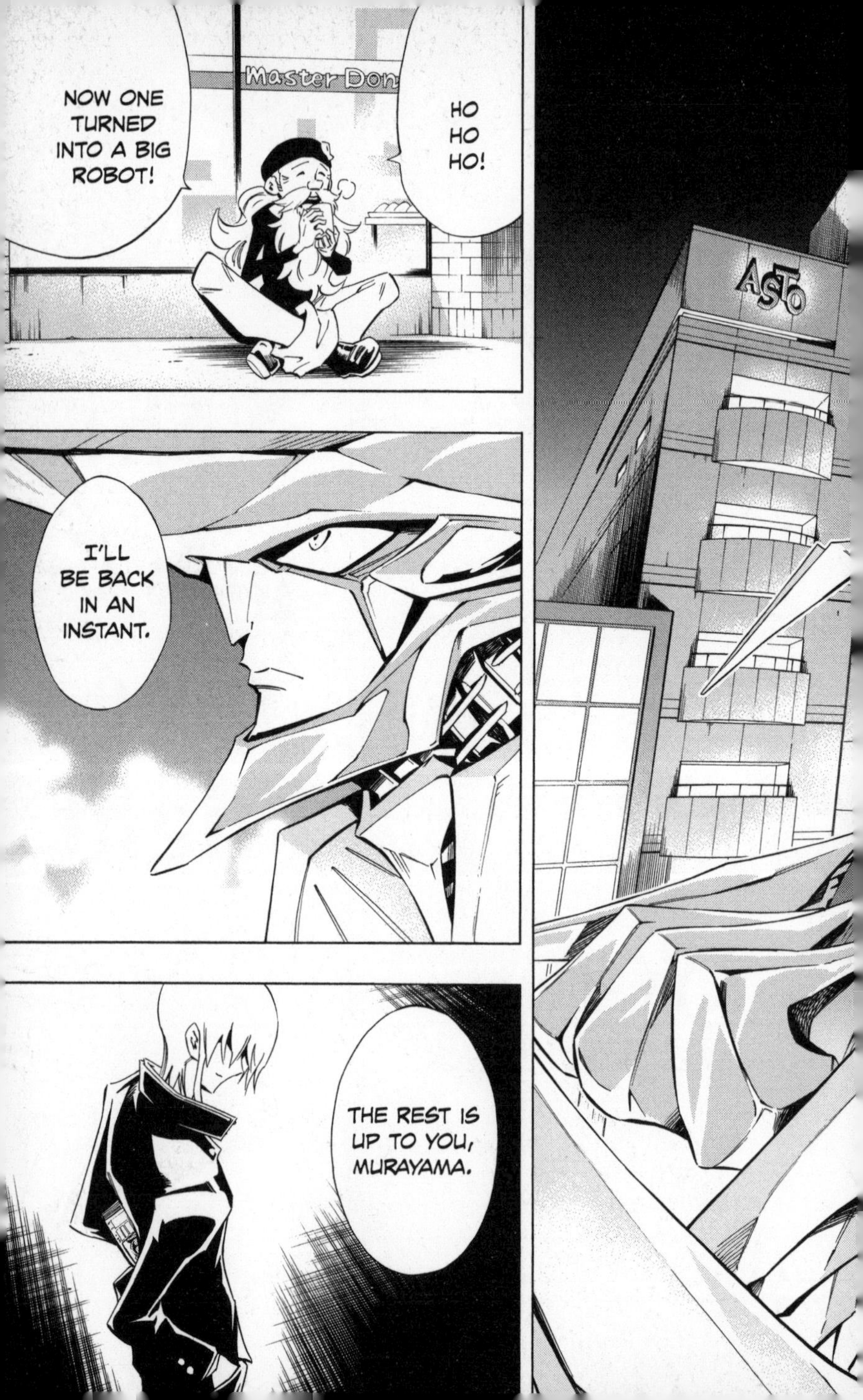
ASTO
Master Don
HO HO HO!
NOW ONE TURNED INTO A BIG ROBOT!
I'LL BE BACK IN AN INSTANT.
THE REST IS UP TO YOU, MURAYAMA.

Noh: Space-time Flight

12th century

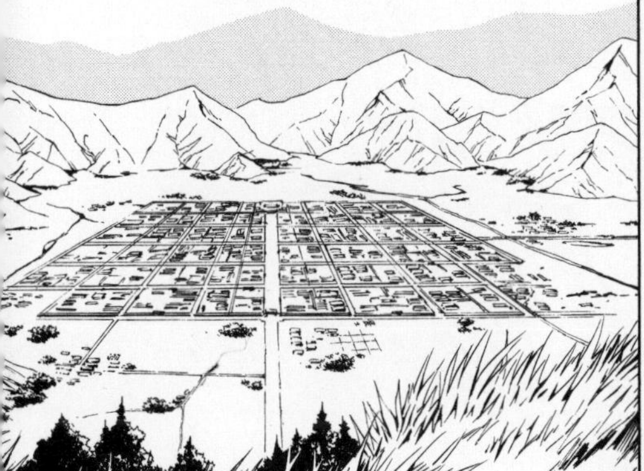

KYOTO Japan

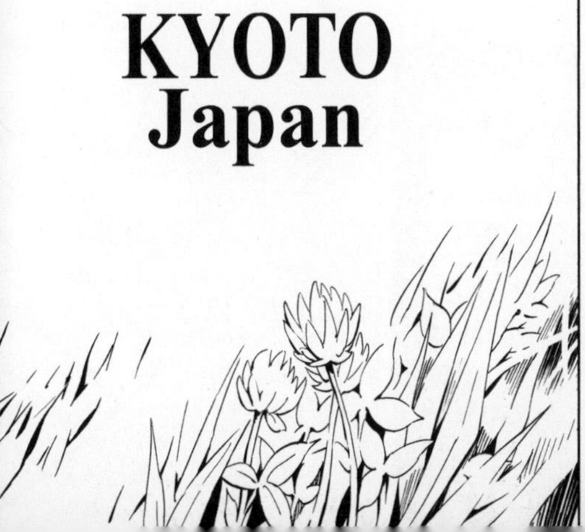

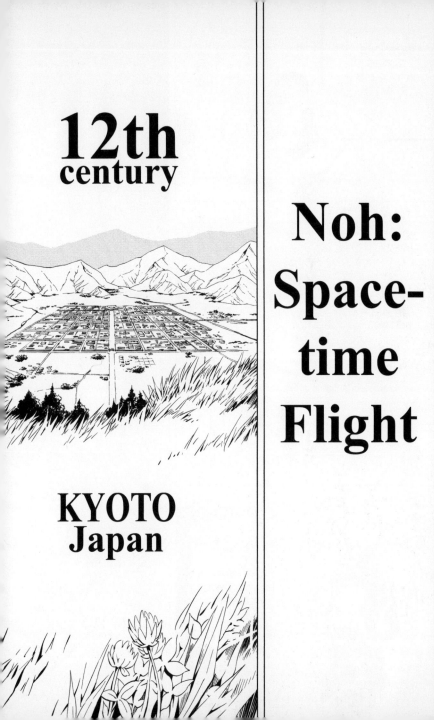

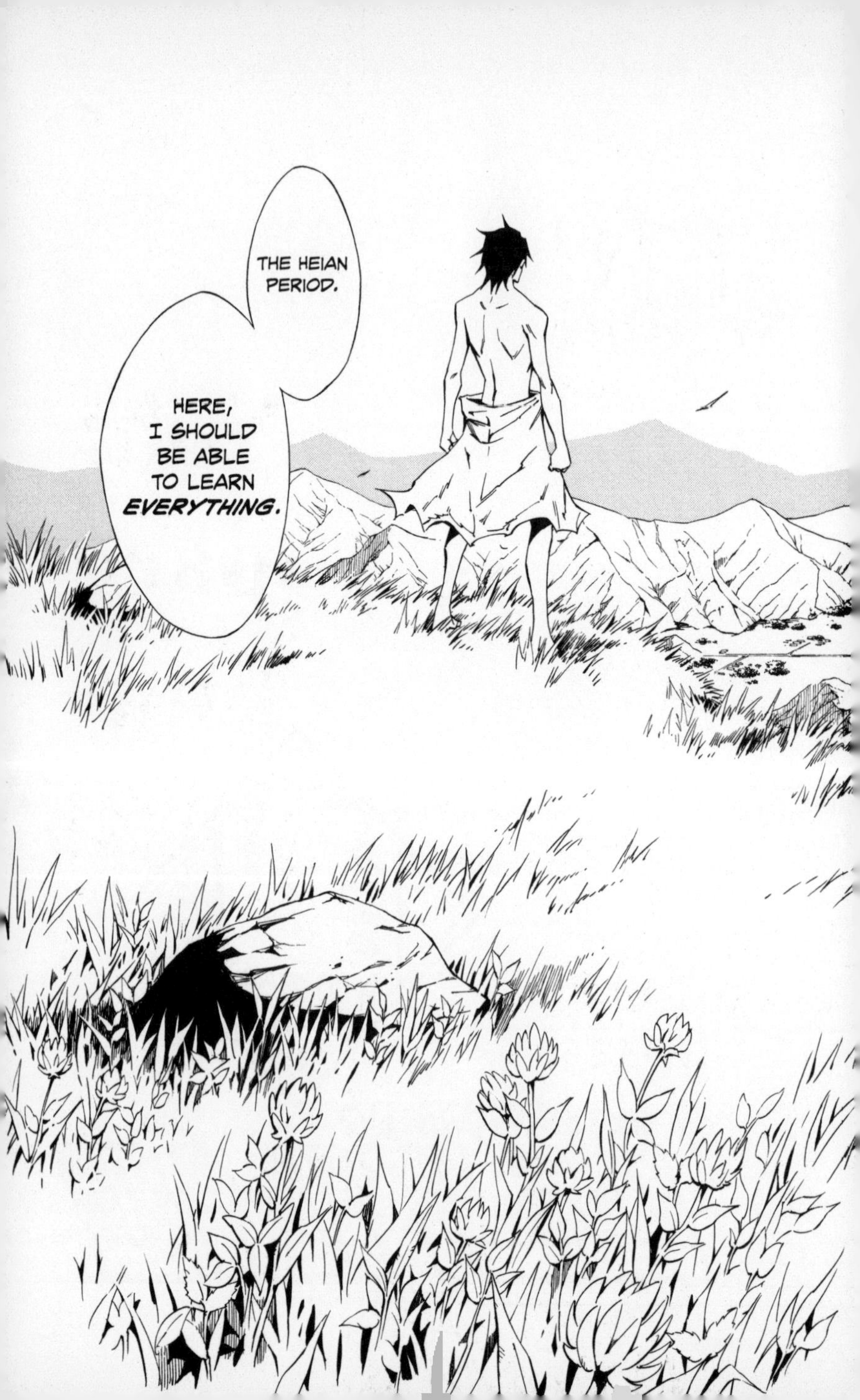
THE HEIAN PERIOD.
HERE, I SHOULD BE ABLE TO LEARN *EVERYTHING*.

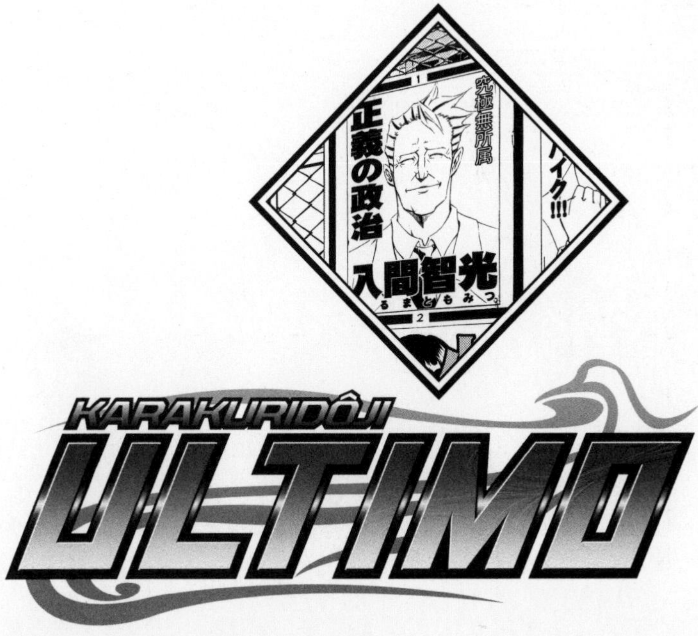

究極無所属
正義の政治
入間智光

KARAKURIDÔJI
ULTIMO

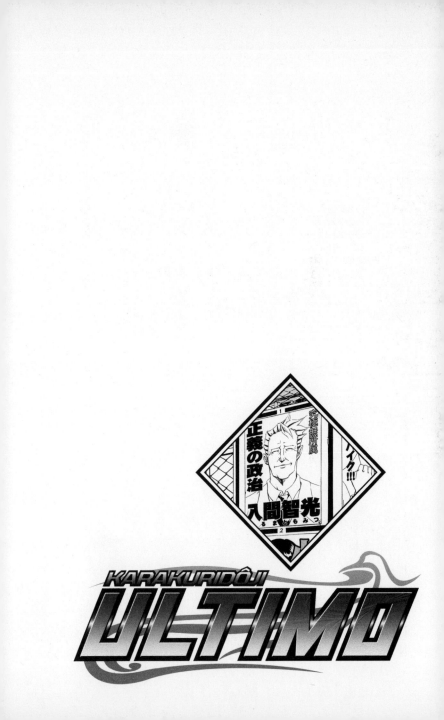

ACT 16 TIME TRAVELER YAMATO

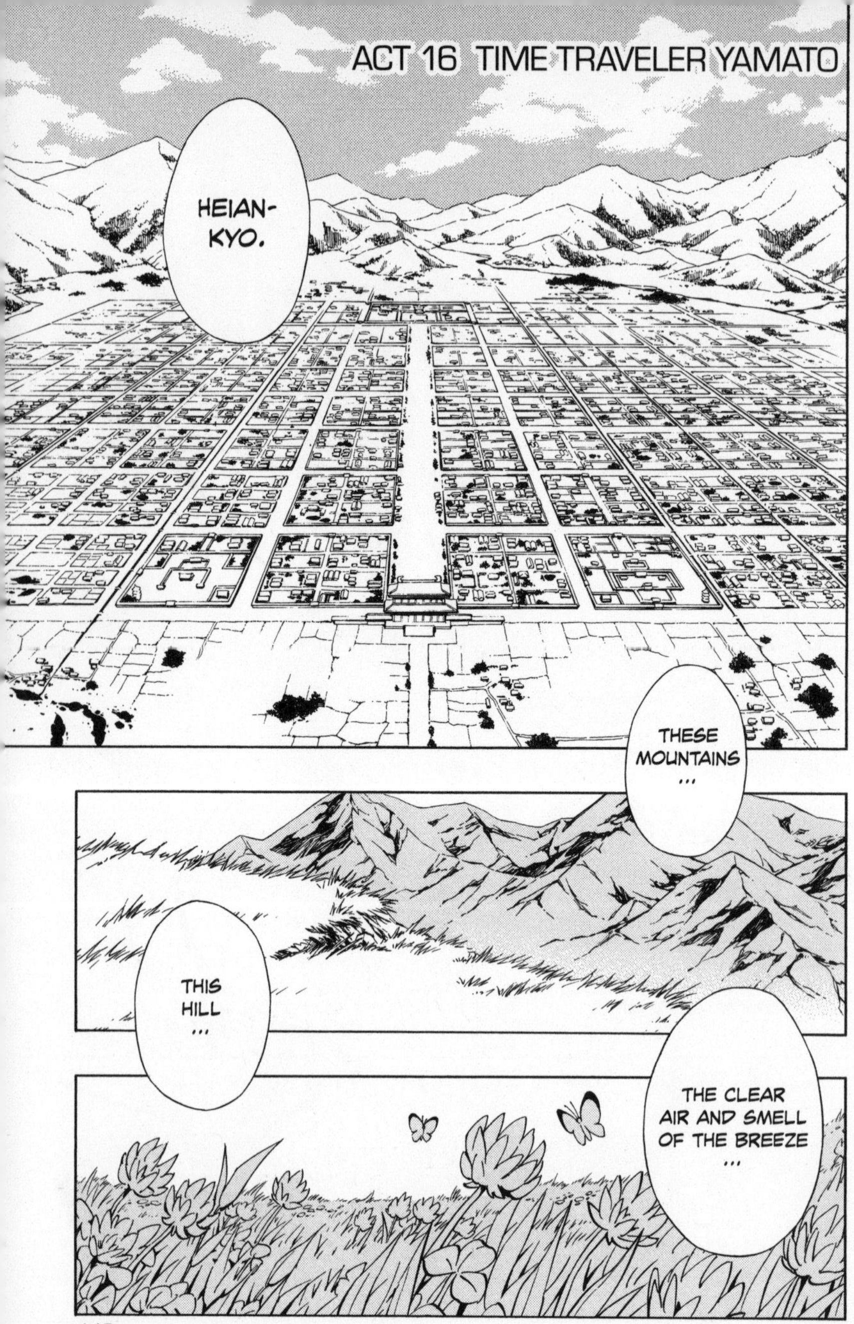
HEIAN-KYO.
THESE MOUNTAINS...
THIS HILL...
THE CLEAR AIR AND SMELL OF THE BREEZE...

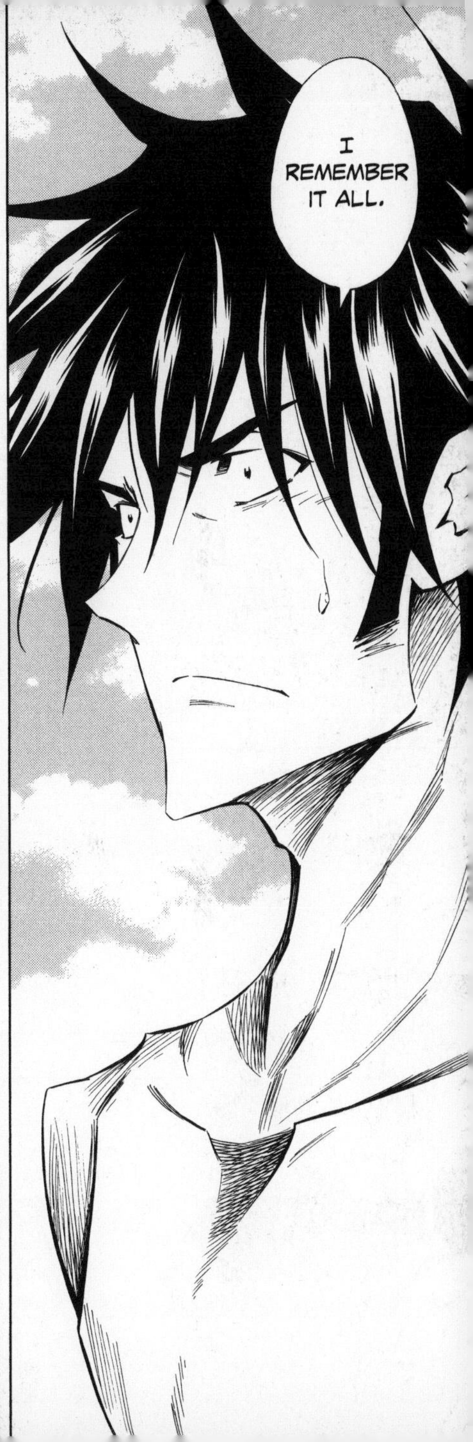
I REMEMBER IT ALL.
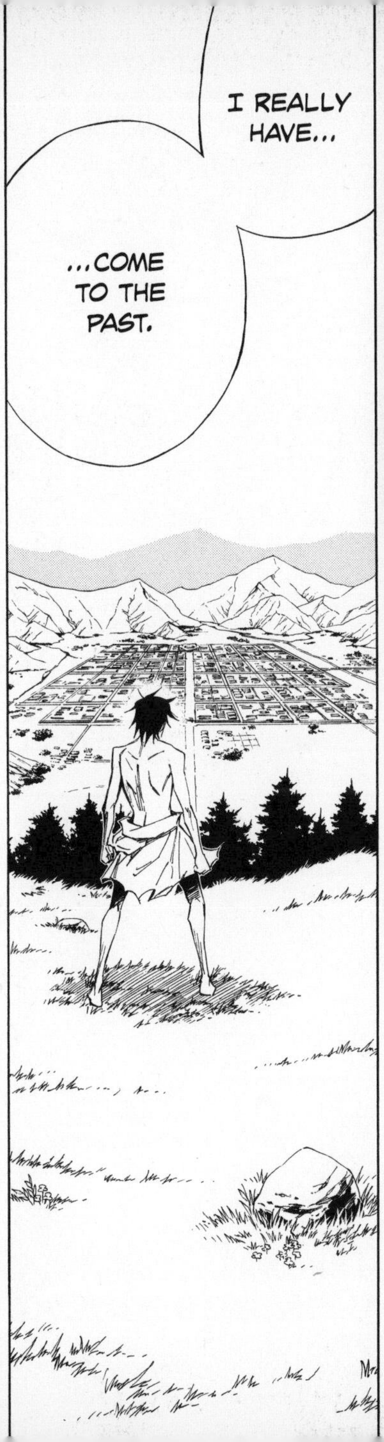
I REALLY HAVE...
...COME TO THE PAST.

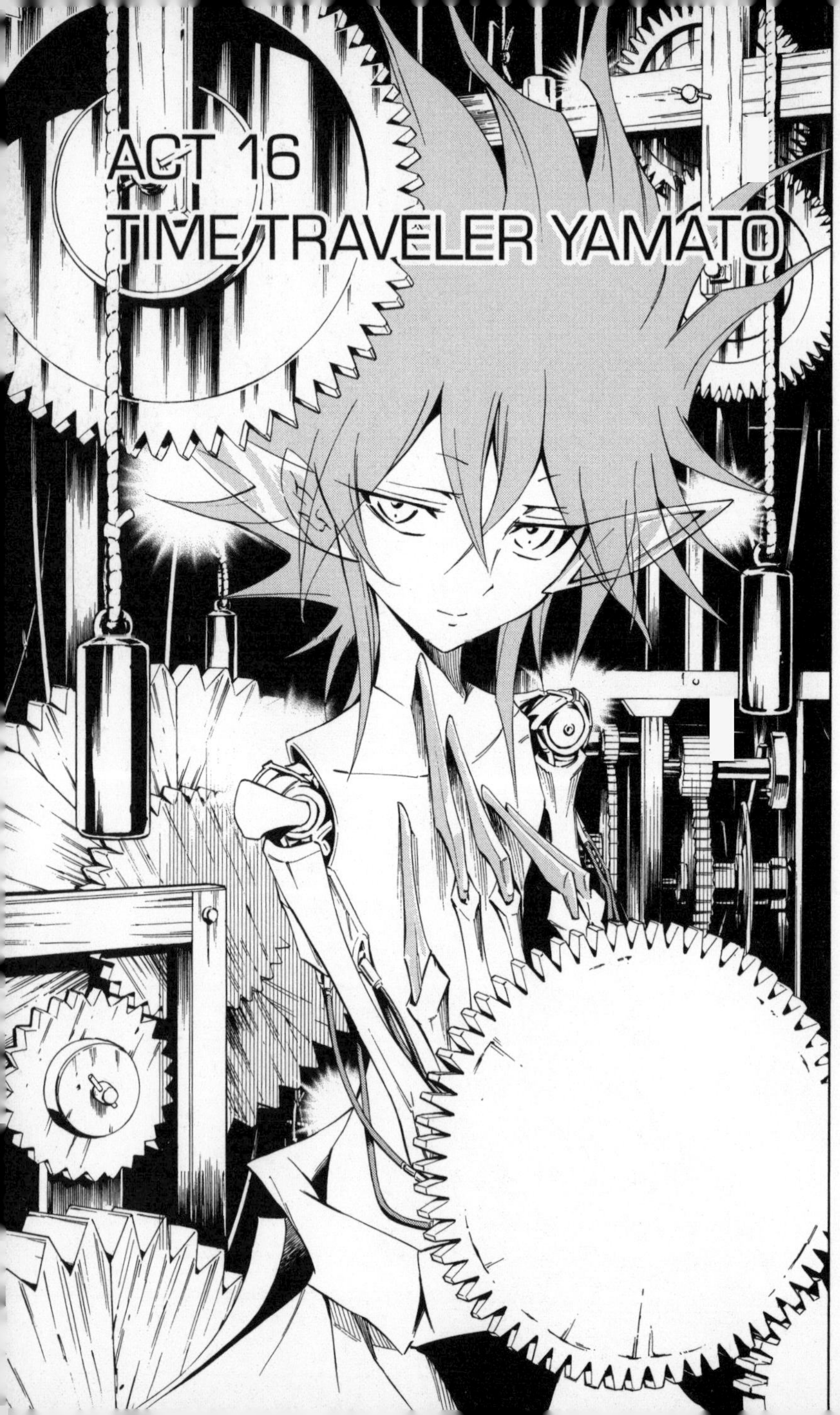
ACT 16
TIME TRAVELER YAMATO

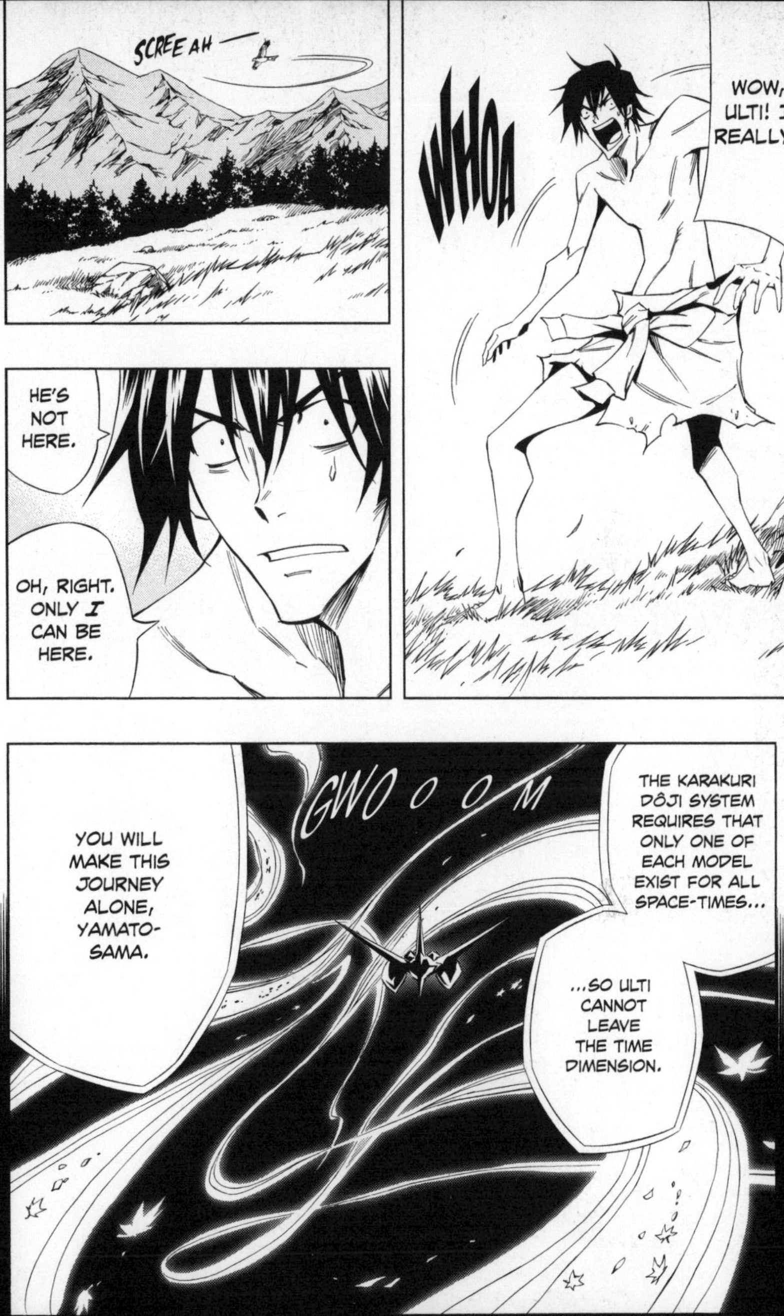
WHOA
WOW, ULTI! I REALLY--
SCREEAH
HE'S NOT HERE.
OH, RIGHT. ONLY I CAN BE HERE.
GWOOOM
THE KARAKURI DÔJI SYSTEM REQUIRES THAT ONLY ONE OF EACH MODEL EXIST FOR ALL SPACE-TIMES...
...SO ULTI CANNOT LEAVE THE TIME DIMENSION.
YOU WILL MAKE THIS JOURNEY ALONE, YAMATO-SAMA.

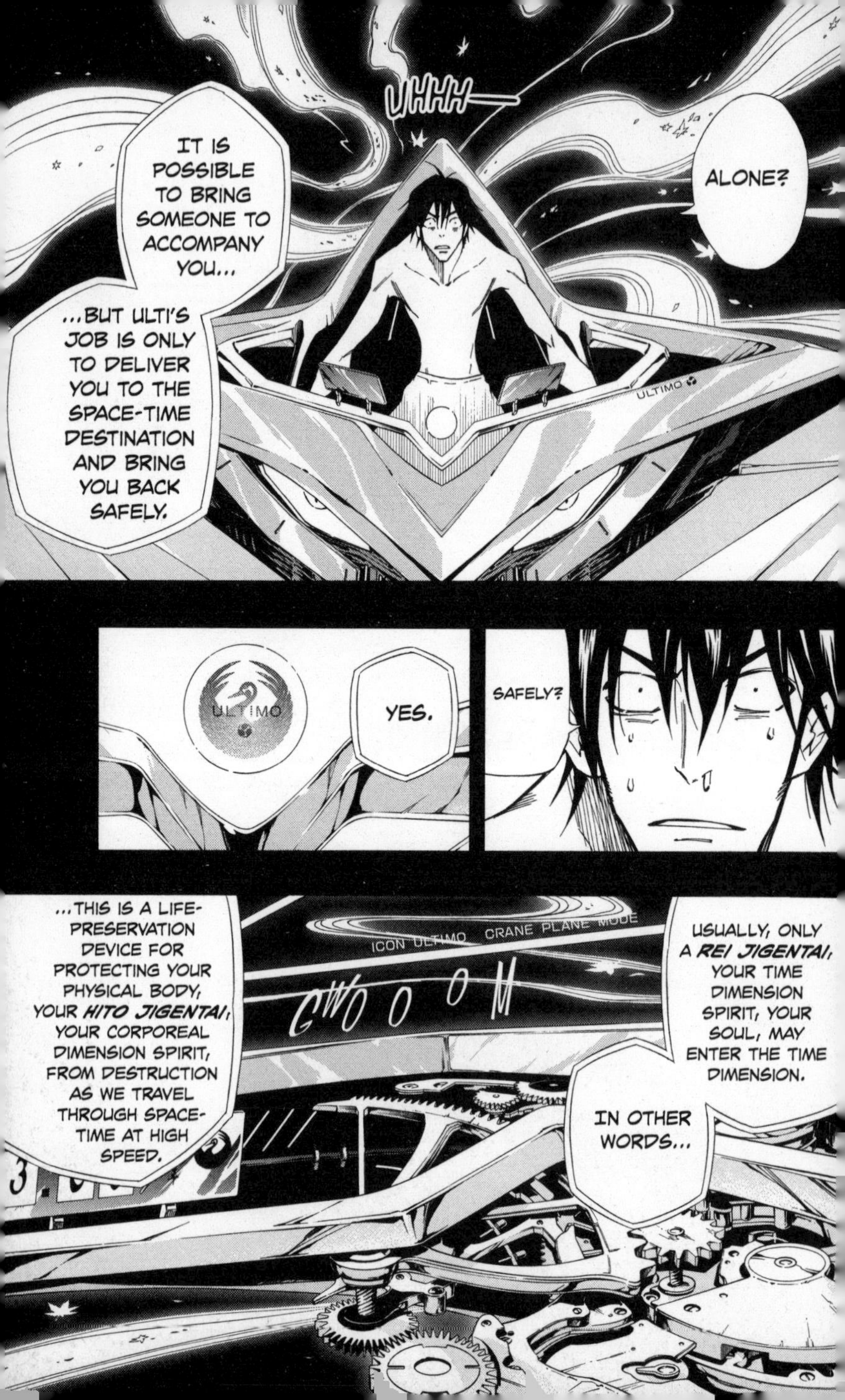
UHHH
ALONE?
IT IS POSSIBLE TO BRING SOMEONE TO ACCOMPANY YOU...
...BUT ULTI'S JOB IS ONLY TO DELIVER YOU TO THE SPACE-TIME DESTINATION AND BRING YOU BACK SAFELY.
ULTIMO
SAFELY?
YES.
ULTIMO
USUALLY, ONLY A *REI JIGENTAI*, YOUR TIME DIMENSION SPIRIT, YOUR SOUL, MAY ENTER THE TIME DIMENSION.
IN OTHER WORDS...
...THIS IS A LIFE-PRESERVATION DEVICE FOR PROTECTING YOUR PHYSICAL BODY, YOUR *HITO JIGENTAI*, YOUR CORPOREAL DIMENSION SPIRIT, FROM DESTRUCTION AS WE TRAVEL THROUGH SPACE-TIME AT HIGH SPEED.
ICON ULTIMO CRANE PLANE MODE
GWOOOM

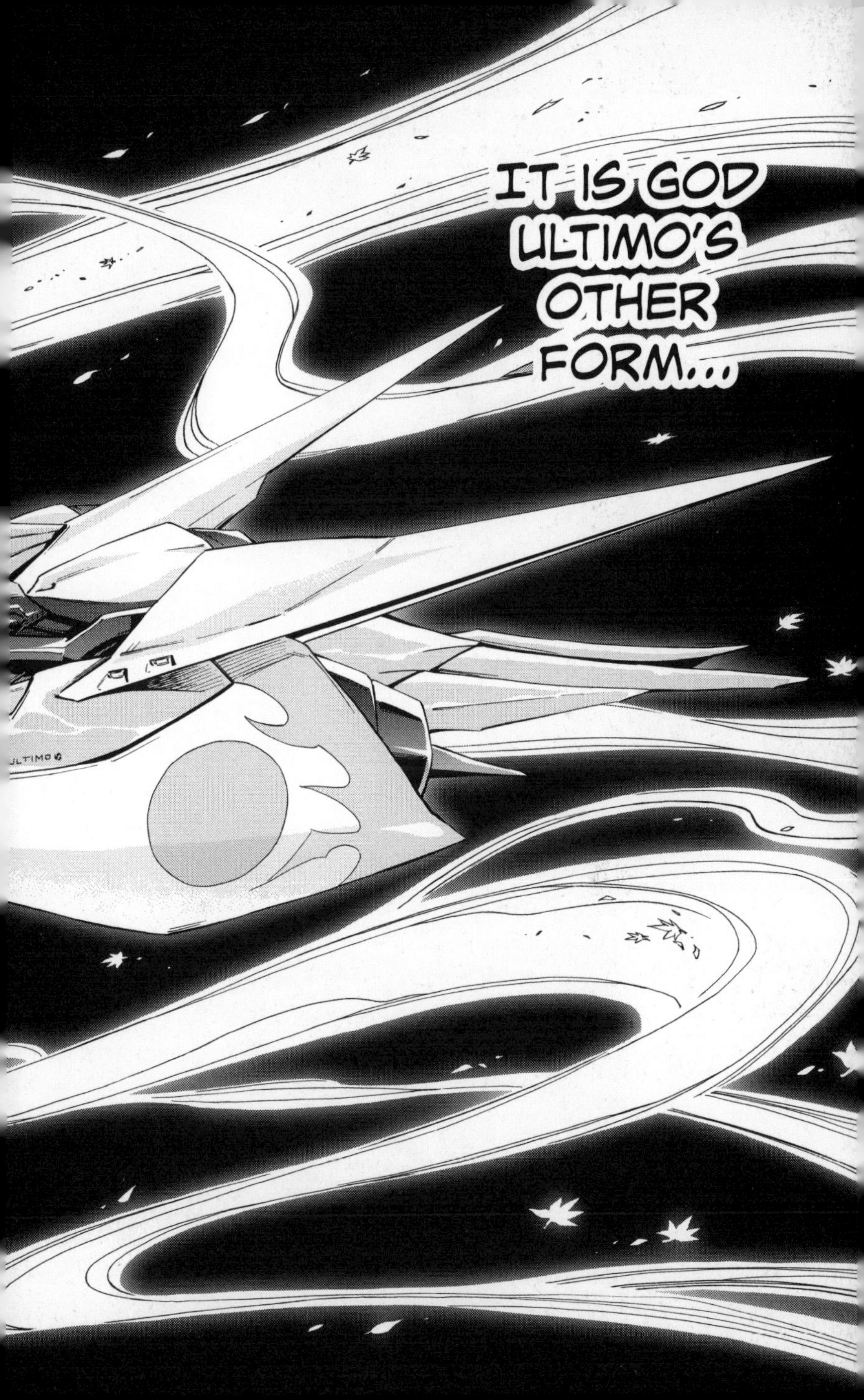
IT IS GOD ULTIMO'S OTHER FORM...

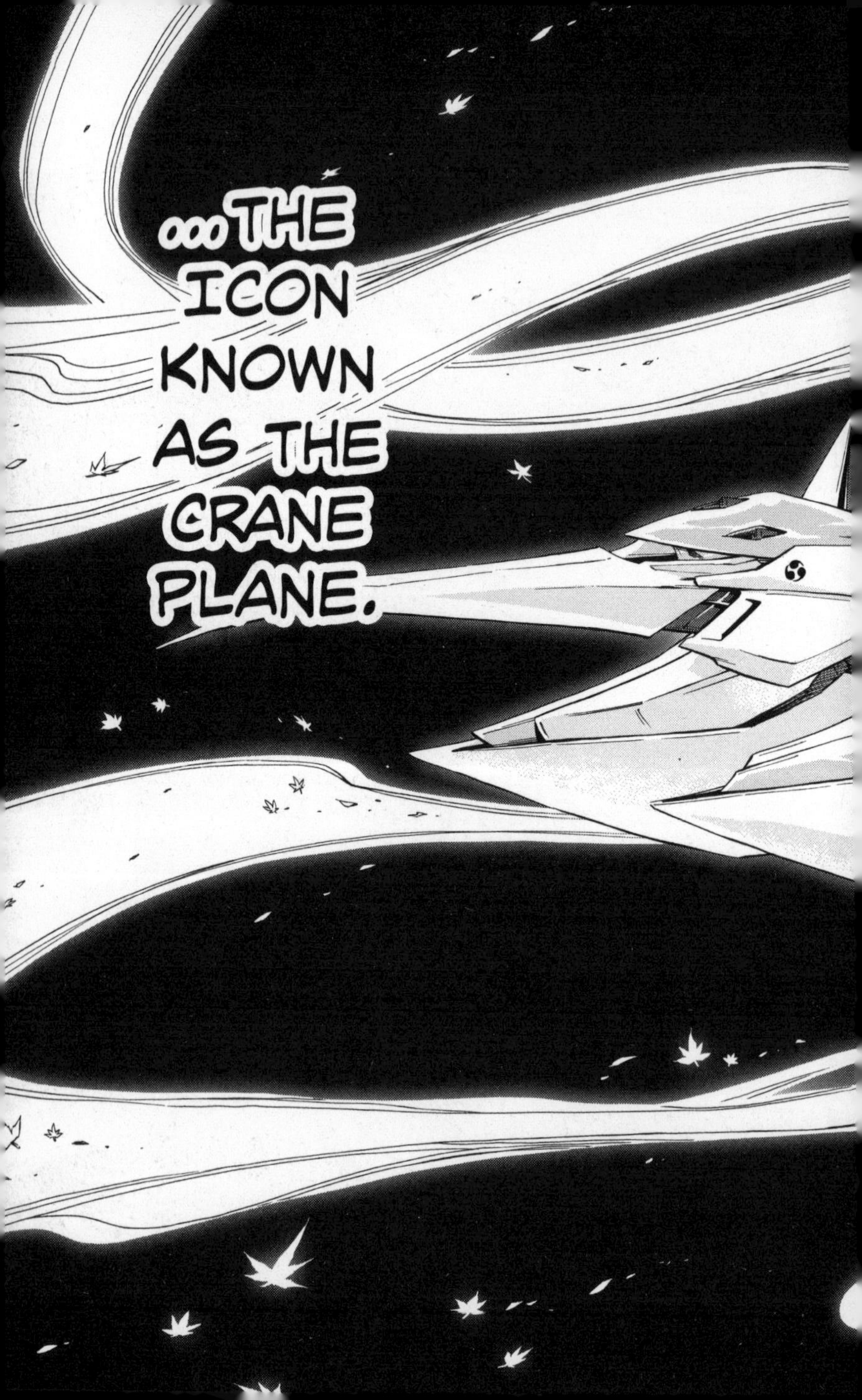
...THE ICON KNOWN AS THE CRANE PLANE.

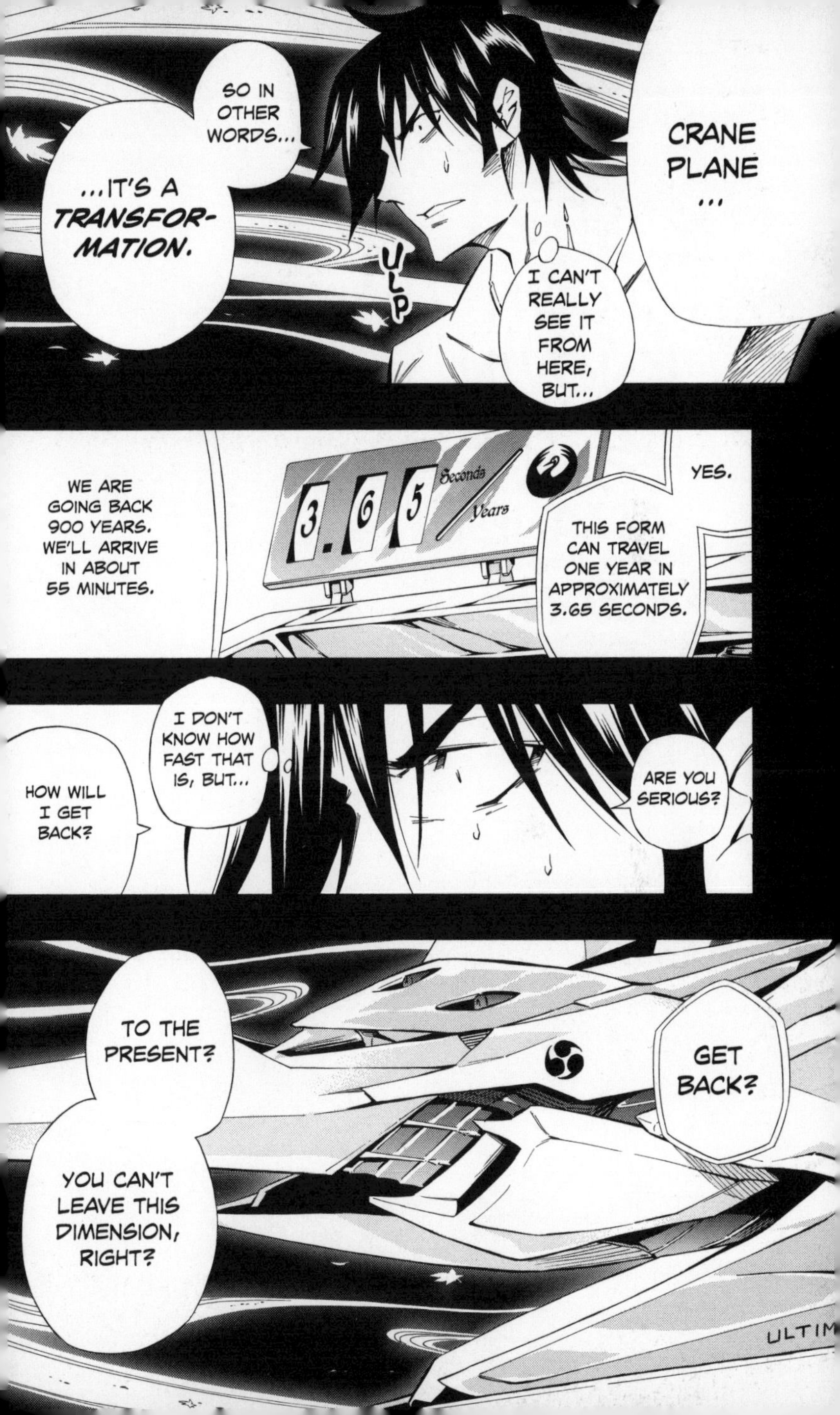
CRANE PLANE ...
I CAN'T REALLY SEE IT FROM HERE, BUT...
SO IN OTHER WORDS...
...IT'S A *TRANSFORMATION*.
ULP
YES.
THIS FORM CAN TRAVEL ONE YEAR IN APPROXIMATELY 3.65 SECONDS.
3.65
Seconds
Years
WE ARE GOING BACK 900 YEARS. WE'LL ARRIVE IN ABOUT 55 MINUTES.
ARE YOU SERIOUS?
I DON'T KNOW HOW FAST THAT IS, BUT...
HOW WILL I GET BACK?
GET BACK?
TO THE PRESENT?
YOU CAN'T LEAVE THIS DIMENSION, RIGHT?
ULTIM

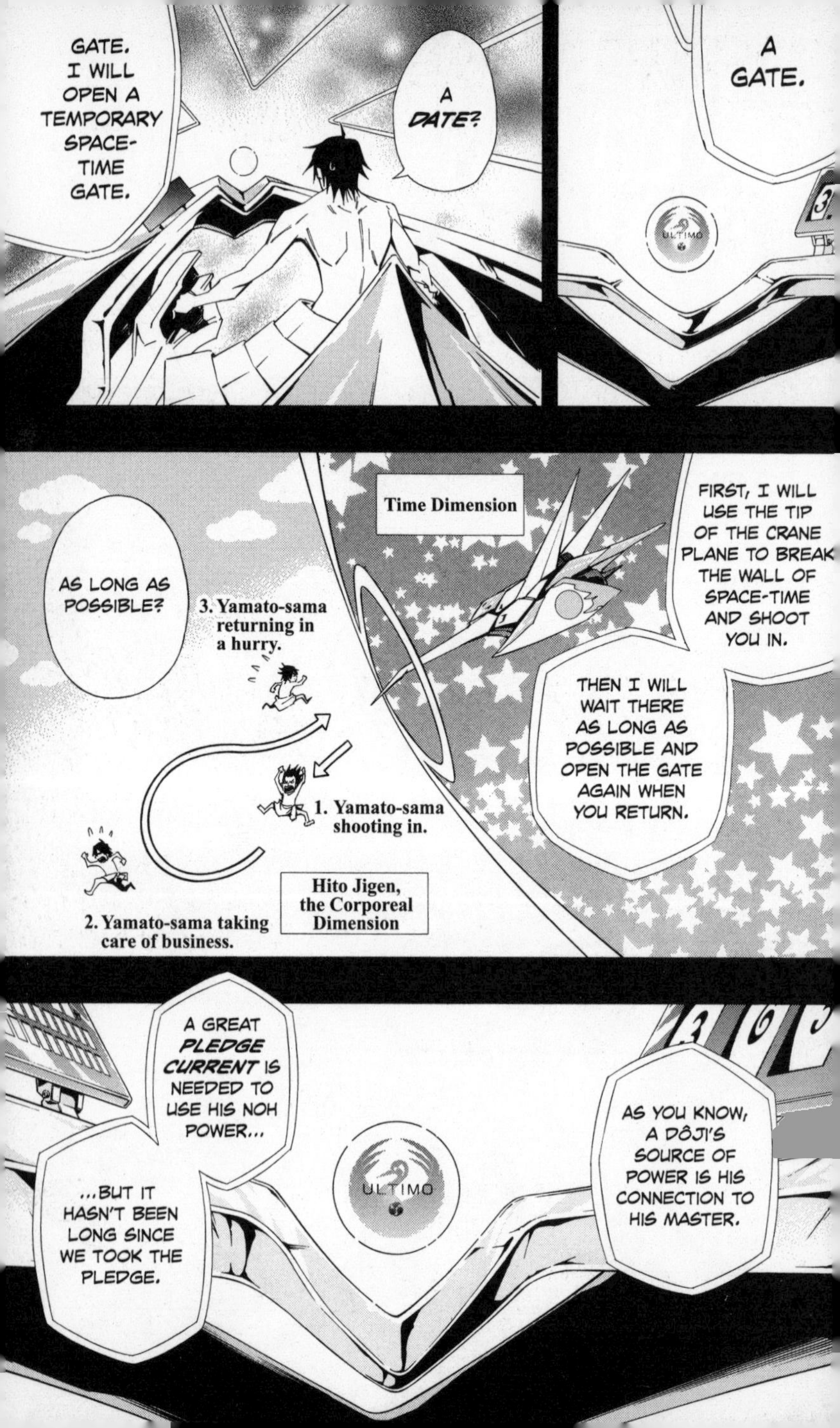
A GATE.
A DATE?
GATE. I WILL OPEN A TEMPORARY SPACE-TIME GATE.
ULTIMO
FIRST, I WILL USE THE TIP OF THE CRANE PLANE TO BREAK THE WALL OF SPACE-TIME AND SHOOT YOU IN.
THEN I WILL WAIT THERE AS LONG AS POSSIBLE AND OPEN THE GATE AGAIN WHEN YOU RETURN.
Time Dimension
1. Yamato-sama shooting in.
3. Yamato-sama returning in a hurry.
Hito Jigen, the Corporeal Dimension
2. Yamato-sama taking care of business.
AS LONG AS POSSIBLE?
AS YOU KNOW, A DÔJI'S SOURCE OF POWER IS HIS CONNECTION TO HIS MASTER.
A GREAT PLEDGE CURRENT IS NEEDED TO USE HIS NOH POWER...
...BUT IT HASN'T BEEN LONG SINCE WE TOOK THE PLEDGE.
ULTIMO

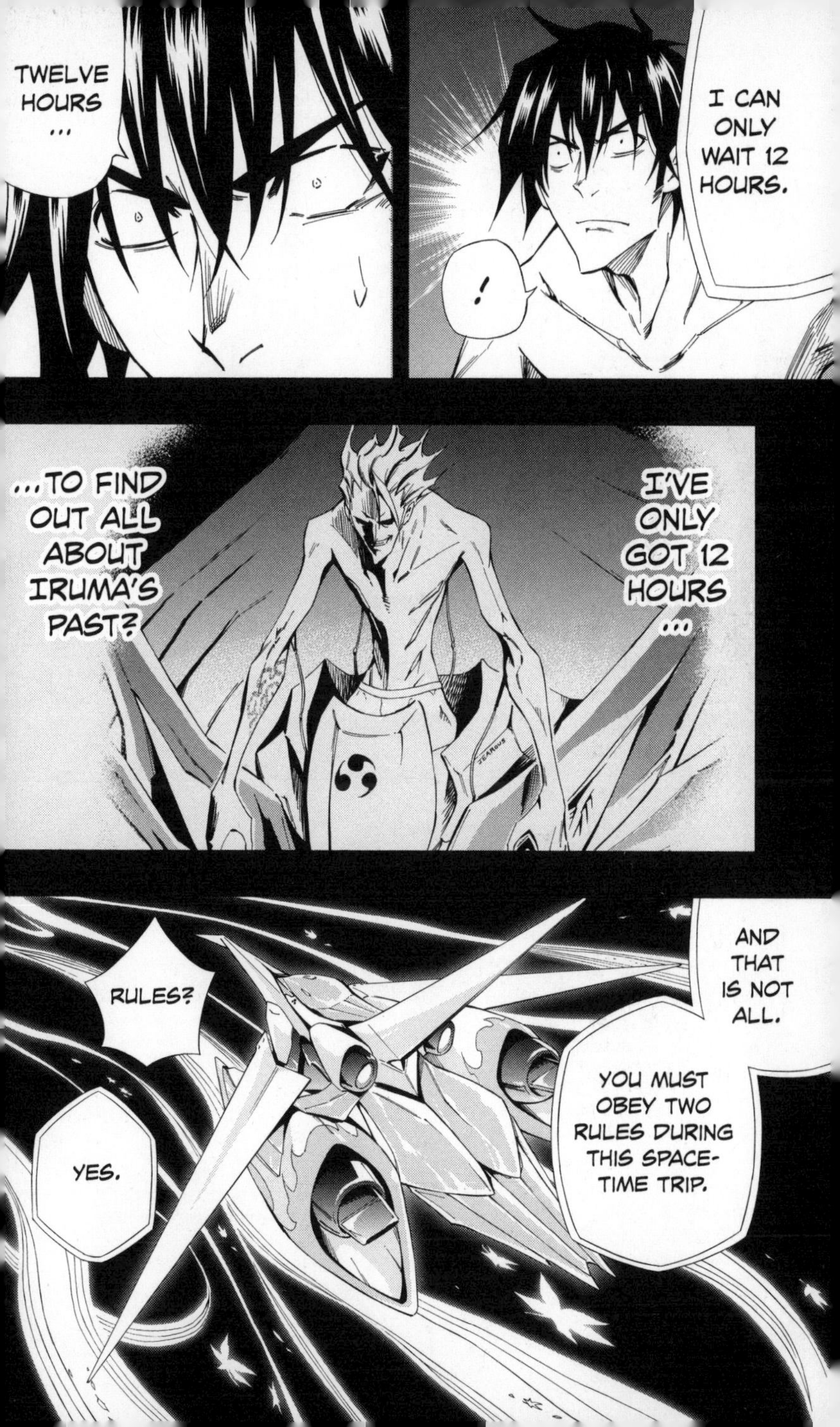
I CAN ONLY WAIT 12 HOURS.
!
TWELVE HOURS ...
I'VE ONLY GOT 12 HOURS ...
...TO FIND OUT ALL ABOUT IRUMA'S PAST?
AND THAT IS NOT ALL.
YOU MUST OBEY TWO RULES DURING THIS SPACE-TIME TRIP.
RULES?
YES.

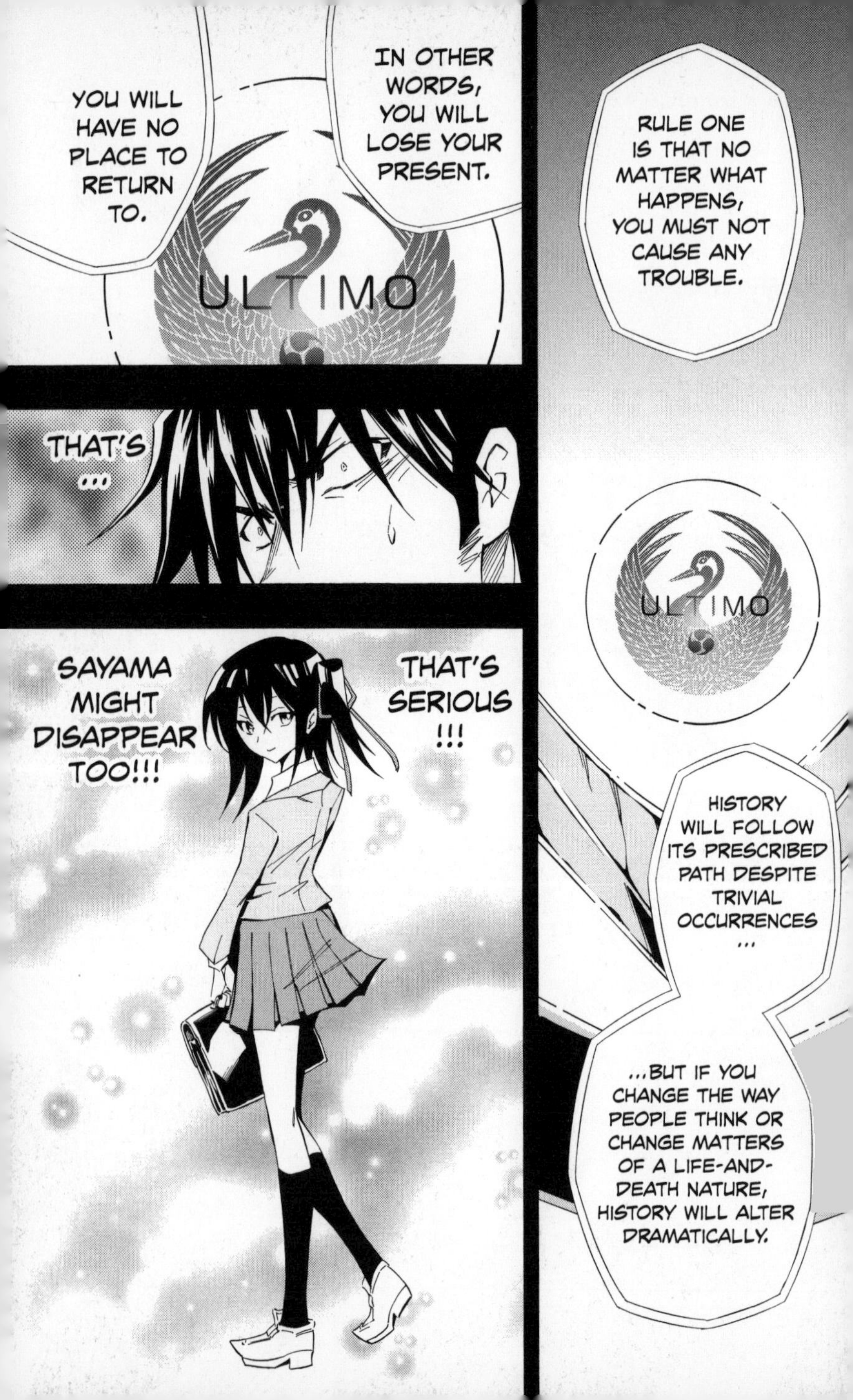
RULE ONE IS THAT NO MATTER WHAT HAPPENS, YOU MUST NOT CAUSE ANY TROUBLE.
ULTIMO
HISTORY WILL FOLLOW ITS PRESCRIBED PATH DESPITE TRIVIAL OCCURRENCES ...
...BUT IF YOU CHANGE THE WAY PEOPLE THINK OR CHANGE MATTERS OF A LIFE-AND-DEATH NATURE, HISTORY WILL ALTER DRAMATICALLY.
YOU WILL HAVE NO PLACE TO RETURN TO.
IN OTHER WORDS, YOU WILL LOSE YOUR PRESENT.
ULTIMO
THAT'S ...
THAT'S SERIOUS !!!
SAYAMA MIGHT DISAPPEAR TOO!!!

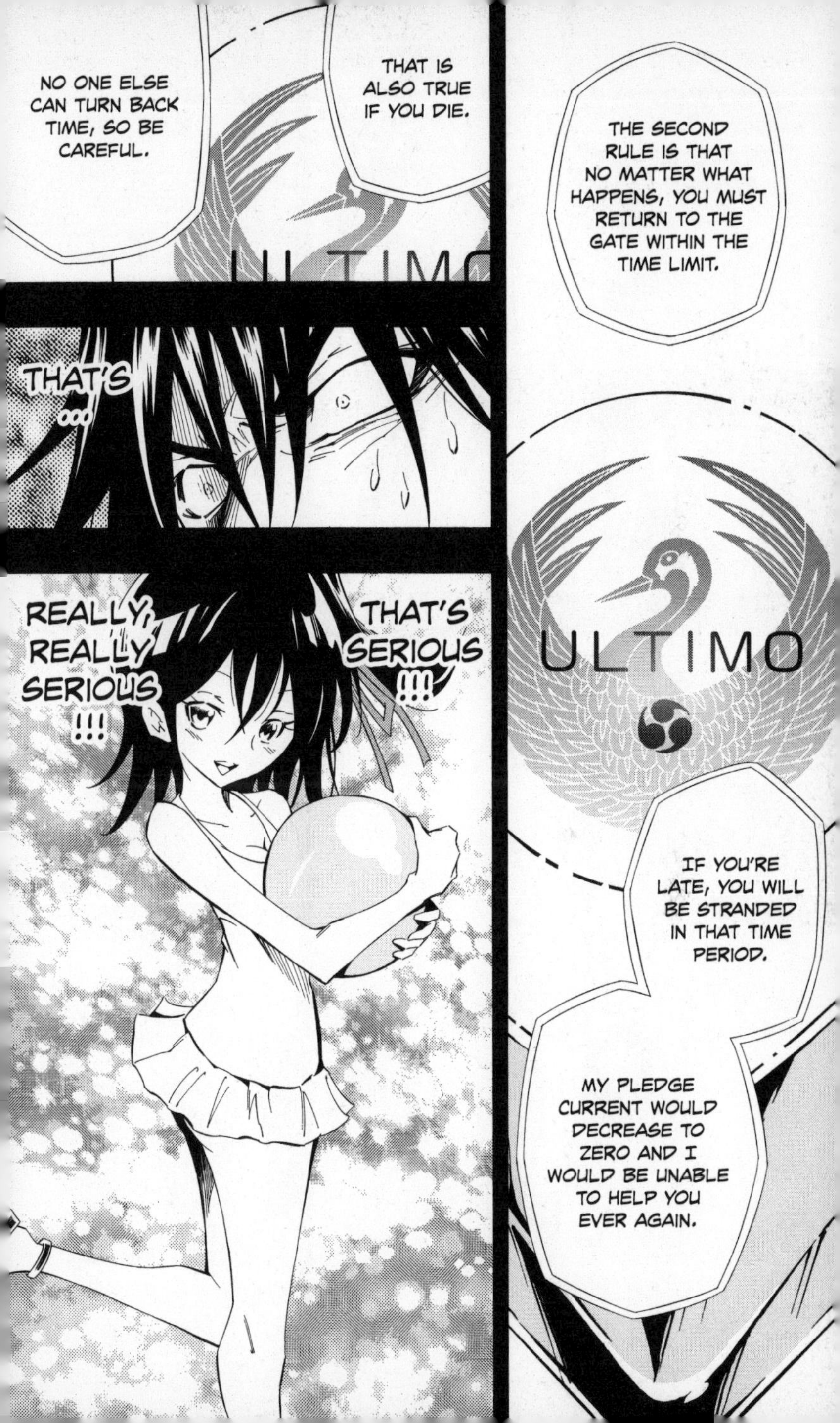
THE SECOND RULE IS THAT NO MATTER WHAT HAPPENS, YOU MUST RETURN TO THE GATE WITHIN THE TIME LIMIT.
ULTIMO
IF YOU'RE LATE, YOU WILL BE STRANDED IN THAT TIME PERIOD.
MY PLEDGE CURRENT WOULD DECREASE TO ZERO AND I WOULD BE UNABLE TO HELP YOU EVER AGAIN.
THAT IS ALSO TRUE IF YOU DIE.
NO ONE ELSE CAN TURN BACK TIME, SO BE CAREFUL.
THAT'S ...
THAT'S SERIOUS!!!
REALLY, REALLY SERIOUS!!!

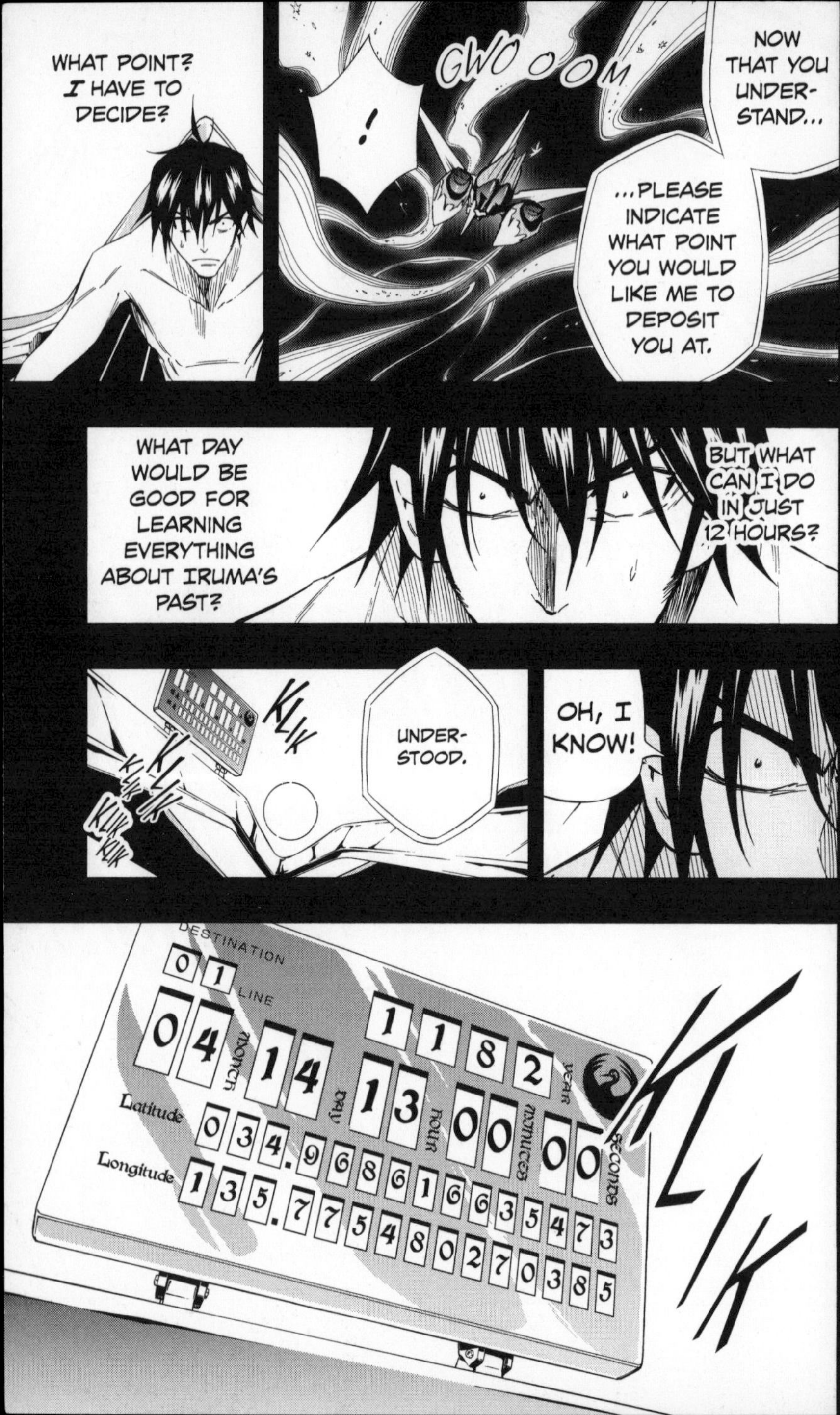
GWOOOOM
NOW THAT YOU UNDER-STAND...
...PLEASE INDICATE WHAT POINT YOU WOULD LIKE ME TO DEPOSIT YOU AT.
!
WHAT POINT? I HAVE TO DECIDE?
BUT WHAT CAN I DO IN JUST 12 HOURS?
WHAT DAY WOULD BE GOOD FOR LEARNING EVERYTHING ABOUT IRUMA'S PAST?
OH, I KNOW!
UNDER-STOOD.
KLIK
KLIK KLIK KLIK KLIK KLIK
DESTINATION
01
LINE
04 MONTH
14 DAY
1182 YEAR
13 HOUR
00 MINUTES
00 SECONDS
Latitude 034.96861663547 3
Longitude 135.77548027038 5
KLIK

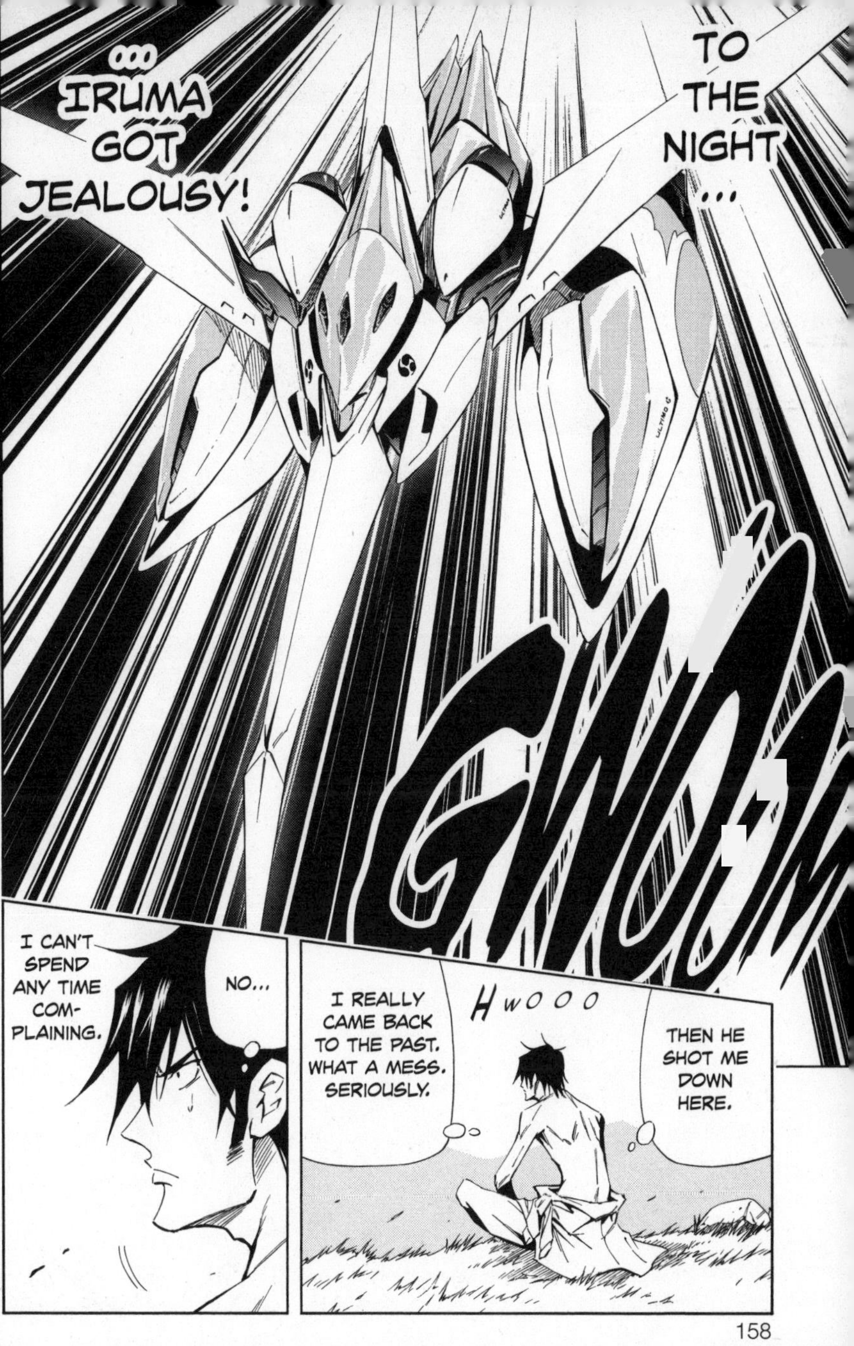
TO THE NIGHT...
...IRUMA GOT JEALOUSY!
THEN HE SHOT ME DOWN HERE.
HWOOO
I REALLY CAME BACK TO THE PAST. WHAT A MESS. SERIOUSLY.
NO...
I CAN'T SPEND ANY TIME COMPLAINING.

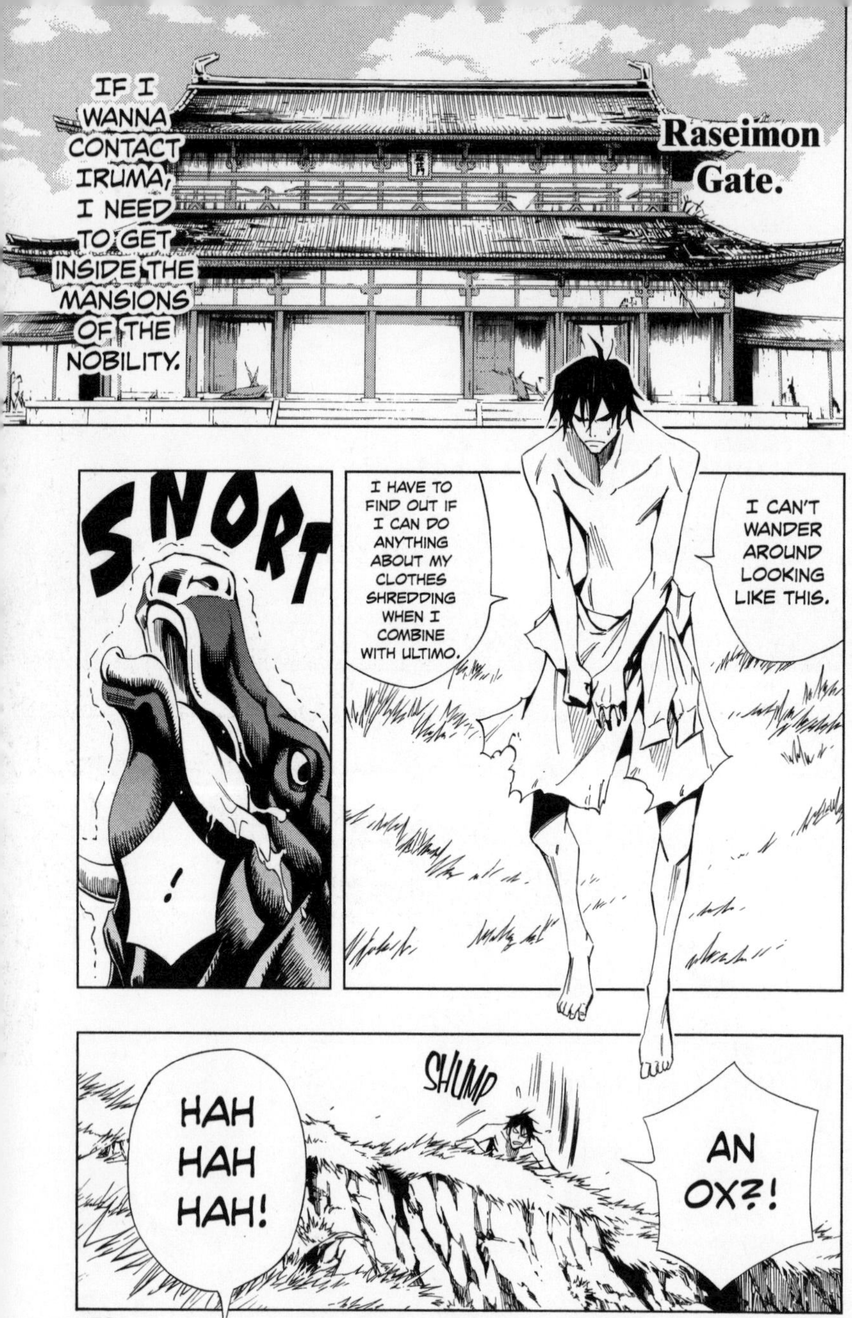
Raseimon Gate.
IF I WANNA CONTACT IRUMA, I NEED TO GET INSIDE THE MANSIONS OF THE NOBILITY.
I CAN'T WANDER AROUND LOOKING LIKE THIS.
I HAVE TO FIND OUT IF I CAN DO ANYTHING ABOUT MY CLOTHES SHREDDING WHEN I COMBINE WITH ULTIMO.
SNORT
!
AN OX?!
SHUMP
HAH HAH HAH!

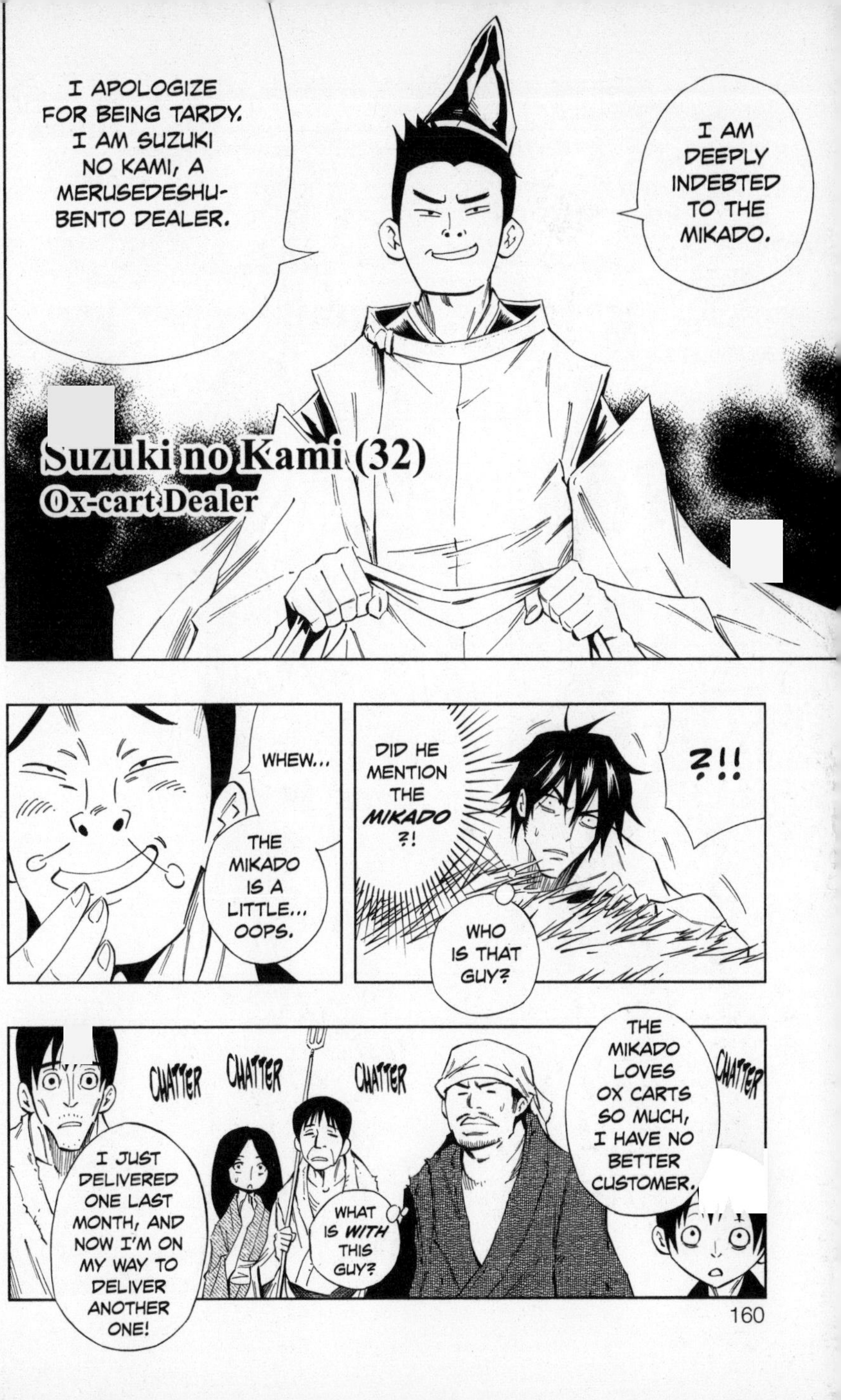
I APOLOGIZE FOR BEING TARDY. I AM SUZUKI NO KAMI, A MERUSEDESHU-BENTO DEALER.
I AM DEEPLY INDEBTED TO THE MIKADO.
Suzuki no Kami (32)
Ox-cart Dealer
?!!
DID HE MENTION THE *MIKADO*?!
WHO IS THAT GUY?
WHEW...
THE MIKADO IS A LITTLE... OOPS.
CHATTER
THE MIKADO LOVES OX CARTS SO MUCH, I HAVE NO BETTER CUSTOMER.
CHATTER
WHAT IS *WITH* THIS GUY?
CHATTER
CHATTER
I JUST DELIVERED ONE LAST MONTH, AND NOW I'M ON MY WAY TO DELIVER ANOTHER ONE!

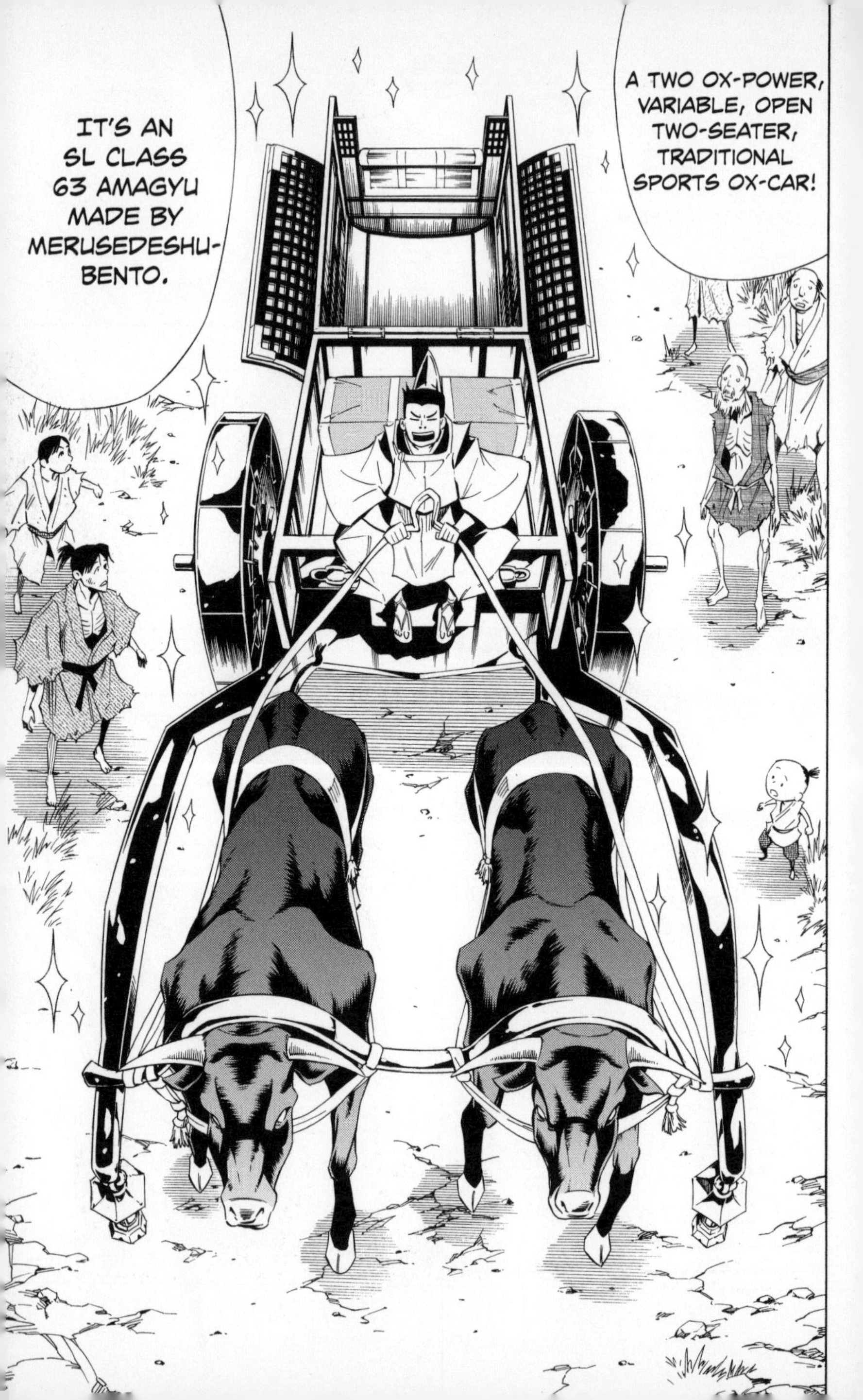
A TWO OX-POWER, VARIABLE, OPEN TWO-SEATER, TRADITIONAL SPORTS OX-CAR!
IT'S AN SL CLASS 63 AMAGYU MADE BY MERUSEDESHU-BENTO.

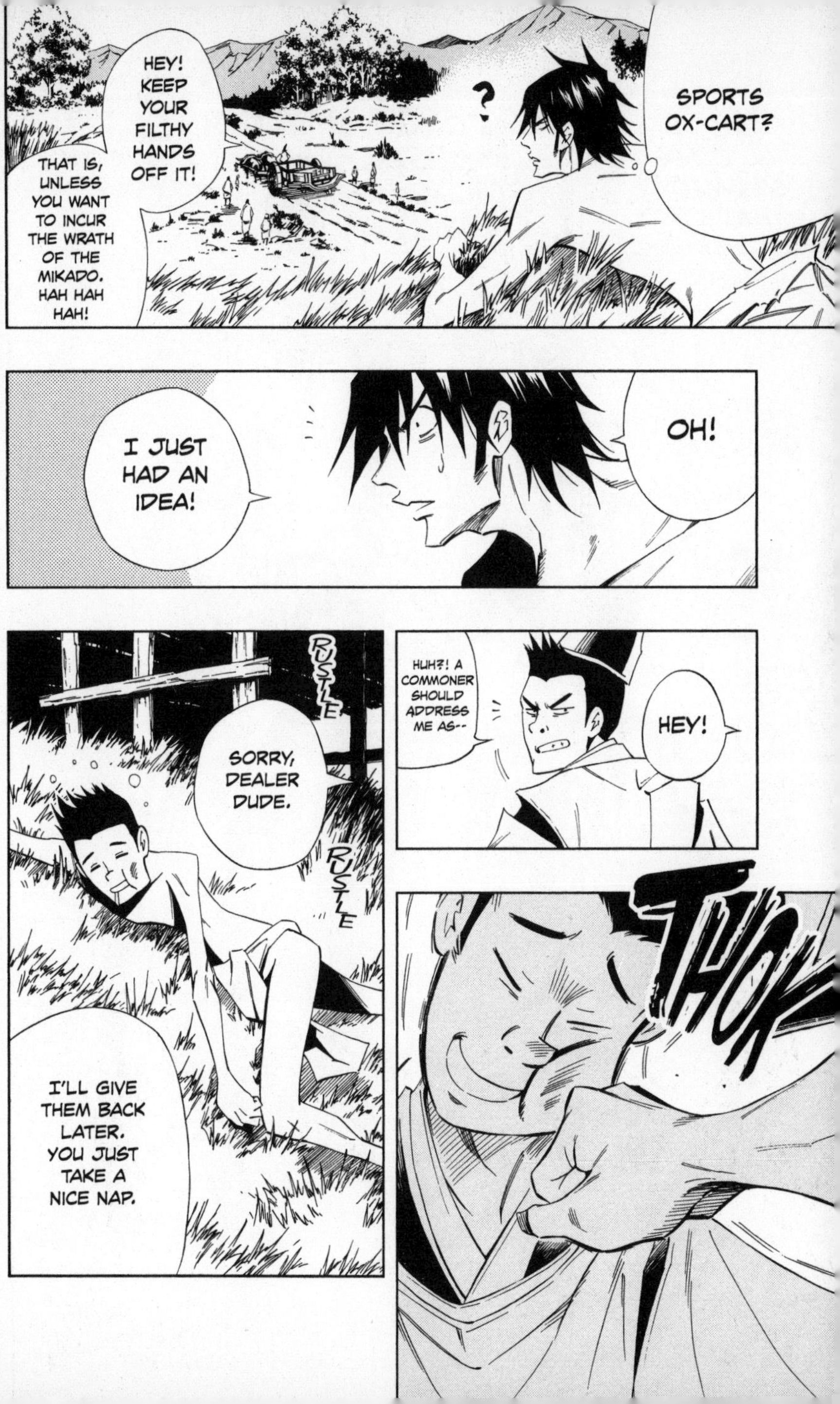
SPORTS OX-CART?
HEY! KEEP YOUR FILTHY HANDS OFF IT!
THAT IS, UNLESS YOU WANT TO INCUR THE WRATH OF THE MIKADO. HAH HAH HAH!
OH!
I JUST HAD AN IDEA!
HEY!
HUH?! A COMMONER SHOULD ADDRESS ME AS--
THOK
RUSTLE
SORRY, DEALER DUDE.
RUSTLE
I'LL GIVE THEM BACK LATER. YOU JUST TAKE A NICE NAP.

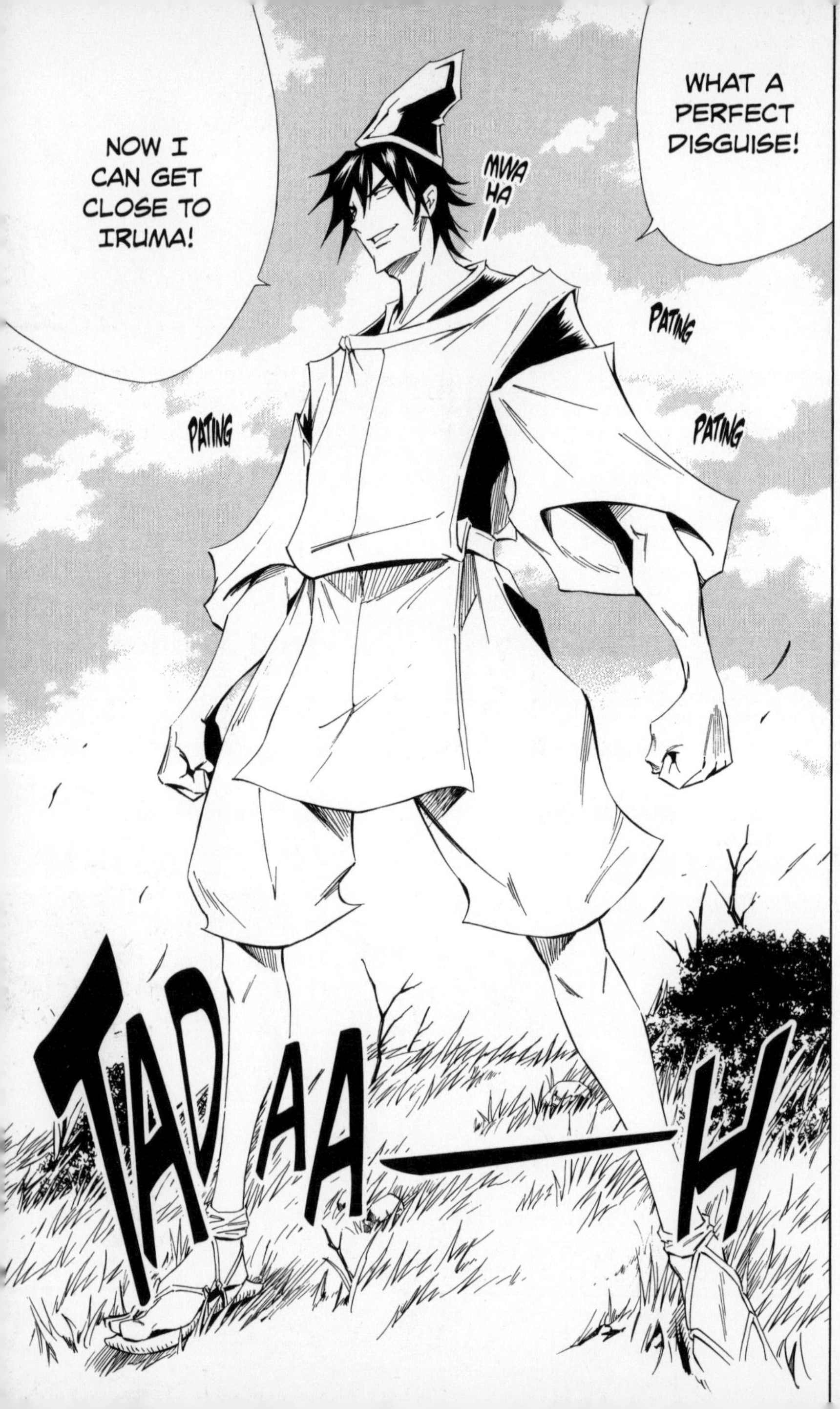
WHAT A PERFECT DISGUISE!
MWA HA
NOW I CAN GET CLOSE TO IRUMA!
PATING
PATING
PATING
TADAA—H

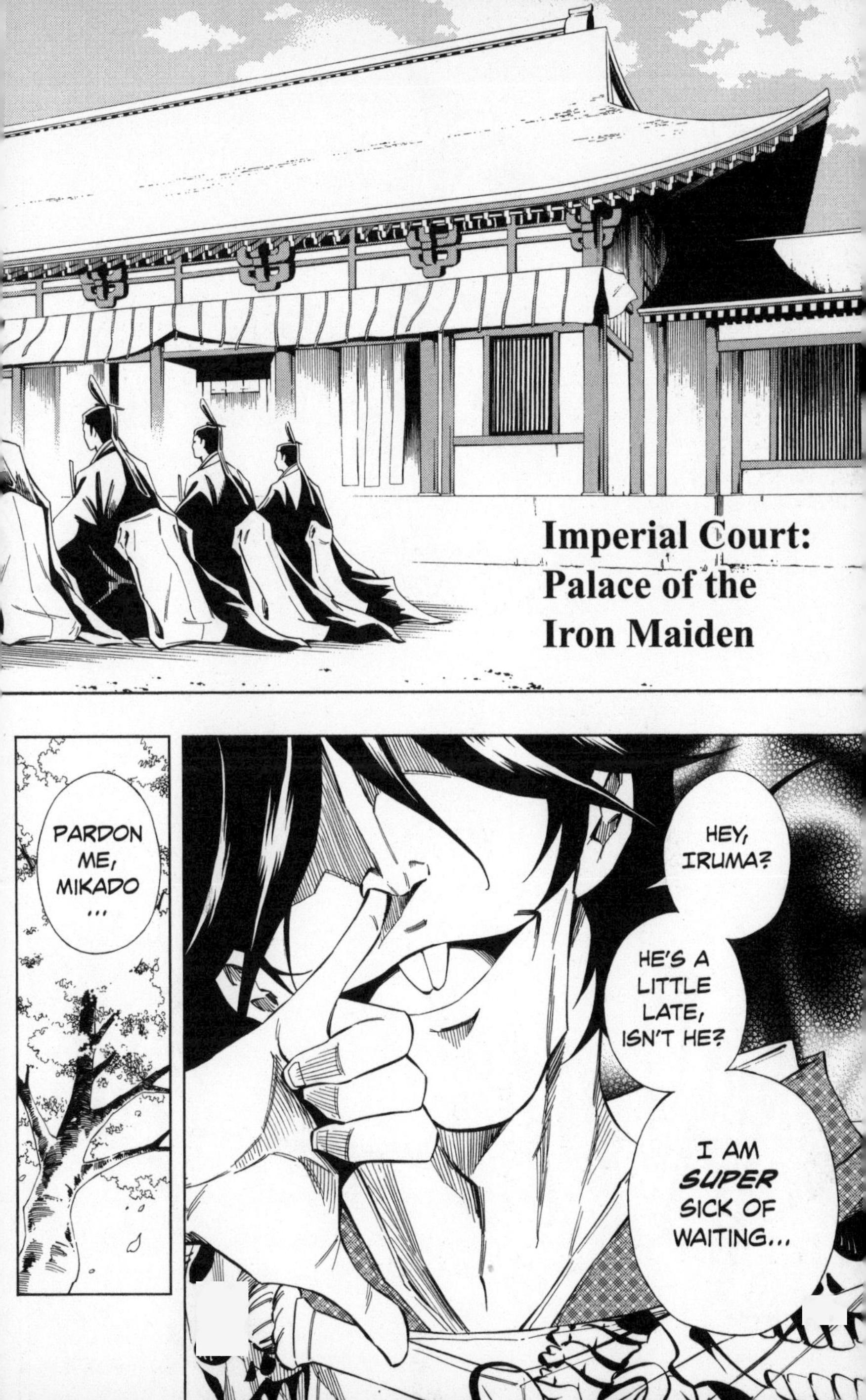
Imperial Court: Palace of the Iron Maiden
HEY, IRUMA?
HE'S A LITTLE LATE, ISN'T HE?
I AM *SUPER* SICK OF WAITING...
PARDON ME, MIKADO...

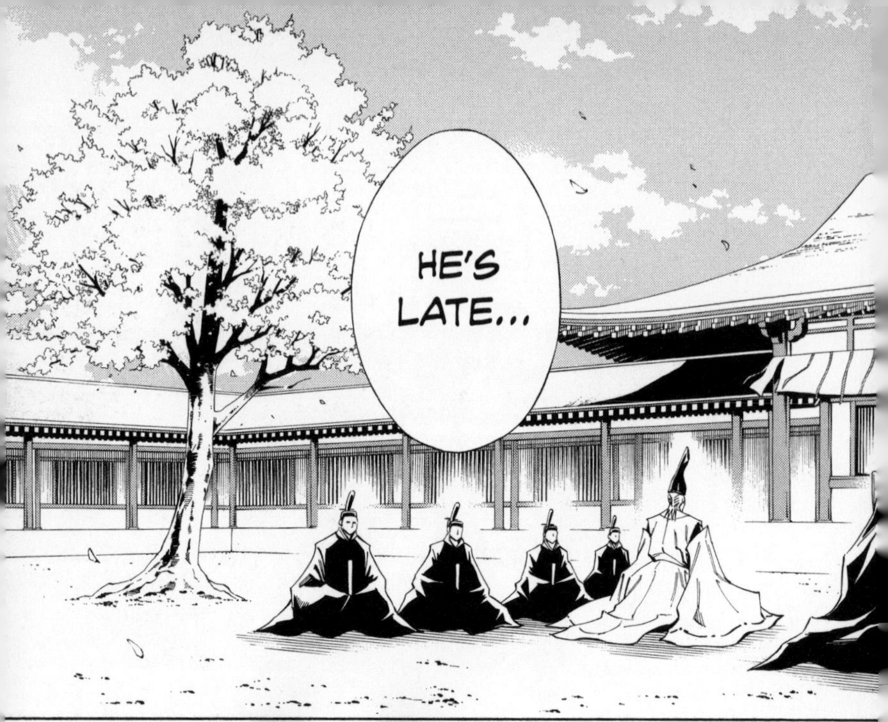
HE'S LATE...

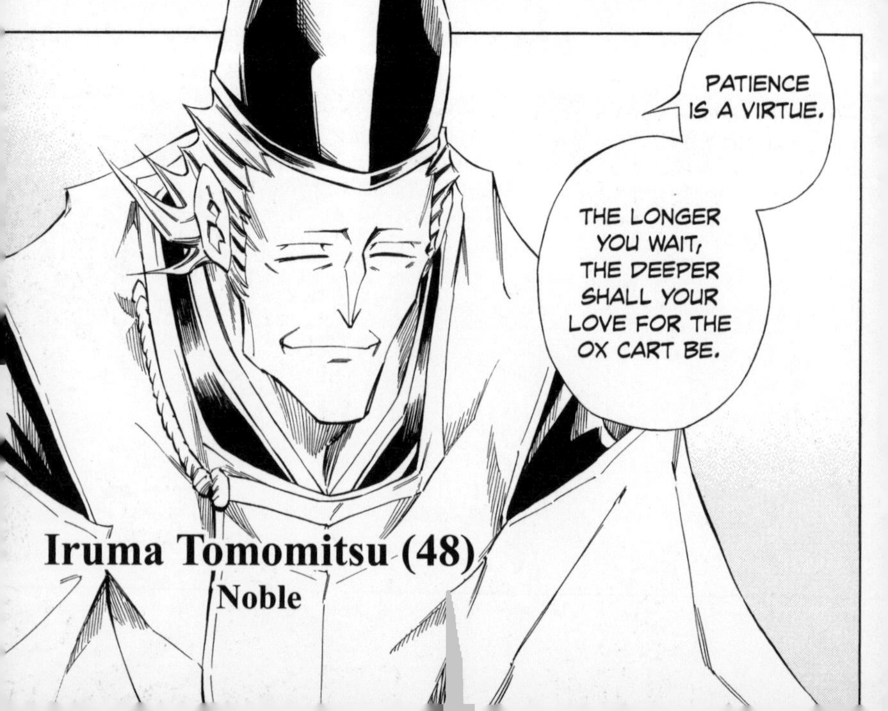
PATIENCE IS A VIRTUE.
THE LONGER YOU WAIT, THE DEEPER SHALL YOUR LOVE FOR THE OX CART BE.
Iruma Tomomitsu (48)
Noble

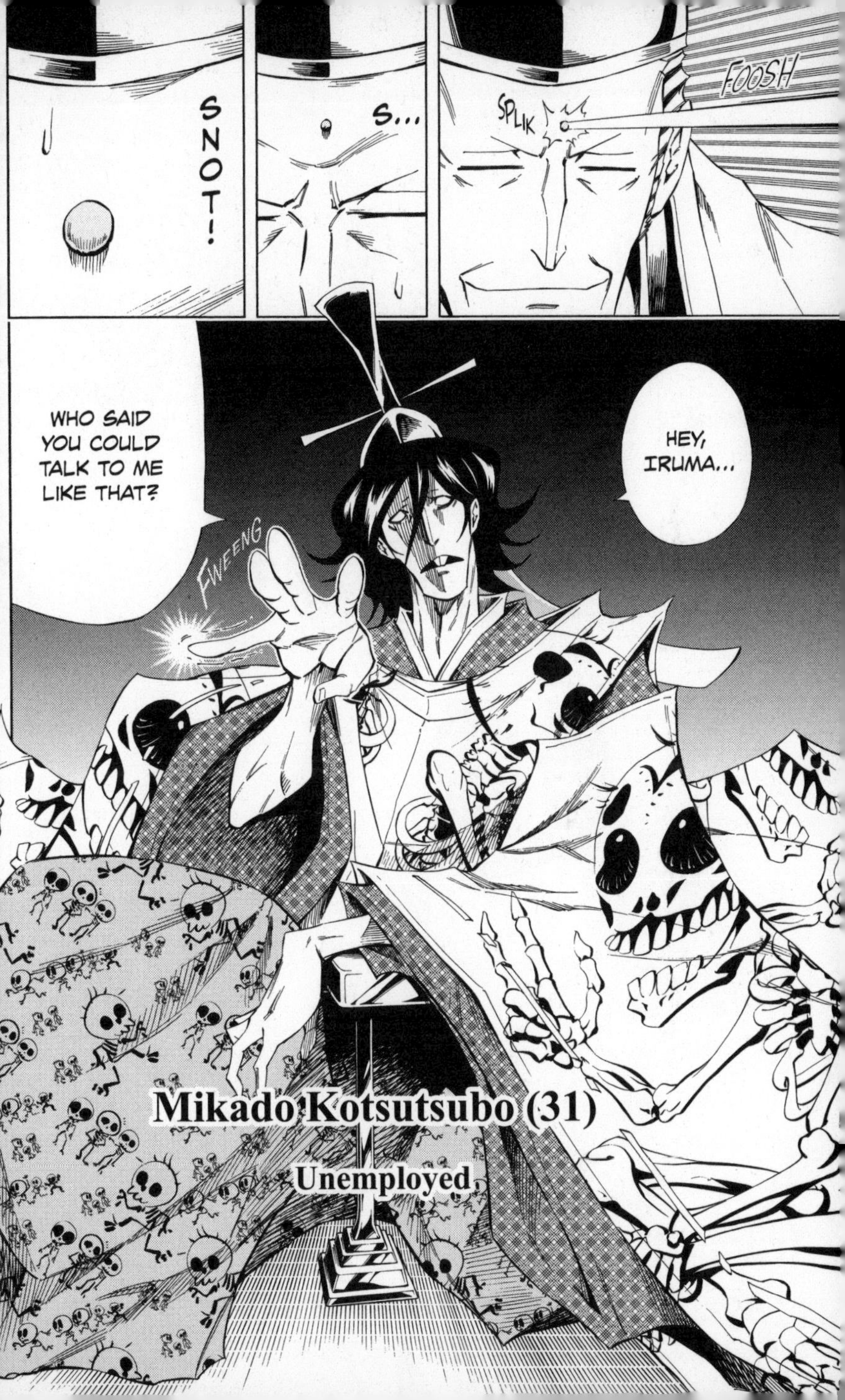
FOOSH
SPLIK
S...
SNOT!
HEY, IRUMA...
WHO SAID YOU COULD TALK TO ME LIKE THAT?
FWEENG
Mikado Kotsutsubo (31)
Unemployed

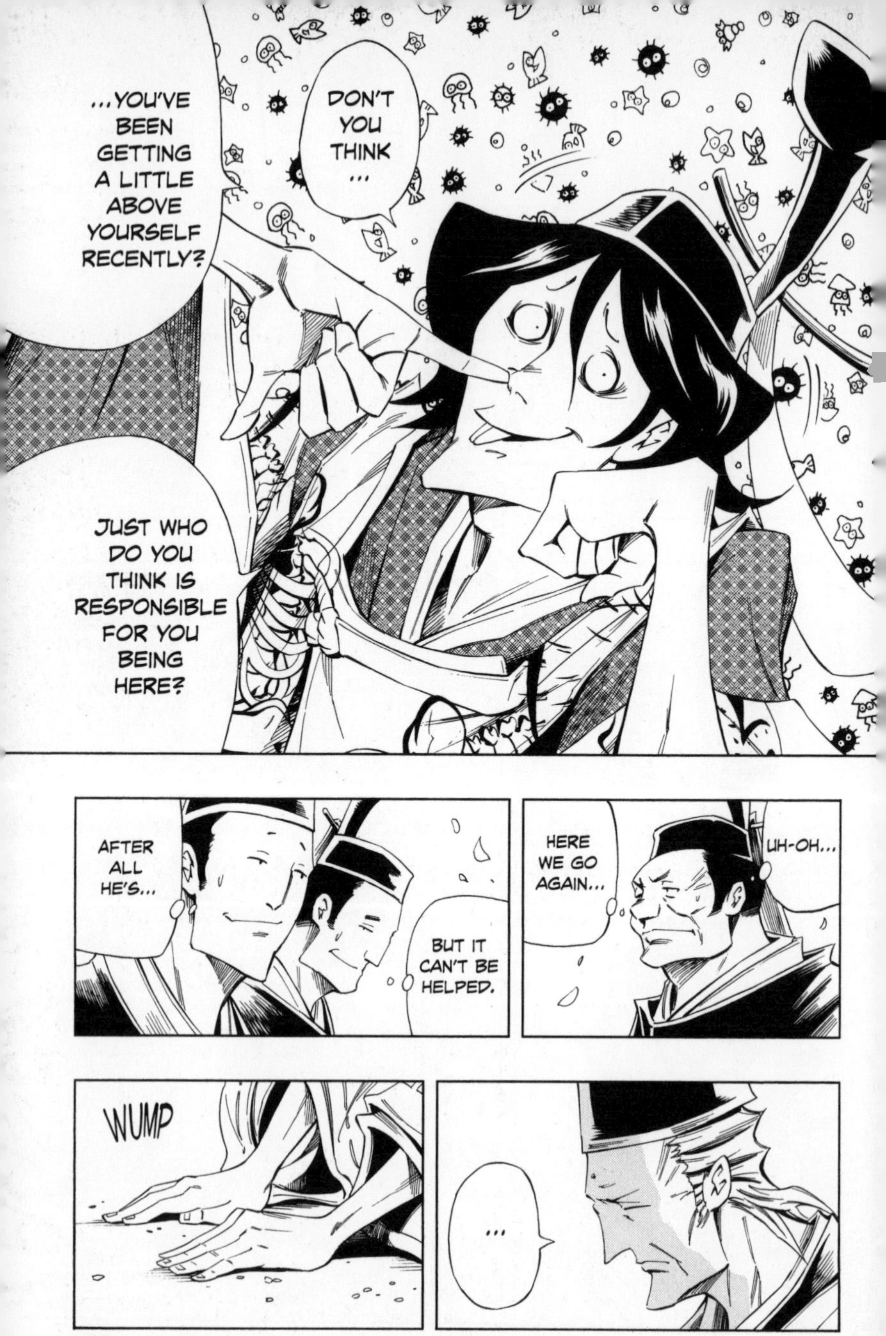
DON'T YOU THINK ...
...YOU'VE BEEN GETTING A LITTLE ABOVE YOURSELF RECENTLY?
JUST WHO DO YOU THINK IS RESPONSIBLE FOR YOU BEING HERE?
UH-OH...
HERE WE GO AGAIN...
BUT IT CAN'T BE HELPED.
AFTER ALL HE'S...
...
WUMP

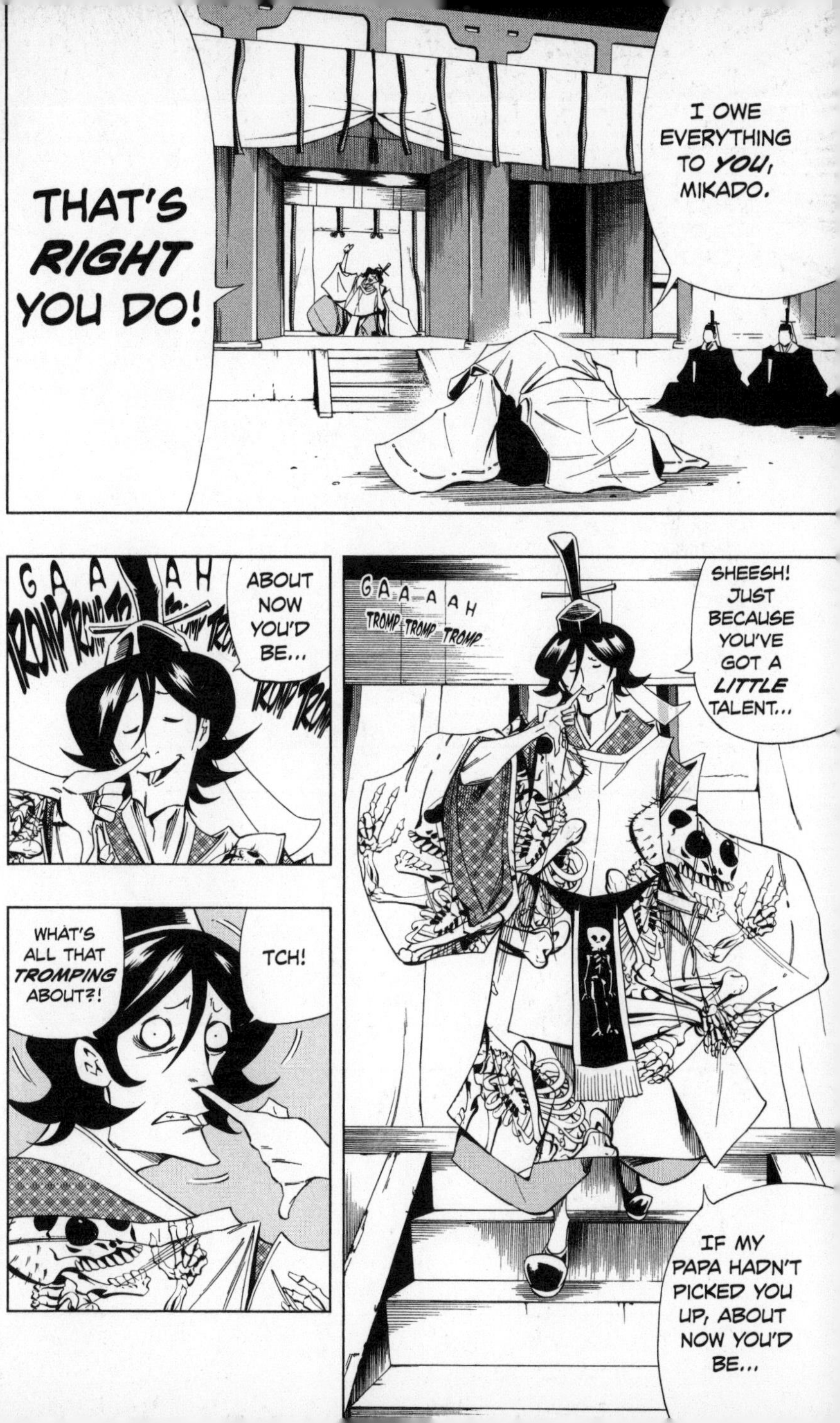
I OWE EVERYTHING TO YOU, MIKADO.
THAT'S RIGHT YOU DO!
GAAAAAH
TROMP TROMP TROMP
SHEESH! JUST BECAUSE YOU'VE GOT A LITTLE TALENT...
IF MY PAPA HADN'T PICKED YOU UP, ABOUT NOW YOU'D BE...
GAAAH
ABOUT NOW YOU'D BE...
TCH!
WHAT'S ALL THAT TROMPING ABOUT?!

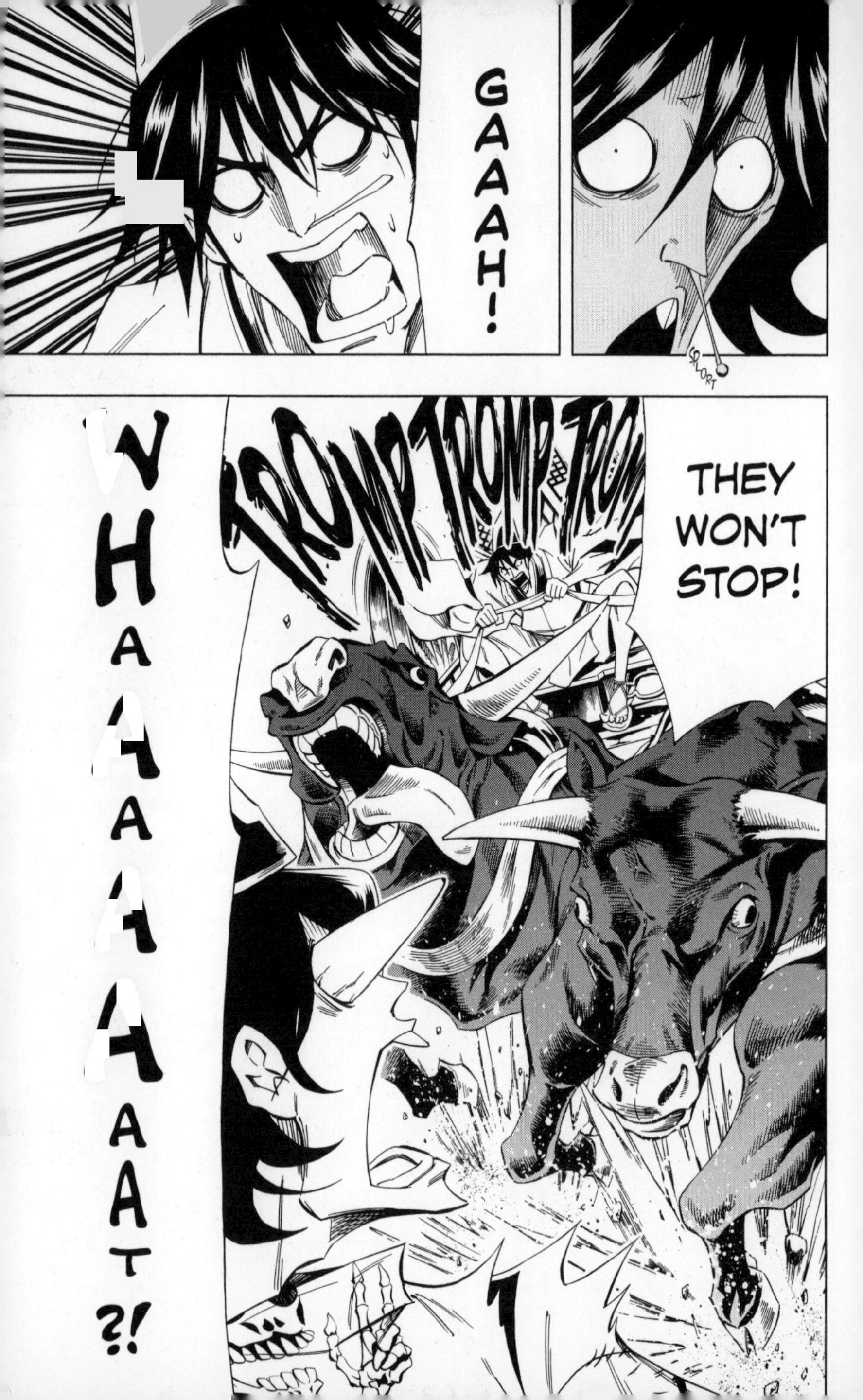
SPLORT
GAAAH!
THEY WON'T STOP!
TROMP TROMP TROM
WHAAAAAAAT?!

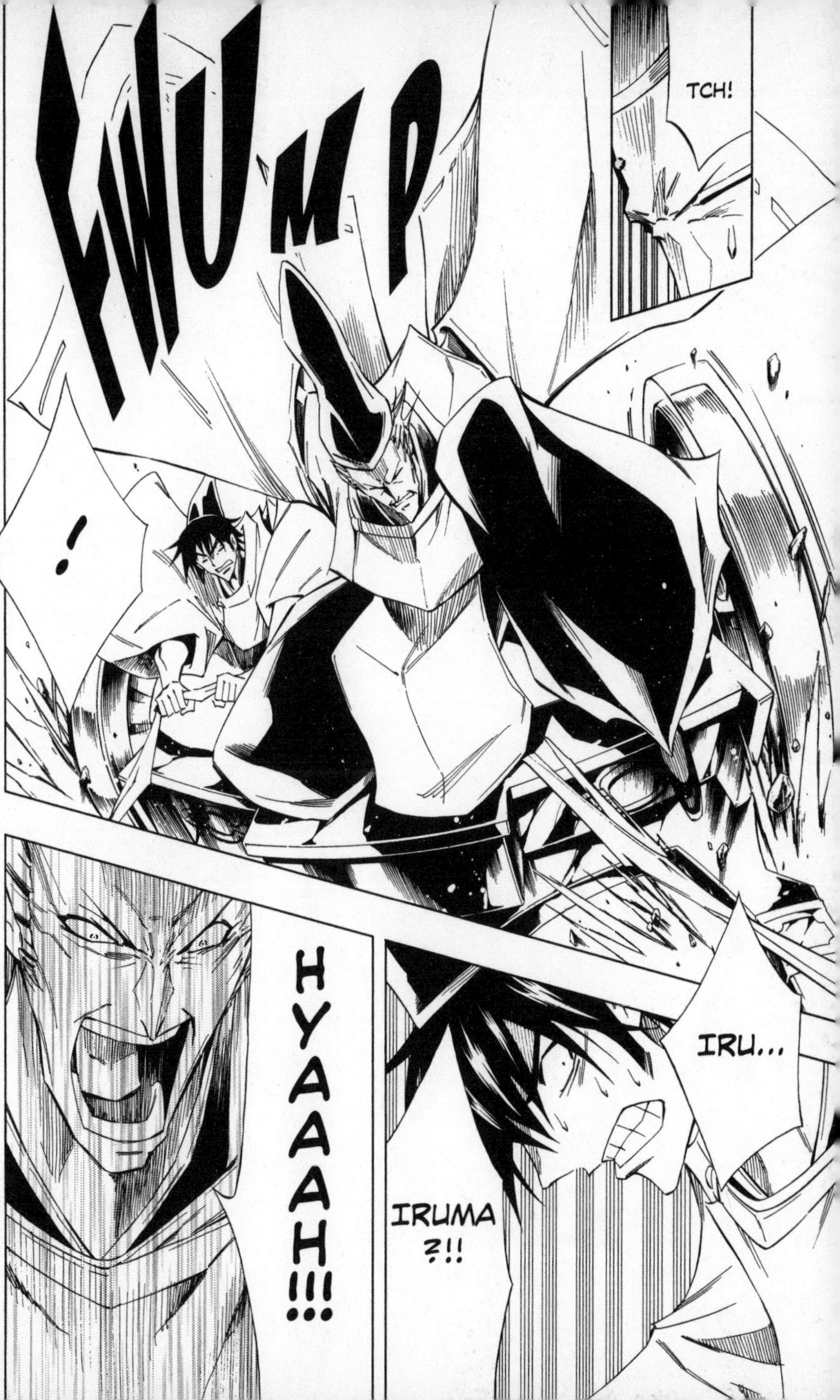
TCH!
FWUMP
!
IRU...
IRUMA ?!!
HYAAAH!!!

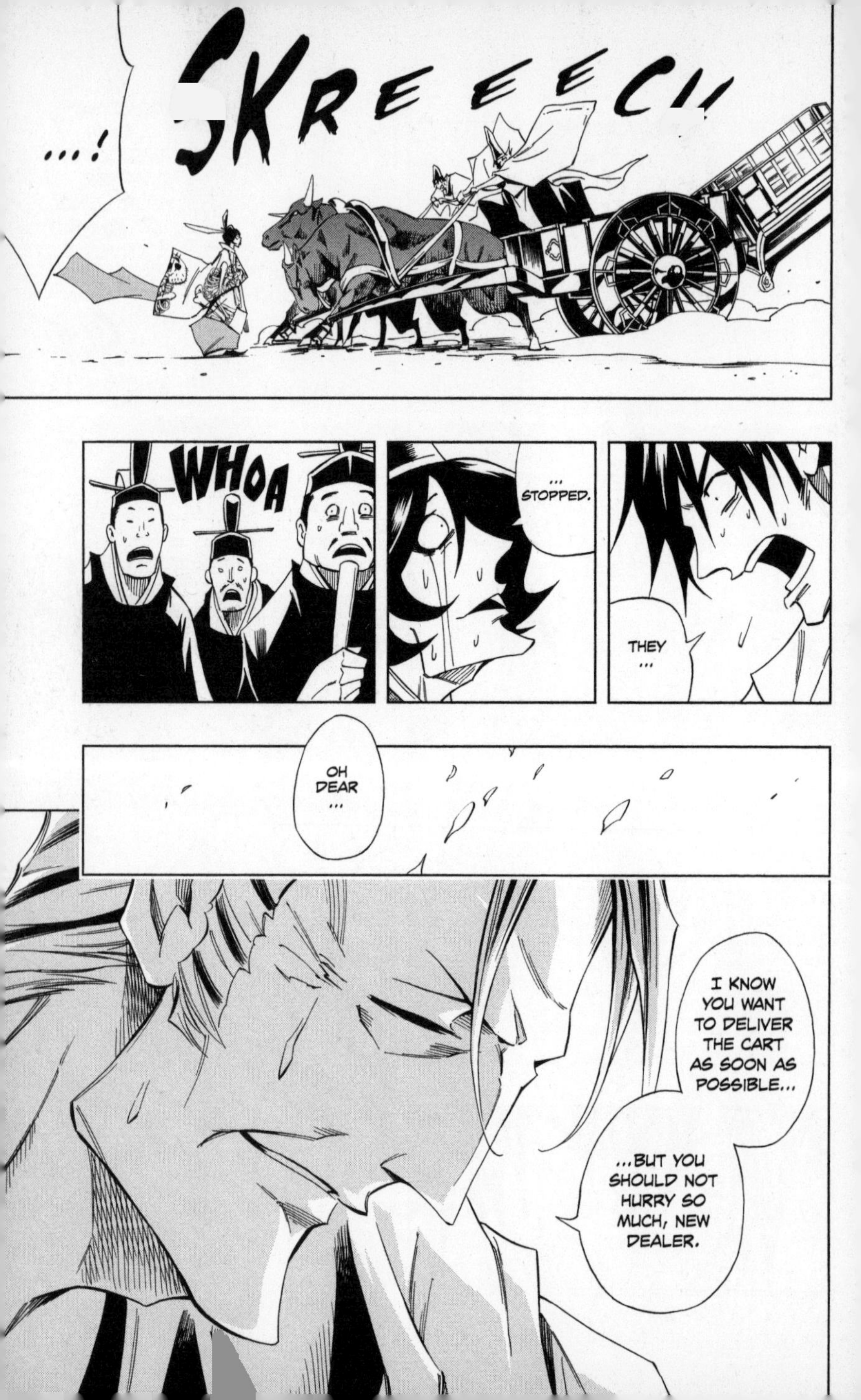
SKREEECH
...!
THEY ...
... STOPPED.
WHOA
OH DEAR ...
I KNOW YOU WANT TO DELIVER THE CART AS SOON AS POSSIBLE...
...BUT YOU SHOULD NOT HURRY SO MUCH, NEW DEALER.

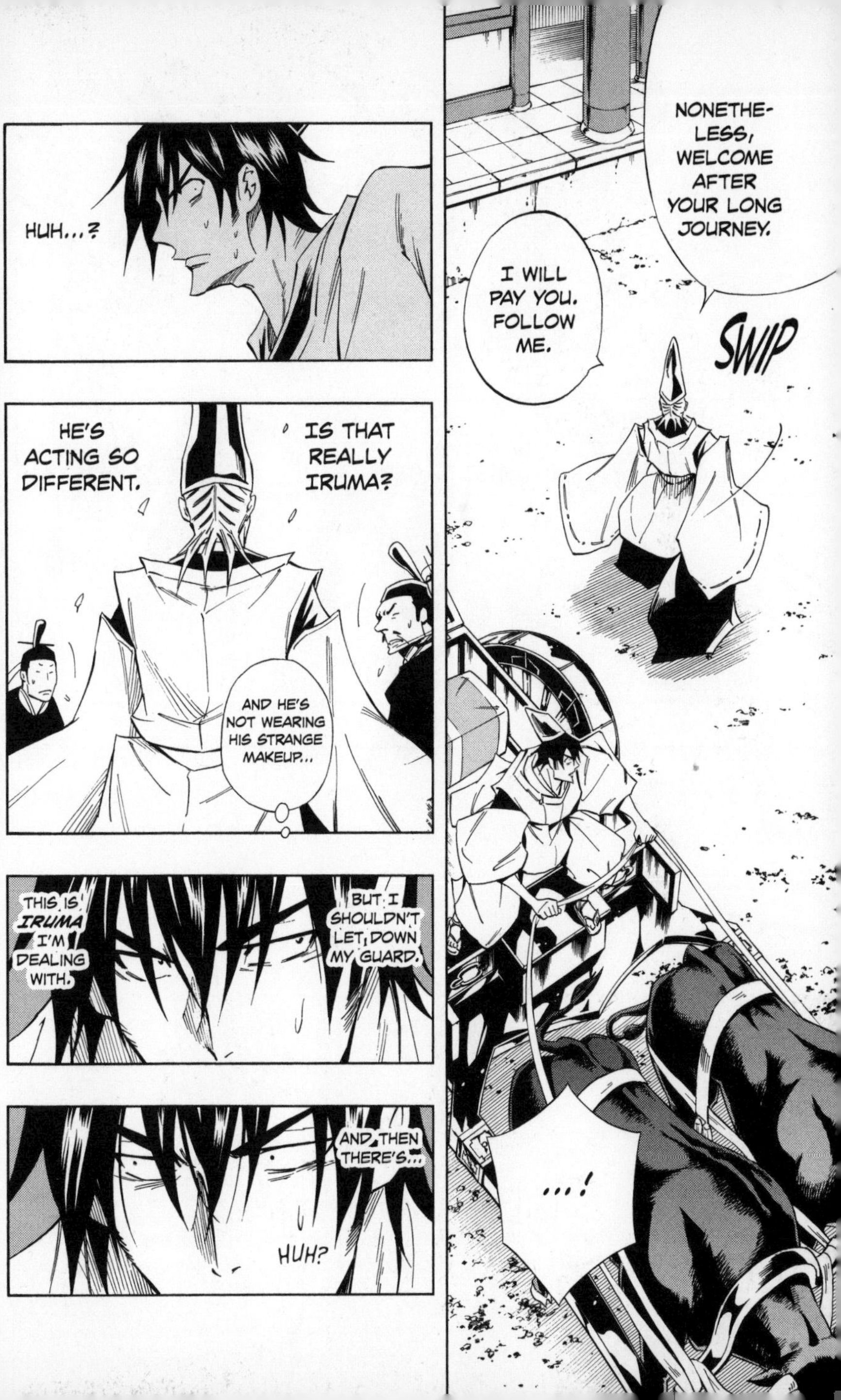
NONETHE-LESS, WELCOME AFTER YOUR LONG JOURNEY.
SWIP
I WILL PAY YOU. FOLLOW ME.
...!
HUH...?
IS THAT REALLY IRUMA?
HE'S ACTING SO DIFFERENT.
AND HE'S NOT WEARING HIS STRANGE MAKEUP...
BUT I SHOULDN'T LET DOWN MY GUARD.
THIS IS IRUMA I'M DEALING WITH.
AND THEN THERE'S...
HUH?

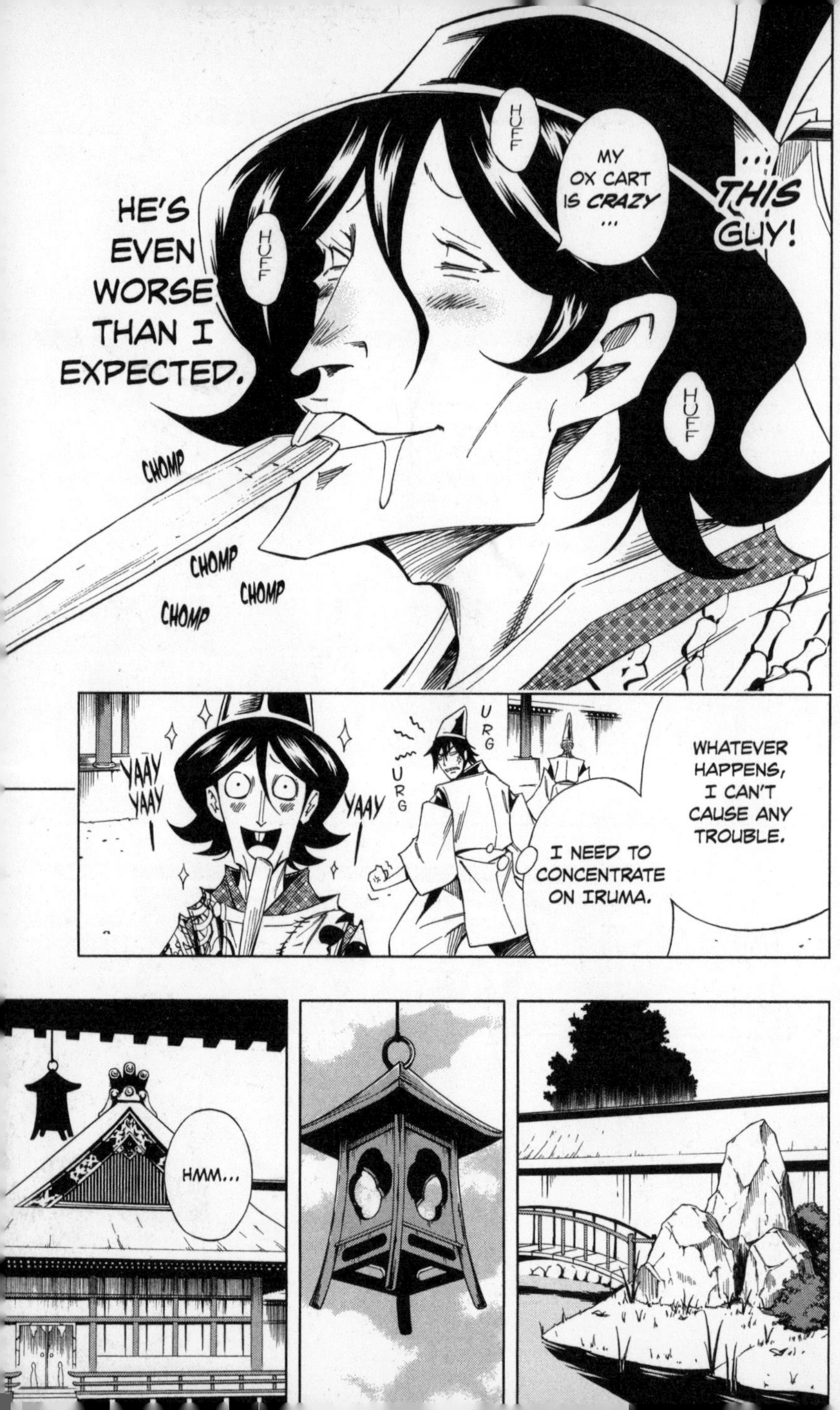
...THIS GUY!
MY OX CART IS CRAZY...
HUFF
HUFF
HUFF
HE'S EVEN WORSE THAN I EXPECTED.
CHOMP
CHOMP
CHOMP
CHOMP
WHATEVER HAPPENS, I CAN'T CAUSE ANY TROUBLE.
I NEED TO CONCENTRATE ON IRUMA.
URG
URG
YAAY!
YAAY YAAY!
HMM...

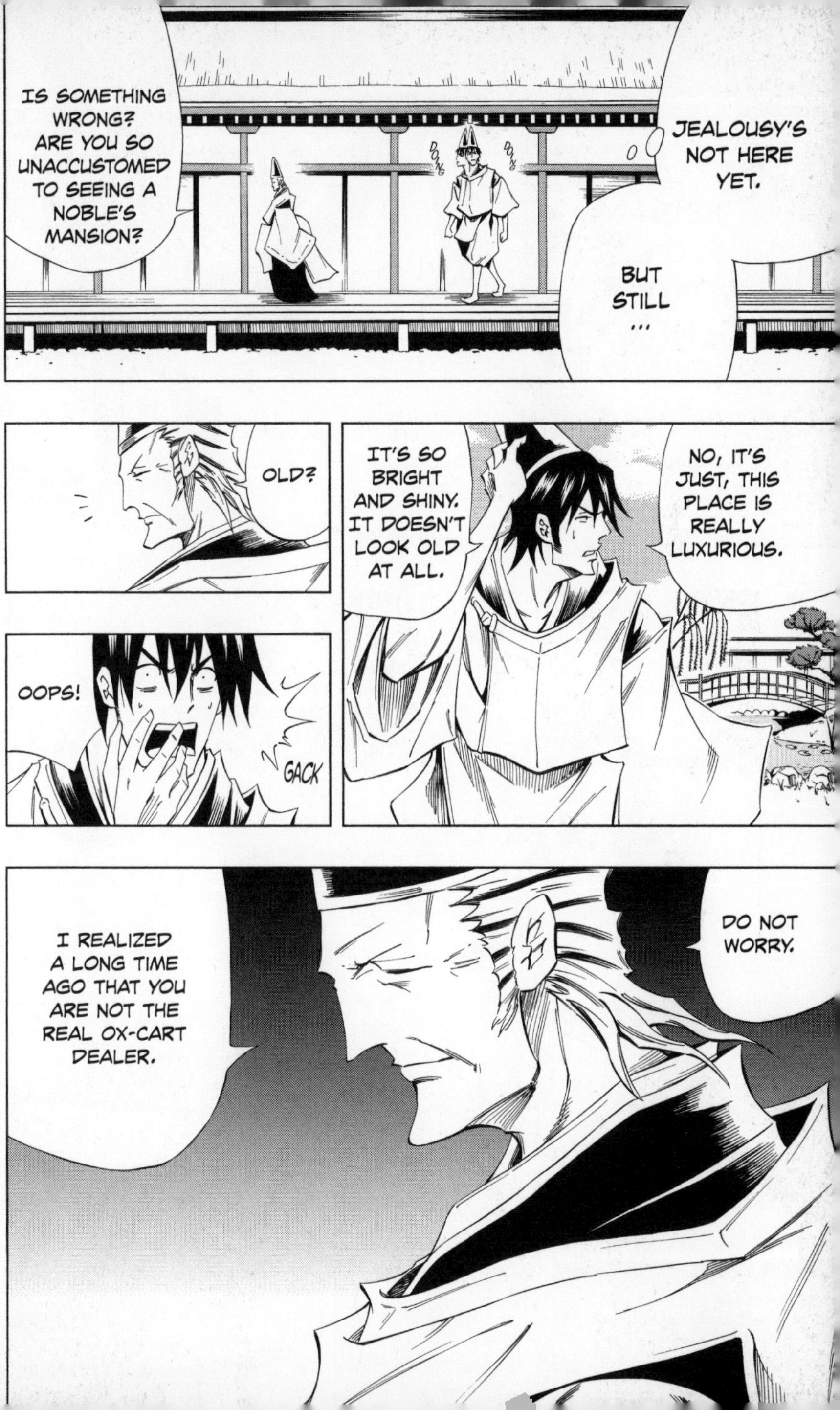
JEALOUSY'S NOT HERE YET.
BUT STILL ...
DONG
DONG
IS SOMETHING WRONG? ARE YOU SO UNACCUSTOMED TO SEEING A NOBLE'S MANSION?
NO, IT'S JUST, THIS PLACE IS REALLY LUXURIOUS.
IT'S SO BRIGHT AND SHINY. IT DOESN'T LOOK OLD AT ALL.
OLD?
GACK
OOPS!
DO NOT WORRY.
I REALIZED A LONG TIME AGO THAT YOU ARE NOT THE REAL OX-CART DEALER.

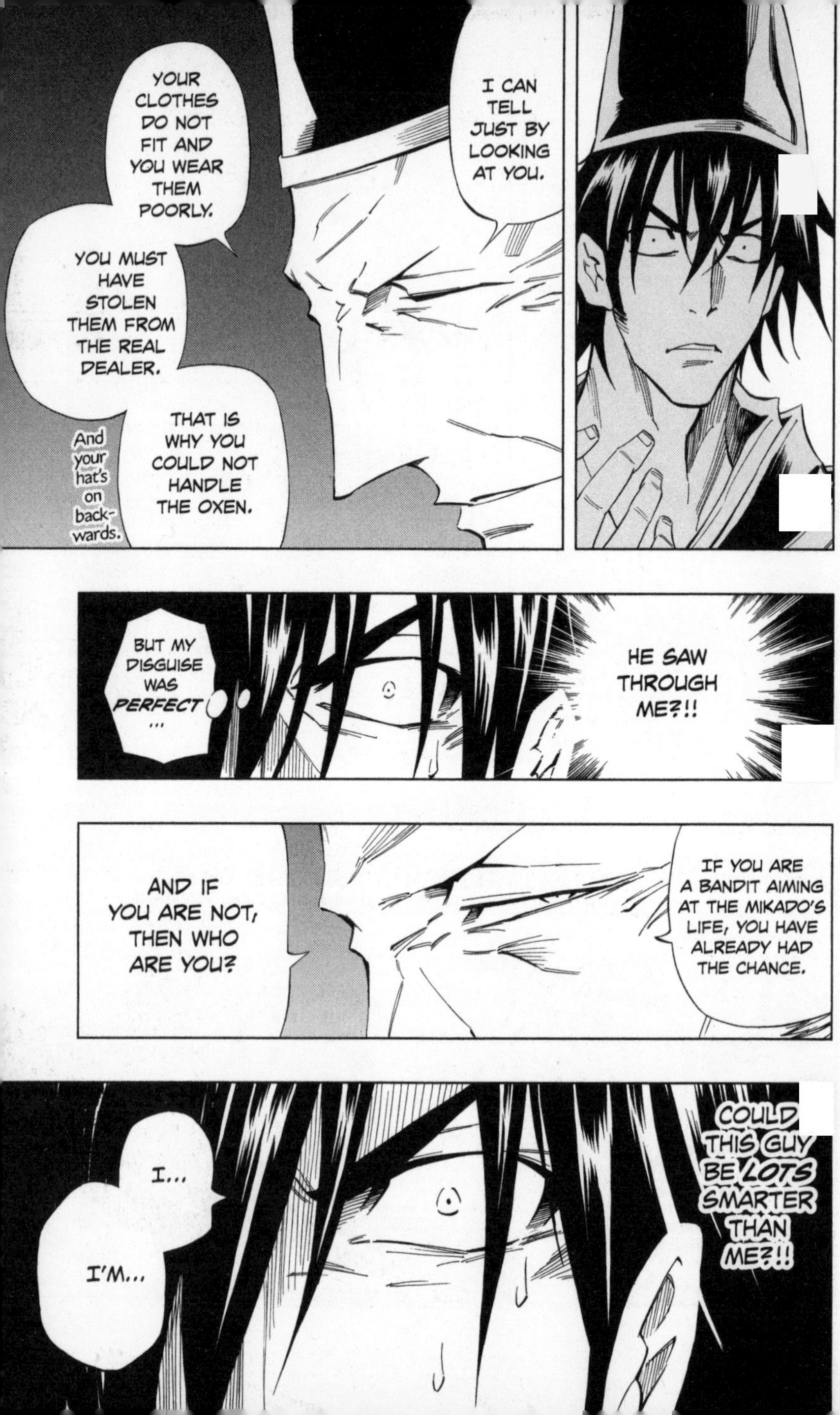
I CAN TELL JUST BY LOOKING AT YOU.
YOUR CLOTHES DO NOT FIT AND YOU WEAR THEM POORLY.
YOU MUST HAVE STOLEN THEM FROM THE REAL DEALER.
THAT IS WHY YOU COULD NOT HANDLE THE OXEN.
And your hat's on back-wards.
HE SAW THROUGH ME?!!
BUT MY DISGUISE WAS *PERFECT*...
IF YOU ARE A BANDIT AIMING AT THE MIKADO'S LIFE, YOU HAVE ALREADY HAD THE CHANCE.
AND IF YOU ARE NOT, THEN WHO ARE YOU?
COULD THIS GUY BE *LOTS* SMARTER THAN ME?!!
I...
I'M...

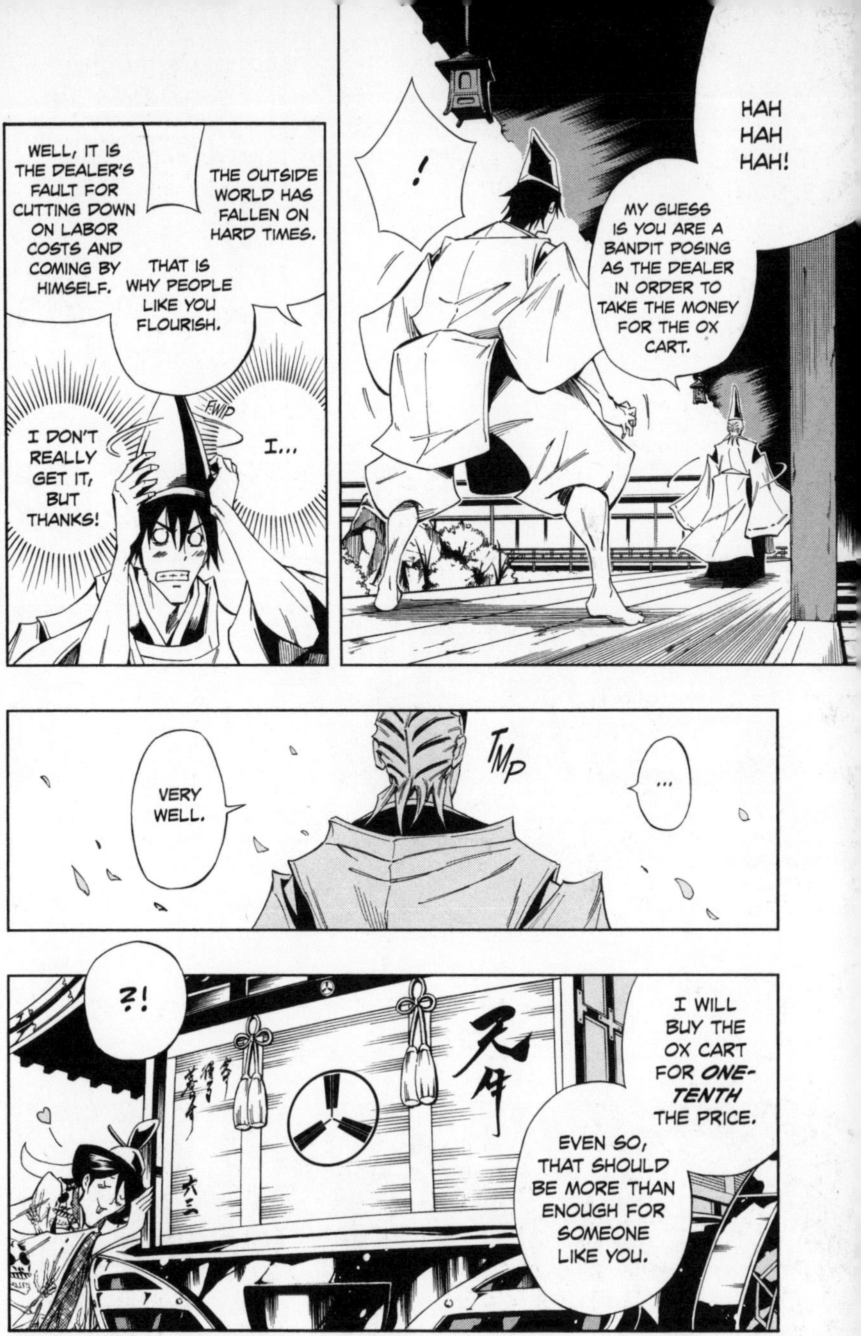
HAH HAH HAH!
MY GUESS IS YOU ARE A BANDIT POSING AS THE DEALER IN ORDER TO TAKE THE MONEY FOR THE OX CART.
!
THE OUTSIDE WORLD HAS FALLEN ON HARD TIMES.
WELL, IT IS THE DEALER'S FAULT FOR CUTTING DOWN ON LABOR COSTS AND COMING BY HIMSELF.
THAT IS WHY PEOPLE LIKE YOU FLOURISH.
I...
FWIP
I DON'T REALLY GET IT, BUT THANKS!
...
TMP
VERY WELL.
I WILL BUY THE OX CART FOR *ONE-TENTH* THE PRICE.
EVEN SO, THAT SHOULD BE MORE THAN ENOUGH FOR SOMEONE LIKE YOU.
?!

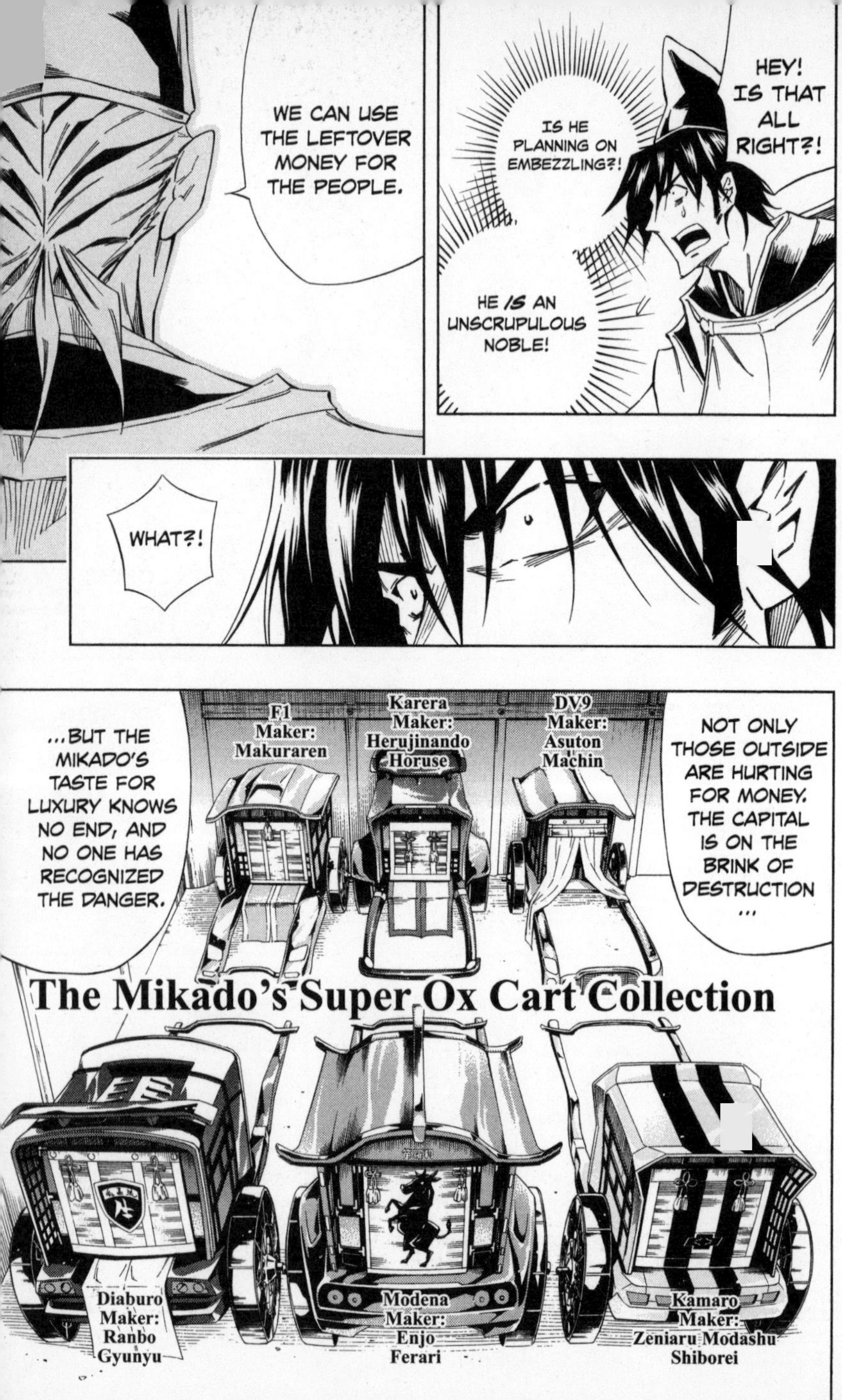
HEY! IS THAT ALL RIGHT?!
IS HE PLANNING ON EMBEZZLING?!
HE *IS* AN UNSCRUPULOUS NOBLE!
WE CAN USE THE LEFTOVER MONEY FOR THE PEOPLE.
WHAT?!
NOT ONLY THOSE OUTSIDE ARE HURTING FOR MONEY. THE CAPITAL IS ON THE BRINK OF DESTRUCTION...
...BUT THE MIKADO'S TASTE FOR LUXURY KNOWS NO END, AND NO ONE HAS RECOGNIZED THE DANGER.
DV9 Maker: Asuton Machin
Karera Maker: Herujinando Horuse
F1 Maker: Makuraren
The Mikado's Super Ox Cart Collection
Kamaro Maker: Zeniaru Modashu Shiborei
Modena Maker: Enjo Ferari
Diaburo Maker: Ranbo Gyunyu

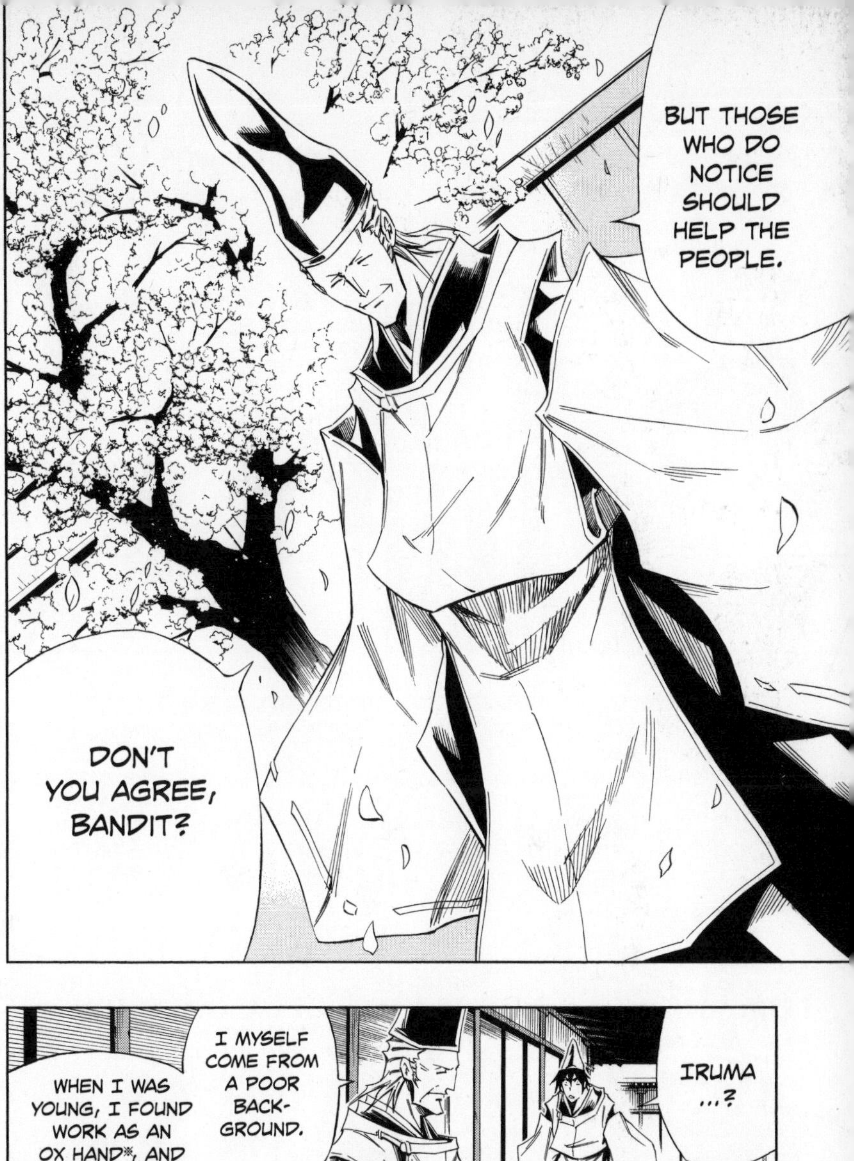
BUT THOSE WHO DO NOTICE SHOULD HELP THE PEOPLE.
DON'T YOU AGREE, BANDIT?
IRUMA ...?
I MYSELF COME FROM A POOR BACK-GROUND.
WHEN I WAS YOUNG, I FOUND WORK AS AN OX HAND※, AND EVENTUALLY BECAME A BODYGUARD※ TO THE NOBILITY. I DID EVERYTHING I COULD TO RISE TO THIS POSITION.

※OX HAND: SOMEONE WHO ACCOMPANIES AN OX CART AND CARES FOR THE OXEN.
BODYGUARD: A BODYGUARD TO THE NOBILITY.

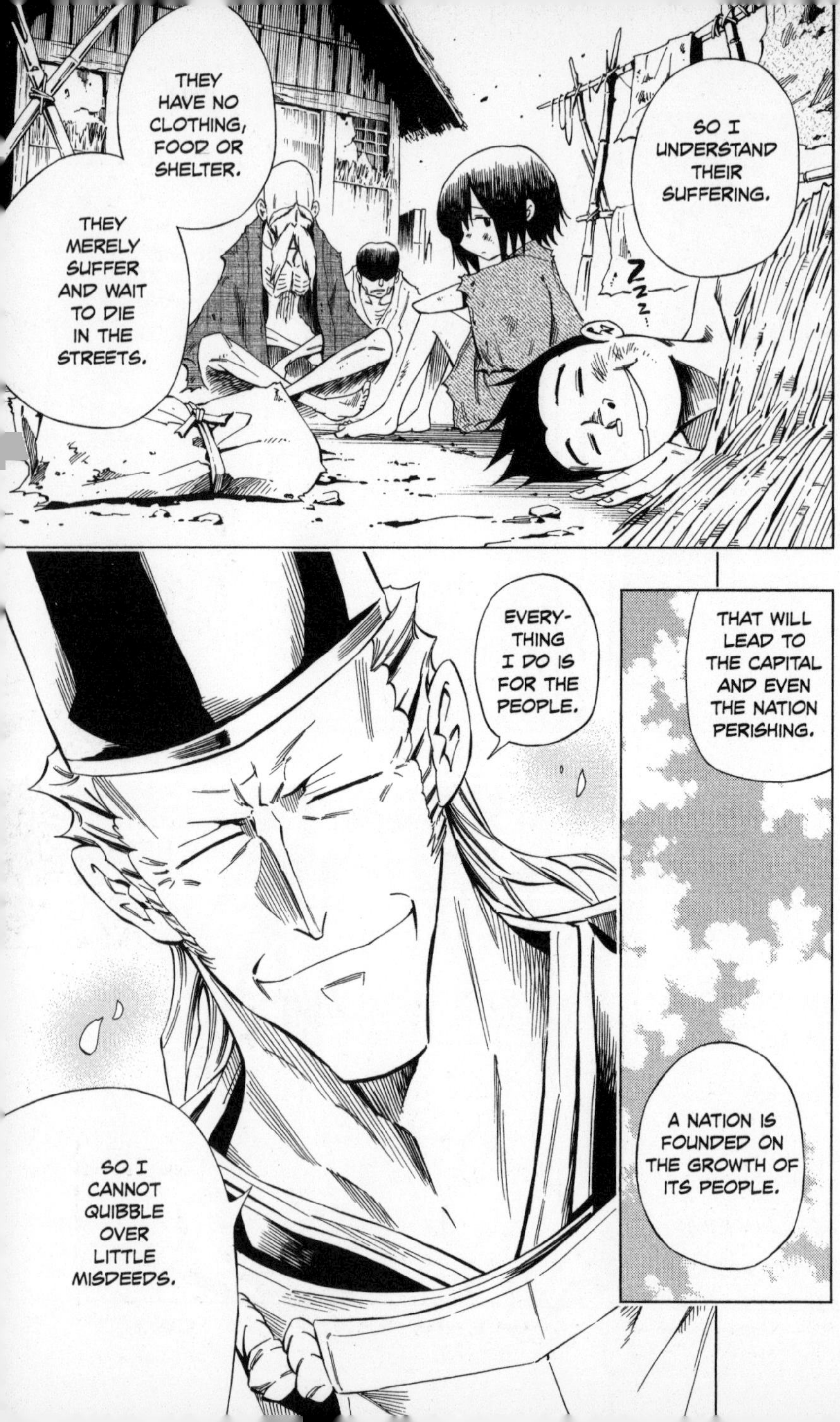
SO I UNDERSTAND THEIR SUFFERING.
THEY HAVE NO CLOTHING, FOOD OR SHELTER.
THEY MERELY SUFFER AND WAIT TO DIE IN THE STREETS.
ZZZ
THAT WILL LEAD TO THE CAPITAL AND EVEN THE NATION PERISHING.
A NATION IS FOUNDED ON THE GROWTH OF ITS PEOPLE.
EVERY-THING I DO IS FOR THE PEOPLE.
SO I CANNOT QUIBBLE OVER LITTLE MISDEEDS.

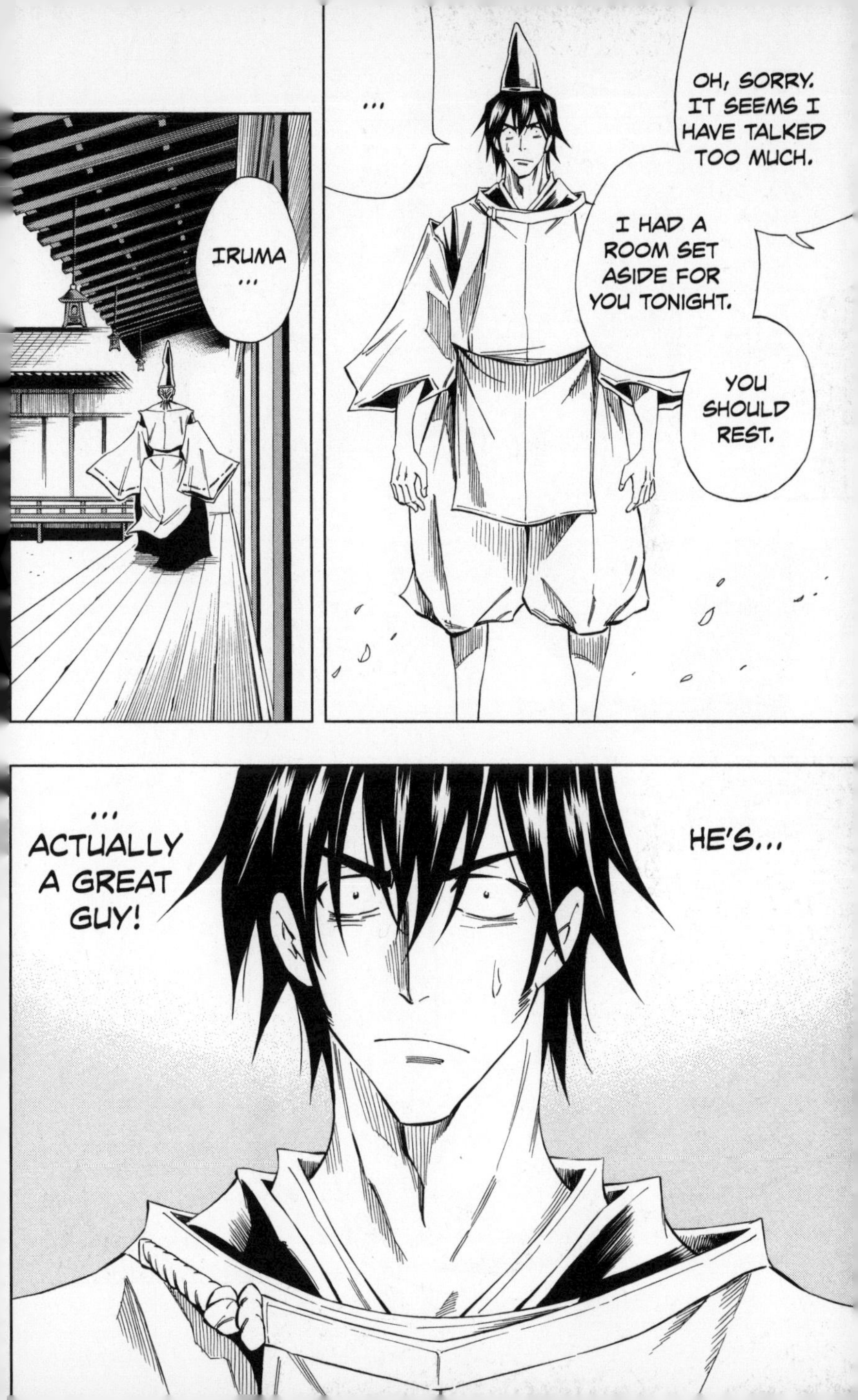
...
OH, SORRY. IT SEEMS I HAVE TALKED TOO MUCH.
I HAD A ROOM SET ASIDE FOR YOU TONIGHT.
YOU SHOULD REST.
IRUMA ...
HE'S...
... ACTUALLY A GREAT GUY!

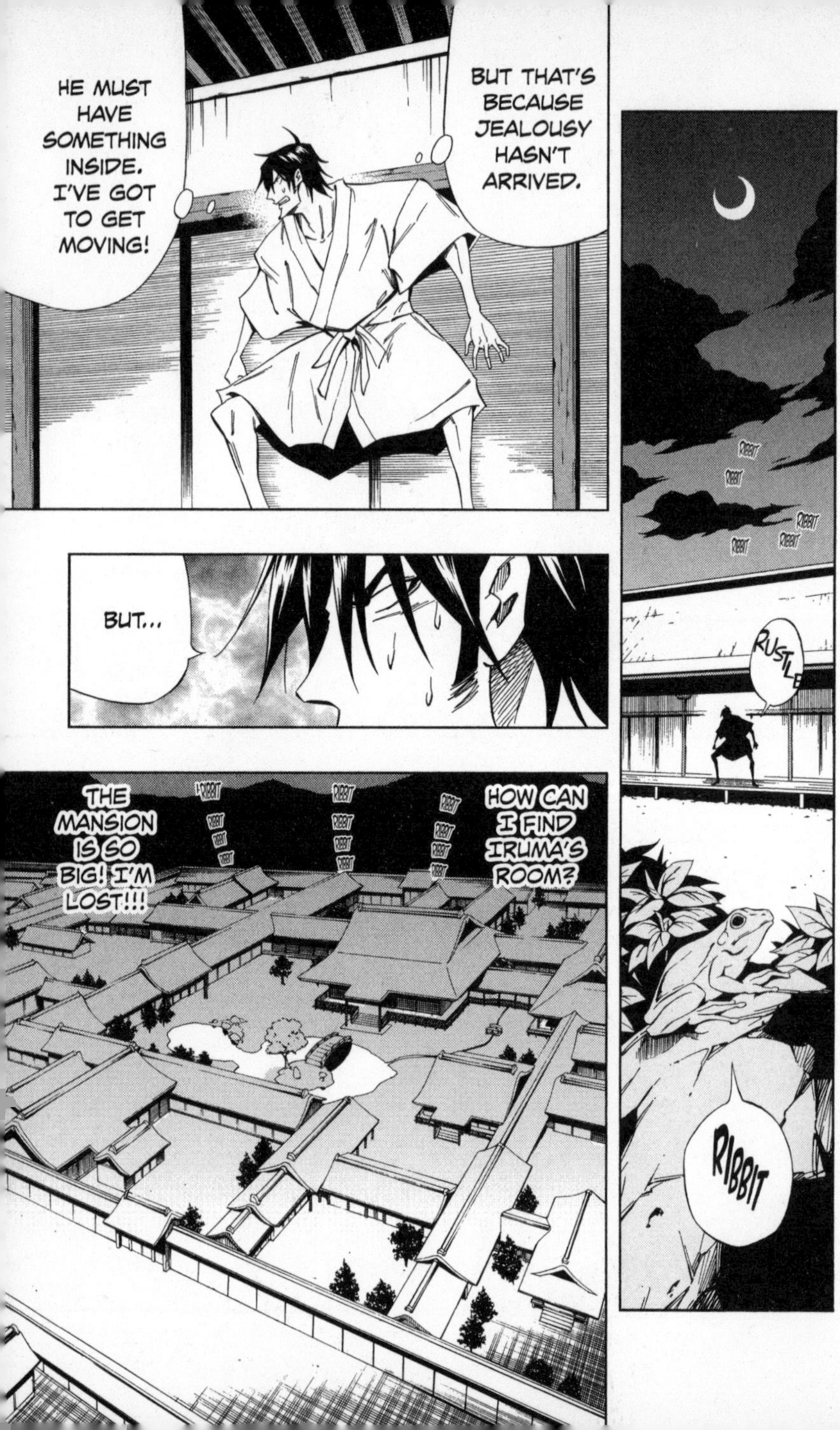
BUT THAT'S BECAUSE JEALOUSY HASN'T ARRIVED.
HE MUST HAVE SOMETHING INSIDE. I'VE GOT TO GET MOVING!
BUT...
HOW CAN I FIND IRUMA'S ROOM?
RIBBIT RIBBIT RIBBIT RIBBIT
RIBBIT RIBBIT RIBBIT RIBBIT
RIBBIT RIBBIT RIBBIT RIBBIT
THE MANSION IS SO BIG! I'M LOST!!!
RIBBIT RIBBIT RIBBIT RIBBIT RIBBIT
RUSTLE
RIBBIT

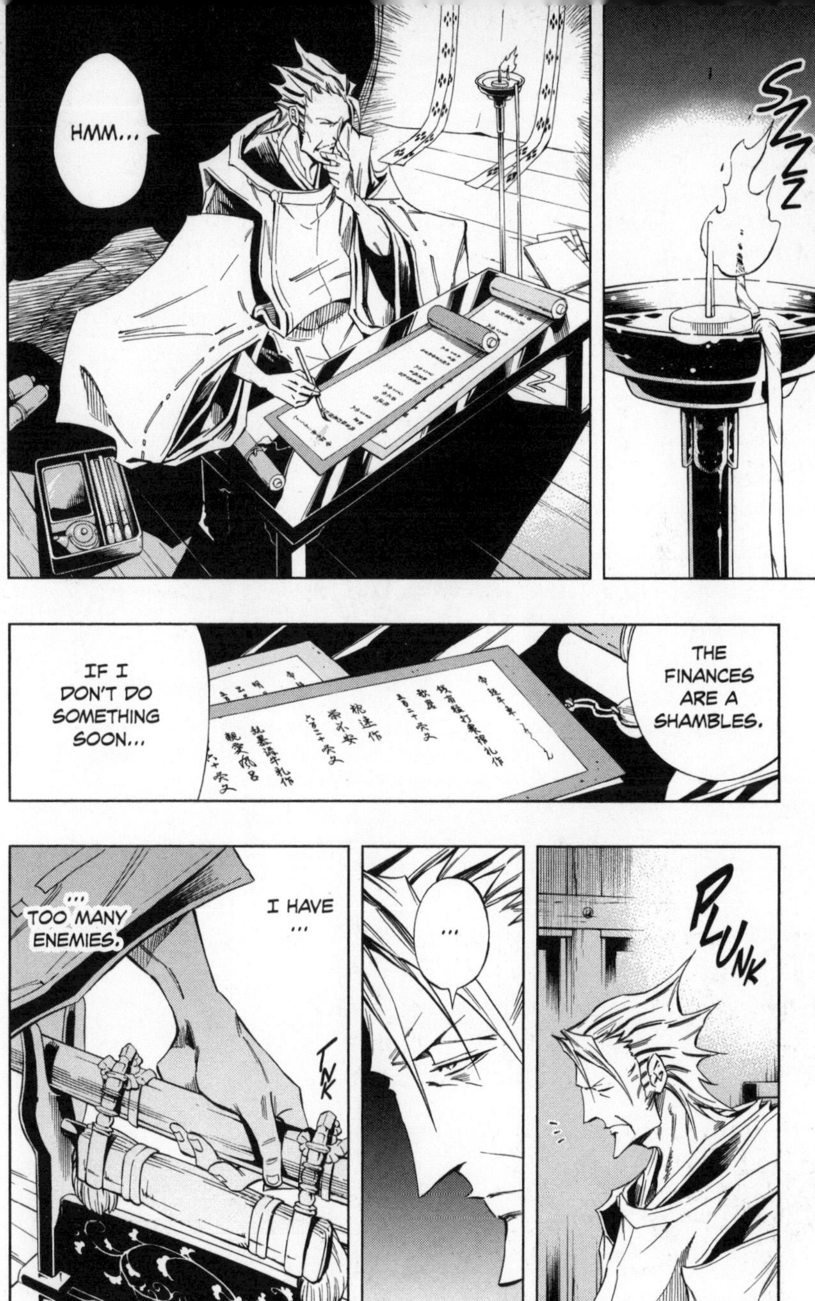
SZZZ
HMM...
THE FINANCES ARE A SHAMBLES.
IF I DON'T DO SOMETHING SOON...
PLUNK
...
I HAVE ...
... TOO MANY ENEMIES.
TNK

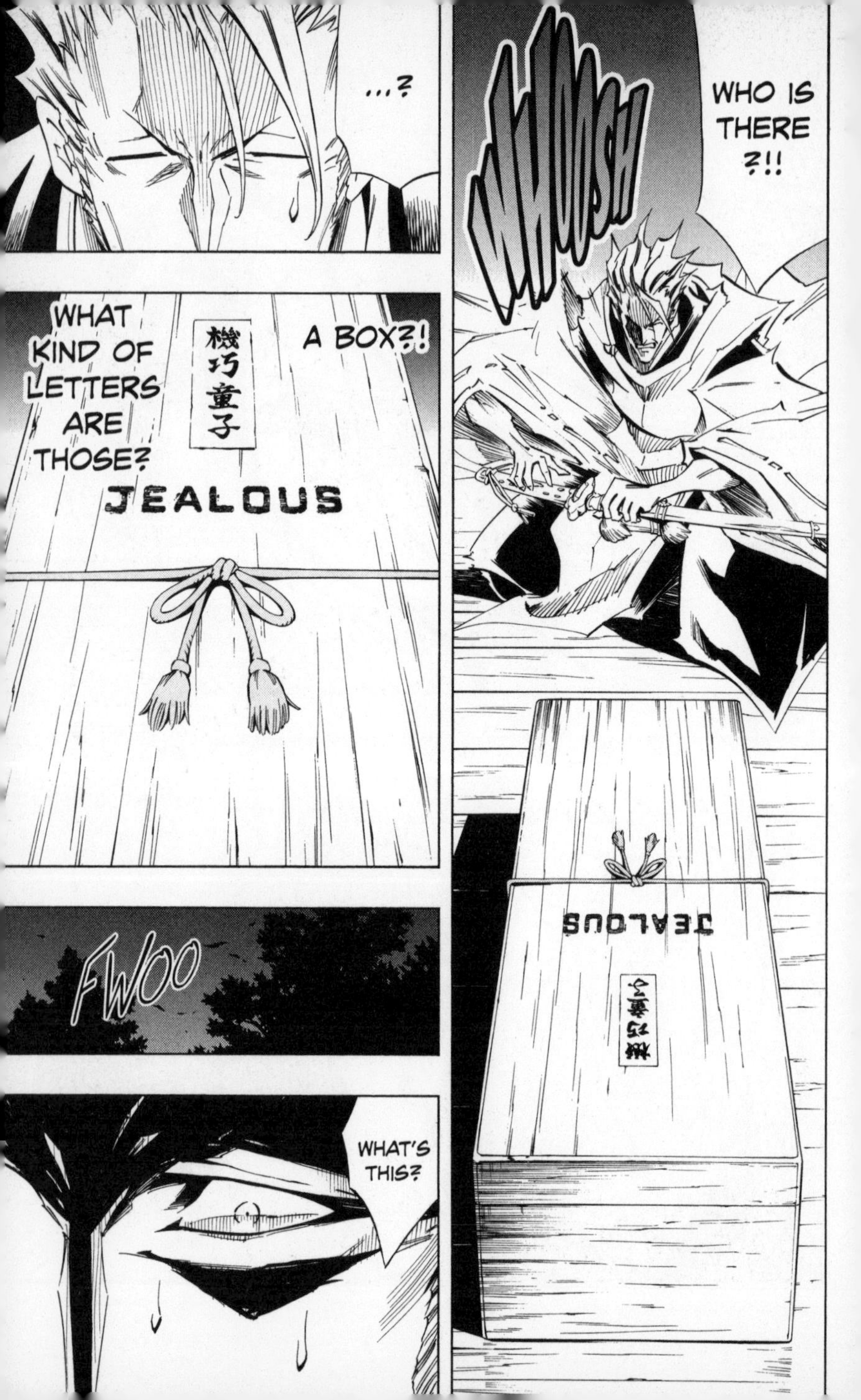
WHOOSH
WHO IS THERE ?!!
JEALOUS
機巧童子
...?
A BOX?!
機巧童子
WHAT KIND OF LETTERS ARE THOSE?
JEALOUS
FWOO
WHAT'S THIS?

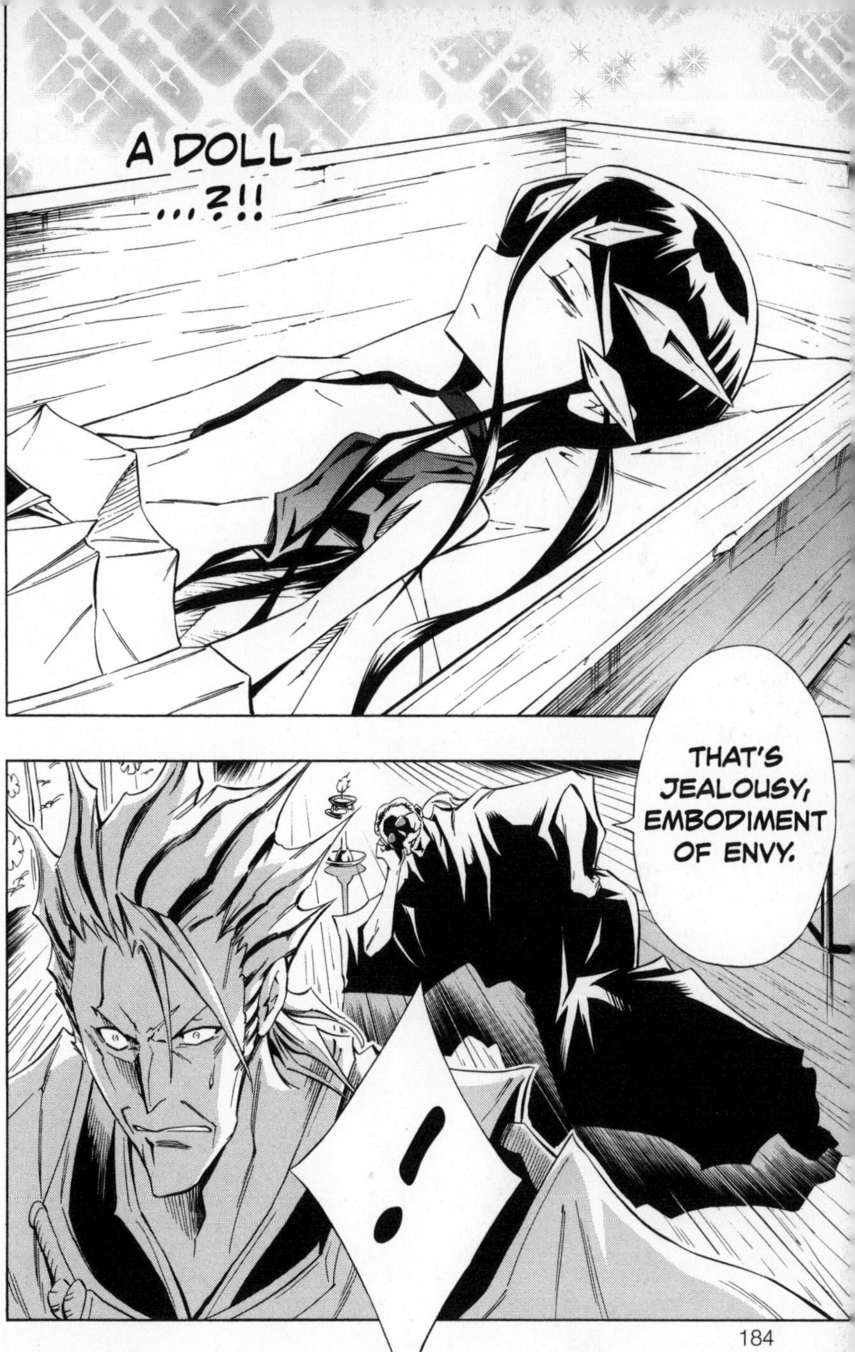
A DOLL ...?!!
THAT'S JEALOUSY, EMBODIMENT OF ENVY.
!

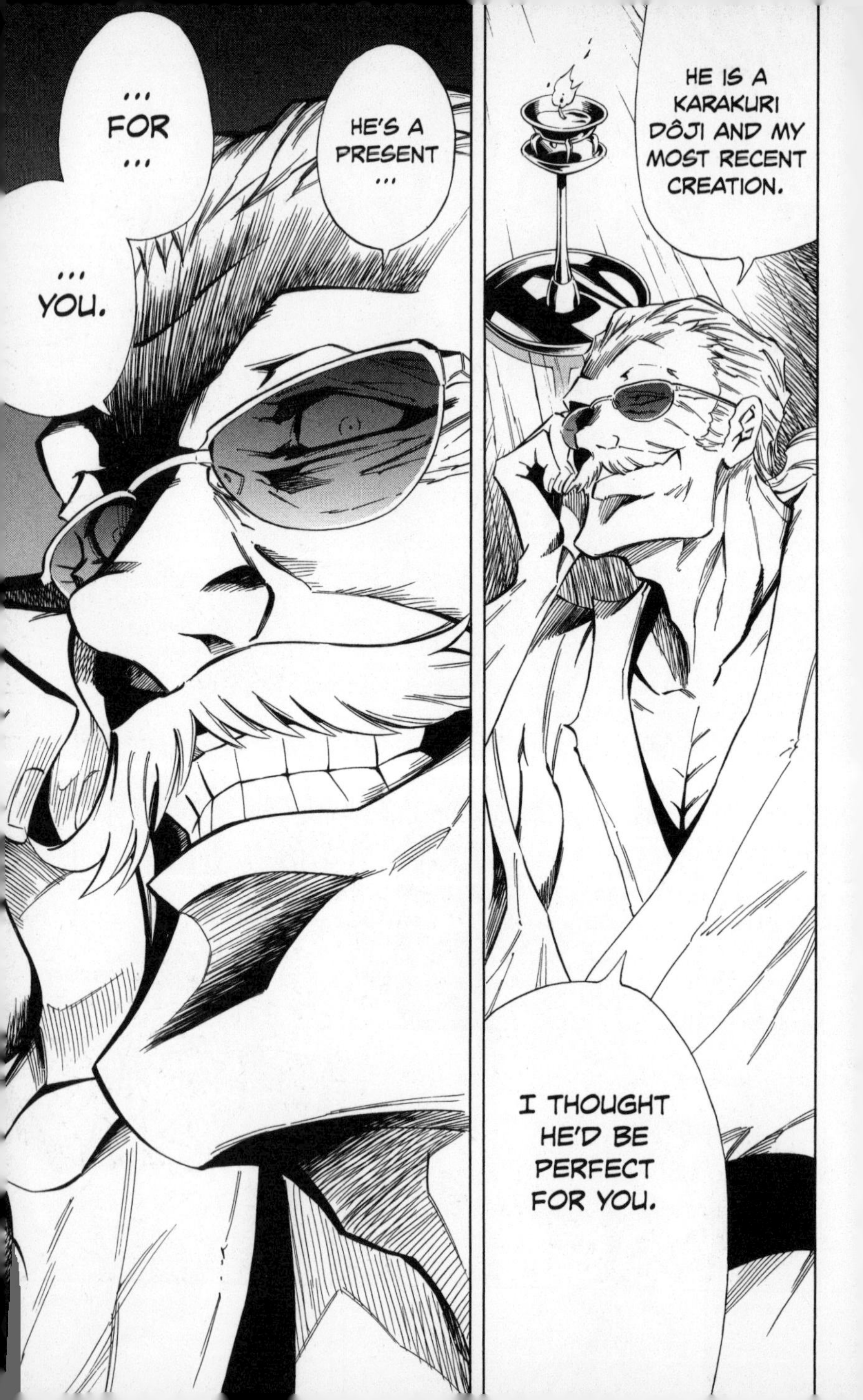
HE IS A KARAKURI DÔJI AND MY MOST RECENT CREATION.
I THOUGHT HE'D BE PERFECT FOR YOU.
HE'S A PRESENT ...
... FOR ...
... YOU.

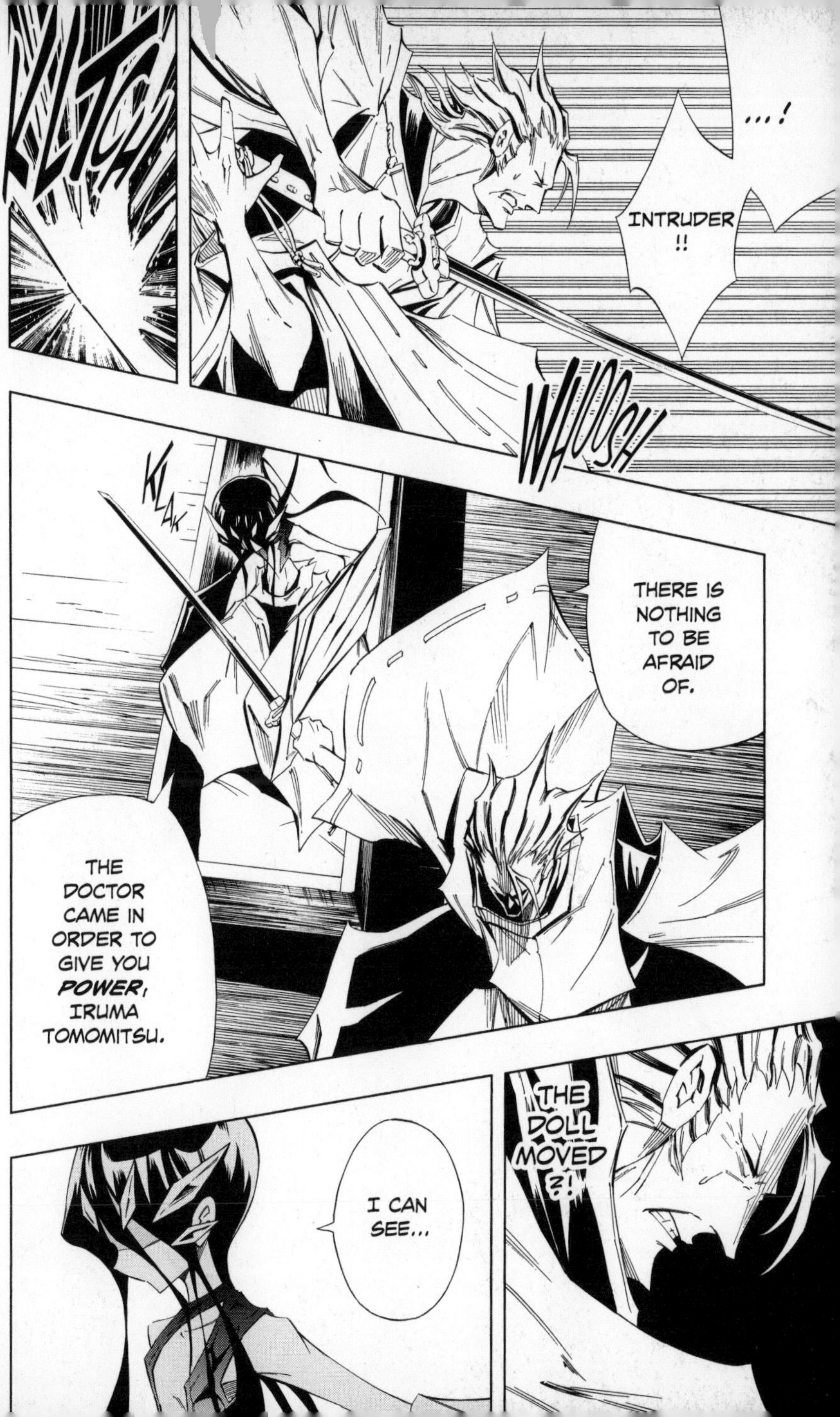
...!
INTRUDER !!
WHOOSH
KLAK
THERE IS NOTHING TO BE AFRAID OF.
THE DOCTOR CAME IN ORDER TO GIVE YOU **POWER**, IRUMA TOMOMITSU.
THE DOLL MOVED?!
I CAN SEE...

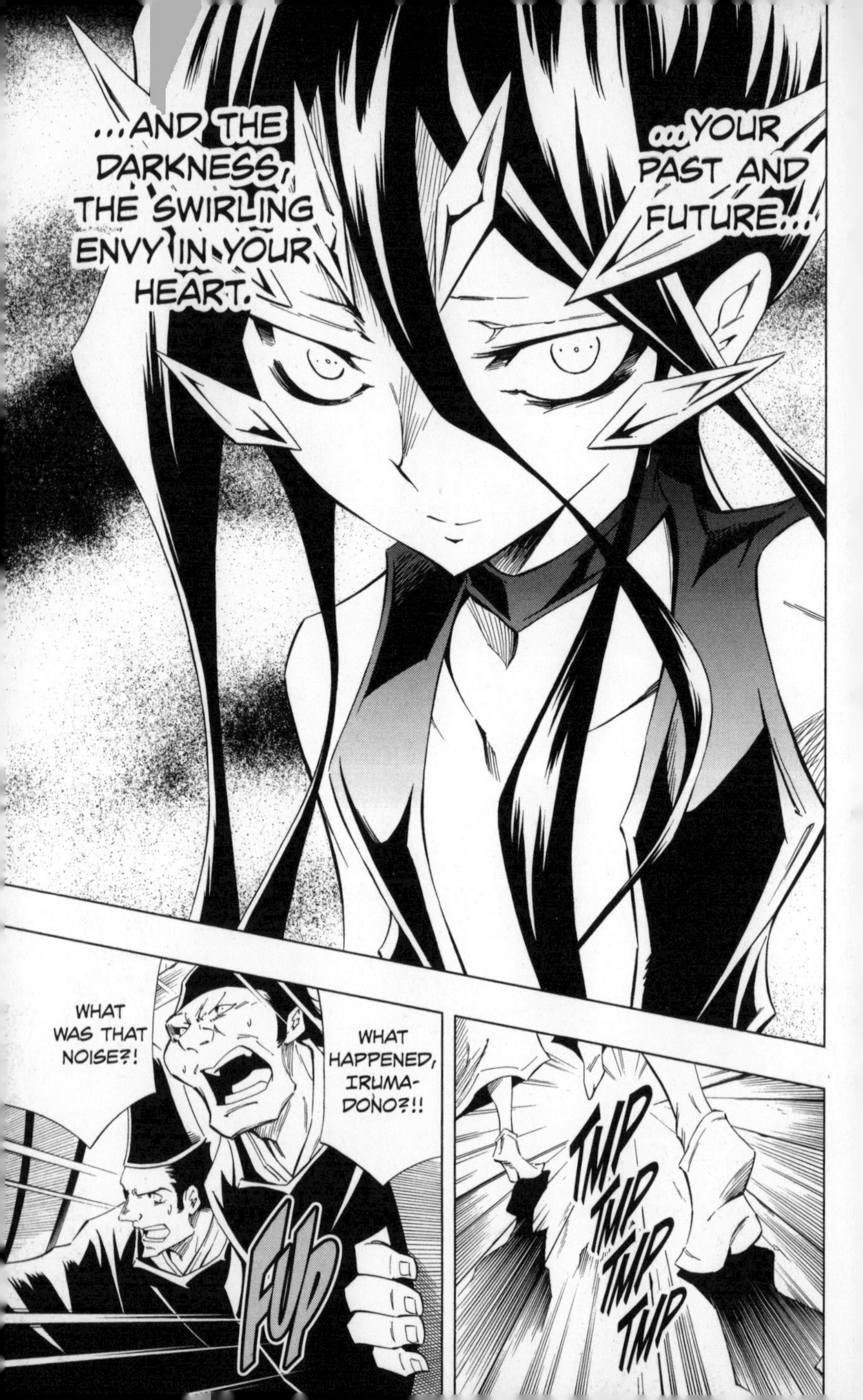
...YOUR PAST AND FUTURE...
...AND THE DARKNESS, THE SWIRLING ENVY IN YOUR HEART.
TMP TMP TMP TMP TMP
WHAT HAPPENED, IRUMA-DONO?!!
WHAT WAS THAT NOISE?!
FUP

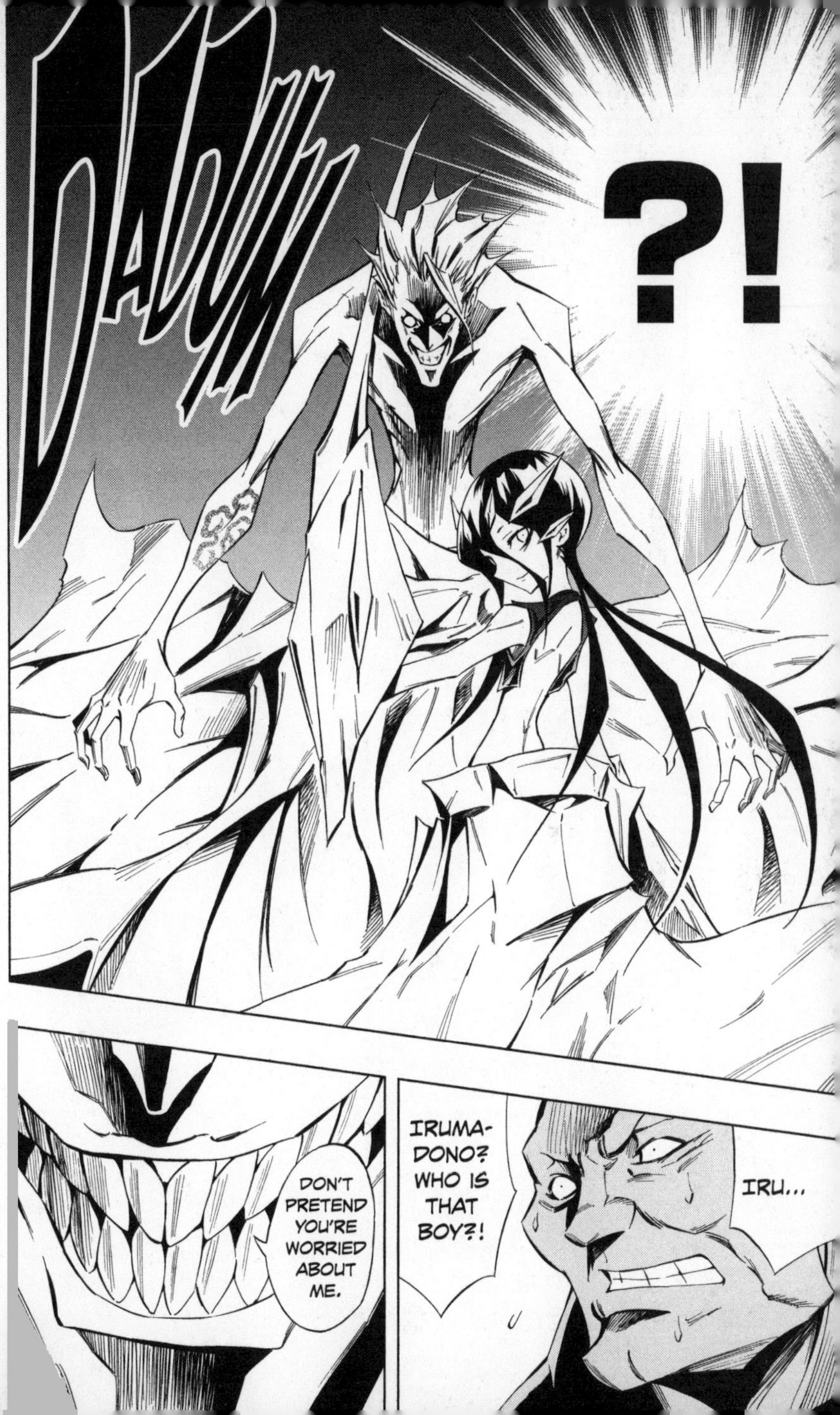
?!
IRU...
IRUMA-DONO?! WHO IS THAT BOY?!
DON'T PRETEND YOU'RE WORRIED ABOUT ME.

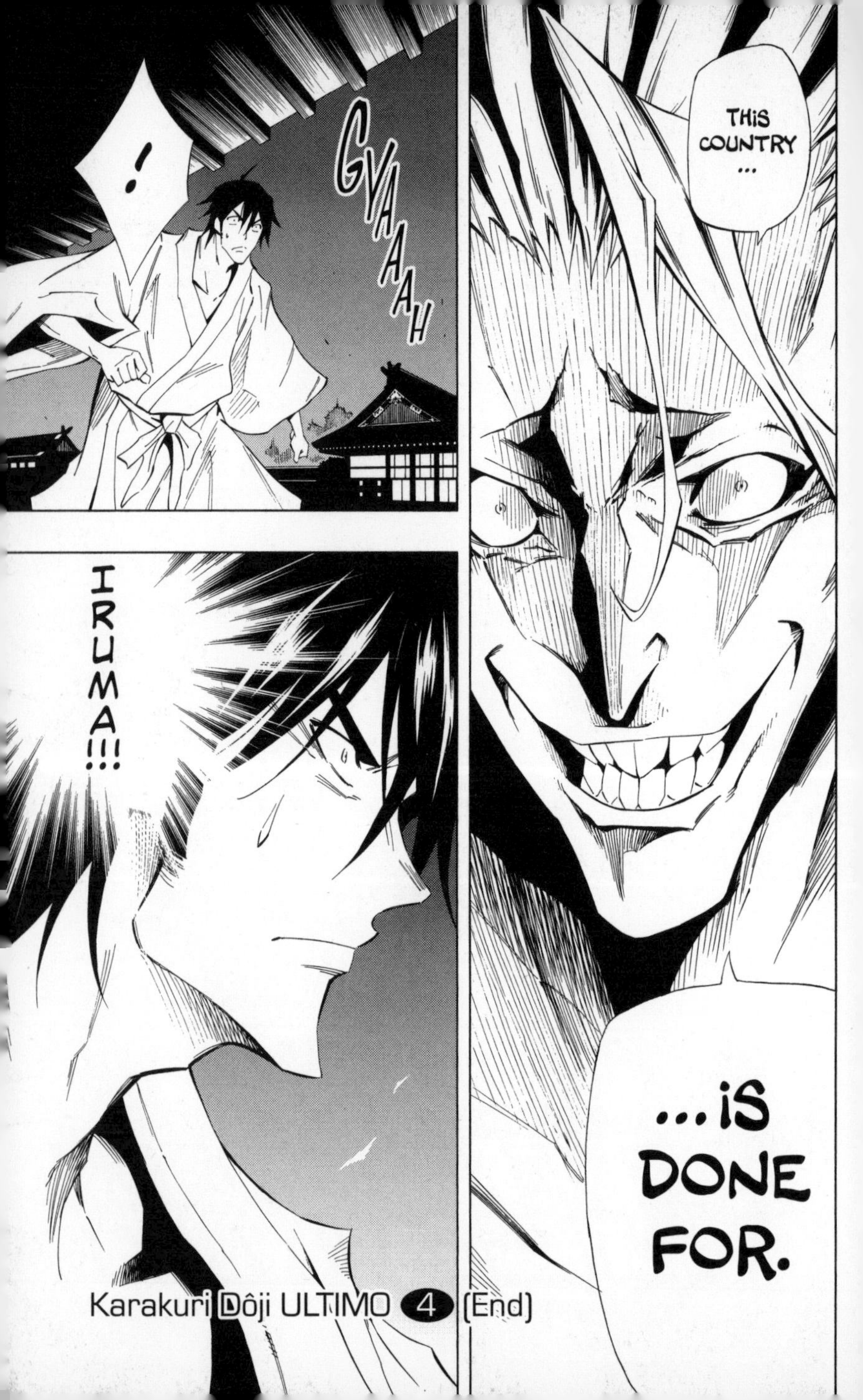
THIS COUNTRY ...
...IS DONE FOR.
!
GYAAAH
IRUMA!!!
Karakuri Dôji ULTIMO 4 (End)

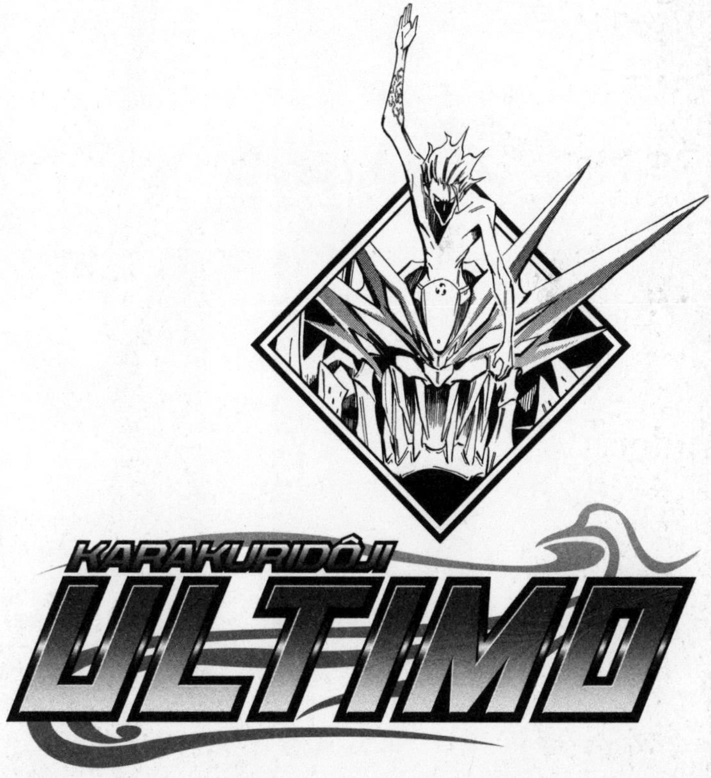

KARAKURIDÔJI
ULTIMO

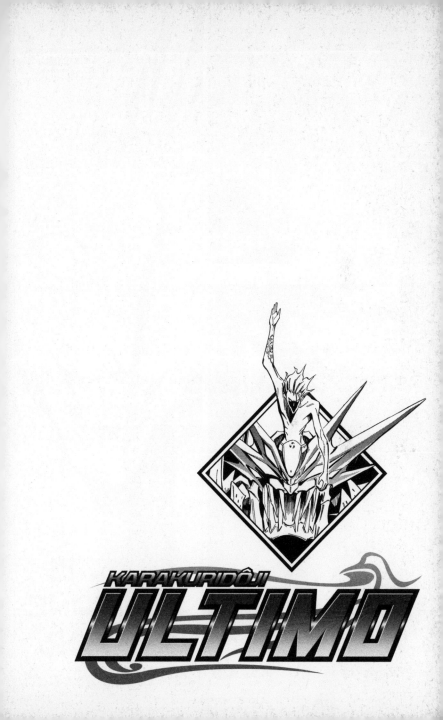

ULTIMO

In the next volume...

Yamato meets the first person in his journey to know.

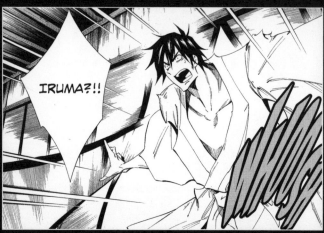

IRUMA?!!

Suddenly, a transformation?!

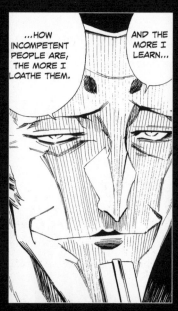

AND THE MORE I LEARN...
...HOW INCOMPETENT PEOPLE ARE, THE MORE I LOATHE THEM.
BECAUSE I *KNOW.*

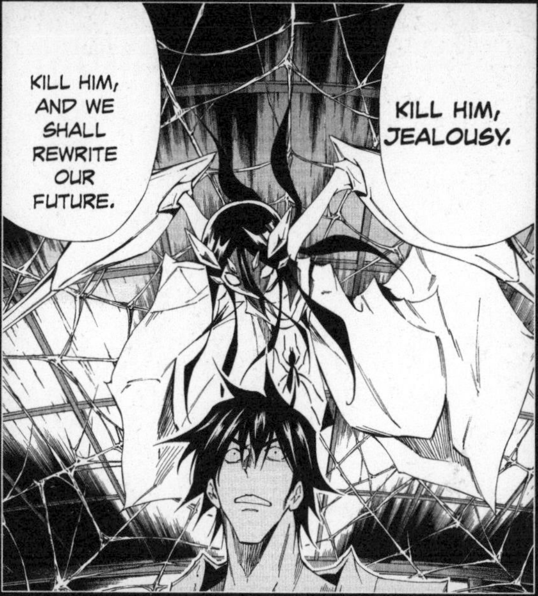
KILL HIM, JEALOUSY.
KILL HIM, AND WE SHALL REWRITE OUR FUTURE.

A sticky situation!!

And suddenly …

…DUNSTAN?!!

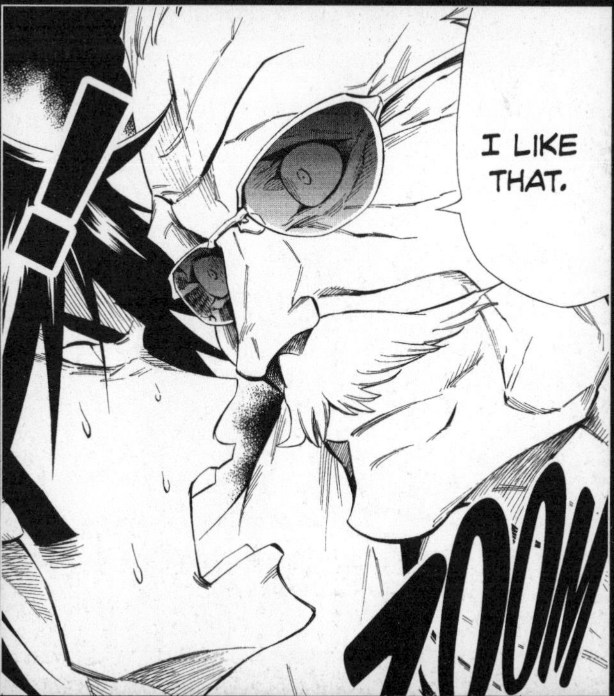
I LIKE THAT.
ZOOM

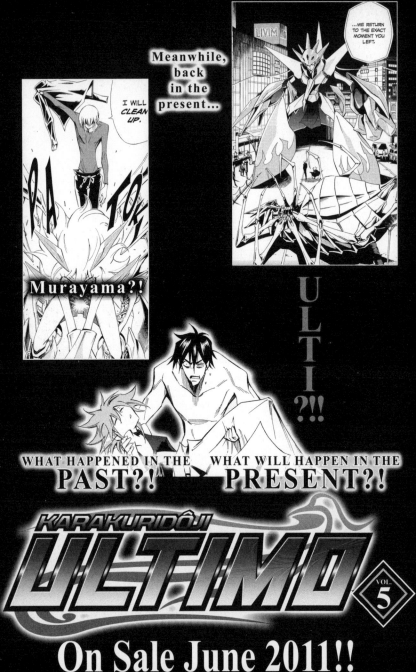

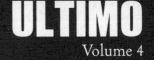

ULTIMO

Volume 4

Original Concept: Stan Lee
Story and Art by: Hiroyuki Takei

SHONEN JUMP Manga Edition

This graphic novel contains material
that was originally published in English
in SHONEN JUMP #91–94.
Artwork in the magazine may have been
slightly altered from that presented here.

Translation | John Werry
Series Touch-up Art & Lettering | James Gaubatz
Design | Fawn Lau
Series Editor | Joel Enos
Graphic Novel Editor | Megan Bates

KARAKURI DOJI ULTIMO © 2008 by Stan Lee—POW!
Entertainment/Dream Ranch, Hiroyuki Takei
All rights reserved. First published in Japan in 2009 by
SHUEISHA Inc., Tokyo. English translation rights arranged
by SHUEISHA Inc.

Printed in the U.S.A.

Published by VIZ Media, LLC
P.O. Box 77010
San Francisco, CA 94107

10 9 8 7 6 5 4 3 2 1
First printing, March 2011

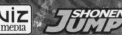

www.viz.com   www.shonenjump.com

STAN LEE

As a kid, Stanley Martin Lieber spent a lot of time dreaming up wild adventures. By the time he got to high school, he was putting his imagination to work writing stories at Timely, a publishing company that went on to become the legendary Marvel Comics. Starting with the *Fantastic Four*, Lee and his partner Jack Kirby created just about every superhero you can think of, including *Spider-Man*, the *X-Men*, the *Hulk*, *Iron Man*, *Daredevil* and *Thor*. Along the way, he wrote under many pen names, but the one that stuck was Stan Lee.

HIROYUKI TAKEI

Unconventional author/artist Hiroyuki Takei began his career by winning the coveted Hop Step Award (for new manga artists) and the Osamu Tezuka Cultural Prize (named after the famous artist of the same name). After working as an assistant to famed artist Nobuhiro Watsuki, Takei debuted in *Weekly Shonen Jump* in 1997 with *Butsu Zone*, an action series based on Buddhist mythology. His multicultural adventure manga *Shaman King*, which debuted in 1998, became a hit and was adapted into an anime TV series. His new series *Ultimo* (*Karakuri Dôji Ultimo*) is currently being serialized in the U.S. in SHONEN JUMP. Takei lists Osamu Tezuka, American comics and robot anime among his many influences.

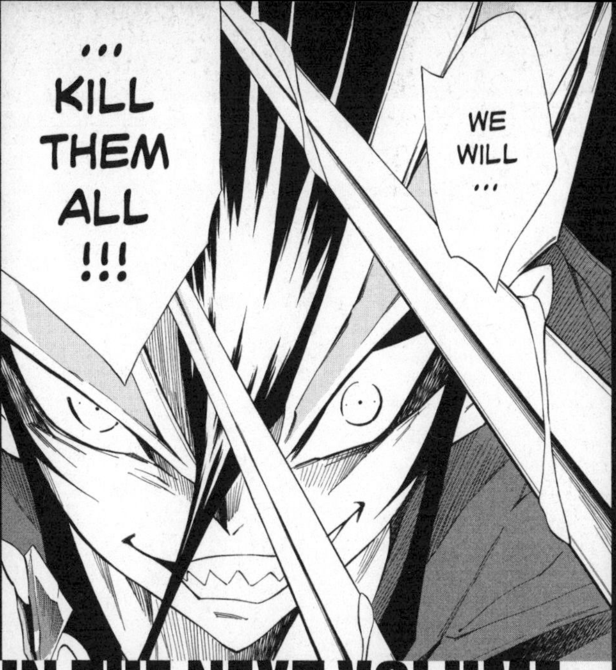
WE WILL ...
... KILL THEM ALL !!!

IN THE NEXT VOLUME...
YAMATO IN TROUBLE

Returning from his time travels, Yamato lands back on the day before the Hundred Machine Funeral. Will his newfound knowledge about Iruma help him divert the inevitable, or will it only help him mess things up more? In a fierce continuation of the battle that started Yamato's first time around, both Maruyama and Yamato are injured. Sensing weakness, Vice takes things into his own hands...

AVAILABLE JUNE 2011!
Read it first in SHONEN JUMP magazine!

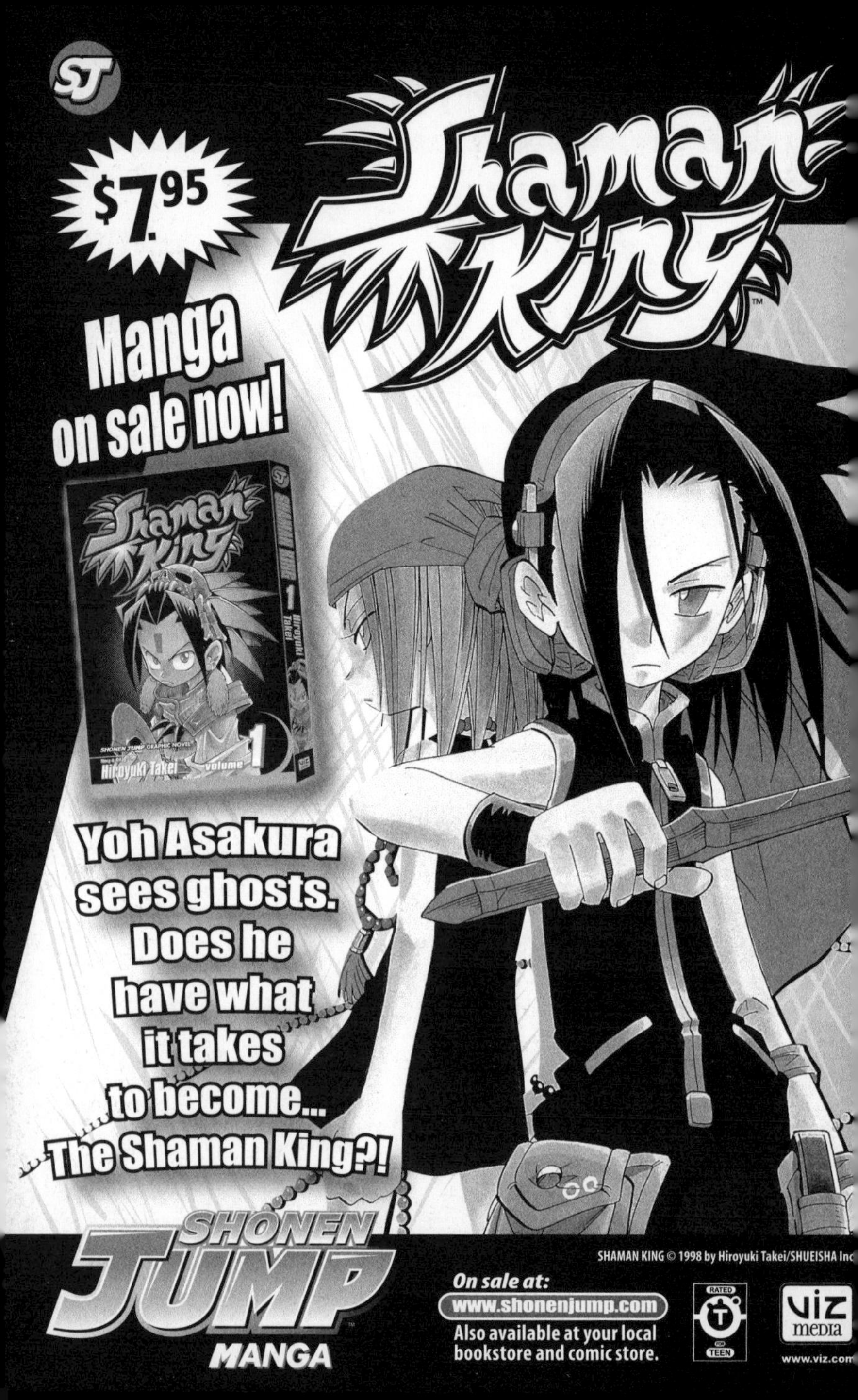
SJ
$7.95
Shaman King™
Manga on sale now!
Shaman King
SHONEN JUMP GRAPHIC NOVEL
Hiroyuki Takei
volume 1
Yoh Asakura sees ghosts. Does he have what it takes to become... The Shaman King?!
SHONEN JUMP MANGA
SHAMAN KING © 1998 by Hiroyuki Takei/SHUEISHA Inc
On sale at:
www.shonenjump.com
Also available at your local bookstore and comic store.
RATED T FOR TEEN
viz media
www.viz.com

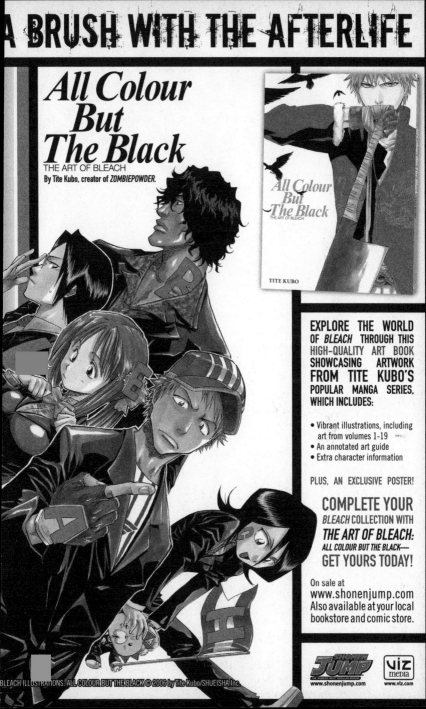

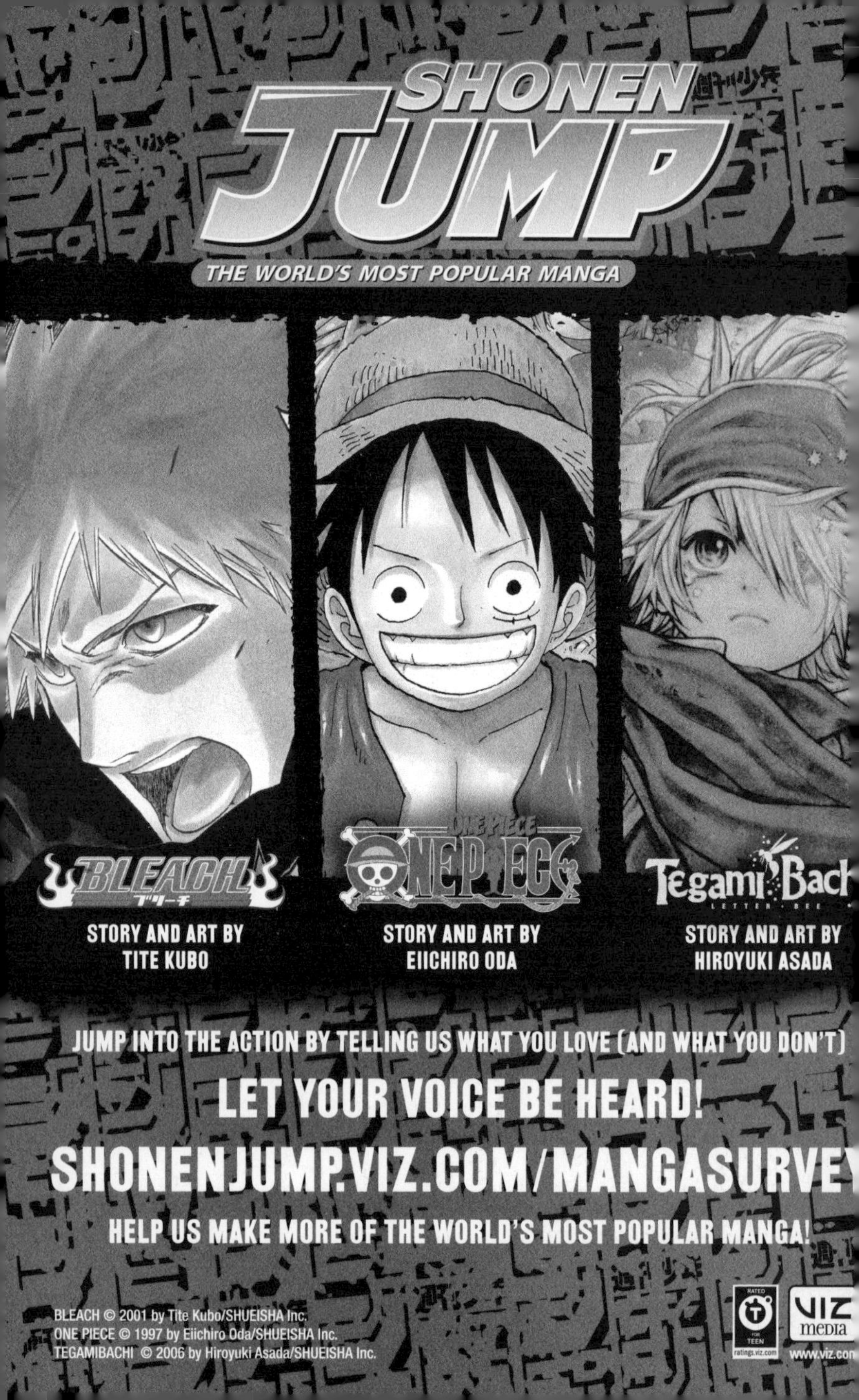
SHONEN JUMP
THE WORLD'S MOST POPULAR MANGA
BLEACH
ブリーチ
STORY AND ART BY
TITE KUBO
ONE PIECE
STORY AND ART BY
EIICHIRO ODA
Tegami Bachi
LETTER BEE
STORY AND ART BY
HIROYUKI ASADA
JUMP INTO THE ACTION BY TELLING US WHAT YOU LOVE (AND WHAT YOU DON'T)
LET YOUR VOICE BE HEARD!
SHONENJUMP.VIZ.COM/MANGASURVEY
HELP US MAKE MORE OF THE WORLD'S MOST POPULAR MANGA!
BLEACH © 2001 by Tite Kubo/SHUEISHA Inc.
ONE PIECE © 1997 by Eiichiro Oda/SHUEISHA Inc.
TEGAMIBACHI © 2006 by Hiroyuki Asada/SHUEISHA Inc.
RATED T FOR TEEN
ratings.viz.com
VIZ media
www.viz.com

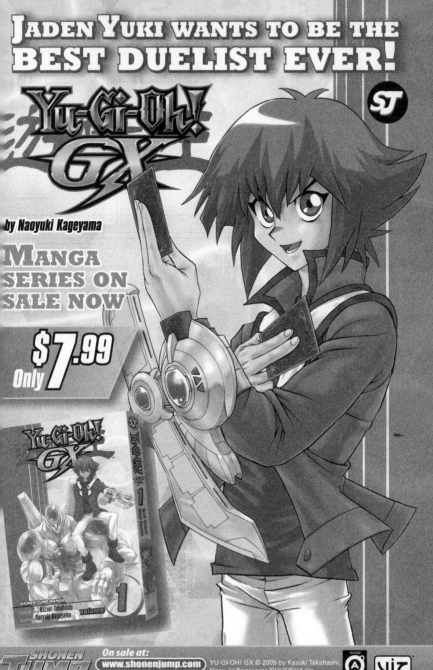

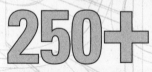
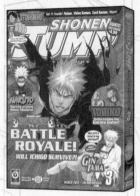 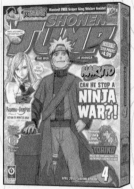 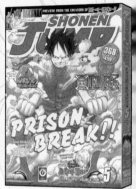